Prisoners of Conscience

Studies in Rhetoric/Communication
Thomas W. Benson, Series Editor

Prisoners of Conscience
Moral Vernaculars of Political Agency

GERARD A. HAUSER

The University of South Carolina Press

Cloth edition published by the University of South Carolina Press, 2012
Paperback edition published by the University of South Carolina Press, 2014

www.sc.edu/uscpress

Manufactured in the United States of America

23 22 21 20 19 18 17 16 15 14   10 9 8 7 6 5 4 3 2 1

The Library of Congress has cataloged the cloth edition as follows:
Hauser, Gerard A.
   Prisoners of conscience : moral vernaculars of political agency / Gerard A. Hauser.
     p. cm. — (Studies in rhetoric/communication)
   Includes bibliographical references and index.
   ISBN 978-1-61117-076-4 (cloth : alk. paper)
   1. Communication in politics. 2. Conscience—Political aspects. 3. Rhetoric—Political
aspects. I. Title.
   JA85.H39 2012
   365'.45—dc23

                        2012019767

ISBN 978-1-61117-188-4 (ebook)
ISBN 978-1-61117-438-0 (pbk)

To Lloyd Bitzer

Contents

Series Editor's Preface

Gerard A. Hauser's study in *Prisoners of Conscience* of what he terms the "thick moral vernacular of human rights" is a work of erudition, scrupulous theoretical reasoning, patient critical analysis, and profound moral seriousness. In his 1999 book *Vernacular Voices: The Rhetoric of Publics and Public Spheres*, also published in this series, Professor Hauser developed an account of "publics theory," an understanding of how public opinion may be understood as a discursive process in which citizens engage in everyday talk that shapes and discloses public interests and the public sphere. *Vernacular Voices* has been a widely influential book, inspiring stimulating new lines of study in rhetoric. Hauser's *Prisoners of Conscience* is likely to be equally influential.

At the core of *Prisoners of Conscience* are five case studies. At Robben Island in apartheid South Africa, Nelson Mandela and his fellow political prisoners were subjected to intimidation and abuse; their response was to enact a practice of what Hauser, adapting the term from Foucault, terms *parrhesia*, a rhetorical figure of speaking the truth with frankness. The prisoners found ways to maintain and represent their humanity, and thereby their sense of self and solidarity, against a regime of total control and degradation. Next Hauser tells the story of Irina Ratushinskaya, condemned to a Soviet prison camp, in the "small zone" set aside for women prisoners, describing the enactment of a rhetoric of indirection in which prisoners performed a silent self-control in the face of indignities and reprisals—winning over their fellow prisoners to a shared sense of human agency and dignity.

In his account of the hunger strike of Provisional IRA prisoners at Maze prison in Belfast, Northern Island, Hauser describes a regime of physical punishment that is met by the prisoner's inversion of and resistance to the system by "self-induced performances of bodily pain"—passive aggression as vernacular moral rhetoric.

Hauser returns his account to Robben Island for an analysis of a memoir by Indres Naidoo, *Island in Chains*, written after his release from a ten-year sentence, in which he depicts how even the body in pain can undermine the authority of the state and affirm an individual human identity.

In a final case study, Professor Hauser examines the circulation of images of prisoner abuse by United States military guards at Abu Ghraib prison in Iraq, arguing that, despite energetic efforts at dissociation, the images came to frame and define the neoconservative supremacy of executive power. In casting blame for Abu Ghraib on a few low-ranking soldiers, the administration attempted to dissociate itself and the high command from the shame. And yet Hauser does not permit his own reader the easy response of self-purification by dissociating from the neocons, feeding our sense of moral superiority by an act of pity or blame. Hauser's nuanced and complex moral reasoning leaves us with no easy answers, but he does bring illumination and balance to a central challenge to human understanding.

THOMAS W. BENSON

Preface

This study began on Chios, before I was born. John Michalakes was a gunrunner in the Greek resistance against Turkish occupation of the island. In 1822, the islanders living on Chios joined the Greek War of Independence agains Ottoman rule. They suffered massive casualties in the ensuing massacre. Fully 100,000 of the island's 120,000 Greek inhabitants were killed, expelled, or enslaved. The lingering animosity in the survivors fueled continuing unrest. In 1910, as tensions were building toward outbreak of the first Balkan War, Turkey was impressing Chiote men into its army. Turkish soldiers grabbed John in the streets of Chios Town, the island's capital city. A fistfight ensued; he broke free and fled. Knowing he could not return home without endangering his wife and children, John made his way to the shore, where he found a tender that took him to the Pagasitikos Gulf city of Volos on the Greek mainland. Although he had found safe haven, the political situation on Chios made it impossible for John to liberate his wife, Marcella Christophos, and their two children, Irene and Christ, from the island. He believed his only chance to reunite with his family was to get himself to America, where he hoped to eventually secure them an immigration visa.

John signed a letter of indenture to gain passage and entrance to the United States, but once processed through Ellis Island he immediately disappeared, assumed an alias, and led a life in the shadows until he had made the necessary connections to get Marcella an immigration sponsor and saved the necessary resources to pay for his family's passage. When she arrived, in December 1916, she had their two children in tow—boys. The older child, Irene, had died. The younger of the two boys—George—John had never seen. My grandmother was pregnant when he had fled.

My childhood was filled with stories of my grandfather's srength and guile. He had supported his family by running a jitney service to the steel mills in Buffalo, New York. His customers were black workers, which brought him grief from the other cabbies who disapproved of his choice of clients. He told them these men had done him no harm and to mind their own business. My uncles would tell of moving often to new flats—whether to avoid being caught by the authorities for not honoring the letter of indenture or from economic hardship they were uncertain. What they did recall was that my grandfather was a shrewd negotiator. The family was growing, and he would use its size to play on a landlord's sympathies. Here he was, a poor immigrant cab driver with six or seven or more mouths to feed. Could the landlord find

compassion for his family? After he had negotiated a favorable rent, he'd then negotiate an equal rate for the other tenants in the building.

He died when I was six, but the stories remained and became a source of moral
instruction from my relatives about the meaning of freedom, democracy, community,
and family. They instilled in me an abiding curiosity to learn more of his adventures,
perhaps because my childhood memories of my grandfather were uniformly fond and
his absence left a void. They also were an opportunity for my family to share other
stories of Greek resistance, struggle, and the resilience of the human will to survive.
This book is, in that sense, in honor of my grandfather and his children, who stoked
admiration for freedom fighters and curiosity about how these underdogs kept their
struggles alive.

Freedom fighters are difficult to write about without falling into snares of romanticizing an oppressed group that in some cases, if given the opportunity, would gladly
visit the same harsh treatment and more on their oppressors. It poses the challenge
of making sense of violent acts committed for political motivations. The truism that
one person's freedom fighter is another's criminal reflects the hopelessly partisan
nature of considering their pleas. It poses the further difficulty of interpreting the
historical context that explains their actions. What, from the insurgent's perspective,
seems a history of injustice is from another point of view a legitimate exercise of
the state's responsibility to steer a political course responsive to the social and economic realities of the times. Still, as my mentor, Lloyd Bitzer, once remarked when
discussing the civil rights movement, sometimes an issue doesn't have two legitimate
sides.

Without gainsaying that insurgents are often, perhaps always, romanticized to
some extent, they emerge in public memory as signal figures that inspire emulation
through the integrity with which they lived their lives. Their integrity is less a matter of memorialized great acts and decisive events than how their ground-level performance of resistance influenced one another through moment-by-moment choices
and interactions. The heroic characters that lead resistance movements are well known
and are powerful figures who inspired masses to solidarity in their fight for freedom.
However, their struggles were not always played out on center stage. Often their most
important moments included time spent in prisons, where they were subjected to
harsh conditions and worse treatment in the state's efforts to break their will to continue the resistance. Figures in the background of the struggle also are important in
the streets and in the prison for sustaining the fight to overturn oppression and in
publicizing the plight of political prisoners to an outside world. Regardless of status,
political prisoners live in a tenebrous region that discloses little of their existence or
treatment and whose harsh realities make constant danger their closest companion.

Those who have gone through violent upheavals have much to tell us. They have
faced starvation, torture, prison, and physical and psychological mistreatment, have
often been reduced to an animal's existence, the threat of extermination, and still kept

records, wrote secret diaries, smuggled information into, within, and out of prison, persisted in resisting when all hope seemed lost, and accepted brutalization and even death rather than sacrifice their conscience. Among the things they have to tell us is the depth to which a political power will sink in order to protect and sustain itself and the equally strong thirst of oppressed peoples for political agency. In the dark places of the prison, this pas de deux is not performed with great speeches. It is part of the everyday milieu of interaction between warder and prisoner, between administration and prison population, in which the political battle that rages on the outside migrates into the prison to be enacted in new forms dictated by the constraints of prison life and no less critical to the ends of both sides.

Regardless of its form, however, the interaction between political prisoner and prison has a distinctive rhetorical function in that it constitutes the prisoners' identity, gives sustained meaning to the struggle, has great bearing on how the prison is run, and ultimately offers proof and refutation of the prisoners' humanness. Moreover, this is a vernacular rhetoric, a rhetoric of everyday microperformances of identity, affiliation, authority, and cooperation or resistance.

By vernacular rhetoric I mean the language of the people, as distinct from the language of the professions or specialized body of knowledge. One does not require a formal education to acquire it; it requires that a person be conversant in the things that matter locally. It also is a language that involves power vectors—those that exclude it from important forums where learned language is the norm, such as the court or the lecture hall, and its own exclusion of outsiders who are tone deaf to subtleties of class, race, sexual orientation, and gender that circulate within its use. Finally, in the case of political prisoners, their vernacular rhetorical appeals for human rights deal with virtue and vice, living in truth, and ultimately justice. It is a *moral vernacular.*

The ambiguity over where the emphasis should go—a *moral* form of vernacular rhetoric, or a *vernacular* form of moral rhetoric—cannot be resolved by stipulative definition. Moral vernacular rhetoric shares in the essential ambiguity that accompanies all rhetoric. Moreover, it is a productive ambiguity (McKeon 1969) that opens to multiple meanings and interpretations inherent to any conversation about human rights and inherent to the way these prisoners engaged in acts of resistance intended to make their person and their cause matter.

Prisoners of Conscience continues the project on vernacular rhetoric begun in *Vernacular Voices* (Hauser 1999b). That earlier work's contention was that, as an alternative to polls and to the statements by officials and leaders, we should pay greater attention to the discourse of ordinary citizens, whose vernacular rhetoric reflects a discursive form of public opinion. This project is concerned more narrowly with vernacular discourse as a mode of rhetoric where the vernacular is the main source of available appeals: the discourse of political prisoners, or more precisely prisoners of conscience (POCs). The project has particular salience at this moment in history, when we are barely removed from a national scandal in the United States over the treatment of enemy combatant detainees at black sites by the Central Intelligence Agency (CIA) and/or foreign governments and, at the same time, the difficulty of tending to and acting on inhuman treatment of political prisoners that raises serious human rights issues: Zimbabwe, China, and most recently Iranian citizens protesting the results of that country's presidential election come to mind.

This book explores how POC modes of resistance constitute a moral vernacular discourse of human rights. Toward that end, it has three central ambitions. First, it is interested in shedding light on how the modes of POC resistance constitute what I call a "thick moral vernacular" of human rights. POCs engage in performances of moral suasion by resisting the deceit of states that would manipulate human weaknesses with false hope for freedom at the expense of personal integrity. They are engaged in unyielding combat with prison authorities in order to protect their lives and, often, in ceaseless efforts to keep the resistance movement alive and to mount international pressure for their freedom and for national reform. Their rhetorical accomplishment is to transform human rights into something more than soft or quasi-legal international agreements or philosophical commitments. Through their advocacy, human rights acquire life as a discourse—a moral vernacular discourse— about what it means to be human and to live free in a human(e) world. It is a discourse of political agency.

Second, this book seeks to clarify how these acts of resistance deploy what I call "rhetorical mechanisms" to expose the state's vulnerability. By "rhetorical mechanisms," I refer to discursive structures that shape rhetorical responses to contingencies. Whether intentionally or not, they animate invention, evidence, argument, pathos, and ethos that constitute the identity of rhetors, audiences, and publics. Because rhetorical mechanisms provide a structure for performing rhetoric, emphasizing them emphasizes how discourse takes form, how rhetorical exchanges are a way of doing as much as an art of speaking and writing. It is in the doing that POC discourse comes onto the horizon of others, engages them, promotes identification, patterns experience of persons and events, and enlivens beliefs and actions by which we constitute a human world. Rhetorical mechanisms provide structures unique to shaping the central concern of performing rhetoric: inventing appeals that constitute identity and agency.

Finally, this book seeks to contextualize the "thick moral vernacular" in social conditions and specific circumstances that acclimatize expressions of conscience. Although POCs sometimes make explicit reference to their human rights, more often they do not. Although sometimes they make reasoned arguments associated with formal appeals, more often they address their immediate audience or an audience of readers and viewers in a way that interrupts what such audiences were doing and demands a response. Moreover, their demands frequently attach moral implications to how their target/audience responds. Part of my concern, in this regard, is to explore how POCs convert universal commitments to human dignity, agency, and voice—often expressed in international agreements with premises lacking transcultural support—into the moral vernacular of the society and culture to which their rights talk is addressed.

Though much of this book focuses on the discourse within the prison, I delve into historical contexts out of which the prison struggles grew. At the same time, much that would be in a history of each period is excluded. I trust readers will not regard these as digressions, since they are essential to understanding the vernacular exchanges that are my focus. In addition, some may find my accounts have an excessively partisan tone. The partiality of the accounts reflects my effort to place the reader in the position of the resisters, whose stories I am attempting to tell.

I hope readers will engage the stories and ideas I am presenting here and wrestle with their implications for rhetoric. But I also hope they will be moved to hear the vernacular rhetoric of oppressed peoples occurring today and, in the spirit of Hannah Arendt (1958), tend to the catastrophic histories of which they speak so that we might better think what we are doing.

Acknowledgments

This project has been in the back of my mind since the waning days of the Cold War, when Polish and Czech dissidents were writing letters and essays concerned with a vision of civil society and Northern Ireland was being ravaged by the "Troubles." It grew with the emancipation of South Africa from an apartheid state. Its outline clarified with Abu Ghraib and publication of the torture memos. During the intervening years, I shared my thinking in a variety of venues where my audiences were generous with comments and encouragement that have proven invaluable and sustaining. I am indebted to the faculty and students who read papers and responded to lectures on the rhetoric of prisoners of conscience, especially those in communication at the University of Colorado Boulder. I presented various chapters to the faculty and students in communication arts at the University of Wisconsin; communication studies at Northwestern University; the Rhetoric Section of the Department of Media, Cognition and Communication at the University of Copenhagen; the Centre for Research in Reasoning, Argumentation and Rhetoric at the University of Windsor; the Department of Information Science and Media Studies at the University of Bergen; and the Department of Communication, Media and IT at Sodertörn University. Their challenges, comments, and suggestions have been a source of insight and encouragement. In this regard, I cannot thank enough my colleagues in the Rhetoric Workshop at the University of Colorado Boulder, who read early drafts of most of what appears here. Your comments have made me rethink and improve my argument at every turn.

I want to give special thanks to Erik Doxtader for his comments on chapters 2 and 3 and conversation about images of violence at Abu Ghraib. Erik has been a source of continuing encouragement and personal support that I treasure. Chapter 4 was first presented at a conference in Cape Town to commemorate the tenth anniversary of South Africa's democracy. I am indebted to Philippe Salazar for inviting me to speak and for his many conversations about South African politics during apartheid. Thomas Farrell, James McDaniel, Larry Prelli, and Dilip Gaonkar offered helpful criticisms of chapter 7. I am indebted to Larry as well for his insightful conversation on the Abu Ghraib images at the point where my analysis was taking form. The research for chapter 6 was conducted in part in the human rights archive at the University of Colorado at Boulder. Jennifer Thackaberry Zeigler was my research assistant and coauthor of a conference paper on Bobby Sands's hunger strike. Sam

McCormick made valuable suggestions that helped me think through some key issues in chapter 6. Bruce Gronbeck read and commented on chapter 6, and was a valued conversational partner on this project from its earliest stages. My colleague Pete Simonson read the first draft of this book with unsurpassed care and insight, for which I am grateful. I also profited from the gifted editorial eye of Kathleen Dominig, who read the manuscript in its second draft. Frank Beer has been my interlocutor and devil's advocate on this, as on all projects dealing with political rhetoric, from its inception. His relentless questioning has kept me uncomfortable about my early conclusions and at the task of interrogating my texts. Finally, thanks to my anonymous reviewers and to Jim Denton, who has had faith in this project from the start. Your patience and encouragement have been sustaining.

Archival work was conducted at the University of Colorado at Boulder, the Mayibuye Archive at the University of the Western Cape, the University of London, Linen Hall Library in Belfast, and the National Archives of Ireland in Dublin. I am indebted to their staffs for the assistance, suggestions, and enthusiasm they exhibited for this project. Special note goes to Mayibuye's Stanley Stello, who offered invaluable assistance in locating and gaining access to materials then not in wide circulation. I also want to thank the Department of Communication, College of Arts and Sciences, and Graduate School at Colorado for grants that supported archival work overseas. Thanks are owed to Jay Hauser, who assisted in preparation of the index. Jean Hauser assisted me in archival research in the fall of 2008, as she has in all matters of life for more than fifty years, with care, patience, and love. Thank you. Finally, this project is a reflection of personal ideals about scholarly work and their relation to the condition of the world we inhabit that were instilled in me by Lloyd Bitzer. He demanded our work have moral worth. To the extent that this project does, I owe him my continuing gratitude and dedicate this book to him.

Portions of this book were previously published. I thank the publishers for permission to reprint them here. These include, in order of publication:

"Body Rhetoric: Conflicted Reporting of Bodies in Pain." In *Deliberation, Democracy, and the Media,* edited by Simone Chambers and Anne Costain, 135–53. Boulder, Colo.: Rowman & Littlefield, 2000.

"Prisoners of Conscience, Self-Risk, and the Wedge: The Case of Dietrich Bonhoeffer." In *Henry W. Johnstone, Jr. and the Dialogue of Philosophy and Rhetoric,* edited by Gerard A. Hauser. Pittsburgh: Pennsylvania Communication Association, 2004.

"Moral Vernaculars and Rhetorics of Conscience." In *Rhetorical Agendas: Political, Ethical, Spiritual,* edited by Patricia Bizzell, 11–24. Mahwah, N.J.: Erlbaum, 2005.

"Demonstrative Displays of Dissident Rhetoric: The Case of Prisoner 885/63." In *The Rhetoric of Display,* edited by Lawrence Prelli, 229–54. Columbia: University of South Carolina Press, 2006.

"Women in Combat: Arguments against Military Women in Combat through Media Depictions of Jessica Lynch and Lynndie England." *Proceedings of the Sixth Conference of the International Society for the Study of Argument,* edited by F. H. van Eemeren and P. Houtlosser, 583–90. Amsterdam: Sic Sat, 2007 (with Virginia Sanprie).

"The Moral Vernacular of Human Rights Discourse." *Philosophy and Rhetoric* (2008) 41:440-466.

"Attending the Vernacular: A Plea for an Ethnographical Rhetoric." In *The Rhetorical Emergence of Culture,* edited by Christian Meyer and Felix Girke. Rhetoric Culture Series, Vol. 4, 157–72. Oxford: Berghan Books, 2011.

PART I. *Theoretical Probes on a Moral*
         Vernacular Rhetoric of Human Rights

I.   *Reclaiming Voice*

During the Civil War, Abraham Lincoln invoked the president's war powers to authorize suspending the writ of habeas corpus when disturbances to abet the South's insurrection seemed to compromise the Union's military action. Lincoln's actions were both extravagantly blessed and hideously cursed. During the George W. Bush administration, U.S. policies of detention and interrogation of suspected members of the Taliban and al-Qaeda evoked similar responses. Their initiation in 2001 near the onset of the war in Afghanistan received benediction from such icons of the Left as Alan Dershowitz (San Francisco Chronicle, January 22, 2002) and Michael Ignatieff (2004), and was reinforced by congressional support for the Patriot Act, which suspended such basic rights as freedom of speech and privacy when the president deemed it necessary in the interest of national security. This was before the American public and the community of nations became aware of the extremes to which these policies led: warrantless wiretapping, indefinite detention, denial of habeas corpus rights or legal representation, torture, and more. These stunning realities called into question the ethos of the United States as the planet's oldest continuous democracy and, as its lone superpower, democracy's moral leader.

Dangerous times, the administration argued, call for extreme measures, but the U.S. Supreme Court ruled the measures must conform to the Constitution. And the court of public opinion, confronted by the graphic evidence of troops-gone-wild photographs from Abu Ghraib, wondered what had become of American honor. The remaining years of the Bush administration, from May 2004 on, played like a Greek tragedy with an abundance of curses: the White House suffered repeated rebuffs from a conservative Supreme Court; the American people suffered the expansion of the state of exception that claimed limitless presidential powers under the unitary executive theory,[1] thereby making the country an effectual dictatorship; allies became disenchanted with Bush's foreign policy doctrines of unilateralism and his intransigence in the face of mounting evidence that these policies put the United States on the wrong course; and the mounting costs in lives and treasure from the U.S. military misadventure in Iraq fractured citizen confidence in the administration's capacity to lead.

Years of Discontent

Retrospection makes it easy to decry the folly of policies so askew with a nation's history and traditions. At the time when fateful decisions were being made, however,

Jeremiahs were scarce, and the chorus of dissidence from such isolated quarters as the American professoriate was easily dismissed as the shrill reaction of a notoriously liberal faction equally notorious for its naive detachment from reality (see Yoo 2006). Up close, ambivalence was the more widespread response. Dangerous times call for extreme measures, to be sure. Terrorists had attacked the United States and threatened more of the same. Intelligence on enemy activities was essential to disrupt further terrorist attempts on U.S. citizens and to capture terrorist leaders intent on causing harm.

At the start, up close, it wasn't clear where to draw the line on the treatment of enemy combatant detainees. It never is when confusion abounds. By the end of the Bush administration, seven years after 9/11, it appeared that the White House either had been unable to gain clarity on the stopping point or, if its war rhetoric was to be believed, was blessed with perfect Machiavellian clarity and no regrets: the only stopping point was the end of terrorist threats to the United States; the end justified the means. For the rest of the country, the strange new vocabulary of "extraordinary rendition," "waterboarding," "Camp X-Ray," and "enemy combatant," not to mention suspension of habeas corpus and warrantless wiretapping, defined a world that the majority believed went too far.[2]

Abusing those who are imprisoned for acts that grow from political ideals has a long history. Rulers have seldom looked kindly on their opponents, and absolute rulers have been inclined to treat them as troublemakers and enemies of the state who required harsh treatment. Gladiators, for example, often were Rome's political prisoners. Their fate was emblematic of the suicidal consequences of political opposition. Today the consequences are no less severe. Through the first eight months of 2008, Amnesty International issued reports dealing with alleged human rights violations in at least thirty-two countries. The treatment by the U.S. government of detainees who were suspected to be members of the Taliban or al-Qaeda was breathtaking only because of who administered it—a government that prided itself on abiding by the Geneva Conventions—and those who were justifying and authorizing it—the Justice Department, the Office of Legal Counsel,[3] the Defense Department, and the Office of the Vice President.

The presence of political prisoners on every continent signals that dissent and opposition, which are a given in political relations, are suppressed in many parts of the world, often with violence. It may be a truism that one group's terrorist is another's freedom fighter, but it is no less significant for the essential contest each political prisoner represents. Their harsh treatment reflects the important stakes in human aspirations for freedom. Political prisoners are often their most eloquent, most passionate, and most imaginative representatives.

This is a book about political prisoners, or, more precisely, prisoners of conscience (POCs), and how their modes of resistance constitute a discourse of human rights. It is a discourse that exercises influence through the rhetorical power of their resistance.

There is moral suasion in resisting the deceit of states that would manipulate human weaknesses with false hope for freedom at the expense of personal integrity, in unyielding combat with prison authorities in order to protect their lives, in ceaseless efforts to keep the resistance movement alive and to mount international pressure for their freedom and for national reform. These are rhetorical transformations of human rights into something other than soft or quasi-legal international agreements or philosophical commitments. Their advocacy gives human rights life as a kind of discourse—a moral vernacular discourse—about what it means to be human and to live free in a human(e) world. It is a discourse of political agency.

Political Prisoners and Rhetorical Paradoxes

Political prisoners occupy a unique rhetorical space. Unlike convicted felons who break the law for personal gain or through criminal recklessness, blind passion, or folly, POCs are incarcerated for the threat of their ideas. Often the only law they have broken is the (unspoken) prohibition against disagreement with a hegemonic power. When their legal violations do involve acts of violence, they stem from embracing ideas at odds with the existing order. Their ability to display an alternative political vision can be so compelling, as recent history has demonstrated, that repressive regimes are willing to liquidate leading dissidents and even entire ethnic groups with genocidal fervor.

In the absence of material penalties, the efficacy of liquidation can become an overwhelming imperative for murderous policies. When, on March 4, 2009, the International Criminal Court (ICC) at The Hague issued an arrest warrant for Sudanese president Omar Hassan al-Bashir as a war criminal, his response was to inform the ICC it could "eat" its warrant (*Belfast Telegraph*, March 4, 2009). Despite compelling evidence gathered over several years that al-Bashir had orchestrated the genocide in Darfur, he had little to fear as far as enforcement went. When world leaders confronted with evidence of human rights abuses, including genocide, more often than not find an excuse to look the other way, al-Bashir's response threw back the obvious question: who was going to arrest him?

Willingness to remove dissidents from society rests on a calculation that once they are off the public stage they will be forgotten, and, if their treatment is horrendous enough, quite possibly they will recant. Consequently, repressive regimes remain willing to take their chances of success at forcing the opposition to be silent. This is not a sure bet, however. The impulse toward a pogrom can be checked in cases where the opposition has made effective use of publicity and its enemy status is defined less on group identity than ideological differences. There prudence dictates that mere incarceration may suffice. Against the risk that the political prisoner will quicken public imagination as a symbol of the state's alien ethos, the regime calculates that removal from public view will toll the dissident's political death knell and possibly deliver a mortal blow to the ideas for which he or she stands. For those still on the streets, the regime banks on intimidation forcing dissidents to avoid the kinds of overt acts that will bring them to the same fate, as the former Soviet Union's practice of show trials grimly testifies. Without public displays of disaffection and alternative visions of the political order, the bet is that opposition politics will disintegrate or, at worst, go underground.

Underground resistance may breed disaffection, but disaffection without the remedy of leading dissident voices often succumbs to the toxicity of cynicism, itself a form of display, albeit unlikely to captivate public understanding or overpower the existing order's claim to legitimacy. By the same token, the political prisoner remains alive as a viable political being only through communication channels outside the official political public sphere. Political prisoners must find ways to be seen in order to have political force; they require at least a counterpublic sphere in which to conduct and sustain dissident discourse (see Asen and Brower 2001; Hauser 1999b, 111–60). Moreover, the prisoner must find ways to display political conscience and consciousness capable of inspiring resistance regardless of personal costs in the service of revolutionary change.

Without rhetorical champions, the aspirations alive in the discursive arenas of a counterpublic sphere are unlikely to captivate public understanding and overpower the existing order's claim to legitimacy. By the same token, the POC remains alive as a viable political being only through the channels of the political counterpublic sphere. POCs address their fellow citizens to sustain resistance against the existing government. Within the enclaved sphere of the prison, their performances of resistance are both acts of political conscience and calls to solidarity among their fellow political prisoners in the prison's ongoing contest over its own terms of engagement. They lodge official protests with the prison authorities and the state in order to establish a record of illegal treatment. And they strive to make their cause known to the international community to invoke not only surrogates who will engage in the thin moral vernacular of human rights discourse but also to bring pressure to bear against the existing regime by marshaling international opinion.[4]

The POC with clandestine means to communicate not only survives but also leads. The POC may be exiled from public life, but this exile contains a political paradox. Imprisonment removes the activist's voice from the epicenter of evolving events. At the same time, it bestows a perverse imprimatur, since removal from society offers tacit state recognition of the prisoner's importance. Prisoners speaking from prison acquire an aura of authority to direct thought and action against the existing order, as Martin Luther King Jr.'s "Letter from Birmingham Jail" eloquently testifies (see Baker 1995, 18–19).

Coping with Terror

The realities of prison are different for POCs than for convicted felons. A dissident poet, say Vaclav Havel detained during the 1980s, or a religious leader, say Stefan

Cardinal Wyszynski detained during the 1950s, becomes a source of rhetorical invention. Their incarceration enters public imagination as a metonym for the body politic, a representation of the morbidity caused by political ills. Partisan appeals memorialize them as models of political principle. Dissident rhetoric transforms the confrontation with authorities into the body politic's struggle for survival. When the state is unable to force such celebrated opponents of repressive regimes as Nelson Mandela or Aung San Suu Kyi to cave, it signals tacit acknowledgment of their cause's superiority. Without rhetoric capable of commanding its citizens' minds and hearts, the state is reduced to using force.

Here we should note that not all political prisoners are POCs. A political prisoner becomes a POC by choosing to remain a dissident in prison. It is a choice that bears resemblance to phronêsis. Donald Verene's (2010, 212) helpful discussion of conscience points out that it has its conceptual origins in practical reason through the Greek concept of *synderesis*. *Synderesis* was the intuition of moral primitives on which practical reasoning depended. It provided the first principles of behavior to be applied in specific circumstances. Conscience guided their application and was capable of error. Although the first principles themselves were true, and therefore, not only general guides for action ("do good"), they also provided a basis for moral content about specific behaviors.

Hegel pushes the epistemic feature of the ancient Greek conception into the realm of moral self-consciousness. In the *Phenomenology of Spirit*, he describes conscience in developmental terms. Conscience is the state of consciousness in which the self ceases to oscillate between self and world and achieves certainty of its own being: "As conscience, it [moral self-consciousness] is no longer this continual alternation of existence being placed in the Self, and vice versa; it knows that its existence as such is this pure certainty of itself " (1977, 481). Apropos to this study, Hegel points to the realization of conscience as present in the human self as a key step in the self-knowledge that results most immediately in duty (1977, 383, 392). In using the term in this way, as a state of moral self-consciousness that results in duty to act, I deviate from the narrower understanding employed by such nongovernmental organizations (NGOs) as Amnesty International, which limits it to those imprisoned and/or persecuted for the *nonviolent* expression of consciously held beliefs.[5] Those discussed here include dissidents who have resorted to violence in service of political resistance. My emphasis rests on the choices made in prison out of conscience to continue their resistance in prison and through vernacular expressions of resistance and identity that carry moral force within their national community.

In the case of leading dissidents—whose treatment gets high-profile attention from foreign states, NGOs, and the news media—refusal to accept the authorities' Faustian bargain of their name for their freedom often gets publicity and even enters history. Such diverse figures as Socrates, Sir Thomas More, Galileo, Peter Zenger, Susan Anthony, Margaret Sanger, and Mahatma Gandhi remind us that recrimination against those who have advocated beliefs or engaged in practices that challenged the existing authority has been a historical constant. For most who lack celebrity, their resistance enacted in daily micropractices that refuse submission to an authority they regard as illegitimate or whose dictates they consider untenable goes unnoticed by the outside world. Regardless of their status, their deep disgust at the deal—things will go easier if you sign a loyalty oath, recant your prior criticism, accept an offer of emigration, inform on your confederates—makes fidelity to the commitments of their advocacy preferable to personal liberty. The prison's disciplinary regime has as its raison d'être to strip them of their political commitments. For political prisoners who survive as POCs, their conscious commitments not only keep them in prison but also individuate them as prisoners of their conscious commitments.

Most political prisoners do not lead lives of the sort that demand to be retold in a book. Nevertheless, refusing the state's offer is heroic; it accepts the terror of prison as the personal price for maintaining an authentic voice.[6] As Jonathan Swift demonstrated in the savage comedy of *Gulliver's Travels,* "humanity" is but a matter of scale. The magnitude of an authoritarian state that can't subdue a lone POC's insistence on the indelible mark of oppositional identity gets diminished in stature. And the smallness of the single resister who accepts terror as the price for maintaining one's commitments gets magnified in a narrative of humanity that transcends his or her constructed identity by the penal code. By choosing not to submit to an interrogator's intimidation, the POC turns the tables and reframes his or her incarceration from the official narrative of the sentence to an interrogation of the state's legitimacy.

Within prison, these dueling interrogations often migrate to the prisoner's body. Publicizing a confession of guilt, recantation, or renunciation of the dissident movement itself can reap the dissident's political demise. Torture is often the state's means to this end. Accounts of prison life such as Elaine Scarry's (1985) meditation on pain; Havel's (1989) detailed letters to his spouse, Olga; or Irina Ratushinskaya's (1989) account of confrontations with her warders chronicle how the prisoner's body comes under assault. And, as Jacobo Timerman's *Prisoner without a Name, Cell without a Number* (1981) graphically portrays, these cruelties come not only from beatings and torture but also from insulting treatment, isolation, physically exhausting and degrading conditions of internment, and psychological abuse. Not least among these is the interrogator's insistence that one's pain and degradation are self-imposed. The prisoner need only recant to gain release from this nightmare. However, to choose one's physical life by such means is also to choose political suicide.

Commitments of conscience make the choice clear, even if not easy. The more salient problem is how to confront terror within prevailing constraints. Physical force is not an option; more likely are tactics that can engage other prisoners, the prison itself, and the outside publics of the nation and world community. Collaboration on where to draw the line for cooperation with the authorities, mitigating institutionalized terror by invoking the structures of law the prison is supposed to follow, smuggling letters to the outside, and inventive means of confrontation testify to the value of resistance and keep the call to identity alive. These are *rhetorical* practices, modes of appeal speaking an alternative language, advancing an alternative political aspiration to the existing power, and indicting the state's alien status in the eyes of those it governs.

The Problem of Voice

The existential condition of the political prisoner is captured by what Giorgio Agamben (2005) calls the "*state of exception*"—a condition that lies between the legal and the political. The ambiguity between the political and the legal makes the state of exception both difficult to define and strikingly descriptive of state power. Agamben, drawing on Francois Saint-Bernard and Allesandro Fontana, writes: "Indeed, according to a widely held opinion, the state of exception constitutes a 'point of imbalance between public law and political fact' that is situated—like civil war, insurrection and resistance—in an 'ambiguous, uncertain, borderline fringe, at the intersection of the legal and the political'" (2005, 1). Conditions of civil war are a decidedly ambiguous region in which laws may be suspended in order to restore political order, and make citizen rights and even citizenship uncertain. He continues: "One of the elements that make the state of exception so difficult to define is certainly its close relationship to civil war, insurrection, and resistance. Because civil war is the opposite of normal conditions, it lies in a zone of undecidability with respect to the state of exception, which is state power's immediate response to the most extreme internal conflicts. Thus, over the course of the twentieth century, we have been able to witness a paradoxical phenomenon that has been effectively defined as a 'legal civil war'" (2).

Agamben uses the case of Nazi Germany as the exemplar for suspension of constitutional rights to deny certain citizens—Jews and gypsies—their citizenship. However, the state of exception has become widespread. Denial or suspension of civil rights, as occurred under South Africa's policy of apartheid; Britain's Criminalization Act of 1976, which provided individuals arrested for terrorist activities, notably those of the Irish Republican Army, with summary trials without benefit of a jury of peers; the Soviet Union's frequent abrogation of the constitutional right to free speech and conviction for expressing views the Communist Party determined did not comply with the standards of socialist society; and the United States' Patriot Act, which suspended privacy rights, habeas corpus rights in certain circumstances, and adherence to the Geneva Conventions on torture, were each justified on grounds of national security and preservation of social order. Each illustrates the politics of biopower. Each denies voice not on the basis of class or citizenship or other more common distinctions on which power has been based. These regimes focus on voice as embodied and deny it to bodies controlled by the state.[7]

Homo sacer

Michel Foucault has argued that biopower initiates a new form of power. Speaking of the two forms of disciplines that studied the body from the Enlightenment forward—the *anatomo-politics of the body*, which focused on the body as a machine that had to be disciplined, and the focus on the species body, which was concerned with its biological functions—he says, "The old power of death that symbolized sovereign power was now carefully supplanted by the administration of bodies and the calculated management of life" (1980, 139–40). The administration of bodies and management of life represent a positive power: control over biological life. The object of governance is no longer explicable in terms of liberties, rights, and social contract, but in terms of the state's capacity to keep society safe and alive. Safety requires that social menaces be controlled, which reflects the presence of biopolitics whenever state powers control the body. Whereas Foucault opposes biopower to old sovereignty, Agamben equates its control over life with the state of exception.

Next to the displaced persons who are sent to the camps, those most obviously placed outside society are prisoners. The state interprets acts that challenge public safety and public well-being, on which its legitimacy rests, as a criminal challenge to its sovereignty.

In the state of exception, common criminals, whether dangerous or hapless, are victims of social forces that the state must regulate in order to maintain public well-being. They are placed in a common location where the state assumes control of their bodies; they are stripped of their citizen rights; and whatever unique marks they may possess as individual humans become irrelevant. They are defined as beings lacking qualification, which makes them unambiguous subjects of biopower and unambiguous signs of the sovereign's power through control of their bodies. Agamben (1998) sheds light on the relationship of sovereign power to biopolitics by drawing on the ancient Roman construct of the *homo sacer*. He points to Pompeius Festus, who, "after defining the Sacred Mount that the plebeians consecrated to Jove at the time of their secession," adds: "The sacred man is the one whom the people have judged on account of a crime. It is not permitted to sacrifice this man, yet he who kills him will not be condemned for homicide; in the first tribunian law, in fact, it is noted that 'if someone kills the one who is sacred according to the plebiscite, it will not be considered homicide.' This is why it is customary for a bad or impure man to be called sacred" (1998, 71).

The construction of the outcast as "that who may be killed but not sacrificed" lies at the heart of a biopolitics under the state of exception. It affords the distinction between natural life marked merely as being alive, or what the ancient Greeks called *zoē*, and the qualified life of public existence as this or that type of person, or *bios*. At the same time, the biopolitics of inclusion/exclusion that lies at the heart of the state of exception includes the excluded body in the meaning of the polity through the sovereign's act of exclusion, inscribing its meaning by this very act of exclusion.

The prototype of the *homo sacer* is the muselmann as described by Primo Levi (1959, 93–106) in *If This Is a Man*. Taken from the German *Musselman* (Muslim),[8] it was a derogatory term used among inmates of World War II Nazi concentration camps to "describe the weak, the inept, those doomed to selection" (94). Those in the lagers suffering from a combination of extreme starvation and exhaustion were listless, did not maintain basic standards of physical hygiene, and were unresponsive to their surroundings and apathetic toward their own fate. The other prisoners derided them since to show them pity would require the more fit to expend emotional energy better conserved for their own survival.

Arendt (1968), commenting on the growing numbers of refugees and stateless peoples since the First World War, reminds us that the excluded body has no place in the public realm where politics occurs. Public life is lived by appearance and expression. The Greeks regarded whoever could not appear or speak as condemned to idiocy. And yet, by being excluded, the body of the *homo sacer* speaks to the most fundamental reality of politics: the sovereign's power. Since the sovereign's ultimate power is over life and death, the *homo sacer* condemned to the liminality of bare life quells the sovereign's apprehension over his or her own sovereignty with its bodily representation of the sovereign's condemnation: "You have no rightful way of life." Sacrifice would qualify his or her life with something symbolic that transcended *zoē*, his or her bare existence as a natural being, a biological life that has had its freedom of association and expression suspended. Transcendence of that sort would make the apprehension a reality.

The prisoner typifies the *homo sacer*, a human reduced to "bare life" or biological life as an existing creature but lacking qualification, which bestows a uniquely individuating public identity. Against an unambiguous sign of the state's sovereignty, however, the political prisoner stands in resistant separateness to the state of exclusion. The rapidity of the sovereign's invocation of the state of exception in response to exigencies of the moment revokes the simultaneity of sense, thought, and event that challenges policies by bracketing them out of the *bios politikos*.[9] Unlike the Jew, who became *homo sacer* not for acts of opposition but for race, the POC is excluded for words and deeds. His or her citizenship is suspended, but with the caveat that repentance, rehabilitation, and readmission are possible. The POC can recant and be freed, or be rehabilitated through political reeducation at a labor camp, either of which preserves the face of the sovereign as sovereign.[10] And, if executed, at least the POC will die in a state of civic grace. In this respect, then, the POC provides a challenge to the fated nature of Agamben's analysis.

Speaking the Truth

Political crimes, being acts of political and often moral conscience, spring from a different motivation than the crimes of ordinary felons. Consequently, the judiciary's sentence for the political prisoner's illegal act is often secondary to the political relationship between the POC and the prison, which is based on the prisoner's commitments of conscience and the prison's dedication to breaking his or her strength. The biopolitics of the prison or the camp ostensibly strips the prisoner's individuating qualification of political conscience. It is enacted through systematic attempts to control the body in a way that puts it beyond oppression, since the oppressed body is one with rights that have been abused. The oppressed body has a claim on justice, which requires consciousness of a right to act with integrity and a conscience that cannot compromise on this. Compromising conscience would destroy that which qualifies the prisoner as self-possessed.

The political prisoner's thought finds its animus through living in truth; its expression is emblematic of what the ancient Greeks called *parrhesia*, fearless speech. Traditionally, parrhesia was spoken to the superior power under the seal of permission to speak candidly with the guarantee that the speaker would not be punished for uttering the truth. The authority comprehended what was said, and tolerated it, in fact, through an appreciation that hearing unwelcome expression of how matters stood was critical to the effective exercise of sovereign power. By contrast, the POC has neither asked for permission or amnesty nor expected it could be granted. The POC's parrhesiastic challenge to the sovereign's vision of a society that is alive and safe precipitates a crisis: it raises the possibility of defying the state's sovereign capacity to decree the *homo sacer* and thereby reduce the citizen to bare life. The POC's fearless speech manifests the tension between the prisoner and the sovereign by speaking the truth to authority in a way that disrupts the biopolitical equation of sovereignty, exposes the limits of state power, and asserts that sovereignty can be challenged and possibly redefined. It puts the division over claims to freedom and rights into the frame of what Arendt (1958) called "common sense" by making them visible and legible to all who can witness them. Making a call to justice visible and legible challenges the sovereign's attempts to naturalize its claims about freedom and rights; it exposes the biopolitical order that strips its citizens of their political identity. POCs demonstrate by their public action—by its publicity—that they can perform that which has been denied them, that they have political agency.

Foucault writes that "parrhesia is a verbal activity in which a speaker expresses his personal relationship to truth, and risks his life because he recognizes truth-telling as a duty to improve or help other people (as well as himself). In parrhesia, the speaker uses his freedom and chooses frankness instead of persuasion, truth instead of falsehood or silence, the risk of death instead of flattery, and moral duty instead of self-interest and moral apathy" (1983).

The Greek formulation of parrhesia, which is fundamental to Foucault's discussion, inexorably calls attention to individual courage. Although parrhesia is not self-regarding, it is an individuating mark of personal character consistent with the Greek concern for *arête*.

For the POC, matters are different. Frank speech requires courage, and the POC is fully aware of and embraces the threat of death that signifies parrhesia as the cost for living in truth. However, the POC does not stand apart from the subjugated, whose pain he or she voices. The POC may speak frankly to power knowing fully that this may result in the loss of freedom, the infliction of pain, or even death, but the POC does not speak alone. Vaclav Havel, writing of the practices of the post-totalitarian state that ground the human spirit to dust, described his oppositional practice as trying to bring the Czech government, which chose to disregard the aspirations of its people, into harmony with the people's desires. While explaining to Western readers the reticence of Eastern and Central European dissidents to accept invitations to attend their congresses and join in their opposition to totalitarian regimes, he instructs:

> Seen from the outside, the "dissidents" present the appearance of a miniscule and rather singular enclave—singularly radical, that is—within a monolithic society which speaks with an entirely different voice. In a sense, they really are such an enclave: there is but a handful of them and the state does everything in its power to create a chasm between them and society at large. They are in fact different from the majority in one respect: they speak their mind openly heedless of the consequences. That difference, however, is hardly significant. What matters is whether the views they express differ significantly from those of the majority of their fellow citizens. I do not think they do. Quite the contrary, almost every day I come across some piece of evidence that the dissidents are really saying nothing other than what the vast majority of their fellow citizens think privately. (Havel 1986c, 164)

Havel's observation suggests that POCs are exponentially dangerous because they speak what everyone knows but is afraid to say. POCs consciously choose to speak frankly in order to preserve their integrity, which endorses the integrity of living in truth. They are the quintessential parrhesiastes.

Frank speech questions an important dimension of biopolitics. Biopolitics represents a new form of governmentality (Foucault 1991, 2008). It is concerned with the problems of society posed by masses, and worries less over the old regime's concern with deciding who would live or die and more with regulation of the population to foster its well-being. Concerns of public safety, public health, economic stability, and education require state intervention to protect the public good. This introduces a novel consideration into an analysis of power whereby the state foregoes dealing with society as a judicial body defined by laws and instead treats society as a population that is the object of governance. Considered as a population, as an organism, society poses scientific and political problems. Maurizio Lazzarato (2002) explains: "The new biopolitical dispositifs are born once we begin to ask ourselves, 'What is the correct manner of managing individuals, goods and wealth within the family (which a good father is expected to do in relation to his wife, children and servants) and of making the family fortunes prosper—how are we to introduce this meticulous attention of the father towards his family into the management of the State?'"

The image of the father insinuates into biopolitics the dangerous conflation of the watchful eye that grows from love with that in the service of power. The much-discussed formulation of power under the rubric of surveillance emphasizes molding subjectivities through policies that rehabilitate a population's unhealthy behaviors, and normalizes and institutionalizes socially healthy ones (see Foucault 1977). Rehabilitation, normalization, and institutionalization are accomplished through preventive measures. They require the police to regulate the population by applying disciplinary knowledge through mechanisms designed to maximize safety and health in statistically significant ways.

Placed in relation to the *homo sacer*, policing also implies the possibility of resistance, since there must be freedom to choose in order for some social behaviors to be considered healthier than others and to rationalize the need to regulate choices. Freedom of choice allows for the possibility of saying no. However, the prospect of resistance remains largely theoretical in a biopolitics that considers all challenges to power from the inside as invoking the state of exception. It denies that there is an outside. That is the point of sovereignty predicated on the existence of the homo sacer. The sovereign, through the state of exception, is able to place the subject outside, reduce him or her to natural life, *zoē*, standing outside political life, *bios*, and thereby define the meaning of sovereignty in terms of its performativity. The POC challenges this framework by enacting resistance from an outside stance that asserts a political identity through searing critique of the sovereign's power. Challenging the reduction to bare life also asserts human rights; it makes a claim to agency and to voice.

Returning to my starting point, the POC speaks on the stage of resistance and reform, which requires artful maneuvering within the constraints set by an authoritarian power in ways that serve these ends. Foucault considers parrhesia to involve address to an audience that cannot be persuaded, and for this reason he holds it is not a form of rhetoric. Allowing for resistance as more than a theoretical possibility, tying parrhesia to the surface feature of direct address—a speaker directly addressing an immediate audience—runs contrary to actual practice. The POC speaks frankly to a number of audiences: authority, fellow prisoners, the underground, human rights agents, the general populace, and international audiences through the press. Although there always is an ostensible audience, it is not necessarily the POC's intended one. Given the austerity of parrhesia as frank speech that critiques its audience by saying what it does not want to hear, the fact that the POC is a prisoner for speaking frankly, and that this type of speech defies the sovereign's power to reduce the POC to bare life, continued address to an intractable audience requires explanation. I believe these conditions, contrary to Foucault, make parrhesia rhetorical speech all the way down.

Its rhetorical character invites us to look at POC discourse for how frank speech may not only speak the truth to authority but also entail rhetorical mechanisms for combating the state monopoly on violence with what the POC does best—speak the truth.

Living in Truth

The POCs' most fundamental commitment is to live in truth. Acquiescing to social, political, or religious structures that diminish if not degrade human life haunts them. They write with passion about the balance point between integrity and hypocrisy. Havel, for example, is remarkably clear about Czech society suffocating from living a lie. Cooperating with a state that denies freedoms and rights simply isn't worth it. That insight is enacted in many forms, but it is always an assertion of voice and a performance of agency. To challenge being reduced to bare life is a human rights assertion; it makes a claim to individuating marks that qualify the person through the transgression of personal choices that cannot be contained by an identity as merely biological, as *homo sacer*. The state of exception gives the sovereign unconstrained power to place those who speak frankly outside the state. Speaking the truth reflects a commitment not to accept the terms of bare life regardless of the consequences.

Having voice and being heard are different matters. For example, Charter 77 (Havel 1977) offered as its rationale for expression of discontent its desire to engage the state in dialogue with hopes that it might produce reform. Jacek Kuron and Karol Modzelewski's "Open Letter to the Party" (1982) was written in the same vein. In both cases, their disagreement with the state's actions and call for reform resulted in arrest and imprisonment. Statements expressing hope for a stronger economy, a more inclusive society, and a more participatory politics were treated as acts of disloyalty. What does it mean when you are always slapped for courting dialogue? Polish dissident Adam Michnik thought it meant the state was incorrigible. It no longer made sense to address it; citizens should only address one another.

In that spirit, after the formation of Solidarity, leaders of Poland's Worker's Defense League (KOR) declared they were interested in a self-limiting revolution. They would cede to the state the reins of government in return for guarantees of an open civil society. KOR specified how members of a genuine civil society would act: they would live their lives as if an open civil society were a reality (Schell 1985, xxvii–xxx). One cannot help but hear Hannah Arendt's (1958) position on reality as in the world in KOR's commitment to talk and act with openness, truthfulness, autonomy of action, and trust. Precisely because the totalitarian state politicizes daily life, it offers a vast terrain for exposing and undermining its reach by living daily life *as if* its reach did not exist. The party's intolerance of being ignored, and of commitments to openness in society generally, led to further denunciations of official "realities" of a "people's republic" as motivated by the party's interests rather than the people's.

Matters are quite different in prison. When you are free and have voice there is at least the possibility of dialogue, mutual accommodation, and reform. Inside, claiming voice is an unmistakable act of resistance; even when it surfaces as an expression of cooperation, it is always an interrogation of power that is tactical in its choice between responsiveness and belligerence. In either event, the POC, whether addressing the state through traditional forms of public argument or tactical quotidian engagements, or addressing fellow citizens, employs a vernacular of political agency that advocates a moral alternative to the political reality imposed by the state.

The POC's rhetorical problem is to express fundamental human rights of dignity and agency, which get expressed as moral universals in human rights documents, such as the Universal Declaration of Human Rights (UDHR), in the moral vernacular of the society and culture he or she is addressing. This expression is not entirely straightforward, at least if we are to judge by the rhetoric of political prisoners. The rhetorical animus of their call to conscience[11] seldom begins with the inherent responsiveness of an audience of virtuous citizens who act on the basis of what moral conviction demands; nor is the rhetorical animus the actor's virtue. Their rhetoric is situated within the frame of the rhetoric to which it responds. To counter the state's monopoly on power and violence, the moral vernacular of resistance flows, instead, from the orientation of the vice to which it responds, and, more specifically, which vice the POC puts first. This defining characteristic is exemplified in Vaclav Havel's "The Power of the Powerless."

Vaclav Havel

In his New Year's Day 1990 address, Havel reflected on the astonishing political developments of the previous year in Central and Eastern Europe. For him, the spontaneity of widespread harmonious revolutionary action posed important questions about political consciousness:

> Everywhere in the world people wonder where those meek, humiliated, skeptical, and seemingly cynical citizens of Czechoslovakia found the marvelous strength to shake the totalitarian yoke from their shoulders in several weeks, and in a decent and peaceful way. And let us ask: where did the young people who never knew another system find their desire for truth, their love of free thought, their political ideas, their civic courage and civic prudence? How did their parents—the very generation that had been considered as lost—come to join them? How is it possible that so many people immediately knew what to do, without advice or instruction? (Havel 1998b, 5)

Havel may not have shared everyone's surprise, since his writings predicted the way these developments transpired.

From a distance, his essays appear to be attacking hypocrisy as the ordinary vice corrupting his nation. Certainly he has hypocrisy in mind when he depicts life in

Communist Czechoslovakia as living within a lie and describes a national yearning for living within truth. More fundamentally, however, Havel was concerned with how post–Prague/Spring[12] life had sapped the reserves of human spontaneity from his fellow Czechs. The problem was less the regime's hypocrisy than its treachery. Close up, his essays and letters during the 1970s and 1980s, a period he dubs "post-totalitarian," are morose reflections on the treachery of a system that strips away all pretense of hope.

The post-totalitarian state no longer required physical violence to gain compliance. Since its subjects believed there was no alternative, they were coerced into obeying appeals detached from their personal convictions in order to avoid trouble. Its treachery lay in requiring citizens to be unfaithful to themselves and, through their infidelity, live a life of hypocrisy.

How treachery evokes conscience is exemplified by Havel's distinguished essay "The Power of the Powerless." Havel wrote the essay in 1978 to explain the significance of Charter 77, of which he was a cofounder. It was banned from official publication in Czechoslovakia, but had circulated as samizdat and was printed in the West (Keane 2000, 281). Through its memorable parable of the greengrocer, it explores the state's violation of the moral universal to respect each person's inherent dignity.

The parable portrays a world of stultified thought and compliant behavior enacted through a poster proclaiming, "Workers of the world unite!" The party had given the poster to shopkeepers, and the greengrocer automatically displays it in his shop window. Its display signifies he is living in a lie. Havel observes that the greengrocer need not believe the mystifications of the state that "enslave the working class in the name of the working class," falsify national history, misrepresent the material conditions of life, and present the very circumstances that degrade the individual as if they were the source of the individual's liberation. But the greengrocer must behave *as if* he believed them. He acts in this way to get along in life, to avoid being reproached for failing to have the right decoration in his window or being accused of disloyalty. He displays the poster with indifference to its semantic meaning and the ideal it expresses for one reason: so he will be left alone (Havel 1986c, 42).

Significantly, the greengrocer was not directed to put the sign in his window. Had a party official instructed him to display a sign proclaiming "I am afraid and therefore unquestioningly obedient," he would not be nearly as indifferent to its semantic content. It would be a source of embarrassment and shame because it would be an unequivocal statement of his degradation and violate his sense of human dignity, even though it spoke the truth. To overcome this complication, the greengrocer's expression of loyalty must take the form of a disinterested sign. It hides him from the low foundations of his own obedience while simultaneously concealing the low foundations of power behind the facade of something high: *ideology.*

Havel positions the power of the post-totalitarian world to control life in ideology's excusatory function. What is wrong with supporting the workers of the world?

How could one question whether they should unite? The sign's ideological content provides those below and above with an *illusion* of identity, dignity, and morality while making it easier for everyone in a post-totalitarian world to *part* from them. The illusion "that the system is in harmony with the human order and the order of the universe" (43) gives ideology a transcendent power. It goes beyond physical power to dominate society by providing power with its inner cohesion and by becoming a pillar supporting the system's external stability. Havel has depicted the treachery of exerting control out of a conscience lacking objective content but infinitely certain of itself, and also the cause of the state's undoing. Its ideology is an unstable pillar because, he says, "it is built on lies. It works only as long as people are willing to live within the lie" (50).

The power of the powerless, on the other hand, lay in their ability to act differently, to decide not to live within the lie. Prefiguring 1989's "Velvet Revolution," Havel continues his parable of the fruit and vegetable store manager:

Let us imagine that one day something in our greengrocer snaps and he stops putting up slogans merely to ingratiate himself. He stops voting in elections he knows are a farce. He begins to say what he really thinks at political meetings. And he even finds strength in himself to express solidarity with those whom his conscience commands him to support. In this revolt the greengrocer steps out of living within the lie. He rejects the ritual and breaks the rules of the game. He discovers once more his suppressed identity and dignity. He gives his freedom a concrete significance. His revolt is an attempt to *live within the truth*. (55)

There will be consequences for breaking the facade and exposing the nakedness of post-totalitarian power. Of course, he will pay a price for his assertion of autonomy. He will lose his position as manager of the shop, be transferred to a warehouse, have his pay reduced, lose his vacation time for a holiday in Bulgaria, and even see his children's success in higher education threatened. Nonetheless, his act will have confronted living within the lie with its alternative, and these two alternatives cannot coexist. People may not queue up publicly to support him, but everyone will know the mendacity of the regime has been exposed.

In the post-totalitarian system, therefore, living within the truth has more than a mere existential dimension (returning humanity to its inherent nature), or a noetic dimension (revealing reality as it is), or a moral dimension (setting an example for others). It also has an unambiguous *political* dimension (57).

Havel's parable of the greengrocer is representative of the problematic addressed by oppositional writers in post-totalitarian states. Unlike dictatorships, which impose their will through violence, the post-totalitarian regime exerts its power through its web of influence in every aspect of life, dividing the person from himself or herself with a force, Havel says, that eludes description.

His argument, then, relies on an ethical commitment to the primacy of human dignity. In this respect it fits with a fundamental argument for human rights in which human dignity is invoked as a universal, albeit ambiguous, first principle from which other moral universals follow. It is important to note that the parable of the green-grocer translates its moral first principle into an East-Central European vernacular. It is questionable whether Western audiences would feel the compelling force to display the sign in the first place or grasp the political understanding of the parable as an exemplar of the moral universal it represents. Havel's efforts here, as elsewhere, explained to Western readers that they typically misunderstood the realities of Czech political stances because they suffered from what I refer to as *the "Todorov problem,"* whereby they habitually misrepresented the local meaning of Central and Eastern European discourse critical of the state through their own filter of Cold War ideology.[13] Havel's concern was to quicken his *native* readers' sense that everyone shared the private thoughts they harbored with each act of self-betrayal. In this supersaturated condition of moral alienation, someone breaking ranks and exposing the nakedness of the regime would be the seed that catalyzed a revolution of independent conduct typical of a functioning and vibrant civil society.

Overview

POCs assert their human rights of agency and voice through a discourse of resistance. They do not appropriate the language of human rights covenants but instead use a vernacular rhetoric that is conditioned by their social conditions and the specific circumstances in which their acts of conscience are called into play. Although they sometimes will make explicit reference to their human rights, more often they will not. Although sometimes they will make reasoned arguments that are associated with formal appeals, more often they will rely on a rhetoric that addresses its immediate audience or an audience of readers and viewers in a way that interrupts what they were doing and demands a response. Moreover, its demand frequently attaches moral implications to how they respond. Because theirs is a vernacular rhetoric, it tends to be specific to its particular culture. Whereas human rights covenants use the decontextualized language of human rights principles, which often are in tension with the cultural and/or political commitments of the human rights abuser, the POCs' expression of human rights emerges in local circumstances and often incorporates the commitments of its oppressor to make its point.

2. *Human Rights and Human Rights Talk*

T he world had hoped the end of the Cold War would usher in an era of peace and an end to human rights abuses. The Soviet empire had collapsed, the peoples of East and West Germany had pounded the Berlin Wall to rubble, the emerging Internet's disregard for national borders had made information control significantly more difficult, and the lure of a market economy, aided by the new media of information technology, had connected former adversaries and longtime partners in its web of globalization. These events intimated hopes would become reality. They have not. Without pressure to align with the powers of the North Atlantic Treaty Organization (NATO) or the Warsaw Pact, centuries-old rivalries have erupted into bloody tribal conflicts. Petty dictators now slaughter their own peoples in tribal warfare; religious zealots slaughter those who do not share their faith; heads of state slaughter citizens along ethnic lines; warlords slaughter those whose allegiances do not advance their political and economic interests; and paramilitary forces, the new warriors of the twenty-first century, fight beyond the control of nation-states with terrorist tactics that disregard the rules of war and render conventional terms of military engagement obsolete. Bosnia, Rwanda, Kosovo, and Darfur have become signatures for how these circumstances have sustained and escalated human rights abuses.

Less publicized is the treatment of boys in Kenya, where ten-year-olds are tortured and forced into the militia (Houreld 2008); of women in Saudi Arabia, who are reluctant to file a complaint in court about spousal abuse since they may not do so without the presence of an obligatory male guardian, who is often the woman's husband ("Our Women" 2008); or of the Roma (Gypsies) in Bulgaria, Romania, and Hungary, estimated at between four and twelve million, who live below the poverty line and are treated with official indifference, which means these governments have washed their hands of concern for their life expectancy, infant mortality, literacy rates, and unemployment ("Bottom of the Heap" 2008, 35). The prospect that incarceration and torture for oppositional beliefs or that official lack of concern for basic survival needs of targeted groups and ethnicities would fade into history books has withered. Even the United States, long the leading voice against human rights abuses and steadfast in its denunciation of torture, now stands accused of both for its treatment of Iraqi, al Qaeda, and Taliban detainees suspected of terrorist activity (Danner 2009a, 2009b; International Committee of the Red Cross 2007; Mayer 2008).

At the same time, the cause of human rights has become among the most visible and supported international agendas of the new century. I say "agendas" with an eye toward how this support is framed. A decade ago, the U.S. Department of State began its 1999 annual report on international human rights practices by observing: "Today, all the talk is of globalization. But far too often, both its advocates and its critics have portrayed globalization as an exclusively economic and technological phenomenon. In fact, in the new millennium, there are at least three universal 'languages:' money, the Internet, and democracy and human rights." Framing human rights in conjunction with money and the Internet suggests too easily that the growing international discourse on human rights exists because moral individualism is somehow joined to economic individualism and that it has become a global language because it serves the interests of the powerful. In fact, the opposite is the case. Money and human rights are more commonly antagonists, as the pressure brought against large conglomerates for abusive labor practices in the developing world demonstrates. And framing human rights in conjunction with democracy places it in service of policies such as the United States' interest during the administration of George W. Bush to export democracy, with force and questionable practices if necessary.

The globalization of human rights is rather a function of localization; its success as an international movement depends on its ability to imbed itself in the language and culture of nations independent of the West. The high ideals of human rights express negative liberties of each human as a priori natural rights. However, the doctrine of natural rights is highly contested, making consensus on practices derived from universal meaning an idle dream. The meaning of human rights, their political and cultural traction, and the capacity of the international community to influence abusive, but nonetheless internal practices of sovereign states is a function of human rights rhetoric; that is, their influence depends on how the international community talks about human rights and how human rights abuses are communicated.

These are not identical. Each is a form of discourse. One is the discourse of human rights talk—a way of translating specific human rights into a locally relevant and culturally specific form of communication intended to curb abusive practices. It is a discourse among nations, international governmental organizations, nongovernmental organizations (NGOs), and news media on behalf of the abused. The other is the localized discourse of resistance—a way of translating specific human rights into locally relevant and culturally specific communication in order to inspire resistance. It is a way of communicating human rights through resistance to oppression, usually expressed through the voice of an imprisoned leader to fellow citizens on the outside but often through concerted expressions of resistance by those who suffer persecution for their political beliefs. Each, I argue, is a form of rhetoric—a discourse that constitutes social realities through its influence on perceptions, attitudes, beliefs, meanings, and actions; more specifically, each is a moral vernacular rhetoric. The former, human rights talk, is the more obvious form of discourse implicit in the vast human rights literature. The latter is relatively unexplored and is the topic of this book.

The Continuous History of Human Rights

Insofar as human rights entail protection of the weak from being subjugated to the stronger or more powerful, it has been at least a nascent concern since c. 1800 BCE when Hammurabi's Code (Avalon Project 2001) regulated social relations by establishing legal rights and penalties, which included the rights of women and their protection. Modern constructions of human rights, however, usually trace to the Enlightenment, especially the philosophical discussions of Locke and Rousseau. Their philosophical considerations were based on the belief that humans are born free. In *The Second Treatise on Government* (1988/1699), Locke argued that there is a natural law that provides each human with the right to live free. When humans enter society, they form a social contract by which they cede certain of these natural rights to the government in order to maintain social order for their collective well-being. Rousseau's *The Social Contract, Or Principles of Political Right* (1997/1762) advanced a similar theory, arguing that humans are born free in a state of nature. When they enter society, they may decide that their individual interests should override society's. However, as a member of the collective, the free citizen puts aside personal interests for the collective good expressed as the "general will." Society is thus governed by popular sovereignty. Both Locke and Rousseau held that the state could not act in an arbitrary way or contrary to the citizens' interests because its powers were derived from the people, and could not exceed the natural powers they themselves had and could transfer. This was an important limitation because it guaranteed basic rights such as free speech, movement, and beliefs; private property; and protection against arbitrary laws and actions by the state as human rights.

For Rousseau, the rights of man tend toward anthropology of the subject in the individual's intersubjectivity as constitutive of the community. The individual as subject is always already both individual and collective, a member of the community reflected in the *general will* and a particular human independent of an absolute authority or sovereign. According to Etienne Balibar (2004, 320), Rousseau introduced "a 'reduction of verticality' brought about by the way the democratic conception of the law places the citizen in a 'two-fold relation' to him- or herself." Locke, on the other hand, offers an individualist anthropology of agent and agency in which the individual's autonomy simultaneously requires responsibility for one's actions. Again according to Balibar (2004, 320), Locke renews the ancient Greek concept of *oikeiosis*, care of oneself, from which he derives the modern idea of self-ownership.

Notwithstanding the general will/self-ownership divide, the idea that all humans had rights to life, liberty, equality, and property, which influenced the thinking of the American and French revolutionaries, provides a platform on which contemporary human rights thinking is based. The Declaration of Independence, the U.S. Bill of

Rights, and the Declaration of the Rights of Man and Citizen set forth guarantees of human rights and liberties based on the Enlightenment's liberal philosophy that held each human had inalienable rights to be guaranteed and protected by the government and on which its legitimacy rested. The lineage of thought and, just as important, legal codes, documents, and other codifications of rights stands as a precursor to today's concern with human rights, most notably expressed in the Universal Declaration of Human Rights (UDHR).

However, the platform provided by Rousseau and Locke contains within both lines of thought implicit limit conditions that suggest the idea of human rights is not part of a natural order but a social compact. Rousseau's "coercion to be free"[1] and Locke's (1988/1699, 284) exclusion of criminals from humanity in order to exclude them from citizenship and legislative power both place the offending party outside the human condition and forfeit claims to human rights. In contemporary thought, Arendt (1968), Ranceire (2004), and Žižek (2005), among others, have argued that human rights are extended only to those who have been placed beyond them, to those whose political condition has excluded them from treatment as humans. In other words, at the level of praxis human rights are rhetorical constructions for which the free citizen has no need since the rule of law guarantees negative liberties and just treatment. At the same time and prefatory to human rights, Doxtader (2010, 373) has argued, "is a recognizing of how we cannot live until such a time as we have dispensed with their need . . . that their value turns within words that we have yet to find and that, in our time, do not yet have a place."

The Hope of Moral Perfectionism

Shortly after World War II had ended and the United Nations (U.N.) had formed, world leaders set to drafting what became the UDHR. It was intended to enunciate the rights of all human beings and the obligations of sovereign states to respect them. This was a remarkable endeavor, considering the condition of the world in 1947 and the differences between states over their relations to their citizens and their respective assumptions of sovereignty. Were it not for the unsurpassed leadership of Eleanor Roosevelt, the endeavor likely would have failed. Her skill at keeping self-interested arguments of national representatives in check and the drafting committee focused were critical.

More challenging than competing interests for the final document's ultimate shape and present-day consequences for human rights rhetoric were deep philosophical differences already present when Roosevelt first convened a drafting committee at her Washington Square apartment in February 1947. At that meeting two philosophers, Peng-Chun Chang, a Chinese Confucian who had studied under John Dewey at Columbia, and Charles Malik, a Lebanese Greek Orthodox Thomist, got into a row over the bases of human rights (Lash 1972, 52). At stake was how far you could go in the direction of pragmatic compromise without putting truth, and thereby moral universality, up for grabs (Glendon 2001, 47). At one point the argument became so heated that Roosevelt concluded the only way to make progress was if West and East agreed to disagree (Ignatieff 2002, 58). Her choice proved wise since it also allowed all parties to avoid the uncomfortable discussion that would have ensued had the skeletons been brought from the closet. The Soviet Union had no more interest in explaining the Red Terror than the United States its Jim Crow laws or Britain its colonial practices. Everyone had something to be ashamed of, but the point was not to embarrass each other with indictments of what *is* but to keep them focused on the high principles of what *ought* to be (Roosevelt 1992/1961, 320).

High principles also skirted the question of enforcement. The UDHR provides no mandate for intervention to stop human rights abuses, leaving Roosevelt's uncertainty whether "a mere statement of rights, without legal obligations, would inspire governments to see that these rights were preserved" (quoted in Urquhart 2001, 32) as the real question ever since. The UDHR left untouched the U.N. charter's guarantee of state sovereignty. "Instead," in the words of Michael Ignatieff, "the delegates put their hopes in the idea that by declaring rights as moral universals, they could foster global rights consciousness among those they called 'the common people'" (1999, 58).

The rhetorical character of moral universalism without the undergirding of a specific philosophy or theology makes the UDHR an affirmation of a secular creed left ambiguous in its justification so as to better move among different political systems and cultural frames (Taylor 1999, 126; see also Doxtader 2010). With Nazi atrocities fresh on everyone's mind, the framers asserted the priority of each person's basic humanity as entailing fundamental rights that nations must agree to accept and respect. It may not have set forth specific consequences for failure to respect these rights, but the world has acted *as if* abusing human rights could go neither unnoticed nor unpunished, at least as this view is reflected in the rhetoric of human rights on the international stage.[2]

The ideals of moral perfectionism, however, are hard to live by, especially when trouble hits. Their abstract righteousness offers a language of antipolitics, which inspires rhetorical neutrality toward national interests in order to privilege the inherent worth of every human regardless of national origin, belief, or creed, or at least it does so from the perspective of accusing nations and NGOs. This rhetorical position is problematic, however, when your nation is under assault. It is difficult to criticize your government when you can be attacked for being unpatriotic. Defending, say, the human rights of "enemy combatant" detainees at Guantánamo accused of being part of the al-Qaeda network or part of the Taliban with the language of moral universals seems, to an audience of angry and fearful citizens, not only unpatriotic but also impudent and irrelevant (Ignatieff 2002, 18). Although the passing of time may abate anger and provide space for deeper reflection on what we are doing, that does not alter the lurking power of circumstances to render the universality of moral perfectionism moot.

Human Rights and the Problem of Moral Perfectionism

In a discussion of its ideological aspirations, Louis Henken (2000, 11) celebrates the UDHR as having made four significant achievements: it helped convert a discredited philosophical idea ("natural rights") into a dominant ideology; it defined a vague colloquialism ("human rights") in an authoritative code, a triple "decalogue" of thirty articles of fundamental rights; it universalized human rights, promoting a constitutional ideology accepted in a few countries into a standard of constitutionalism for all countries; and it internationalized human rights, transforming matters that had been subject to exclusive domestic jurisdiction—"sovereignty"—into matters of international concern, putting them permanently on the international political agenda, and providing the foundation for a sturdy edifice of international norms and institutions.

As a statement of accomplishments, Henken sets forth what the West would like to believe. Judged by existing realities, however, it is a convenient fable. All nations profess to honor human rights, but on their own terms. Human rights are understood and lived so differently as to defy categorization as a "dominant ideology," as, for example, such perspectives as those of personalist-communitarian and critical law attest at the level of theory (Leary 1992) and China, say, at the level of praxis (Jingsheng 2000). Moreover, in light of interminable East-West wrangling over human rights abuses versus insistence on national sovereignty in the treatment of citizens, it seems fair to assert the UDHR is anything but authoritative with respect to actual practices. Nor is it clear that the standard of constitutionalism, which has been adopted by postcolonial states, always results in practices aligned with human rights accords, Rwanda being but one example. Although there is much rhetorical hand-wringing about human rights abuses, only the most egregious violations capture the international community's attention. When they do, the accused state, contrary to Henken's portrayal, frequently retorts with an explicit assertion of state sovereignty: treatment of its citizens is an internal matter. Few states are willing to challenge the alleged abuser's claim that "what happens within our borders stays within our borders." Unless a state's security is in question, a policy of noninterference also provides a convenient buffer against challenges to its own sovereignty. Henken's optimistic reading loses sight of how the UDHR[3] came about, the difficulty of enforcement that concerned its framers, and why, in all likelihood, it can never be what he purports it has become.

Conflicting Interpretations of Human Rights

Original misgivings about enforcement of the UDHR were not misplaced. Samantha Power (2002) has documented in exhaustive detail the chilling reality of genocide since World War II and the sorry performance of state leaders, who consistently have vowed they would not idly stand by if genocide occurred on their watch, only to settle for plaintive protests when called upon to act.[4] The priority of national interest coupled with the rhetoric of public denunciation provides a convenient mask for a policy of nonintervention.

Equally inhibiting is the unavoidable ambiguity of what the UDHR's thirty universal rights mean. Disputes over their meaning often have taken the form of dialectical debate to establish the rational priority of each side's fundamental claims. The purpose of debate, however, is not necessarily to reach agreement. Often it is to prevail. Failure to recognize that disputes have an inherent rhetorical dimension does not obviate its presence as an agency of influence. Core cultural and ideological commitments are seldom open to change. Detachment from the other's core beliefs and failure to recognize that human rights arguments must engage the desires and interests of those accused of abuses only intensify differences that make enforcement and compliance difficult.

From the outset, this ambiguity has fostered a continuing moral universalism/ moral particularism divide. Universalism holds to a deontological position that considers rights to be a moral primitive (Donnelly 2003, 42). In practice, on the other hand, political interpretations of human rights lead to differences over a person's status as a subject and citizen, which, in turn, lead to conflicting rhetorics. For moral universalists, human rights are not merely matters of internal affairs; they are universal norms that transcend cultures while having expression in all cultures (Jingsheng 2000). Particularists, on the other hand, argue that human rights must be understood against the backdrop of cultural and social differences, such as exist between individualist and collectivist cultures (Alford 1992).

The universalism/particularism divide also is reflected in how each side grounds human rights. Universalists ground them in human dignity, particularists in cultural autonomy. The rhetoric of universalism affirms such positions as the meta-ethical argument for the moral obligation that sovereign states have to protect the rights of all humans to reason and act, or the moral obligation to protect "the possibility of a rational social and political order based on individual rights that, over time, could facilitate happiness for humankind as a whole" (Falk 1992, 45). Universalists consider these state obligations as rational dictates. This assumption lies behind the rhetoric of such arguments as those of Soviet dissidents who commonly cited the UDHR and other human rights covenants in court proceedings, protest letters, and the like in order to marshal the pressure of world opinion against their government (Romanov 2000).

The rhetoric of particularism objects to the foundational rhetoric of universalism, which makes it difficult to establish a human rights regime acceptable to everyone (Gutmann 2001, xvii). In fact, the particularists' dialectical position suggests that the very idea of "human" is itself a social construct. Anthropologist Rhoda Howard (1992), for instance, argues that although most societies have a concept of *rights,* they do not have a concept of *human* rights. Historically, she points out, most societies have made a social determination of who is or is not human, with slaves and foreigners dealt out of the game. On her assessment of particularist terms, human dignity does not refer to an *inherent* right to respect, but something *granted* at birth or by incorporation into a community. It is concomitant with one's ascribed status, and therefore not private, individual, and autonomous but public, collective, and prescribed by social norms (84). That is why, for example, under Shari'a criminal law, which is given precedence over the secular legal code in many Muslim countries, certain crimes may be punished by dismemberment. It is a severe punishment dictated by the Qur'an. It may be cruel, but it is not regarded as degrading. To question it is not only a sign of losing one's faith but may result in severe social chastisement and possibly death as an act of apostasy (An-Na`im 1992b, 35).

Finally, both moral universalism and moral particularism are vulnerable to favoring one group over another. Universalist arguments typically favor Western over non-Western or developing world cultural practices. On the other hand, colonial practices are notorious for subordinating indigenous peoples to a dominant power. By the same token, conflicts between ethnic rivals, as in Darfur and the Balkans, show a dominant culture's equal enthusiasm to victimize a subordinate one by excluding its members from the public sphere, proving intransigent in negotiation over inclusion, or engaging in genocidal warfare (Falk 1992, 45).

These problems arise from an understanding of human rights as moral commitments, codified in declarations of rights and in accords. For universalists, they are regarded as *customary international law*, binding their signatories to honor treaty-like codes of conduct. They are a system of lawlike rules that sets forth sanctions for violations. However, these covenants lack the sanctioning power of laws; they are quasi- or soft legal instruments that ratifying nations assume responsibility to enforce under the supervision of a global body. From a Western perspective, violators are open to sanctions, and individuals who have committed egregious offenses may be tried before international tribunals and, if found guilty, subjected to punishment, including execution. From a particularist perspective, attributing soft legal status to human rights accords has the appearance of a rhetorical ploy to impose a Western conception of the good life on expressions of value that are open to interpretation. Exporting its moral commitments, it is argued, and imposing them on another ignores those moral commitments specific to a particular culture. From this perspective, universalist claims constitute a form of hegemonic moral imperialism.

The stalemate between these positions is illustrated by the inability of the International Criminal Court (ICC) to arrest and extradite accused human rights violators for trial before an international court. A case in point was the refusal of the Sudanese government to honor the ICC's charge of genocide against President Omar Hassan al-Bashir for "masterminding attempts to wipe out African tribes in Darfur with a campaign of murder, rape and deportation." The government responded that it did not recognize the jurisdiction of the ICC ("Sudanese President" 2008).

In addition to the cultural divide, principles of human rights do not assert claims easily translated into a system of enforceable rules without violating fundamental principles of national sovereignty. Framing human rights as moral a prioris or as meaningful only as culturally inflected norms makes it impossible to heal this divide without one side foregoing its self-understanding (Anderson 2006; Agamben 1998). Here, again, the international community's commitment to honor national sovereignty makes unilateral intervention extremely problematic. Most allegations of human rights abuses are raised with respect to specific individuals, groups, or events that do not constitute genocide. Opposition to an authoritarian regime may result in arrest, torture, and even execution, but these responses may be regarded as internal matters that raise concerns about the treatment of nationals but are not regarded as so egregious and widespread as to constitute justification for armed intervention. The U.N. has addressed these cases with resolutions and diplomacy rather than military force. Even when it appears that atrocities against a national group are widespread, the difficulty in overcoming a veto by a permanent member of the Security Council has made military intervention unlikely.[5]

When force has been used, it has been outside the U.N., undertaken by joint efforts of several nations rather than unilaterally, and justified with the rationale that there are alternative legal bases for authorization than that of the U.N., such as international law or humanitarian mandates to stop genocide. In the case of NATO's intervention in Kosovo, for instance, its five members sitting on the U.N. Security Council claimed military action was necessary to avoid a "humanitarian catastrophe" (Terry 2004). However, a humanitarian rationale is not necessarily invoked in such cases. When President Clinton appeared before the U.N. General Assembly to explain U.S. participation in the bombing of Serbia-Montenegro, he stated: "By acting as we did, we helped to vindicate the principles and purposes of the U.N. charter, to give the U.N. the opportunity it now has to play the central role in shaping Kosovo's future. In the real world, principles often collide, and tough choices must be made. The outcome in Kosovo is hopeful" (Clinton 1999). Clinton's rationale reflects political considerations rather than humanitarian ones, and speaks to the difficulty of translating moral universals into a system of enforceable rules without violating fundamental principles of national sovereignty.

The clash between universalist and particularist commitments places moral perfection out of reach. That is a good thing because it suggests the need to reframe human rights as something other than moral imperatives that are not shared. Abandoning the quest for moral perfection removes the discussion of human rights from acceptance of natural law as a grounding principle, a perspective based on acceptance of the a priori condition of each person as an entitlement not to be treated in ways that compromise human dignity. Since there is no agreement on the definition of this a priori condition, but there is agreement that for a person to be considered a human, he or she has inalienable rights that are inherent in his or her humanness, however these may be understood, the focus should be on principles of human rights, such as those expressed in the UDHR. Setting aside a deontological understanding of human rights, the principles enunciated in the UDHR are better thought of as providing terms to which signatories to human rights accords have ascribed validity for conducting specific discussions concerning human rights abuses. In other words, they provide the lingua franca of a reticulate public sphere (Hauser 1999b, chapter 3) in which nation-states, NGOs, religious bodies, news media, and international organizations engage in the ongoing negotiation over the human treatment of individuals and groups under the control of a specific state.

In *Human Rights as Politics and Idolatry*, Michael Ignatieff (2001) makes the argument that human rights language cannot be "parsed" into nonindividualist or communitarian perspectives, that it is inexorably individualistic and "nonsensical outside that assumption." From his perspective, the individualistic nature of human rights language accounts for why human rights are so attractive worldwide and have become a global movement. They are "the only universally available moral vernacular that validates the claims of women and children against the oppression they experience in patriarchal and tribal societies" (68).

Ignatieff's assessment accentuates the inherent political dimension of human rights. Dealing with human rights abuses as if they were "moral aspirations" and rights conventions as if they were "syncretic syntheses of world values" fails to address the concrete reality of "conflicts that define the very content of rights" (67). Human rights conflict is between, in his words, a "rights holder" and a "rights withholder." This is a political conflict better understood in terms of a discourse in which human rights provide a language for negotiation, hence the value of human rights language, in Ignatieff's view, as a moral vernacular.

Reading human rights accords in a way that reframes human rights as a discourse foregoes the dialectic of first principles for the inventional possibilities inherent to rhetoric. Human rights talk is a rhetorical form all the way down, with its own mechanisms of discursive influence, central among which is the moral vernacular. Moreover, Ignatieff's repositioning of human rights from philosophical foundationalism and moral trump cards to a language of politics moves away from the realist presupposition that privileges state sovereignty over external actions on behalf of individual rights and into the realm of discourse and rhetoric (Beer and Hariman 1996). At the same time, his claim that human rights are a discourse is underdeveloped, and his claim that they are a moral vernacular is an incomplete if not flawed formulation for its failure to consider the vernacularity of human rights themselves as distinct from their universality. These two claims must be considered separately because they involve distinctions that have significance for the main concern of this book: the moral vernaculars of political prisoners.

Human Rights as a Discourse

The moral panic inspired by savage cruelty directed at persons and groups for their identity and beliefs is as ancient as the mayhem that followed Antigone's placing of her familial obligation to Polynices's slain remains above the edict of a spiteful king. To make sense of her resistance required that she explain not only to Creon but also to herself why she had to pay final service to her brother's corpse. She prefaces her explanation with a question: "What is the law that lies behind these words?" (Sophocles 1973). It is a question that pertains to all human rights issues. Since its adoption, the UDHR has invoked the natural right of every human being to the liberties it sets forth as the law behind its words.

Yet laws are abstractions, and natural rights is a particularly nettlesome abstraction because it creates difficulty in formulating human rights as a discourse that can avoid the mire of irresolvable problems inherent to moral perfectionism. For most people in the United States and many in Western Europe who did not suffer in the Nazi camps, abusive practices are removed from experience; they lack a human face when couched in national values and abstract legalisms. That changed in the U.S. context after 9/11, and in disturbing ways. Images of Iraqi, al Qaeda, and Taliban detainees held in U.S. facilities at Camp X-Ray and Abu Ghraib captured U.S. military personnel abusing them. Their actions were a contradiction of a national self-understanding that the United States did not engage in torture and raised questions of who knew about this treatment, was it authorized, and did the answers lay in the Oval Office?[6]

Human rights discourse mirrors this experience of abstract and concrete rhetoric. On the one hand, there is official discourse about abuses, abusers, and the abused conducted between governments, and frequently involving NGOs. Advocates for the abused, especially for political prisoners, speak as surrogates for those whose faces we do not see, whose voices we do not hear, and whose pain we do not witness. There is a second form of discourse that comes from the abused and, by showing us their human face, gives presence to their pain and immediacy to their plea for help.

With respect to the former, which is my present concern, Ignatieff's suggestion that we reframe human rights as a discourse complicates our understanding of the UDHR and other human rights agreements. By a discourse, Ignatieff points to the fact that when human rights are regarded as moral imperatives, they impose an essentialist conception that ignores the nature of political legitimacy. In his words, "political legitimacy is always local: power translates itself into legitimate authority by exploiting and using traditions and symbols of the local political culture" (2001a, 172). Taking this into account, Ignatieff affirms that his proposed construction of human rights as a discourse offers a *minimalist* human rights program, but one with prospects for concrete achievements.

Several points related to discourse are germane to this discussion. "Discourse" is a polysemous term. From one theoretical/analytical perspective associated with the work of Foucault (1972, 1977), "discourse" refers to a set of acceptable statements within a discourse community formed by these statements. Their meanings constitute its social practices and articulate its truths, which both distinguish it as a community and legitimate its regimes of power. The discourse itself creates relationships regarding who is or is not included in the community and who can or cannot speak. For example, those outside a democratic culture typically are excluded from its discourse community, as is the case with authoritarian leaders (Touraine 1997). Even when they profess their states to be democratic, as did leaders of Communist democratic republics during the Cold War, they are excluded by nonauthoritarian states from the discourse called "democracy." Equally, cultural norms—as exist, for example, in patriarchal or theocratic states—have the power to exclude voices of women and the unconfessed. Put differently, discourse constitutes both the subject and agency. As noted above, although every culture professes that a human has certain rights that qualify that person as human, the term is applied differently in different cultures and time periods.

A discourse of power is a social practice; it is concerned with a culturally inscribed way by which power is manifested. In patriarchal and theocratic states, it is manifested in the person of authority, who acquires this status by birth or by relationship to that culture's sacred texts. Power, in these cases, is displayed in the language of cultural beliefs, which are often expressed by traditional norms or sacred texts. In democratic societies, power may be expressed through modes of speaking and acting that are inclusive and that reflect sensitivity to identities, and is legitimated by those outside of power through myriad expressions of public opinion. Equally, democracies also have their rules of exclusion. Children may not vote; those who speak may be required to meet certain, sometimes most undemocratic, qualifications, as was the case in the United States when Jim Crow laws excluded blacks from voting; organizational and institutional structures may place restrictions on those who may participate in decision making, as was the case in the Canadian parliament's annexing of indigenous people's water rights (Kempton 2005), and so forth.

This understanding of discourse encounters difficulties with respect to human rights because it describes the conversations and the meaning behind them by a group of people who hold certain ideas in common. It reflects an ideology, manifested in its institutions, and their power to define lived reality. However, beginning with ideological assumptions about human rights ignores the nature of political legitimacy, which does not necessarily honor external ideological givens and leaves them without traction in localities that do not share them. Moreover, it does not fully capture the counterdiscourse of those who are excluded and act in ways that resist exclusion not just through what is spoken but also what is performed.

A second sense of discourse, not entirely divorced from the one just described, views it as an ongoing process of exchange that includes the practice of deliberation. Deliberation occurs in a context of choice and decision. Parties to deliberation have different beliefs, opinions, feelings, and allegiances that give rise to differing ends and often lay at the core of disputes. Deliberation functions as their means to resolve public problems through whatever decisions are reached. It is a method for discovering ways to reach acceptable ends within the limits of differing commitments. The involved parties advocate, exhort, and dissuade with presentations of fact, arguments about what is the case, and forecasts of the future if events are shaped by agreements or if left to themselves. Deliberation situates discourse within the public sphere and within rhetoric, which has, from the time of Aristotle, been concerned with the useful, the just, and the honorable.[7] Because deliberation is situated within rhetoric, it is concerned with what is desired, not with what is desirable in itself. This important distinction moves discourse into the realm of the contingent, where ideology is subordinated to efficacy with respect to prevailing exigencies.

This sense of discourse opens the field of human rights rhetoric to alternative possibilities. Exhortation and dissuasion are the means for deriving future policy. The meaning of human rights becomes a human invention, not an ideological derivative. Judgments are concerned with how to treat those who are guilty of atrocities, and, as a form of appeal with the end of justice, it includes the possibility of reconciliation (Doxtader 2000, 2001, 2007). Demonstration seeks agreement on acts that deserve esteem. It extols honorable practices and holds them up as models for others to emulate, while it condemns dishonorable ones and derides their agents as outside the community. An understanding of human rights as a deliberative discourse fashions the meaning of any specific human right at any given time as provisional. It recognizes that "political legitimacy is always local: power translates itself into legitimate authority by exploiting and using traditions and symbols of the local political culture" (Ignatieff 2002, 172).

The Impasse of Imputative Rhetoric

Considering human rights as a discourse helps us understand the mode of rhetoric that produces the irresolvable stasis between moral universalists and moral particularists. Both rely on fundamentally different assumptions that are difficult to translate into the other's perspective; each treats its assumptions as a priori moral principles, a commitment that manifests in the rhetoric of *imputation*.[8] Imputation holds all persons duty-bound to observe precepts and maxims that are universal and asserts objective values (McKeon 1960). Moral universalists interpret human rights as conditions for justice. They consider them to derive from a priori universal laws applicable to each person as an individual and that therefore require observance by all persons. The thirty articles of the UDHR are, by this account, absolute goods. Its articles are not merely adequate but true ideas of justice because they refer to specific objects or behaviors. The moral universalist assumes that all parties have a similar regard for these referent behaviors as guaranteed rights of each person and, moreover, that denying them to any person is prosecutable in the name of justice. When that assumption is denied, we are on the path to polemic where differences of beliefs result in irreconcilable disagreements over reality and irreconcilable moral commitments about justice. The universalist's interpretation of human rights as categorical imperatives regarding justice stands apart from whatever functional efficacy human rights may have as means to ends (McKeon 1960, 192).

Moral particularism also relies on the rhetoric of imputation. It assumes the primacy of its value system's maxims and rules of action, which are validated by tradition. It argues that fundamental values are culturally specific and that "the communal group—whatever that might be (tribe, village, or kinship), and not the individual—is the basic social unit" (Pollis 2000, 11). If human rights are meaningful only in a frame specific to a cultural or political system, then there is no higher good that makes the specific claim meaningful beyond the benediction of being good because it is desired. Although it may be the case that humans do not desire something because it is good but find something good because it is desired, cultural relativism neither supports meaningful dialogue over change nor promotes arguments that will be regarded as sensible outside its own frame of reference.

For both universalists and particularists, imputative rhetoric relies on premises without supporting assumptions that can be translated across cultures; it is a problematic rhetoric for resolving human rights issues. From a partisan perspective, one's side's moral judgments express obvious truths and accepted values; the other side's statements are considered propaganda intended to manipulate power or to advance that side's interests or ideology. Imputation thus reflects a cognitive position in which arguments function only as a form of justificatory rhetoric. It assumes the moral imperative of a human right as derived from natural law and asks the violator to justify "bad" practices in terms of assumptions it does not hold, that is, the accuser's, usually Western, interpretations of the UDHR. Or it assumes the moral imperative of tradition to interpret the meaning of a human right and objects to the moral hegemony of those who do not allow for cultural differences.

From each of these partisan viewpoints, the other side's imputative rhetoric appears to frame human rights with a rhetorical gambit. To particularists, it seems to foist the accuser's moral position on the accused; to universalists, it seems to use cultural autonomy as a justification for what it considers "abusive" practices. Both positions—one framed in the decontextualized language of moral universals, the other in the privileged language of a specific culture—require expression adapted to local demands of specific human rights talk or conversion of a priori assumptions into rhetorical arguments. Both positions lose touch with the fact that questions of human rights, when considered within rhetoric's domain of public moral argument, cease to be answerable with the exclusive warrants of moral absolutes or cultural autonomy. Rhetoric transforms human rights into a discourse that occurs at both the general level, where types of practices are under review, and the particular level, where a specific person's treatment is a matter of public deliberation in the reticulate public sphere (Hauser 1999b, chapter 3) of human rights talk. Human rights provide a language that transcends national borders and adjudicates practices and treatment of persons to whom agency and justice lay claim.

The Thin Moral Vernacular of Accountability Rhetoric

Reading the UDHR as a rhetoric-inducing document that supports a discourse of human rights talk manifests a thin version of the moral vernacular. Each of the rights it enumerates stands as a claim of accountability. Human rights talk in terms of consequences need not address the ideological value structure of an abuser if it can convert assertions of human rights into the accused's frame of reference and vice versa. Conversion requires attention to the characteristics of a human rights precept. Most obviously, as expressed in the UDHR it is a *universal* statement. A human right applies to all people in all places at all times, simply because they are humans. It is a *culturally neutral* statement. A human right cannot hold for one culture or state and not all. This does not mean a human right will have the same expression in all cultures or that it will manifest identical lived realities. Cultural neutrality does prohibit a human right from being prejudicial against a culture; it must, however, be meaningful within the culture. A transcultural human rights claim requires a particular rhetorical means for *transforming* it from one culture to another. Finally, a human rights claim is *nonjustificatory.* The UDHR does not offer justifications for its articles. They are assumed to be human rights, which are validated by the signatories' mutual silence. This silence carries over to the human rights culture.[9]

The human rights culture draws on the UDHR for the language of both sovereign nations and NGOs to address questions of human rights abuses and a topical system for generating human rights arguments and appeals. In some cases, human rights talk allows the international community to adopt a juridical stance against atrocities, such as those committed in the savage ethnic and religious wars in Kosovo and Kashmir. By the same token, the openness of each article to divergent interpretations makes any attempt at concerted action subject to objection and opposition as unwarranted and quite possibly itself unjust. Although human rights discourse seldom achieves unanimity, it sets the terms of engagement in talk, which proffers the promise to avoid conflict or at least retard its spreading.

Human rights discourse provides the thin moral vernacular for what Ignatieff (2002) calls a "thin theory" of human rights. His thin theory regards the universal commitments implied by human rights documents as a discourse that can be compatible with a variety of ways of life. These commitments are only universal as "self-consciously" minimalist agreements, "the definition of the minimum conditions for any kind of life at all" (56). By any measure, agreements on the minimum conditions for any kind of meaningful life are suboptimal at best, but they have the advantage of fixing acceptable standards of responsibility and accountability. These agreements are reached through the rhetoric of *accountability.*

The unavoidable rhetorical dimension in every human rights argument delimits different orientations toward what we understand by "human rights" and the arenas in which human rights arguments about abuses are made. The most common understanding of abuse arguments, as distinct from performative appeals, is that they are made in official public spheres[10] by states, international bodies, and NGOs directly engaged in assertions of abuse against another state and are calls for it to desist. No state accused of a human rights violation is going to admit to it, and either will build a defense for its conduct or claim it is an internal affair. That does not necessarily end the matter. Human rights talk, talk that construes human rights to be a discourse, begins as advocacy for the victim who is entitled to representation as long as he or she seeks relief. In the official public sphere, human rights documents provide premises for arguments. They are agreed-upon reference points for discussing specific actions. Human rights talk shifts from imputation's tendency toward diremption, where arguments are based on the nonnegotiable first principles of natural law or cultural identity, to accountability rhetoric that moves from moral debate to political deliberation and negotiation over the conditions and consequences of action and responsibility.

A significant practical consequence of this discursive shift is that human rights talk focuses on abuses, which are always specific, rather than the abstraction of human rights principles. The argument against an arranged or forced marriage, say, is not the moral imputation that the person has an inherent dignity as set forth in Article 1 of the UDHR, but that individuals have the right to enter into marriage of their own free will and mutual agreement, as set forth in Article 16. It is an argument on behalf of victims whose specific human right has been violated. The argument is to agency.

In fact, human rights talk is all about agency. Unless arguments for the primacy of human dignity are set aside, human rights talk becomes dismally idealistic and futile. Arguments to human dignity encourage dialectical debate over what it means to be "human," what constitutes "dignity," and whether dignity is the foundational principle that proscribes certain practices. On the other hand, the efficacy of specific arguments to agency depends on their engagement of a cultural discourse that defines social power and cultural identity, and is consequential for human possibilities. Cultural discourse delimits spaces of appearance, discursive arenas, and rules of inclusion and exclusion. It constructs the human subject, so that what constitutes a human and who qualifies as included in human rights talk can, itself, be understood as a rhetorical construction. Nor can agency be understood apart from cultural discourse because it, too, is constituted by cultural discourse.

Official political arguments to agency, of course, make reference to specific situations, individuals, and practices. They employ the rhetoric of accountability that encourages deliberation and negotiation, which in turn must acknowledge the relevance of the cultural discourse that stands behind practices (Cohen 1997), even if it is invoked as a cover for bad acts. That is the point of public human rights talk: to talk about a specific case in search of remedy and to use the negative liberties established by covenants and conventions to advance rights that the state may not take away and must protect. Human rights talk proceeds from the assumption that a violation is best addressed through rhetorical engagement and that human rights accords provide a moral vernacular of starting premises that do not require justification; they express at least minimal agreement on what is necessary for the good life while recognizing that each right may be lived differently. Although it is difficult to imagine an acceptable rationale for imposing a vision of the good life on those who are happy with the one they are leading, neither can a state's sacrifice of a portion of its people go unnoticed. Accountability rhetoric is almost always directed at overcoming the use of cultural discourse as a cover for brutality, and compliance is almost always the product of moral suasion addressed to the conditions and consequences of freedom of choice.

The challenge of human rights talk, then, is to translate meaningful ideas from one frame to another. Accountability rhetoric is the architectonic art for doing this. Human rights are inventional; they function as places for generating arguments that can cut across ideological boundaries. They intersect with practices that open possibilities for talking about humans in new terms and uncovering alternative political and social relations. At the same time, the efficacy of human rights talk rests on finding permutations resonant with political desire, which is not always achievable with the thin moral vernacular of official public spheres. This brings us to nonofficial human rights discourse involving the victims and the moral vernacular.

The Problem of the Abused

As noted earlier, reframing human rights as a discourse accentuates their political dimension. Moreover, moving human rights from the deontological realm into the political also places them in the realm of rhetoric. As a species of rhetoric, they provide a political language with which human rights talk can conduct negotiations. This has special relevance for the content of human rights.

For discourse to make progress producing mutual understanding and resolving common problems, participants must share meanings. Where they do not exist, one function of discourse is to produce them. The rhetoric of give and take, as is the case with deliberation, can establish and even change our interpretations of experience. Negotiation is specifically concerned with arriving at a set of shared interpretations that will govern future actions in ways that are mutually acceptable, regardless of how wide or narrow the range of acceptability may be. With respect to concrete contests between rights holders and rights withholders, the contests themselves define the content of rights. Their reality is quite literally forged through the rhetoric of negotiation.

In this vein, human rights talk is concerned with political judgment, which emphasizes phenomena understood as appearances,[11] as what is manifest; its concern is with determining their facticity as phenomena rather than classifying them as objects under an ontological category of universal meaning. Political events have the characteristic, perhaps uniquely their own, of creating their own space of appearance.

But their appearance within this space is always marked by uncertainty and requires the sort of discrimination that relies upon representative thinking[12] in order to reflect upon what is not there—the missing evidence and future consequences of choice and action.

The space of appearance that human rights talk creates for itself need not be available for public scrutiny. Its concern is to protect human agency, which encompasses any treatment that would abridge an individual's or group's freedom to make choices about how they will lead their lives, including protection from unlawful imprisonment and torture. Its objective does not always require marshaling public opinion to bring pressure for change. Secret negotiations are typically more efficacious for the empowered to reach a mutually acceptable resolution to an impasse. Whether in open or back channels, these recognized arenas allow those with the power to act—governments, international bodies, NGOs, the church, and the news media—to engage one another in serious deliberation over questioned practices.

The difficulty confronting advocates for human rights is to find shared perspectives with those whose practices they question or for their defense before those who raise challenges. This is often a problem of overcoming the insularity of ideologically inscribed experiences. Meeting the challenge of insularity depends on our respective abilities to affirm something outside ourselves, or to engage in the representative thinking just noted. In Hannah Arendt's words, "Only where things can be seen by many in a variety of aspects without changing their identity, so that those who are gathered around them know they see sameness in utter diversity, can worldly reality truly and reliably appear" (1958, 57). Arendt's observation reminds us that reality and our understanding of it are social and are formed through critical processes; we decipher the sense of words and actions in light of our partisan and collective experiences.

These considerations highlight the rhetorical problem of the political prisoner. The thin moral vernacular of human rights talk is seldom available to those whose rights have been violated; it is used by those who speak and write on their behalf. Because surrogate discourse is concerned to gain cessation of a specific practice, whether treatment of a group or individual, its appeals are made in the name of justice. Human rights talk gives justice political meaning. Human rights embody justice through their political function of affirming agency. As an expression of negative liberties, they affirm the person's right to have an authentic role in shaping his or her own destiny. Justice affirms equality of freedom. All persons have the human right to judicial protection against discrimination based on gender, race, religion, sexual orientation, ethnicity, political beliefs, or other individuating traits. They also have the right to participate freely in the political process, which includes free access to information, freedom of speech and the press, as well as freedom to assemble and to dissent. As a political expression, justice requires that individuals and groups have the right to be secure against arrest, torture, and imprisonment for their beliefs, as well as protection of their personal, social, and cultural rights. In the name of justice, persons and groups are guaranteed economic rights to earn a living and receive fair compensation for their labor. This list could continue and, as is evident, as a political language it would include all the provisions of the UDHR construed as required because justice demands them.

The political concerns of POCs are more immediate. Their circumstances make the abstraction of justice secondary to the realities of their situation and their lack of power. They do not have access to the public realm in which one finds human rights discourse of the sort Ignatieff espouses. Their struggle is not deliberative; their discourse addresses exigencies they and their society confront that require direct attention. They speak to their interrogators, warders, or other inmates to mitigate threats to their physical and mental well-being, and even to their survival. When personal safety is not their foremost concern, and, for some, even though it is, their attention turns to a wider audience to inspire resistance. The urgency inspiring their arguments and appeals is less action in the name of justice than for the demands of conscience on which their political identity depends and which holds them relentlessly captive.

The rhetoric of POCs manifest in such forms as prison writings, bodily performances, and coordinated actions have a moral vernacular of their own that I refer to as a *thick moral vernacular*. In contrast to the thin moral vernacular of human rights talk, thick moral vernacular does not use the language of the UDHR and other human rights conventions to construct the meaning of human rights in a specific context. In fact, the UDHR and like conventions are rhetorically useful only as inartistic proofs. Their covenants are invoked as matters of fact, as if they are moral universals whose meanings are evident and which their governments, as signatories, are duty bound to respect. The thick moral vernacular is not a deliberative discourse. It migrates from the logic of deliberation to the postmodern logic of discourse communities that define and are defined by the statements acceptable to it. This moral vernacular's discursive logic is dependent on culture. It is a discourse on virtue and vice; it is a performance of agency and power that is contesting, if not in conflict with, that of the state; it constitutes and sustains political community through appeals banished from official public life, though not necessarily from the general public's view. These rhetorics of conscience offer insight into the thick moral vernacular as a locus of resistance with the potential to invert society's ostensible power vectors and that they have relevance to present political conditions.

3. Thick Moral Vernacular and Human Rights

Beginning in 1942, the Nazis invented a new way to dehumanize Jews and gypsies. At Auschwitz and in the Lagers, registration numbers, which already were sewn on the prisoners' clothing, were now tattooed onto their left forearms. Soon the tattoos were further coded to mark each prisoner's identity with greater precision. Men were tattooed on the outside of the arm, women on the inside. Gypsies had their numbers preceded by the letter Z, Jews reporting from the beginning of May 1944 on were preceded by an A, which shortly thereafter was replaced by a B. When children started to arrive, after September 1944, all of them, including infants, also were tattooed (Levi 1988, 118–19).

For the Nazis, the tattoos served the formal function of coding each prisoner as if an inventory item. Assigning registration numbers was not unique to the Nazis; they are part of the prison regime's accounting system that must keep a register of each prisoner's location, assignment, and health history, track his or her behavior, and catalog anything else that pertains to its bureaucratic necessities of biopolitical management.

Quite apart from these administrative requirements, erasing the prisoner's name and assigning each a number in its place is a form of dehumanization. The Nazi invention of tattooing a registration number on the prisoner's body extended the scope of this systematic dehumanization. It was a performance of gratuitous violence, which Primo Levi describes as "an end in itself, pure offense. "Were the three canvas numbers sewn on pants, jackets, and winter coat not enough? No, they were not enough: something more was needed, a nonverbal message, so that the innocent would feel his sentence written on his flesh. It also was a return to barbarism, all the more perturbing for the Orthodox Jews: in fact, precisely in order to distinguish Jews from barbarians, the tattoo is forbidden by Mosaic law" (1988, 118).

Separate from its intended consequence on the prisoner's psyche and that of the Nazis, the tattoo had the unintended consequence of entering the vernacular that constitutes the Jewish survivors' identity. Levi writes: "At a distance of forty years, my tattoo has become a part of my body. I don't glory in it, but I am not ashamed of it either; I do not display or hide it. I show it unwillingly to those who ask out of pure curiosity; readily and in anger at those who say they are incredulous. Often young people ask me why I didn't have it erased, and this surprises me: Why should I? There are not many of us in the world to bear witness" (1988, 119–20).

Among the noteworthy dimensions of Levi's narrative, three are particularly salient to my present purposes. His reflection on the tattoo's status forty years later indicates that what it stood for and its present meaning and significance are commonly known, is part of the ongoing interrogation of Nazi atrocities, and serves as a tacit critique of the Germans who inflicted permanent violence on Jewish bodies; it is an indelible reminder of the Holocaust. Second, as part of a Holocaust vernacular, the materiality of the tattoo is situated within a larger moral discourse that invites instruction, interpretation, and even judgment of others who are both its audience and, in that, inscribed by the double reality of their own form of witnessing a sign of inhumanity. His anger at those who say they are incredulous is perhaps roused by their illiteracy in vernacular expressions of Nazi violence that betrays them as having been inattentive to those who have borne witness since the end of World War II and as outside the community of caring constituted by the moral vernacular of their witnessing. It is equally informative that his response to the queries of youths as to why he has not had it erased is to instruct them on the Holocaust vernacular and its language of witnessing. Moreover, by giving his explanation, "Why should I? There are not many of us in the world to bear witness," he reflects that his decision is an act of conscience. To have it erased would put an end to a part of his testimony about the Holocaust, which would betray the reality he says is now part of his body and his identity as a Holocaust survivor.

In our day, oppression and atrocities are no less real than those of which Levi writes. His account of the tattoo is an exemplar of the way those who are subjected to oppression and atrocities speak of their condition and invite interlocutors, audiences, and publics, who have it within their power, to respond. They speak with a vernacular that is not only an expression of their treatment but, through their bodies, also comment on the condition of the body politic. Sometimes they call to those who share their circumstances, sometimes to those on the outside who share the struggle, and sometimes to the larger world audience to bear witness and to solicit their support and intervention. They make moral pleas rooted in convictions that transcend their own well-being and that conscience will not allow them to betray. They are prisoners of conscience (POCs) both in the material sense of being imprisoned for resistance born of conviction and the moral sense of being prisoners to their own commitments of conscience. These appeals are a different form of human rights discourse than the deliberations and negotiations with rights withholders conducted by states, international bodies, and nongovernmental organizations (NGOs) on behalf of rights holders. They form a thick moral vernacular. Before taking up its thick form in the rhetoric of POCs, I want to consider some of the qualities of vernacular rhetoric per se.

Rhetoric's Paradigm Shift and Vernacular Rhetoric

Until the middle of the twentieth century, critical work in rhetoric was tied to traditional views of text, most commonly a speech, essay, or debate that was bounded by time and situation and presented in a public forum. With notable exceptions of those who sought political inclusion and rights, critics also focused on the rhetoric of the empowered, such as presidents, legislative assemblies, and political and religious leaders. At the same time, the turmoil following World War I and during the Great Depression exposed the inability of this critical orthodoxy to offer a satisfactory account for social influence, which, after all, is basic to a rhetorical view of language. I. A. Richards's *Philosophy of Rhetoric,* published in 1936; his collaboration with C. K. Ogden on *The Meaning of Meaning* (1946), first published in 1923, and which included as a supplement Bronislaw Malinowski's (1946) account of Trobriander language and the islanders' performative uses of words; Kenneth Burke's (1953/1931, 1969/1950, 1984a, 1984b) development of a dramatistic theory, begun in the 1930s with the first edition of *Counter-Statement,* followed by *Permanence and Change* and *Attitudes toward History,* and then developed more completely in *A Rhetoric of Motives,* which appeared in 1950, in which the forms of symbol using patterns are considered as enactments that influence social joining; and M. M. Bakhtin's (1981) work in the 1940s that develops a theory of the inherent critique emergent from the clash of centripetal and centrifugal forces in language use add up to a paradigm shift in what counts as rhetorical.[1] Prior to that time, rhetoric was understood as an art of producing an effective speech or essay. Doubtless the tumultuous period of the 1930s encouraged a more linguistically and sociologically sensitive turn that focused attention on the relationship between language and circumstances contributing to its social discord.[2] And undoubtedly discord situates meaning in practices that, by extension, include consideration of how human symbolic practices, or their rhetoric, influence social practices and how rhetorical performance is itself a social practice.

The extension of rhetoric's scope to consider sources of influence in all human uses of symbols includes the ordinary exchanges of the everyday—a *vernacular rhetoric* of interaction within a discourse community that depends on local knowledge, concerns, meanings, modes of arguments, value schemes, logics, traditions, and the like shared among ordinary people who neither act in any official civic capacity nor have an elite status that is an entrée to established power. It is a rhetoric rooted in their indigenous language. The vernacular of ordinary people is important because it has particular rhetorical salience. Those who speak it share identity as a community, whether they are neighbors, a class, or any other signifying group. Its everyday use is their primary mode of symbolic influence, forming bonds of identification, fostering communal coordination and concerted action, and constituting a communal world that ascribes meaning and value to persons and events.

Although not the discourse of power and officialdom, it nonetheless adheres to the fundamental rhetorical demand for *propriety.* For instance, in the working-class neighborhoods of the Northeast where I was raised, neighbors commonly communicated a shared understanding of their neighborhood by how they maintained their property. Their lots may have been small and their homes modest, but what lawn they had was neatly kept. Front porches were decorated with colorful flowerpots, shrubberies were trimmed, and domiciles had well-maintained exteriors that, collectively, created a vernacular landscape expressing their shared identity as neighbors. Their vernacular landscape also expressed demands of propriety: good neighbors maintain their property; it is unseemly not to do so.

In much the same way, vernacular exchanges more generally indicate bonds of affiliation; they speak a legible and intelligible rhetoric of shared values and solidarity. Adherence to the demands of propriety produces a surplus of symbolic value or symbolic capital that governs the community's life.

Michel de Certeau and his collaborators' study of a working-class neighborhood in Lyon (1998) exemplifies the place of symbolic capital in its construction of its and our own self-understanding. Its residents had hierarchies of status based on age and function. Everyone knew the subtleties that distinguished one block from another. The butcher shop was a place they frequented to keep up with developments in their neighbors' personal lives. They had stylized ways of seeking information without seeming to pry, and the right way to communicate disapproval without giving offense. They also conveyed status for functional reasons. Robert, the butcher, was not only a source of information but also the person who could help you save face when the after-hours emergency of an unexpected guest required a good cut of meat. It was best to stay on his good side.

Although Lyon's middleclass originally considered this working-class neighborhood as undesirable because it was on a steep hill located at the fringes of the city, its elevation gave it clean air, which its denizens valued enough, it turned out, that they had no interest years later in offers to buy from young professionals who found its view and fresh air an attractive alternative to Lyon's congestion and pollution. Why, they shared among themselves, would they want to leave their neighborhood blessed with these virtues they have enjoyed all along? How these neighbors presented themselves in dress and manner, spoke to one another, referenced shared exemplars of social knowledge, in short how they participated in the social field was the sine qua non for membership in the community and freedom to circulate in its network of relationships without necessarily having mastered them all.

Propriety within vernacular rhetoric often manifests in a discourse that implicitly critiques outsiders, usually official power. Bakhtin explains that this critique is accomplished through the power of language to question and interrogate, or dialogize the symbolic practices of the outsider. References to class differences, say, through double meanings, innuendo, speaking by indirection, intonation, hack phrases, commonplace utterances, puns, parodies, and other ways of dislocating conventional meaning interrogate the outsider. The vernacular rubs against the outsider's taken-for-granted meanings; it opens a space for meanings hidden in the taken-for-granted to emerge.

Equally, and without necessarily expressing social critique, locally salient ways of communicating can serve the community's internal political function of negotiating how its members shall act and interact. Clifford Geertz's (1987) much cited study of "deep play"[3] embedded in Balinese conventions for wagering on a cockfight discloses how propriety is expressed through stylized cues that indicate a desire to make a wager, conventions for locating an intermediary to arrange a wager, local etiquette governing a relationship one must honor with a supporting bet, and the like. In a more contemporary American vein, Melissa Harris-Lacewell's (2004) study of discourse within the African American community shows how the language and form of everyday exchanges in the barbershop and church have a direct bearing on the political thought within the local black community. This is vernacular rhetorical work in which the community tells a story about itself in its own terms. It is more than the voice of community; it reflects a rhetorical culture expressed through the banal exchanges of quotidian micropractices. Whatever else we might consider these exchanges to be, they are inducements to an attitude that organizes the ordinary person's social and political life.

At the same time, a culture's vernacular rhetoric places it in tension with *antivernacular* representations of power. These are the discourses that function within the hierarchy of an overarching system of power. They may be formal addresses and policy statements, bureaucratic rules and directives, or even the presentation of self that is a display of public authority. They are sometimes monological, often employ specialized vocabularies and logics, and, even when nuanced, reflect authority attached to person, class, and position. They also are reflected in official regimes of oppression. In these ways the antivernacular functions as an elite discourse, and those who speak it enjoy the elite's capacity to disseminate information, opinions, and decisions while evading direct interrogation. The antivernacular tends to normalize its reification of reality through the ideological realism of official rhetoric. It stands in opposition to a "perspective by incongruity" (Burke 1984a), or seeing the given case from outside its assumptions about experience and meaning to facilitate social critique. Those in power can be counted on to own public issues. Toward that end, code switching through marketing and politics that speaks in the language of the one down in order to imitate vernacular rhetoric in its appeals to the ordinary citizen can marshal an effective albeit cynical rhetoric. A politician speaking like "Joe six-pack" to suggest he is just an ordinary person and that his policies will protect the average citizen's interests when in fact the opposite is the case usurps a vernacular rooted in class to establish issue identification. These mimetic performances dampen and deflect the dialectic between elite interests and the everyday discourse whereby ordinary citizens make sense of their experiences.[4]

Once we recognize vernacular rhetoric as the natural extension of rhetoric's paradigm shift instigated during the 1920s and 1930s, it is difficult to imagine any venue in which it does not have bearing, or any venue in which it is not functioning as counterpoint to the official. Whereas performances of official rhetoric are akin to the formalism of a fugue, vernacular rhetoric is akin to jazz—an ensemble performance of free-form call-and-response. Although it may not be the centerpiece of all rhetorical practices, it is always operating in the background, reflecting how social actors understand and participate in construction of their social world. One of the more obvious practices in which it occupies a central place is political resistance.

A Thick Moral Vernacular of Human Rights

As noted previously, Michael Ignatieff advances the provocative thesis that human rights is a discourse. It is, he says, "the only universally available moral vernacular that validates the claims of women and children against the oppression they experience in patriarchal and tribal societies" (2001b, 68). His claim that it allows dependent persons to act against culturally authorized oppression and legitimates their protests against oppression has validity. However, in practice the actual discourse of human rights as he conceives of it occurs in negotiations with a sovereign state about its alleged abusive practices. It is the lingua franca in a moral economy of human rights talk and establishes the language in which human rights discussions occur. Set against the analysis of vernacular rhetoric I have just developed, Ignatieff's conception is a *thin* moral vernacular. It reduces "vernacular" to the specialized language of the Universal Declaration of Human Rights (UDHR) used by those in power to speak on behalf of rights holders to rights withholders. His thin theory makes any specialized rhetoric a vernacular rhetoric, blurs the essential distinction between languages of the people and the official realm, and obliterates the fundamental distinction between official and vernacular discourse with respect to power. This distinction regarding power points to a thick theory of the moral vernacular that enables the powerless, who often are not literate in the elite languages that populate official public spheres, to contest for rights withheld under conditions of oppression.

The common expression of local affiliation and identity used by the people of a country or district or even a culture is the basis for the moral vernacular. The language of the working class, peasants, certain ethnicities, and the marginalized is situated in a particular local or national setting. Its very utterance performs a critique of power because it is the local language spoken and understood by those who are not among the power elite and who often lack the opportunity, even if they possess the skills, to speak on their own behalf in official forums (Ono and Sloop 1995). Insisting on the distinction between the official and the vernacular allows us to give serious attention to the actual communication practices of the oppressed and the richly inventive ways in which they use rhetorical resources and rhetorical mechanisms to achieve their liberatory aims.

Ordinary Virtues and Ordinary Vices

A thick moral vernacular of human rights discourse is not about human rights principles but about the implied virtues of rights holders and vices of rights withholders. The champions of resisters and within resistance movements occupy the spotlight in official domains. They serve an important representative function for human rights holders. Their rhetoric publicizes the plight of the oppressed by translating it into other cultural frames, and it issues formal calls eliciting international response. They direct our attention to leaders of resistance, such as Aung San Suu Kyi or Nelson Mandela, as emblems of their nation's oppressed, often as victims of horrific treatment, and as evidence that human rights abuses have occurred. Although such dissidents and POCs may be celebrated as heroes, thick moral vernacular is less a celebration of heroic than ordinary virtues. Although oppressors may be monsters, thick moral vernacular is less an indictment of their monstrosity than their venality. Myanmar's ruling generals kept Suu Kyi under house arrest out of fear of her capacity to unite her people in opposition, not out of monstrous vice. Their venality resulted in the treachery of using a misguided American's violation of her house arrest by swimming to her residence as a pretext to extend her sentence.[5]

Thick moral vernacular does not abide heroism comfortably. Heroism calls attention to the individual performer, who often views action in terms of courage and timidity, patriotism and treason, heroism and cowardice. Heroism ascribes virtue to extraordinary actions in service to an ideal that demands our loyalty, such as national solidarity. As heroic virtue, loyalty stands apart form the ideal because it is a personal trait; it confers ethos. Heroism's ultimate expression of loyalty is not just the hero's willingness to sacrifice his or her life but the lives of others as well if doing so advances the cause.

Heroic virtue benefits an abstraction. Although we may celebrate the hero who died for a cause, heroic virtue's embrace of the extreme shows loyalty to history, where it lives through narratives and dies without them. In this it shares in the classical model of the hero whose *arête* required acts so exceptional that the *demos* judged them heroic. Heroic virtue is not part of the moral vernacular; it is a conferred trait (see Todorov 1996; Arendt 1958, 1964). It is personified by actions and performed on the type of stage beyond the personal experience of the ordinary person. It invites us to become spectators of its grandeur, rather then witnesses to human suffering that we can imagine befalling us because it happens to people like us on stages we sometimes populate. As Todorov has observed, it is easier to watch someone die in battle than to watch your neighbor subjected to harsh treatment for nothing more than his or her ethnicity or race, which you may well share (1996, 23).

Ordinary virtues, by contrast, place personal dignity first. They are expressed through acts of personal will, or agency, that show self-respect and ensure membership in the human race. This separates ordinary from heroic virtues. Ordinary virtues are modest, and their modesty lies in the reasons for acting. An act of self-sacrifice, for instance, is not committed as an act mandated by a cause but by one's humanity. Even such a publicized actor as Irish hunger striker Bobby Sands, whose death from self-starvation in 1981 was celebrated as an act of Irish Republican Army (IRA) martyrdom, did not persist to death for the IRA but, as discussed later, in protest over the treatment of Provisional IRA prisoners in Long Kesh prison. Ordinary virtues may lead a person to accept that preserving one's humanity is more important than preserving one's life. Choosing death for what one believes is always a personal choice as a means to an end, since life is the ultimate resource of the individual who seeks to affirm his or her dignity and the ultimate expression of the moral vernacular.

Here we find another marker between ordinary and heroic virtues and the moral vernacular. Ordinary virtue does not choose death without regard for others since the goal is to preserve personal dignity, not to enter history. Although ordinary virtues may reflect a commitment to some values as more precious than human life, they also show respect for the sanctity of the life of others and an inhibition to act in a way that would cost others their lives. For example, Adam Michnik's letter from prison, "Why You Are Not Signing" (1985b), cautions against the condemnation of those whose circumstances may have led them to make less than heroic choices in order to protect their loved ones, such as signing a loyalty oath rather than see their family persecuted (see Hauser 2001). Manifestations of ordinary virtue reflect a regard for persons that is marked by caring, a willingness to look after and even sacrifice for their welfare. It is not an act for humanity but for an individual human being. It reflects bonds of civility that benefit other individuals rather than a cause and that lay at the heart of a civilized society (Todorov 1996, 3–43), although it may also be in service to such a cause.

If ordinary virtues reflect aspirations to a life of human dignity, their contrast with ordinary vices captures the moral contests of the body politic in a way that contrasts between heroic virtues and monstrous vices do not. Rhetorical performances of a thick moral vernacular interrogate the oppressor with a language that exposes its distinctive venality. Judith Shklar, who felicitously renders these moral corruptions as "ordinary vices," argues that moral contests of the body politic are "between cruel military and moral repression and violence, and a self-restraining tolerance that fences in the powerful to protect the freedom and safety of every citizen, young or old, male or female, black or white" (1984, 5). Cruelty, hypocrisy, snobbery, brutality, misanthropy, treachery, dishonesty, tyranny, betrayal, meanness, malice, arrogance, cowardice, revenge, and the like normalize monstrosities behind the veil of their banality.

In the context of institutional power, as Arendt's (1964) analysis of Adolf Eichmann suggests, whether wittingly or not, this is the inevitable consequence of ordinary vices. They normalize monstrosity by denying people's freedom to choose and act for their own well-being, stripping their dignity, denying their humanity, and denying them justice. They also act as screens for reproducing monstrosity in ways that go unnoticed by their perpetrators. During the 1970s, Argentina's commandants in charge of dealing with captured resisters did not regard themselves as monsters when they forced the women they tortured by day to accompany them as escorts at night. In fact, they blamed these women for making them despise their wives. These women's militant insurgence, ability to handle a weapon, and skill at engaging the commandants in wide-ranging conversation gave their torturers erotic pleasure and fulfilled their fantasies of exciting femininity in ways, they raged, their wives never could (Actis et al. 2006, 162–63).

The logic of a thick moral vernacular of human rights differs from that of official rhetoric. It does not engage its opponent in debate. Even formal documents, such as Mandela's "The Struggle Is My Life" (1961) and Michnik's "What We Want to Do and What We Can Do" (1981), often avoid making arguments to the state, refer to the state as bestowing legitimacy on their resistance by the way it has responded, and overtly dismiss the state as irrelevant to their liberatory goals while addressing the people as the only relevant audience to affect them. These public statements also do not invoke the language of governance. A thick moral vernacular summons cultural memory embedded in a people's language, national history, and significant expressions of tradition and belief to inspire allegiance and support. It relies on native assertions of identity and right. Nelson Mandela used the "Freedom Charter" (Congress of the People 1955), Jacek Kuron his "Open Letter to the Party" (Kuron and Modzelewski 1982), and Vaclav Havel the Charter 77 manifesto (1977) as a mechanism for mobilizing the publicity principle.[6] These cultural touchstones of political identity asserted an alternative authority about their human rights and the national interest in respecting them.

The moral vernacular does not have a monopoly on speaking of a people's oppression. Its distinctiveness lies in the recuperative power of performing resistance to human rights violations; through performances of opposition and agency it can reclaim rights that have been withheld. Whereas a thinly construed moral vernacular seeks to negotiate agreed-upon practices and accountability for adhering to agreements, thick moral vernacular is more combative; it is always a critique of power. Slaves in the American South may have spoken with deference to their master in public places for their own safety and well-being, but in slave quarters and churches they spoke a vernacular of identity and resistance (Evans and Boyte 1992; Harding 1981). They also made public moral vernacular performances of "subterfuge, sabotage, trickery, foot dragging and other behavior patterns of resistance [that] were insinuated into the daily intercourse as a tactic of simple survival" (Wilmore 1972, 17). Before human rights had been codified, slaves were fully aware that they held them and found ways to express them.

A thick moral vernacular of human rights is a discourse of power. When state authority is normalized, seemingly disinterested behaviors become willing acts of compliance. Normalized power shields the state's subjects from the low foundations of their own obedience, as Havel argued (see chapter 1), while simultaneously concealing the low foundations of power behind the facade of official ideology. The moral vernacular's power resides in its capacity to speak an alternative, indigenous language that both denormalizes the patterns of thinking and acting that support oppression and discloses the rhetorical mechanisms of power that encourage obedience. The power of the powerless, as Havel (1986c) showed, lies in their decision not to live within the lie and instead to act differently.

The moral vernacular's dialogizing of power—rubbing up against it in ways that disclose hidden meanings, expose its menace, and create new political meaning—is not always understandable from outside the oppressed community. Displays of opposition to conditions of servitude and constraints on basic freedoms are contextual and can only be deciphered fully within their cultural and national historicity. Scott's *Domination and the Arts of Resistance* (1990) details how the hidden transcripts of subjugated peoples are specific to a particular set of actors in a given social site. These transcripts of their stylized social practices enter human rights discourse through coded subversive performances that challenge the power to abuse. When Algerian women removed their veils in response to appeals of the French colonials, their setting aside of a basic cultural marker of modesty disguised the revolutionary intent behind their unveiling. Their unveiled appearance in the European city attracted the attention of French men, whose desire for the Algerians' exotic femininity blinded them to the objects of their desire planting bombs and proved a distraction from the movement of Algerian men intent on overthrowing the French colonial government (Fanon 1965). The vernacular of dress became a complex form of deception, misread by its target, but understood by the resistance community.[7]

The discourse of conscience that grows from these characteristics of thick moral vernacular rhetoric issues a call to personal authenticity and group solidarity. It is a culturally resonant articulation and performance with a capacity to translate the moral universals of the UDHR into that culture's understanding of what it means to be human: the primacy of individual rights, collective identity, historicity, and agency. It is a human rights rhetoric that calls its audience to act, and, when translated back to the more universal language of human rights talk, beckons the world to intervene. One is a call to resist, the other a call to protect the body and spirit of the oppressed; one to political vision, the other to human rights. Both are calls to witness, to civility, and to moral responsibility.

Tensions between Good and Evil: Two Cases of the Moral Vernacular

From the vantage point of the West, there is a strong temptation to valorize those who are pitted against what its lights deem to be an oppressive regime or exploitative system. Without gainsaying the admirable strength and commitment in their valiant displays of conscience, dissidents do not always advocate passive resistance, and often they reject a Western discourse they regard as at the base of their subjugation. In fact, their condition may insist on and explain the necessity for resistance, including violence. We should not forget that when South Africa's African National Congress (ANC) was forced underground, it formed *Umkhonto we Sizwe* (Spear of the Nation, aka MK) as a paramilitary wing to engage in sabotage through guerrilla warfare and eventually invasion intended to culminate in a national uprising, with no less an icon of resistance than Nelson Mandela as its commander-in-chief. Nor should we forget its communist leanings, which, during the Cold War, often made it critical of the United States. Their rhetoric is not always reflective of Western ideals, but it is informative of the tensions between good and evil that are part of commitments to conscience. We see these tensions exemplified in the stark difference between the rhetoric of Dietrich Bonhoeffer and Frantz Fanon as they explain why they resist as they do. Examining these apparent polar opposites will illustrate the cultural specificity of moral vernacular appeals and offer an antidote against romanticizing the appeals of the oppressed at the expense of analyzing them to better understand what they tell us about the moral vernacular of human rights and political conscience.

Dietrich Bonhoeffer and the Price of Costly Grace

Historically, profession of religious conscience has been a major justification for extreme measures taken in defense of faith. Sometimes this has inspired the faithful to risk grave personal penalties or to withdraw from the world to act in accordance with their conscience. For example, Christianity's fundamental belief in redemption has long manifested itself in an attempt to escape the distractions of the material world to focus on an afterlife. Martyrs willingly sacrificed their lives before their faith. Prayer and meditation, even withdrawal from the world by embracing a monastic life, have been regarded as a road to salvation from sin and fulfillment of an aspiration for eternal paradise. Not every person of faith has been so inclined, however. Luther, after all, left the monastery to follow Jesus in the material world.

Once the monastery is abandoned, matters get complicated by life's imperfections, which are difficult to ignore, and by personal weaknesses that challenge self-regard as a faithful Christian. Living in the world instantiates the Kierkegaardian paradox of faith in forgiveness while knowing you inevitably will sin again. For this brand of believers, following Jesus in the world has meant living the virtues Jesus preached in the Sermon on the Mount. They distinctively command the believer not to separate faith from secular life while serving as guidelines for the nonbeliever who hopes for a secular world of justice and peace. Yet the commands "Thou shalt not kill" and "Love they neighbor" are difficult to reconcile when you are witness to evil.

For Germany in the 1930s, the line of conflict between good and evil was not clearly drawn. The evil of nazism was not as evident to the majority of Germans as it was to those in the occupied territories of France, Holland, and Norway, where issues of sovereignty and human rights sparked resistance movements. Germany's terror was confused by the semblance of legitimacy enjoyed by a National Socialist government that appeared to be legal, respectable, and even clean (Burke 1973). The

Nazi promise of national rebirth, overcoming economic crisis and unemployment, and breaking from the chains of Versailles, and its vision of *Volksgemeinschaft* overcoming the haggling of party interests and class, proved a great temptation (Stern 1987). Resisters in Germany were without widespread social support; they were called "'strangers' among our own people" (von Klemperer 1992, 144). Even within the Lutheran Church, invoking the tenets of Christianity as a command to confront Hitler was not well received by the church's hierarchy, as Dietrich Bonhoeffer learned.

Bonhoeffer was a Protestant theologian whose writings from the late 1920s through the 1930s earned him international acclaim. He held a faculty appointment at the University of Berlin; served as a pastor; was a founding member of an ecumenical protestant sect, the Confessing Church; and was a pacifist. He also was active in the German counterintelligence group within *Abwehr*, the Nazi intelligence agency, and had participated in the ongoing plot to assassinate Hitler, for which he was hanged, at age thirty-nine, on April 9, 1945, mere weeks before Germany surrendered.

Bonhoeffer maintained that the true Christian is not a member of a religion but a believer who sees Christian life in this world and who acts, as we must, for peace and social justice while accepting that what is required of us will not be delivered by a shaft of divine light. Christians could not, as Karl Barth and the Confessing Church had advised, "entrench ourselves persistently behind the 'faith of the Church,' and evade the honest question as to what we ourselves really believe" (von Klemperer 1992, 203). Asking "what does it mean to do good?" raised the wrong question. Since evil exists in the world, it must be confronted by manifesting Christian moral agency through worldly practice. The real question, Bonhoeffer insisted, is "what is the will of God, what is required of us at this time, what are we called to do?"

During the 1930s, Bonhoeffer had urged the Lutheran Church to take a stand opposing Nazi oppression of Jews and war. In terms of ordinary vices, the Nazis were guilty of cruelty, and Hitler was its public exemplar. Shklar argues that philosophers and moral thinkers have been reluctant to put cruelty above any other ordinary vice because "to put cruelty first is to disregard the idea of sin as it is understood by revealed religion. Sins are transgressions of a divine rule and offenses against God; pride—the rejection of God—must always be the worst one, which gives rise to all the others. However, cruelty—the willful inflicting of physical pain on a weaker being in order to cause anguish and fear—is a wrong done entirely to *another creature*" (1984, 8). Bonhoeffer's theology of discipleship, however, while retaining the idea of sin, places Christianity in the secular world. A profession of faith does not express discipleship to Christ. "Instead, it is the obedient deed" (Bonhoeffer 2001/1937, 57), which manifested accepting Jesus's command, "follow me." Obedience was expressed by accepting the cost of acting in the face of evil, accepting the repercussions that follow from acting in ways that might be ethically irresponsible but required by Christian conscience. While pride is first among personal vices in turning from God, to place other concerns before the willful infliction of pain on a weaker being is itself a form of pride. Bonhoeffer maintained that false faith professes the depth of one's belief by placing the problem in the hands of God alone without heeding the call to personal action.

Bonhoeffer's indictment of the Church specifically accused it of retreating from its moral responsibility to speak out against Nazi atrocities against the Jews. The Church and the ecumenical movement seemed to be gripped in fear inspired by cruelty. They had chosen a path of accommodating Hitler's persecution of Jews under the state of exception by remaining silent rather than accepting the political repercussions of frank speech. Silence in the face of cruelty leaves morality an abstraction, a convenient self-deception and form of hypocrisy that makes cruelty easier by quieting the one voice able to dissent with moral authority. The Church had succumbed to what Bonhoeffer called "cheap grace," grace without the cross (2001, 41–102). Christians could only defeat evil with "costly grace," attained through the discipleship dictated by the Sermon on the Mount. The price of following Christ's homily, whose political trajectory leads to activism and passive resistance, was high: "Whenever Christ calls us, his call leads us to death" (Bonhoeffer 2001, 87).

Confronted by evil, these morally righteous Christian believers had collapsed under the weight of their own ineffectual rationalizations. Civilized and cultured Germans were living in cheap grace by which they justified their retreat from confronting evil, confident that by faith alone their failed efforts were excused when they placed combat with evil in the hands of God.

At the same time, Bonhoeffer's commitments of conscience as a pacifist, a Christian, and a pastor were not easily reconciled with acts of duplicity, violence, and the risk of death for the sake of Christianity and Germany's honor. The costly grace of discipleship sometimes leads to acts that are ethically conflicted but that conscience demands. Sometimes you must violate God's commandments to combat evil. Nonetheless, violating Christian morality for a righteous cause is still a violation of fundamental Christian commitments.

Bonhoeffer (1967b) had these considerations in mind when he wrote his Christmas letter at the end of 1942, "After Ten Years," to assess the consequences of Hitler's decade in power and the work he shared with Claus Oster and Hans von Dohnanyi, his collaborators in the resistance and to whom, along with his friend Eberhard Bethge and his parents, the letter was sent. The letter is a remarkable synthesis, drawing together thoughts and actions of resistance during the preceding decade; it is an aria to agency.

The letter is written from the perspective of outcasts and those who suffer, seeing the great events of world history from below. In this frame his friends and he had acted in ways that violated their conscious commitments. He writes of the toll this has taken and the fundamental question it raises: "We have been silent witnesses to evil deeds; we have been drenched by many storms; we have learnt the arts of equivocation and pretense; experience has made us suspicious of others and kept us from being truthful and open; intolerable conflicts have worn us down and made us cynical. Are we still of any use?" (16).[8] Against cruelty, the question, "Are we still of any use?" haunts his reflections. He returns to it repeatedly in his search for a stance of effective opposition capable of reconciliation with God.

The problem of resistance went deeper than acting from political conviction. Evil was disguised to appear as "light, charity, historical necessity, or social justice" (2). For Germans, whose traditional virtues placed community above the individual and encouraged acting out of duty, the disguise was bewildering. Being of use meant finding a moral anchor that would hold against Nazi depravity. How could a people to whom every available alternative seemed equally intolerable, repugnant, and futile have become paralyzed by philosophic misanthropy? Responsible Germans, horrified by nazism and in a constant state of outrage, lacked firm ground beneath their feet. Foreshadowing the emphasis his prison letters would later place on this as *a world come of age,* Bonhoeffer captures this Kantian theme[9] in his assessment of their dilemma. Resisters hoping to displace the authority of the state's totalizing claim to agency could no longer rely on the counterauthority of traditional Christian righteousness. Resistance must come from their sense of Christian responsibility.

Bonhoeffer's argument is theologically based. He writes, "The great masquerade of evil has played havoc with all our ethical concepts" (2). *Reason, enthusiasm, conscience, duty, freedom,* and *private virtue*—moral traits that had sustained earlier generations—had become quixotic weapons and, therefore, the wrong weapons for this battle. Each arose from a sense of its own efficacy for overcoming the monsters that had taken control of German life, only to find itself lost in the fog of self-deception and resigning in defeat. The values of the human world—the German tradition of custom, history, and culture—had crumbled before an evil beyond its horizon of experience and to which it had become an unwitting accomplice.

Reason, enthusiasm, conscience, duty, freedom, and *private virtue,* each an ordinary virtue under normal circumstances, respectively offered only an illusion of agency while absent civil courage; each was a reflection of cheap grace. His opening catechism inverts these traditional German virtues, recasting them as ineffectual and guilty of the primary Christian vice, pride. In their place he invokes the values of faith.

Who stands fast? For Bonhoeffer, it is the large-hearted Christian. "We are not Christ, but if we want to be Christians, we must have some share in Christ's large-heartedness by acting with responsibility and in freedom when the hour of danger comes, and by showing a real sympathy that springs, not from fear, but from the liberating and redeeming love of Christ for all who suffer. Mere waiting and looking is not Christian behavior" (14). The spiritual basis for his argument justifying the conspirators' moral transgressions and answering the question "Are we still of any use?" is the theology of faith without religion. It is the moral vernacular of a Christian faith that foregoes the precedent of the preceding 1,900 years when Christianity had rested on a religious a priori (Bonhoeffer 1967c, 139). It is adapted to the last 100 years, when "man has learnt to deal with himself and all questions of importance without recourse to the working hypothesis called 'God'" (Bonhoeffer 1967d, 168). If a solely religious understanding of Christianity made Jesus disappear from sight, as Bonhoeffer believed, and with him the rationale for action found in the Gospels, his large-hearted Christian would find the path back to responsible action, to resuscitating the ordinary virtues Germans traditionally espoused, through communion with God. He would not require recourse to abstract principles of ethics, which ran counter to what a person was called to do in the face of evil, but would act, Bonhoeffer concludes, in "a bold venture of faith while believing that there is forgiveness and consolation to the person who becomes a sinner in that venture" (5).

One could do nothing to overcome the monstrosity of National Socialism unless one could drive a wedge between habituated practices tied to moral commonplaces without understanding their ethical basis. On the one hand, a misguided response to the threat as a threat, and not as a stimulus, carries the consequence of defeat, resignation, and compliance or complicity. On the other hand, an unthinking response is the means by which wicked people naturalize acts of terror against the targeted Other. They fuse data and response to construct a world of mass compliance that serves as a barrier to conscious awareness of what we are doing.

Bonhoeffer relentlessly transcends the evil of his times; he challenges our sense of the ground beneath our feet on which our personal agency stands by exposing its illusory firmness. The only possibility for solid ground is a fundamental moral commitment that transcends shifting circumstances—the primacy of human dignity. Even the nonbeliever who shares an ethical imperative of personal integrity based on the primacy of human dignity can enter the letter's moral economy. We bear responsibility for the chaos of our times because we bear an unshakeable burden of responsibility for the structure of our society and for the world that future generations will inhabit. His emphasis on human dignity separates personal integrity from the mystification of nationalistic rhetoric that, in Nazi Germany, naturalized acts of terror against the Jews. It opens the possibility of a nonreligious God that forgives problematic action taken to claim a future of amity and hope rather than surrender our integrity as qualified beings to a sovereign who would declare us *homo sacer*. Bonhoeffer's positioning of an agential stance outside an internal dialectic of ideological justification offers identity based on self-awareness of acting freely and taking responsibility. His moral vernacular aligning the ethos of Christian ethics with rehabilitated ordinary virtues leads to the important recognition that agency entails becoming a prisoner of our own conscience.

Frantz Fanon

Frantz Fanon, the noted theorist of colonial oppression, is notorious for his advocacy of violence. On the surface, his argument for confronting oppression with force seems to have its natural opposite in the pacifism of Gandhi. The tension between their respective embrace of violence and nonviolence cannot be denied. However, the more revealing tension is with Bonhoeffer, whose participation in the plot to assassinate Hitler was a commitment to violence no less firm but in a different moral register. Both were plagued by the crisis of conscience that comes from standing idle in the face of evil. As Bonhoeffer turned to violence as his last resort to combat evil, Fanon did so as the only means for liberation from colonial oppression. Bonhoeffer's choice is praised for his courage to intervene at the cost of his life to spare the lives of others; Fanon is often criticized for apparently extolling the efficacy of bloodshed over diplomacy. Matters are not as simple as this reduction makes them appear. Fanon saw the subjugation of Africa's natives by racist colonial regimes as rule by violence. Deposing them was a moral requirement and violence, in most cases, the only means available to combat the intransigence of its ordinary vices.

Fanon was not a revolutionary; he was trained as a psychiatrist and arrived at his conviction that violence was the only means for Algerian liberation from French colonial rule as a result of his psychiatric care for natives, settlers, and colonizers. His experience of black consciousness, as he experienced it in his native Martinique, became linked to cultural influences during his psychiatric residency under Francois de Tosquelles, a Catalan radical who emphasized the importance of culture in psychopathology. Fanon left France for Algeria to accept a position as head of psychiatry at Blida-Joinville Psychiatric Hospital. Following the outbreak of the Algerian revolution in 1954, he joined the Front de Liberation Nationale (FLN).

His study of the cultural world in which his patients lived informed his understanding of its consequences on their mental health. Whereas Europeans attributed the natives' disorders to their primitivism and ascribed personal responsibility for their actions, Fanon's studies supported the hypothesis that their disorders stemmed from cultural beliefs and reactions to "the bloodthirsty and pitiless atmosphere, the generalization of inhuman practices, and the firm impression that people have of being caught up in a veritable Apocalypse" (Fanon 1963, 251; see Macey 2000, 199–300). Fanon concludes *The Wretched of the Earth* (1963) with case notes from his psychiatric files at Blida. One of them is from the file of a torturer who was concerned about his growing propensity to violence in all aspects of his life. He had no intention of resigning his police position; he wanted Fanon to help him continue without suffering behavior problems. Fanon comments: "With these observations we find ourselves in the presence of a coherent system which leaves nothing intact. The executioner who loves birds and enjoys the peace of listening to a symphony or a sonata is simply one stage in the process. Further on we may find a whole existence which enters into complete and absolute sadism" (270). This case was emblematic of the colonial system's inexorable violence that had to be confronted on its own terms.

In addition to his medical writings, his frequent contributions to *El Moudjahidi*, an FLN guerrilla bulletin, and attendance at psychiatric conferences brought him to the attention of the colonial authorities. Upon learning his name was on a list to be assassinated, he resigned his position at Blida-Joinville and went into exile. His resignation letter states, in part, "For long months, my conscience has been the seat of unforgivable debates. And their conclusion is a will not to lose hope in man, or in other words myself. . . . I have resolved that I cannot face my responsibilities at any cost on the fallacious grounds that there is nothing else to be done" (Massey 299).

In this context, Fanon wrote his famous essay "On Violence," which was included as chapter 1 in *The Wretched of the Earth*. The essay is a polemic against French colonialism that develops its attack in three parts: it opens with a largely theoretical discussion of colonialism. He argues it is always violent; the colonial government and settlers are committed to racist practices that dehumanize the natives and exploit them for their own economic gain. He then discusses how negotiating with the colonial power co-opts the attempts of nationalist movements to calm brewing unrest. He concludes his argument with a consideration of why the natives must be and are prepared to repel the colonizers with force.

Fanon writes in a voice that appears to speak to whomever might be his reader, but in fact the natives are his audience, putting into words their consciousness of colonial exploitation and giving expression to their rationale for violent resistance. Because we can overhear it, we who are implicated in their oppression—whites, colonizers, and imperialists alike—become the target of a violence that is at once reciprocal and terrifying.

If Bonhoeffer's letter is an aria to agency that finds justification of violence in faith, Fanon's agential aria finds its justification in counterviolence. In a much-quoted passage near the beginning of his essay, he contrasts the settler town, with its paved streets, bright lights, and denizens whose bellies are always full, with the "Negro" town with its natives living in crowded squalor, lacking food and adequate shelter, and looking toward the settler's town with envy and lust (1963, 39). The cultural violence colonialism inflicts on indigenous Algerians turns them against themselves and leaves them withered by their sense of inferiority.

Fanon's depiction of the native lost in self-loathing echoes the cruelty he explores in *Black Skin, White Masks* (1952). There he analyzed the impact of French colonialism on black Martiniquans. He argued that the practices of white colonialists created a Manichaean world in which white was equated with virtue and good, and black with vice and evil. The choice to the native was clear: "turn white or disappear" (100). In response, the black man accedes by accepting a veil. He defines himself in terms of whiteness, which, at the same time, alienates from his own identity. Fanon finds the black man expresses his need for healing the wound of self-alienation by his desire, upon arrival in France, to have a white woman. "Once this initiation into 'authentic' manhood had been fulfilled, they took the train to Paris" (1952, 72).

The white woman possessed heals the black man's feeling of impotence by affirming his manhood. At the same time, finding his identity through a white woman perpetuates the veil of whiteness. The veil masks the authenticity of his own blackness, makes him invisible unless he defines himself in terms of whiteness. Fanon formalizes the veil of invisibility as representing a Manichaean world on which colonial power insists. Fanon believes the racial tension between white and black, the colonizer and the colonized, reflects Aristotle's Law of Mutual Exclusion. The archetypal Western philosopher provides the basic premise for a racialized epistemology that categorizes and classifies in endless hierarchies and oppositions, each with its inherent logic that values up over down, in over out. It is a divide that casts whites as civilized, cultured, and virtuous, and blacks as primitive and evil. Fanon's moral vernacular is born of this tension. The colonial world is built on the ordinary vice of deceit. It relies on fraud and force to deceive the natives into thinking that it acts for their betterment, while defining human worth in terms that dehumanize them, turn them into animals by speaking of them in zoological terms, "of the yellow man's reptilian motions, the stink of the native quarter, the breeding swarms, of foulness, of spawn, of gesticulation" (1963, 42) that alienate the natives from themselves. It practices a biopolitics that reduces the natives to "bare life," to mere biological animality lacking culture, learning, and political competence. It makes the natives and their qualifications invisible behind the veil of colonial definitions of culture, civilization, and virtue. These acts of violence to culture and identity thrive on the terror of those who fall under its thumb. The sovereign's mandates that strip them of their human worth equally strip their visible signs of identity of individuating meaning.

Contrary to the Aristotelian Law of Mutual Exclusion, Fanon finds liberation for the natives' consciousness in the Hegelian possibility for reversal, represented by the master-slave relationship. The native knows "he is not an animal; and it is precisely at the moment that he realizes his humanity that he begins to sharpen the weapons with which he will secure its victory" (1963, 43). Discovering that the settler's skin is of no more value than the native's skin "shakes the world in a very necessary manner. All the new revolutionary assurance of the native stems from it" (45).[10]

Fanon acknowledges that his argument for reversal only substitutes one form of Manichaeanism for another (35), but his argument is predicated on a distinction between the violence of the colonizer that oppresses and of the native that is a liberatory form of self-defense. The reversal unveils the deception on which colonialism rests, and this is terrifying to the colonizer and the settler alike.

There is no mistaking Fanon's view that physical violence is necessary: "Decolonization is always a violent phenomenon" (35), it must be to throw off exploitation "carried on by dint of a great army of cannons and bayonets" (37). He rationalizes the famous FLN leaflet that stated "colonialism only loosens its hold when the knife is at its throat" as not seeming too violent to any Algerian native since it "only expressed what every Algerian felt at heart" (61). The cycle of violence spiraling through Algeria cannot be contained because violence is the ever-present specter in the native's opposition to the colonizer's will and the ever-present threat of the colonizer's force. Fanon's declaration that "the existence of armed struggle shows that the people are decided to trust to violent means only" (83–84) is merely an extension of the violence inherent in stripping away the veil of superiority.

Violence has a second sense that circulates through the text. After his initial admonition that the moment of reversal brings terror to the colonizer's heart, Fanon turns his attention to intellectuals and adherents to the nationalist movement, each of whom tries to avoid violence by negotiating with the colonial power. In a protracted analysis, Fanon argues that theirs is a futile effort. Attempts at political remedies are no more than assertions of rights lacking teeth (59). The colonial government charges the nationalists to calm native unrest so that discussion of accommodation may proceed. Yet accommodation with the colonizer on a program of self-determination is limited to a political vision based on electoral processes. Although the nationalists put matters bluntly to the colonialist bourgeoisie—"Give us more power"—Fanon indicts the elite for their ambiguity on the specific question of violence. They are "violent in their words and reformist in their attitudes" (59); they seek compromise, not independence. Compromise ignores the peasantry, who are inclined toward revolution because they are the most abused by the colonizers and settlers.

Nationalists never consider armed resistance as a possibility because they "are in fact partisans of order." They are perfectly willing to permit the colonizers to retain their monopoly on violence in order to gain greater autonomy in areas of self-interest. "What the factory-owners and finance magnates of the mother country expect from their government is not that it should decimate the colonial peoples, but that it should safeguard with the help of economic conventions their own 'legitimate interests'" (65). This is not a demand for independence. In fact, he considers political solutions a disguised form of violence. The nationalists, whose conscience has been colonized, are not liberated from the colonialists. Rather than removing the veil that keeps the natives invisible, of insisting on their humanity and equality, the nationalists accede to the sovereign's insistence that they restore order, that they deny the natives' political identity and keep them in their place of subservience. Their accommodation of power, in fact, veils colonial violence intended to reinforce the natives' sense of inferiority to the white man.

If the colonial power has made the colonized racially invisible, for their part the colonized have embraced their own veil of invisibility by remaining distanced from the colonizer. Unlike the nationalists, who suffer from an understanding of power that perpetuates their subservience, the peasants' detachment has allowed them to delimit the power of the French colonials. They have never been deceived; they understand perfectly well that accommodation is not liberation (68). The peasants, whose consciousness has never been colonized, refuse participation in a politics that lacks teeth and perpetuates their political meaning in terms of their mere animality as biological beings without human rights.

The Manichaean reduction of white/black into good/evil, their identification in zoological terms; their equation with foulness; their treatment as livestock that may be freely arrested, beaten, and starved; the restriction of their movement; the legal presumption of their guilt; and their control at the end of a bayonet places them outside humanity. This permissible violence inflicted on the *homo sacer* is met by a peasantry ready to resist. Their question, Fanon writes, expresses a quest for agency: "When do we begin?"

Fanon's assault on the Manichaean veil of French colonialism gives the natives visibility. By understanding that they must confront colonial violence with violence, they are, he says, "political animals in the most universal sense of the word" (81). Their guerrilla tactics assert social, political, economic, and cultural identity. As vernacular assertions of agency, they pull aside the veil of whiteness that has rendered them invisible and force the French to recognize them as having power. They violate the colonizer's assumptions about the natives' political meaning and, in that, "denegrifies" them. It is a short step from here to an assertion of the natives' right to defend their identity as humans. To deny their right to counterviolence would be tantamount to denying the legitimacy of those who were assigned to the camps to fight for their freedom. It shares the moral imperative that would make questioning the violent resistance of Jews in the Warsaw ghetto seem ridiculous, if not idiotic.

Fanon's rhetoric of the veil sustains a tension between bare life and political life. It leaves violence nondescript and free-floating (see Kawash 1999, 237). It does not rest on specific deeds since, within the culture of colonial violence, the natives assert their identity as more than bare life at each moment they meet violence with counterviolence. Their self-defense is a rupture of the violence that is always already in colonial discourse and appropriates its surplus of meaning that can never be contained, only resisted. Fanon's moral vernacular of violence advocates the inherent right of the subjugated to assert their identity as more than *homo sacer*. In asserting this right, it also lays claim to its moral efficacy. Violence of this sort is an act of duty demanded by conscience. It recognizes the natives' identity as rising from the land that sustains their natural and cultural life, and their right to reclaim it.

Conclusion

I have argued that human rights, as instantiated by the UDHR, has faced the continuing problem of diremptive frames for interpreting their meaning. The point of the UDHR was to avoid the atrocities committed by the Nazis from ever recurring. Yet differences among its signatories led to a document without specified justifications for its articles or means to enforce them. As a result, moral universalists and cultural particularists have had a continuous clash over its underlying assumptions and application.

As an alternative to considering the UDHR as a quasi-legal document or a codification of moral absolutes, I have followed the lead of Michael Ignatieff, who suggests human rights would be better thought of as a discourse, and argued that its articles provide a moral vernacular, that is, a language for achieving minimal agreement on the necessary conditions for a life worthy of being lived. Contrary to Ignatieff, I have distinguished between thin and thick moral vernaculars. One is a discourse of human rights talk manifested in official public spheres and back channels suited to the discourse of those who speak as representative voices for rights holders to rights withholders. The other is a discourse of opposition and resistance manifested in a performative rhetoric of ordinary virtues and vices. One is a rhetoric of accountability suited to overcoming the stasis of imputation between moral universalism and cultural particularism. The other is a vernacular rhetoric suited to empowering the oppressed to disrupt the regime of power imposed by its oppressor. Both human rights talk and thick moral vernaculars are important transformations of human rights principles into a rhetorical praxis for confronting abuses and atrocities. Both reinterpret human rights in terms that encourage conceptualizing them as a mode of rhetoric. Without distinguishing between them, however, we lose purchase on the unique capacity of everyday interactions to assert identity and rights as rhetorical performances with the capacity to constitute agency through rhetorical manifestations of choice and deed. We also lose purchase on how our own sympathies are mobilized and dispose us to act.

It is hard to imagine anything more extreme than the genocides witnessed during the twentieth century. The UDHR, as a codified refusal to let the slaughter go unnoticed and anaffirmation of the value of every life, is genocide's renunciation. Yet its mobilization of political power to oppose the inhumane exercise of obliterating entire peoples often undergoes a curious inversion when its moral universals are challenged by the practices of realpolitik. Paramilitary forces, the new warriors of the twenty-first century (Ignatieff 1997), and repressive regimes often do not observe the rules of war prohibiting atrocities, but international intervention on behalf of the abused is rare. When confronted by evidence of such practices, sovereign states often say they look more like the results of civil war than a crime against humanity. Such rhetorical dodges work when we lack a sense of being implicated in the problem's underlying causes. They work because the problem has not been translated into our moral vernacular. Without thick moral vernaculars that connect oppressive political and economic practices to our moral universals, it is difficult to imagine how we will escape being tossed by the waves of emotion that rationalize responses but do not resolve political, moral, and spiritual problems of human rights and honor their claims to justice.

Prelude

The cases of Bonhoeffer and Fanon are illustrative of the thick moral vernacular rhetoric explored in this study. This type of rhetoric is a means of empowerment. It is a form of human rights discourse that can enable the oppressed to disrupt the regime of power imposed by their oppressor. It stands apart from the official discourse of states, international bodies, and NGOs in that its appeals are not made directly to rights abusers, may be directed to audiences lacking the power to bring abuser states to justice, and yet are appeals in the name of justice. They are as wide ranging as these two cases illustrate. They are illustrative of how a thick moral vernacular performs important transformations of human rights principles into a rhetorical praxis for confronting abuses and atrocities.

Both human rights talk and a thick moral vernacular reinterpret human rights in terms that encourage conceptualizing them as a mode of rhetoric. Without distinguishing between them, however, we lose purchase on the unique capacity of appeals made in the language of the native and at times imbedded in everyday discourse to assert identity and rights. Perhaps our most valuable lessons on how to respond to oppression come not from states (or from political theory) but from the writings of dissident activists and their vernacular performances of resistance. Their rhetorical achievements, to which I now turn, suggest agendas for confronting the moral panic that accompanies, uninvited, the masquerade of vice.

PART II. *Case Studies in a Thick Moral Vernacular of Political Agency*

4. *Parrhesia at Robben Island*
Prison Reform from the Inside

In 1994, South Africa became an inclusive democracy. That there is a democracy in South Africa is a testimony to political vision and perseverance in the struggle that overthrew apartheid. With most opposition leaders imprisoned and its citizens of color subjected to the harsh social, economic, and political realities of the Afrikaner regime, the odds were stacked against organizing a successful resistance movement; they were even greater against a spirit of truth and reconciliation prevailing should one succeed. Although the social triumph of "truth and reconciliation" remains tenuous,[1] the resistance movement to create a politically inclusive democracy did succeed, and a principal reason for its success was the instruction in political identity and organization that occurred in the least likely place, the state prison on Robben Island.

Robben Island is located eight miles to sea off the Cape Town coast. Its history as an exile for the damned dates to 1525, when a Portuguese ship reportedly left some prisoners there. Since then it has been the place of banishment for South Africa's outcasts: the chronically ill, the insane, lepers, and prisoners. By 1931, the chronically sick, insane, and lepers were no longer treated on the island and the sanitariums were burned to the ground, but the prison remained. The island itself is inhospitable: the waters surrounding it are frigid; the weather conditions tend toward the extremes; its landscape is poorly suited for agriculture and offers only meaningless labor in its rock quarry.

Beginning in the early 1960s, Robben Island became the principal place of incarceration for political prisoners convicted of crimes growing out of their opposition to apartheid. After the Rivonia Trialists[2] arrived in 1964, its population included most of the opposition leaders, Nelson Mandela, Govan Mbecki, Walter Sisulu, and Ahmed Kathrada, among them. Within a short period, white prisoners were transferred to other facilities, leaving only felons as inmates with the newly arriving politicals. The criminal convicts had been organized into rival gangs and, although segregated in lockup from the political prisoners, included them among their targets for intimidation, sexual assault, and physical brutality. The guards, for the most part, were uneducated, sadistic racists without prospects for professional advancement. Their treachery included using the prison gangs to totalize the prison's environment of terror. The island, in short, was a location in which South Africa's racist structure was mirrored by the racial composition of the inmates and conduct of their warders.

Confronted by conditions so extreme that survival had to be each man's foremost concern, the political prisoners soon determined that they could not count on the state or the prison system to initiate humane reform and took it upon themselves to change the prison's culture. Were we to follow the panoptic theory of power set forth by Foucault's *Discipline and Punish* (1977), we would predict their efforts were doomed to fail. Remarkably, however, they succeeded in transforming Robben Island from a culture of violence to one that recognized the prisoners' human dignity, and from an environment in which physical survival was paramount to a "university of resistance."[3] Their success is all the more interesting in that it challenges the Foucauldian position, which focuses on how the biopower of the penal system constitutes subjects, by suggesting that resistance has its own productive capacity, that it is capable of halting an oppressive power by constituting a biopolitics of its own. We are led to ask, what made such a transformation possible?

The answer lies in the role of the moral vernacular in bringing about prison reform from the inside through mobilization of parrhesia as a rhetorical mechanism. There are two stories of the moral vernacular in this reform. Initially, the prisoners on Robben Island opened a space for frank speech in which speaking the truth reformed the prison quotidian. In the process of reforming the culture of violence within the prison, a second story developed. The reformed prison quotidian made it possible for the prisoners to engage in a different form of resistance through a prison paideia that was a projection of the South African democracy to which they aspired. It was intended to advance the struggle on the outside and eventually change South Africa's political structure.

Parrhesia and Rhetoric

Foucault's impressive discussion of parrhesia includes the assertion that it is not a rhetorical mode of speech. Foucault invokes a narrow view of rhetoric in making this claim by reducing it to "technical devices" employed to "veil what [the rhetor] thinks" in order to "prevail upon the minds of his audience (regardless of the rhetorician's [sic] own opinion concerning what he says)" (2001, 12). Setting aside the Neo-Platonic reduction of rhetoric to verbal sleight of hand, which raises issues beyond the scope of this project, the fundamental flaw in Foucault's assessment is that it ignores the fact that critique is more than speaking one's mind. It is addressed presumably to an audience capable of considering and responding, preferably by reforming its ways. Ignoring this dimension of parrhesia misses the subtle ways by which telling the truth elicits change from those with the power to alter prevailing conditions.

That the podium at times has been the locus of parrhesia and its practitioners on occasion have been orators of considerable merit is a matter of historical fact. No less a figure than Cicero, the most renowned Roman orator, came to a bad end precisely for speaking frankly against Antony and the Second Triumvirate. In fact, he did so fourteen times in his "Philippics." Having heard enough, the Second Triumvirate added his name to the proscription list and dispatched a military contingent to hunt him down. His assassins returned his decapitated head and severed hands to Rome for public display. Before the material remains of his extraordinary powers of *actio* were set before the public, however, Antony's wife, Flavia, who was the widow of Clodius, Cicero's enemy from childhood, had her own grudge to settle. Consumed by wrath against Cicero for his defense of Milo, who had issued the warrant to butcher her husband, she took his decapitated head in her hands and vented her hatred by mocking him and spitting on his face. Then, using her hairpins, she repeatedly stabbed the tongue that had argued so eloquently against her husband and in defense of his murderer. After her fury was spent, she relinquished his head, with tongue impaled, to be placed on the Rostra in the Forum Romanum as a public warning about the consequences for speaking against the sovereign (Cassius Dio 1917, 132–33). Cicero's political machinations notwithstanding, his Philippics are consistent with his long-standing political advocacy in support of the Republic and opposition to anything and anyone who threatened it. It is difficult to imagine how Cicero's Philippics would be excluded from parrhesia or from rhetoric. It is equally difficult to imagine that the Second Triumvirate, the spiteful Flavia, or Romans viewing Cicero's grisly remains understood them as anything other than frank speech.[4]

Perhaps the most celebrated parrhesiates of the late-twentieth century was Vaclav Havel, who memorialized "living in truth" as the ethos of opposition to the post-totalitarian state. The expression is apropos of the parrhesiastes' ethos, who, Foucault tells us, has made a conscious decision to speak the truth. Foucault clarifies the status of truth in parrhesia when, in his concluding remarks to *Fearless Speech*, he observes that it is the truth-teller, not *the truth* in a philosophical sense, that is his objective. "My intention was not to deal with the problem of truth, but with the problem of the truth-teller, or of truth-telling as an activity. By this I mean that, for me, it was not a question of analyzing the internal or external criteria that would enable the Greeks or Romans, or anyone else, to recognize whether a statement or proposition is true or not. At issue for me was rather the attempt to consider truth-telling as a specific activity, or as a role" (2001, 169).

Still, the reflexivity of speaking the truth presupposes the truth-teller knows what constitutes it. Havel addressed this concern in a number of his writings and speeches. He put it most directly in acceptance remarks for an honorary degree conferred by the University of Michigan. There, while distinguishing between information and truth, he says, "truth is also information but something greater. Truth—like any other information—is information which has been clearly proved, or affirmed, or verified within a certain system of coordinates or paradigms, or which is simply convincing; but it is more than that: it is information avouched by a human being with his or her whole existence, with his or her reputation and name, with his or her honor" (2000). Because the truth is information that the truth-teller avows with his or her whole being, for Havel the commitment to truth means standing firm to that belief regardless of whether it yields returns, recognition, success, or their opposites.[5]

Living in truth has special reality for the prisoner of conscience (POC). Shortly after his release from prison in February 1983, Havel expressed this reality in concrete terms when, during an interview, he commented on the difference between the political prisoner and the common criminal. He noted that even though they are classified as criminals, political prisoners are singled out in ways that mark them as a menace to sovereignty:

> Political prisoners are surrounded by informers and kept under constant surveillance, punished for the slightest of pretexts, have no hope of conditional release, others are punished if they try to contact them (and this in the most "collective" institution of all!!); the prison authorities think up all kinds of ways to make life harder for them, for example, by assigning them work in which they cannot fulfill their norms and thus rendering themselves liable to yet more punishment; and I have personally had the experience of other prisoners being secretly bribed to harm me. . . . Yet, the politicals are held in high esteem by the others . . . [who] regard the politicals as innocent, as people who—in the laconic prison jargon—have been jailed "for the truth." (1992, 242–43)

Against official rhetoric that portrays their offenses in terms of the criminal code, prison vernacular reframes them through its implicit critique of their jailers, while valorizing prisoners like Havel, jailed for their words, for having had the courage to speak it.

From Havel's perspective, he is obliged to speak the truth because of who he is. When his interviewer asks how he views being considered the leading Czech opposition speaker or dissident voice, he specifically distances himself from that characterization. He is not a politician or professional revolutionary or "dissident." He is a writer who gets involved because he considers it his duty as a citizen and a writer. As a public figure, he has access to the media and gets opportunities to speak that are not available to the ordinary citizen. His public status carries a different responsibility, he says, whether he likes it or not, to express his views more loudly. His responsibility is not to be a spokesperson for any ideology or group; he criticizes his government "not because it happens to be a communist government but because it is bad." His interest is with speaking the truth, which means expressing his conviction regardless of its consequences. "If I serve anything, then only my own conscience" (247).

Havel's attitude and performance make him a model of the Foucauldian parrhesiastes, who "makes it manifestly clear and obvious that what he says is his own opinion." Equally true to Foucault's prescription, Havel "does this by avoiding any kind of rhetorical form which would veil what he thinks." Instead, Havel "uses the most direct words and forms of expression he can find" (Foucault 2001, 12). His fearless authoring of letters and cosigning declarations that were addressed to the government, including the president, both criticizing its actions and policies and calling for reform, did not avail themselves of the sorts of rhetorical inducements that would dull their barb. As a consequence, Havel was sent to prison.

At the same time, this restricted understanding of rhetoric limited to discursive forms of seduction does not discount the polyvocality of frank speech. Havel's speaking the truth was neither lacking eloquence nor without intent to bring about change. His open letters made arguments that were rooted in Czech history, cultural commitments, constitutional and treaty obligations, and national experiences, all directed toward moving his reader to respond, even if the reader happened to be the president. And so what if the president was not moved? Havel was not speaking the truth in a private audience but in a public letter. Stating his views publicly was what he was obliged to do. His letters were read by the larger society, for whose concerns he was a voice and to whom his appeals also were meant as a form of influence on thought and action. As he had predicted in "The Power of the Powerless" (1986c), and then famously reported in his 1990 "New Year's Address to the Nation" (1998b, 5–6), that influence was manifest when, at the right moment, everyone knew where to go and what to do without being told. There had been a social dialogue among the citizens that brought them to yearn for living in truth, and when the moment arrived, they seized it.

Parrhesia is more than speaking frankly to authority without interest in persuading. It is more than conveying information. It is speaking truth that is grounded in fact and conviction. The parrhesiastes speaks the truth first because he or she *must* as an obligation to himself or herself, but also to speak it to the other, who may not want to hear it. Parrhesia is not soliloquy; it has an audience, there is the possibility of change. In the case of public figures like Havel, there also is another audience that witnesses how the addressed audience responds and judges accordingly. Even in prison, Havel's criminal jailmates recognized that the back-and-forth between him and his jailers was not about jailhouse behavior but about something larger—truth— and how they stood in relation to it. At every turn, parrhesia carries political stakes that grow from the fact that serious remarks are addressed to someone with the capacity to effect change. For this reason, parrhesia cannot escape being rhetorical speech. Although we can make sense of parrhesia in terms of the subject's articulation of conscience as an obligation to personal authenticity for living in the world, it defies sense as a political speech act without understanding it as rhetorical, as an expression addressed to an audience with the possibly of effecting change. Living in truth, for Havel, is both. His obligation to speak reflects that he is not called solely to articulate for himself but for others, and to accept the heavy burden of consequences that might befall others for the words he speaks.

Stripping the Citizen of Agency

Havel's commitment to living in truth locates agency at the center of authentic public life and is clear in its assessment that agency is exactly what is always under assault in a totalitarian political environment. Erving Goffman's *Asylum* (1961), which considers the altered reality that defines the total institution, provides clues to the techniques of totality. Mental hospitals, nursing homes, penitentiaries, boarding schools, convents, and so forth, are set apart from the rest of society and designed to function on the basis of a uniform set of rules and expectations that are different from those their "residents" follow in civilian life. These institutions are organized to handle large groups of people who are managed by a small supervisory staff. There is a structural divide between "residents" and staff, says Goffman, that breeds mutual suspicion and hostility, grossly restricts social mobility, and often prescribes social distance, even to the point of tone of voice when speaking across the divide. The animosity engendered by the total institution's structural arrangements are certain to encourage those who are "in" them to balk and make control of its population an institutional imperative.

The person entering the institution comes with a "presenting culture" derived from a "home world," in Goffman's words, "a way of life and a round of activities taken for granted until the point of admission to the institution" (12). This way of life, regardless of the "recruit's" personal organization, was part of a larger civil environment of persons and organizations that provided a range of experiences from which he or she could form a tolerable self-conception. Importantly, Goffman notes, the range of experience also "allowed for a set of defensive maneuvers, exercised at his own discretion, for coping with conflicts, discreditings, and failures" (13). Severing the "residents'" connection to this external world as the "reality" they must negotiate in daily life and establishing patterns of conformity to institutional rules provides the institutional logic for how its "residents" are managed.

The penal/juridical system adheres to the logic of the total institution. It is predicated on severing the prisoner's relationship to the outside world and the multiple roles he or she occupies as a free person.[6] It systematically assaults agency with a series of requirements that, in their performance, are intended to reduce the prisoner to a state of confusion and obedience. Quite apart from whatever may have occurred at the time of arrest and interrogation, immediately upon internment prisoners are presented with *deference obligations*, usually in the form of an immediate obedience test. They are placed in a situation structured to instigate balking. They must choose either to resist and pay the consequence or to humble themselves by keeping their peace. This may be as mild as verbal harassment by the guards or as strong as rough physical treatment. They must defer to the prison's imposition of a number for their name, must wear standard-issue prison garb, which in the case of political prisoners often is ill-fitting and ill-suited to the prison's living and work conditions. They must refer to guards in specified ways that perform acts of deference as part of the daily routine of performing their new role of prisoner. Prisoners are subjected to *personal*

defacement with the loss of their names, the loss of their civilian clothing, the loss of
spatial autonomy, and the loss of multiple roles by which the free person structures
daily life and constructs personal identity. These violations of personal boundaries are
encroachments on the self that are likely to involve acute psychological stress.

The Prison of Apartheid Society

The techniques of dissociation from self and society characteristic of the total institution mirror the techniques of social organization and control used by South Africa's
National Party (NP) to retain political power, secure white economic advantage, and
suppress political dissent. The separation of races had a long history in South Africa.
Near the turn of the twentieth century, as the British were struggling to retain control of the country from the insurgent Afrikaner population, the natives were originally disposed to support their cause on the belief that if the British won, they would
be extended suffrage. Their hopes were dashed when the Treaty of Vereeniging ceded
Crown responsibilities to a coalition of Afrikaner and British settlers who were
adamant on retaining white rule (Frederickson 1995, 44–45). Official commitment
to separation of races was placed at the head of the political agenda when Union
prime minister J. B. M. Hertzog marked the opening of a campaign against the fran-
chise in a speech to his constituency at Smithfield in November 1925: "The time has
arrived for a definite native policy, a policy which will remove all doubt from the
native mind about the position which he will hold in political society . . . but he will
have to be told in the most unequivocal language that the European is fully determined that South Africa shall be governed by the white man, and the white man will
not tolerate any attempt to deprive him of that task" (quoted in Ashforth 1990, 69).

Within a decade, Hertzog's position was given the benediction of a distinct
name when intellectuals began to use the word "apartheid," which means apartness
(Thompson 1996, 186). It also received "scientific" reinforcement from the 1932
Report of the Native Economic Commission, which addressed the "Native Question"
with the language of economics and ethnology to argue that the natives thrived in the
pristine conditions of the reserves, where their unique social system, reflecting their
primitive mentality, contained the laws of their own growth, while the white Europeans, whose identity was constituted economically through the "money economy,"
had their natural location in the towns. If the hapless backward race, with its "primitive," "subsistence," "nonmoney" economy, were placed in contact with the money
economy of the Europeans, contradictions would result, making conflict inevitable.

The economic realities of 1930 found the natives migrating from rural areas,
much to the chagrin of settler farmers and mining interests that wanted their cheap
labor, to towns and urban areas, where there was sufficient secondary industry to keep
them employed. The "Native Question" was further complicated by the fact that
natives living in urban areas included an educated segment who were better qualified
for higher-paying positions than many poorly educated whites. In the commission's

view, the solution was for the state to take control of education, which was then in the hands of the provincial councils, and institute measures to retribalize the natives. Education, the commission maintained, was "not only a condition of his advance in civilization, but of his final survival in a civilized environment." It was hoped that through education, the "lackadaisical" natives would be instilled with a more industrious work ethic and relocate to agricultural and mining regions where they would supply a cheap labor pool (Ashforth 1990, 69–113). State-controlled education also would ensure that what the natives were taught was in keeping with aspirations appropriate to the station in life that was their destiny under white rule. Retribalization would provide the natives with reservations where they could exercise their political voice in the domain appropriate to their political condition, while denying them a say in the governance of the nation.

By 1948, when the NP came to power and made apartheid state policy, the economy of South Africa was firmly resting on the shoulders of cheap native labor, and the tribal reserves were established as quasi-political entities, with tribal chiefs wielding considerable power in their respective domains, although their inhabitants were still South African citizens. The NP quickly moved to transform the administration of the South African population. It used its majority in parliament to solidify the power of the chiefs. It eliminated the voting rights of Colored and African people.[7] It grouped the reserves into eight (eventually ten) territories. These territories became "homelands" for potential African "nations," administered under white tutelage by a set of Bantu authorities. The idea was that Africans would be citizens of the homeland, losing their citizenship in South Africa and any right to involvement with the South African parliament, which held complete hegemony over the homelands (Thompson 1996, 191). The government made certain the chiefs received financial benefits to ensure their staunch support for the system and moderation in their rhetoric about living conditions on the Bantustans (Mandela 1994, 141–96).

The NP aggressively codified apartheid through a series of laws that were intended to preserve white economic interests, solidify white political hegemony, and institutionalize the separation of the races. Starting in 1949, with the Prohibition of Mixed Marriages Act, and extending to the Bantu Homeland Citizens Act of 1970, the NP had put in place structures that forced nonwhite South Africans, more than 75 percent of the population, to behave in ways that stripped them of human agency (see the list at the end of this chapter). Collectively, these laws defined nonwhites out of the category of free persons, and black people out of the category of "human" beings endowed with "rights." Nonwhites were definitionally and structurally positioned as inferior beings that might contaminate the white race by making contact with it.

Not surprisingly, South Africa was awash with human rights abuses. A partial list under the policy of apartheid includes arbitrary arrests and detentions without trial, denial of basic civil and political rights to more than three-quarters of its population, systematic press censorship, denial of equal social and economic rights and opportunities to its people, denial of freedom of movement and residence to three-quarters of its people, denial of freedom of peaceful assembly and association to three-quarters of its people, and torture and extrajudicial executions. Its violations were a matter of statute and public policy that embedded racist structures in all aspects of South African public life.

Apartheid's agenda of white supremacy was given the political cover of a program ostensibly intended to celebrate diversity by allowing the different races to develop in ways that were most harmonious with their cultural differences. This agenda then was given biblical sanction by the General Synod of the Dutch Reformed Church, South Africa's state church, which provided ethical and moral underpinnings to apartheid in its 1974 statement, "Human Relations and the South African Scene in Light of the Scripture" (Doxtader and Salazar 2007, 38–41). In addressing the question of "whether Gen. II.1–9 can serve as a Scriptural basis for a policy of autogenous development," it answers with a qualified "yes," citing differences of languages and nations, and the sinful arrogance of the builders of the tower of Babel, who thought they could create unity through human design, as evidence of diversity among peoples as an essential human condition. It continues to find a basis in the New Testament for biopolitical design. "In specific circumstances and under specific conditions the New Testament makes provision for the regulation on the basis of separate development of the co-existence of various peoples in one country."

From the fact that the existence of a diversity of peoples is accepted as a relative, but nonetheless real, premise, one may infer that the New Testament allows for the possibility that a given country may decide to regulate its inter-people relationships on the basis of separate development—considering its own peculiar circumstances, with due respect for the basic norms which the Bible prescribes for the regulation of social relations . . . and after careful consideration of all possible solutions offered. When such a country honestly comes to the conclusion that the ethical norms for ordering social relationship, i.e. love of one's neighbor and social justice, can best be realized on the basis of parallel development, and if such a conviction is based on factual reasoning, the choice of parallel development can be justified in the light of what the Bible teaches. (39–40)

The best that can be said of this statement is that, through tone and sentiment, the church accepted the possibility that social justice was better served by separation of races when the belief in racial differences had a history of social dislocation and exploitation that had left a significant segment of the population poorly educated and resentful. It also provided the church's moral sanction for racism.

The Vice of Racism

Racism is an ideology. It is also a system of social and institutional policing. By definition, it categorizes people on the basis of either ethnicity or biological characteristics on the belief that members of each racial group possess distinct characteristics or abilities that separate them from one another. It then orders the separate races in a hierarchy according to these distinct characteristics or abilities, and attaches values to the hierarchy. Inevitably, the hierarchical value of "up" as a cut above "down" kicks in, which results in claims of racial superiority. An ideology is not itself a vice; however, it may lead to habits and practices that are disorienting of moral order and can be considered depraved, which brings us into the arena of vice.

Vice is habituated behavior that serves a disordered end. As Aristotle wrote in the *Nichomachean Ethics*, virtues and vices are developed through practice and, once habituated, become part of our character. They influence how we see the world, reason about it, and talk. Thus, he observed, we assess a person's character (*ethos*) by observing his or her habituated responses (*hexis*) in problematic situations. These habits are formed through our social experiences. The processing of everyday experiences occurs in the context of families, school, work, friendships, and social life in which we inherit how others, including significant others, think and talk about the contexts and episodes of social life. We learn who we are as we learn which group we belong to and suffer the gentle violence[8] the group exerts on its members to assimilate its narratives of life-in-the-moment and the values they contain. Although we tend to talk of vice in terms of a specific behavior, we should not forget that vices are constituted by the cluster of behaviors that reinforce how we think, experience, talk, and behave in habituated ways that serve a disordered end.

In the case of South Africa, the practices of apartheid systematically discriminated on the basis of race and color. The vices, or habits, that inclined Afrikaners to institutionalize and enforce racial discrimination made their racism more than a belief that one race was superior to others. It was a habituated pattern of thought in which the assumed inferiority of one group of people because of skin color, language, customs, place of birth, and so forth, was used to justify certain behaviors toward that group, all of which served the disordered end of upholding white privilege.

When the hierarchy of racial differences is translated into institutional practices and public policy, it results in discrimination that challenges the human rights of those who are the object of its prejudice on the basis of the assumed right of the superior race to dominate the inferior one(s).[9] Certainly cultural beliefs may sanction social practices that reproduce racial discrimination as part of that culture. However, as these beliefs are institutionalized, they lead to group-based privileges built into the legal and economic structure of the society. Apartheid was such a system.

Biopolitics has as its central concern regulating the population in order to protect and advance public health, safety, and well-being. Apartheid extended this concern to its regulations based on race. Discriminatory practices based on an a priori are not necessarily a vice. For example, all states have regulations that pertain only to children based on the a priori that children are less competent to care for themselves than adults, and therefore the state has a responsibility to exercise a guardian function to protect their well-being. The difference in the case of apartheid is that it began with an a priori assumption of the native's racial inferiority in mental ability, social organization, economic mentality, and cultural development or civilization. The state then instituted measures to establish legal and structural obstacles to the native's political empowerment and economic advancement. In short, it imposed barriers to agency, effectively denying each person of color the power to make choices about matters that affected his or her health, safety, and well-being.

A belief in white supremacy, of course, may be considered a vice of pride. It leads to practices of bigotry and arrogance, which apartheid institutionalized. In addition, for those who may have had misgivings about apartheid, its institutionalization gave rise to despair that anything could be done, which led either to withdrawal in the face of habituated disorder or undirected acts of rage. For its agents charged to enforce it, especially police and prison personnel, it induced them to acts of cruelty. This intertwining constituted racism as a collective vice.

These racist structures permeated the state's treatment of political prisoners at Robben Island. They were a reinforcing agency for attitudes of superiority among the white warders at the prison, who had little education and no meaningful contact with South Africa's nonwhite population outside the prison. They had a deadening effect on moral sensibilities that would inhibit wanton brutality toward its political prisoners and gave Robben Island Prison the aura of bare life akin to that of the Nazi camps.

Conditions at Robben Island

From the moment they entered the penal system, South Africa's political prisoners experienced its world of regulation and control. As with the common prisoner, their sentence established an official relationship of space and time, a chronotope[10] of sorts, that tempered any and all of the prisoner's daily negotiations with power. For political prisoners, this negotiation was complicated by an ever-present awareness, shared with the authorities, that the isolation of prison remained outward looking; although removed from society's normal places of civic and private concourse, the political prisoners never relinquished hope of engaging society's consciousness. Consequently, the authorities did whatever they could to isolate the politicals from the outside world. They were denied newspapers, radios, or other means for learning of outside events. Their communication privileges of mail and visitors were limited and often abrogated. The chronotope of the politicals' sentence was meant to sever any connection to an externally inhabited local place and historic time that might have reinforced the meaning of resistance by harboring an alternative understanding to the official chronotope of the prison.

They also experienced the common prisoner's reality of bodily insufficiency. They worked, slept, ate, and relaxed in a world of systematic control and ubiquitous observation. Movement was confined to the cell, the mess hall, the prison yard, the workshop. When they passed beyond the prison walls, it was to march to the quarry, where labor was hard and dangerous. There was no personal space under their control, no privacy from the other's gaze.

Unlike common prisoners, most political prisoners also were subjected to human rights abuses. *Personal defacement* was extended to routine strip searches, periodic searches of prisoner quarters, and dispossession of their property. They were subjected to *personal disfigurement* through beatings and denial of food. They were routinely subjected to *mortification*: movements were restricted; their heads were shaved; they were at times forced to perform bodily functions in a pail in their cell; they were fed a sparse and unbalanced diet of inedible rations slopped into a bowl or onto a tray one item on top of another; they were forced to submit to strip searches; their use of the toilet on work detail was restricted; and they were forcibly sodomized by the criminal prisoners and warders. The International Committee of the Red Cross (ICRC) report, issued to the South African government on June 18, 1964 (Hoffmann 1964), listed no fewer that twelve human rights concerns, including physical and psychological maltreatment, sexual abuse, and racial discrimination (see at the end of this chapter the list of specific human rights concerns mentioned in the ICRC report authored by Georg Hoffmann [1964]).

Although South Africa was not alone in violations of human rights, the fact that the NP came to power in 1948, just as the United Nations was in the process of drafting the Universal Declaration of Human Rights, made it conspicuous for overtly moving in the opposite direction from the rest of the international community. The government's detachment from international norms was recorded in its response to the ICRC report, when, after finally making it public (International Defense and Aid Fund 1967), the government employed a mode of rebuttal that anticipated what became known during the Watergate scandal as "plausible deniability."

The abusive practices employed at Robben Island to enforce total institutional control went beyond the physical and temporal arrangements of prisons. The spatialization of the penal system includes its historically conditioned spatiotemporal patterns of social action and routine reflecting a vision of a social world (see Sheldrake 2001, 21). Robben Island Prison, as a specific place, refers not simply to a geographical location but to the dialectical relationship between its environment and the human narratives that occurred there. Its narratives were conditioned by the use of power through inflicting humiliation that was intended to deny prisoners' access to a rhetorical place, an inventional location from which to argue back for their human rights.

Biopower and Parrhesia at Robben Island

In words that echo Havel's account of living in truth, Foucault writes: "When you accept the parrhesiastic game in which your own life is exposed, you are taking up a specific relationship to yourself: you risk death to tell the truth instead of reposing in the security of a life where the truth goes unspoken. Of course, the threat of death comes from the Other, and thereby requires a relationship to himself: he prefers himself as a truth-teller rather than as a living being who is false to himself" (2001,17).

This describes the discursive choice by the POC. Certainly not all political prisoners are parrhesiastes. The authoritarian state is only too eager to offer a devil's bargain to change the political prisoner's circumstances. Sometimes it is promise of an easier time in exchange for collaboration, sometimes it is freedom in return for the prisoner's name, sometimes it is coerced through threat of harm to family and loved ones, sometimes it is coerced through force. No one is in a position to judge the political prisoner who caves under extreme duress. By the same token, not all political prisoners are POCs. The POC must make a deliberate choice to embrace danger and sacrifice much that is dear as the price for preserving his or her integrity. This is a difficult personal accomplishment. To generalize commitment to integrity over personal safety within the total institution of prison and achieve solidarity among the prisoner population is a significant rhetorical accomplishment. It is a rhetorical accomplishment because prison norms are antithetical to agency that might coordinate acts of conscience.

Bodily displays of deference, personal defacement, disfigurement, and mortification can function as a deceptive form of inducement to an attitude of exclusion—a misshapen but extremely effective form of what the ancient rhetoricians called *energeia*, whereby the witness experiences a sense of energy or vigor through observing the action of others (Quintilian 1958, VIII.iii.89). For the warders, each display that stripped the prisoner of human traits was an exciting agitation to greater acts of cruelty, and each cruel act reinforced their attitude of inherent racial superiority to their prisoners. Confronted by conditions so extreme that survival had to be each man's foremost concern, the political prisoners soon determined that they could not count on the state or the prison system to initiate humane reform and took it upon themselves to change the prison's culture. Against such intoxicating and seductive displays of power, the prisoners mounted vernacular performances of counterrhetoric reframing their warders' acts of depersonalization.

Indoctrination: Welcome to Robben Island

Indoctrination into the prison system was accomplished in a series of experiences intended to sever the prisoner's relationship to the external word and replace them with deference obligations discussed earlier. In most cases, the prisoner would have had to endure a long trip to Robben Island, since trials were likely to occur in the administrative capital of Pretoria, Johannesburg, or Durban, each 1,400 kilometers or more distant from Robben Island. Prisoners were transported by flatbed truck shackled in pairs with leg irons and handcuffs. The trips took more than one day, which meant they were exposed to stifling heat in summer and frigid cold in winter. There were no latrine stops, and the truck was rank with the stench of human waste.

Usually there was an intermediate stay at one of the labor prisons, which lasted any-where from two weeks to two years. Leeuwkoop Prison, just north of Johannesburg, was among the more frequently used in this capacity. Prisoner narratives paint a ghastly scene of daily strip searches and beatings. When they arrived at Cape Town, they were transported by boat to Robben Island, again manacled in pairs. Strong cur-rents made for rough passage to the island. Prisoner narratives describe being tossed about by the seas and being bruised by their restraints, as the lurching motions of two adult male bodies in rough seas tightened their handcuffs about their wrists.

When they arrived at Robben Island, guards would pull them off the boat and toss them into a waiting tumbril, as if they were bales of hay. Nkosinati Fihla, convicted of sabotage in 1965, tells of his arrival on the island:

> When [the trials] were all completed between the 6 of us then we were brought together at Robben Island. Of course hand cuffed, leg irons and all that. In fact we—the picture then it was—it looked as if we—sort of during the time of slavery when people were leg ironed and all that, that was the picture we had then. When we arrived at Robben Island it was terrible then because we were taken—we crossed with a boat and then were taken by—you know these tip lorries, we were put on those tip lorries. Then when we arrived there we were kicked by those—with those leg irons and hand cuffs so we just fell against each other as if they were tipping animals. (c. 2000, 4)[11]

The newly arrived prisoners were marched to the reception center where they were processed into the prison. Prisoners commonly report that they stood in the elements for two hours before they met with a prison official. Indres Naidoo (1982), sentenced in 1963 to ten years for sabotage, reports that upon arrival the new prisoners were taken to the yard where they were forced to stand spread-eagle while the white warders subjected them to a humiliating hand frisk. When they were given prison issue—short pants made of canvas, a lightweight jersey, a cap, sandals with wooden soles, three thin blankets, and a mat—it was ill-fitting, unsuited to the demands of work and the elements, and worn thin.

Philip Silwane, a schoolteacher convicted of sabotage in 1966 at a summary trial and sentenced to ten years, reports the indoctrination warder barking, "'Jy moet onthou kaffir, jou naam is 25866. Wat is jou naam?' 25866. 'Sê dit weer.' And you repeated your name, this is your name." He was told to write it on all his clothing. The language divide between warder and prisoner, which marked the initiate prisoner as lacking an essential human capacity to communicate, was institutionalized when the guards insisted they be addressed only in Afrikaans. Silwane was assigned to D section, which was reserved for those who were given the fewest privileges and where most political prisoners were initially assigned. "As soon as I walked in there this chap said: 'Ja outside you was in control, now we was in control of you here.' He couldn't even speak English this chap. You was in control, now we was in control of you here.

Het what this chap say!" (Silwane 2000, 42). Silwane's incredulity at the warder's inability to speak English is an important marker that the language divide worked both ways, as will become evident momentarily.

The personal defacement of these indoctrination episodes was part of Robben Island's vernacular of subjugation. Given the choice between balking and being beaten or subjecting themselves to ritualized humiliation by holding their peace, many chose resistance. Moses Dlamini, who also arrived in 1963, recalls the new prisoners being assembled for registration and issued the instruction: "All of you listen . . . when your name is called, you must run to the office." Then a convict came with a list and began calling their names. The warders shouted at them to run, but someone behind the first line of prisoners whispered "trot with dignity comrades." Dlamini reports that as each tried to maintain his dignity as his name was called, the warders rushed him wielding batons and beat him on the shoulders and ribs, being careful to leave no marks on his face. After the group had been registered, their act of resistance was more formally punished when the warder in charge ordered them to stand in the scorching midday December sun. Two men collapsed from the heat. Then, now exhausted, new prisoners were taken to their work site where some men were unable to perform their assigned tasks. Later, after the work detail had returned to the prison yard, Chief Warder Theron appeared. The names of seventy men were called. "He looked at them sneeringly for some seconds. 'Two meals off,' he said and moved away." One of the gang members who was Theron's stooge reminded them of the prison's power: "You don't want to work . . . therefore you deserve to be starved" (Dlamini 1984, 24–26).

Setting Boundaries: Two Can Play That Game

The new political prisoners also received an orientation from those already on the island. African National Congress (ANC) prisoners, especially, were organized and had a leadership structure. From at least 1964, they provided an alternative reading to the violence that lay in store and what was necessary for survival. Joseph Mati, who arrived in 1964, says that the ANC leadership met with the new prisoner to brief him on what he must and must not do. In his words, they would say: "Comrades, you must know that we are arrested here—we are in prison and the conditions are bad. So you must understand that the struggle continues. We have got to make the conditions better in prison. We are going to fight for many things. And fighting for these things will entail suffering" (2000, 17). This political frame informed a specific praxis of everyday interaction in the prisoners' dialogue with terror.

The prisoners providing this counter-indoctrination were clear about the likely extent of suffering. Under prevailing conditions in 1964, manhandling by the warders was inevitable; each had to set boundaries for their treatment. Since most of them had already been subjected to physical and psychological violence during police interrogations, they knew what to expect but also that the warders were not free to act as they pleased. South Africa's apartheid-based law enforcement establishment, as is true of most repressive regimes, was skilled at disciplining the rebel body by placing it in situations of controlled violence. Torture was common during their police interrogations. Steve Biko (1978) explains how knowing that the interrogator acts under instructions influenced his responses during interrogation. He would cooperate as long as his interrogator talked with him, but if he tried bully tactics, Biko would cease communicating, and if he became violent, Biko would reciprocate. If he hits you, Biko reasoned, he does so under instructions to take matters only so far.

> If I react sharply, equally and oppositely, to the first clap, they are not going to be able to count the next four claps, you see. It's a fight. . . . You see, the one problem this guy had with me: he couldn't really fight with me because it meant he had to hit back, like a man. But he was given instructions, you see, on how to hit [that is, so many times, where, and so as not to leave visible marks] and now these instructions were no longer applying because it was a fight. So he had to withdraw and get more instructions. (Biko 1978, 153)

Similarly during the 1960s, the politicals were instructed that they could not mitigate the unrestrained terror of the prison unless they set boundaries for what was and was not acceptable, for how far the individual was prepared to go, and where to draw the line. They were cautioned not to resist in ways that placed their lives in jeopardy; each must draw his boundaries for personal sacrifice. They were always to remember that they were in prison: never challenge the authority of their warders on prison matters, cooperate with reasonable requests, and be courteous in their manner of addressing their warders. However, it would be a mistake to think that by submitting to degrading treatment their sentence would be more tolerable; it would be worse as soon as they were perceived as weak. They were political prisoners and must never forget that the goal of their keepers was to break the resistance against apartheid.

One boundary condition was refusal to be complicit in their personal degradation. An oft-cited example was refusal to participate in the humiliating ritualization of the common strip search, called "*Tausa!*" ("Dance!"). The command was issued as part of the strip search that took place when the prisoners returned from their work detail. Guards were ordering the naked prisoner to leap in the air and spin while opening his legs and clapping his hands overhead. He was to land making a clicking sound with his mouth, legs apart and body bent forward to expose an open rectum to the warder's inspection.[12]

Another boundary condition was refusal to obey unreasonable orders. Mandela, who began his life sentence on the island in 1964, tells how the prisoners commonly engaged in go-slow strikes to protest excessive and unfair work demands (1994, 386). Naidoo recounts an incident where prisoners had been ordered to enter barefoot a stagnant pool of water polluted with slime and dead seagulls and whose bottom consisted of jagged stone. Naidoo refused and defended his action with a reasoned defense based on the necessary conditions for an order to be valid. He was told his reason had no place in Robben Island's world. His only course was to follow orders blindly, and he was found guilty of insubordination. His punishment was to receive four lashes with a bamboo cane.[13]

Mostly the politicals set boundaries in everyday interactions with the warders and administration by generally refusing to be bullied. Mandela's autobiography contains numerous instances where he and others stood up to the authorities and, in return, spent time in solitary confinement and were denied food. Others accepted consequences of another sort rather than comply with racist demands. Dlamini recalls the meanness of the warder Delport and others who did not allow the men to relieve themselves until they referred to the warders as *baas*. "If you don't say 'baas' then you can't relieve yourself. . . . Otherwise you must sweat the urine out." The men refused, "and so," Dlamini continues, "we had to work with our bladders loaded to capacity. Some whose resistance was weak messed themselves up. What did it matter? After all, the trousers dried up quickly. It wasn't so easy to say 'baas'" (1984, 34). Dlamini's reframing of personal humiliation as of no consequence reflects a compassion and kindness that minimizes the sting of degradation intended by the warders' cruelty. It makes the mortified prisoner whole by keeping matters in perspective. Urine-soiled trousers will dry; the loss of personal dignity caused by complying with demands to call their warders *baas* would strip personal integrity in a way that left a permanent scar.

The older prisoners were inventive in meeting the anathema of calling the warders *baas*. They had refined *baas to meneer* (mister or sir). Hector Ntshanyaya credits Philip Chilwine with devising the hidden transcript of saying "baas" loudly and then adding softly "tard." "Tell yourself that you are not saying Baas! Say BAAS-tard," Chilwine advised. Whenever your name is called, say "Ja-BAAS-tard" being "careful that the second part is not heard." The prisoners' refusal to comply with the prison authorities' insistence that they speak Afrikaans, refer to their warders as "*baas*," and acknowledge references to them as "*bandiet*" [prisoner], or with the racially inflected terms "*kaffir*" [a racial slur for a black person] and "*coolie*" [a racial slur for an Asian person], were a quotidian rhetoric of autonomy and eventually led to changes. Hector Ntshanyana, who arrived on the island in 1963, recalled that when an informant reported this hidden transcript, the officer in command called the prisoners together and said, "Look people, these people are really bosses, so there's no need for you to baas them. From today on, you call him by his rank, if he has a rank. If he's a Sergeant, call him Sergeant, if he's an ordinary warder, call him by his surname, forget this baas thing" (quoted in Buntman 2004, 258–59). Within the prison vernacular, refusing to demean themselves and inventive modes of naming and address were rhetorical acts of gentle violence that kept a steady critique of the warders' behavior in play and served as a goad to acts of solidarity among the prisoners.

Some refusals took a more formal and concerted form. For example, the prisoners invoked the law as a form of counterintimidation to countermand capricious behavior. At one point, the warders began a practice of selective intimidation. For two months they had singled out a prisoner each day to be charged with malingering, insubordination, or some other petty offense. They were taken to the prison's administrative court, where the presiding magistrate would be a judge brought by boat from Cape Town. In response, the prisoners established a legal committee to advise the prisoners on how to conduct themselves in the prison's administrative court. When the charges were capricious, Mandela advised the prisoner "to do one thing and one thing only: ask the court for 'further particulars.'" The prisoner's right as a defendant was to require that the particular acts leading to the charge be documented. Mandela reports that one warder in particular, Van Rensburg, was continually stumped by this request, which meant the court then had to be adjourned while he went out to gather "further particulars." The judge, meanwhile, had to be ferried back to Cape Town, sometimes enduring rough seas. When particular acts could not be documented, the charge had to be dismissed, which provoked the ire of the judge, whose time had been wasted, and embarrassed the prison authorities. Such actions were small victories for the prisoners, and kept the warders on notice that the prisoners had means of response that were consequential for warder conduct (Mandela 1994, 432–33). They also afforded a rhetoric of solidarity among the prisoners.

The prisoners were able to go beyond inconveniencing the system to actively harass the guards in ways that proved consequential for their warders' careers. Ian Kitson, convicted of sabotage in 1964 and sentenced to twenty-nine years in Pretoria Prison, where white political prisoners often were held, recounts how prisoners used the Department of Prisons (DOP) rules against the warders. The DOP rules contained a paragraph stipulating that warders had to set an example for prisoners as part of their rehabilitation. When Helen Suzman, who as a member of the ICRC team, visited the prison facilities where the politicals were housed and asked if the prisoners had any complaints, they would say the warder had not conformed to paragraph 72b, which would then go in the warder's dossier. At the end of the year the warder would be reviewed. A list of complaints would block promotion. The prisoners coordinated this activity by forming a committee to lodge complaints. For example, if a warder shattered glass, they would lodge a complaint that he was not setting an example. The institutional committee reviewing the dossier typically did not have firsthand knowledge of conditions in each prison; it only saw the complaints. Kitson (1993), using the ancient trope of prosopoeia, speaks the consequence in the voice of the committee: "Being a warder is dealing with people, applied psychology, and you can't do it. Sorry, we can't promote you this year."

By framing each choice as an assertion of consciences, the prisoners made their cooperation or resistance an affirmation of their human dignity. This intersection of choice with human dignity, within the constraints of prison, invented an expressive idiom for asserting their human rights. Cooperation and resistance became statements in themselves. Moreover, as an expressive idiom they made claims of agency that sometimes challenged institutional logic and could not be ignored. During the 1960s, for the most part, these interrogations of the prison's rationality, these moments of parrhesia, were dismissed with impunity. Sometimes the appearance of due process was observed, and a formal complaint was filed before the prisoners were punished. In many instances, however, the response to resistance was less formal, immediate, and stunningly brutal in its degradation of the prisoner's being.[14] The point, however, was that balking interrupted the prison's logic. It forced the warders and officials to respond to a moral claim. Although some warders remained impenetrably sadistic, not all were able to remain completely closed to a prisoner behaving as a human and demanding respect as a human. Setting boundaries embraced the personally dangerous risk of challenging the efficacy of harsh treatment. It was a form of frank speech that chose to directly defy orders and accept the consequences rather than to cooperate in one's own mortification. It spoke the truth about the human dignity of the prisoner and was a declaration of intent to live in truth. It called for a response, and thereby made the prisoner a discursive node, a point of articulation of the prisoner's right to be treated as a human. It also opened the possibility of negotiation over the prisoner's participation in the material practices of the prison.

Norms of Goodwill: We Care for You

Within their boundaries for acceptable conduct, the prisoners adopted norms of goodwill, or what the Greeks called *eunoia*. They attempted to relate to the guards as humans, engage them in conversation, be helpful and respond to them in generous ways whenever possible, and seek openings where they could show compassion, sympathy, beneficence, and the like. Mati says if they found something a warder lost, they'd return it. Johnson Mgabela, sent to the prison in 1964, tells of kidding the warder in charge of the hospital, Schoeman, giving him a nickname, Schoentjie, and engaging him in banter and serious conversation (2000, 44).

Another norm of goodwill was the ANC prisoners' refusal to be baited into physical confrontations that would have blocked further attempts to humanize the prison's environment. When the prison gangs mocked them with songs that parodied the ANC's political aspirations, they responded by singing songs that could be taken as statements of political protest. "For a number of weeks," Mandela reports, "our two groups sang as we worked, adding songs and changing lyrics. Our repertoire increased, and we were soon singing overt political songs" (1994, 408). Eventually the politicals bested the gangs both in their enthusiasm for singing and in their repertoire. The contest ended, but the worksite songfest continued until a guard fluent in Xhosa recognized they were singing resistance songs and ordered them to stop.

Perhaps the most significant norm of goodwill was engaging in what appeared to be gratuitous acts of caring and altruism. Mandela reports, for instance, that he had adopted the policy of attempting to befriend gang members whenever the opportunity presented itself. His intent was to reframe his relationship with the individual gang member from "enemy" to "recruit." Even when matters didn't pan out as he had planned, such as when he offered to write a letter of protest on behalf of one of the prison gang members only to have him accept a bribe for not filing charges, the fact that his gang had been terrorizing the politicals made extending a hand of kindness a means of reducing the level of hostility within the prison (1994, 408–9). Moreover, it allowed Mandela to awaken the gang member to standing fast to protect his own human dignity. The success of these displays of caring at politicizing the criminal prisoners was a major reason why the state decided to place the vast majority of political convicts on Robben Island rather than risk their converting a larger segment of the general prison population. It also contributed to transferring the criminal prisoners to other facilities, which ended gang terrorism in the prison.

The most influential act of *eunoia* occurred through a structural oversight by the Pretoria government that joined the warders and prisoners in an unanticipated common cause. The policy of apartheid, along with the institution of state capitalism, created a structural need for a vast bureaucracy to administer and enforce a policy that was to control 75 percent of the population by limiting its freedom of movement, education, employment, political activity, housing, property rights, and more, and to oversee and regulate the economic sector. Total control of such magnitude required that a significant portion of the white population be employed as civil servants. The English population, which was well educated and had strong ties to the private sector economy, had little need for civil service jobs. On the other hand, the Afrikaners, who were a ready pool of potential public employees, were poorly educated in general and therefore poorly equipped to perform the duties required to sustain a vast administrative bureaucracy. By 1970, nearly 50 percent of the all economically active Afrikaners were employed by the public or semipublic sector, as compared to only 17 percent of the English-speaking population (Price 1991, 25). This problem touched the prison system in two ways. Most of its personnel lacked a high school education, which limited their chances for advancement and contributed to the brutal atmosphere of its prisons in general. Moreover, its inmate population included Afrikaners, many of whom lacked the education necessary to participate in the economy, which may have been a contributing factor to their criminal acts. To address this problem, the 1959 Prisons Act encouraged the DOP personnel and well-behaved prisoners to take classes.

This law applied to Robben Island Prison, where there was a vast difference between the levels of education of the political prisoners and their warders. In the mid-1960s, as Robben Island was becoming a location for incarcerating political convicts, most of the new prisoners were educated to some degree. Many were close to completing a high school diploma—called Matriculate Certificate, or "matric"—or were in a position to pursue undergraduate and even postgraduate studies. This disparity was a source of embarrassment to the DOP. As long as prisoners had not achieved their Junior Certificate,[15] uneducated warders, indoctrinated with an ideology of racial supremacy, were insulated from feelings of inferiority by their hatred of blacks and the official policy of harassment. However, the DOP could not tolerate a situation in which prisoners would be better educated than their guards. The warders' embarrassing conduct resulting from a disparity in education would make it difficult to regulate the prison on the DOP's own terms.

When the politicals agitated to take courses, for which they technically qualified under the Prisons Act,[16] the prison system stepped up its encouragement for the warders also to take classes. This facilitated an unanticipated structural relationship. Warders and prisoners often were enrolled in the same courses. The warders' sense of competition led to boasts that their "racially inferior" African, Indian, and Colored charges were incapable of matching them in intellectual achievement. When grades were posted and the unthinkable had occurred, the prisoners invented a space for a vernacular rhetoric that performed hospitality.

Hospitality is an ordinary virtue rooted in availability and openness. In an interesting exploration that links hospitality to hope, Dale Jacobs (2008) reminds us that the Latin root of hospitality, "hostis," means "stranger" or "enemy." It is extended not just to those who are known and beloved but to strangers who may be hostile toward us. It commences with conveying our availability to the other, on which intersubjectivity depends. It also depends on listening to what they have to say, which means hospitality defines an open space where invention of relationship based on mutual respect is possible. Whereas the hostile person might expect resistance and opposition, hospitality does just the opposite by conveying care for the person of the other, even if the ideas of the other are not shared.

Relationships of mutual regard are antithetical to polite silence in the face of disagreement. Instead, they require that the person extending hospitality show himself or herself unambiguously as a person of a certain sort with certain ideals and lived commitments. By doing so, Jacobs argues, hospitality transforms the person extending it from a "nobody" into a "somebody," which is requisite for a relationship to develop.

Jacobs maintains that the dialogic character of hospitality places it in relationship to hope. "At its core," he argues, hope is "thoroughly intersubjective, a horizontal relationship of mutuality that looks toward a shared future. . . . Through a conception of hope that involves this kind of radical intersubjectivity, we internalize our responsibility to others as we move towards collective action that is rooted in, rather than outside of, material reality" (2005, 786–88).

Robben Island's prison narratives report how the prisoners met their warders' disbelief at being outscored by their "racial inferiors" with acts that restructured hostile relationships through the hospitality of sincere offers of assistance. Prisoners began advising warders about education as in their self-interest. Mati reports the prisoners' appeals to the guards' self-interests to encourage them to study: "Look, man, you will never get promotion. You must do something; you must study. Sacrifice some of your time and money and pass JC (Junior Certificate), pass matric. You cannot become a lieutenant if you don't have matric—so you must study" (2000, 18–19). Mati says they offered to assist their warders with their courses and included them in the prisoners' study groups, even providing tutoring. Those on night duty would take their written work to the cells of the more educated prisoners, including Mandela, who would correct them. Prisoners in single cells who had been teachers in civilian life even tutored some of the warders. Mati reports, "When we arrived there, they were told by their superiors: 'These people are very dangerous. You must not befriend them.'" Helping them with their schoolwork introduced a relational change. Mgabela explains how this act of hospitality led to behavioral changes. He tells of his fleeting conversations with Delport, the warder whom Dlamini earlier had cited as refusing the prisoners' request to relieve themselves:

Sometimes Delport and I would talk, only briefly, but still: "*Oom* Dellie, one thing is wrong with you. You are not educated. These Afrikaners misuse you." "How do you mean they misuse me?" I explained to him that he will stay where he is because he didn't have higher schooling; that there was no future for his son whilst he only held a low rank. He agreed that he would come to the cells after hours and that we would organize him a teacher for each of his subjects—Afrikaans, English, Maths, History, everything. He came and he passed standard six. He did JC and passed JC. He did matric and passed matric. It changed Delport's life. He became a kind man. He even spoke out against people who had a bad attitude and filled other people with hatred. When we were on a hunger strike it was Delport who would take us to the quarry and who suggested that we must go to the sea and collect food to eat. (2000, 43–44)

The friendships that did form were of a particular kind. The islanders were still prisoners, and their warders were still responsible for imposing the prison's regime of oppression. The senior guards during the 1960s, for the most part uneducated older men in their forties and fifties who were used to thinking of the prisoners in deeply racist ways, remained hostile. Work in the quarry was hard, conditions were severe, and often treatment of the prisoners was demeaning. Whatever friendship formed between the prisoners and those they were helping had limited opportunities for reciprocity. Regardless of the limitations, the important point is that through acts of goodwill the prisoners opened a discursive space where they could speak frankly to their warders about their own exploitation under apartheid and the government's need for them to fill a role not necessarily in their own best interests. Even modest attitudinal and behavioral changes encouraged by acts of goodwill contributed to reforming the prison. As the case of Delport suggests, it was possible for the guards to see their prisoners as humans and to respond to them in terms of their humanity.

Norms of Reciprocity: Do the Proper Thing at the Right Time

The prisoners' attempts to establish a climate of civility at Robben Island were not entirely other-regarding. In civil society, relationships often are strategic and marked by the principle of quid pro quo. This was true on Robben Island. Seemingly simple exchanges of favors could carry significant political import. Mandela recounts how a warder had approached Mac Maharaj for help. A newspaper had announced an essay contest. The warden wanted to enter and hinted there would be something in it for Maharaj if he helped him write the essay. Maharaj agreed, and a few weeks later the excited guard returned to report he was now a finalist. If Maharaj would write another essay for him, he would smuggle him a cooked chicken. Maharaj had qualms of conscience and discussed it with Mandela and Walter Sisulu. Should he help the warder? Should he accept the bribe? What if he refused? They went back and forth but told him that if he helped, taking the chicken would carry the appearance of looking out for himself. Maharaj decided to act strategically. He asked the warder for a pack of cigarettes instead. The next day he reported he now had leverage on the guard, since he had the pack of cigarettes with his fingerprints on it. In return for his silence, the guard would provide him with newspapers, among the prisoners' most prized contraband since, as politicals, they were systematically denied contact with the outside world and its political developments.

Mgabela, who was an uKwaluka on the outside—a person who performs circumcisions—reports a less coercive exchange. By the mid-1970s, Robben Island received a flood of teenage boys convicted of anti-apartheid crimes. Because they were so young, they had not been circumcised, which was the rite of passage practiced by Xhosa and other tribes. The circumcision was to have taken place at least by age eighteen. This passage to manhood, importantly in the context of the prison, made the young male's conduct responsible to the community of elders. As these boys were becoming physically adult, their lack of discipline posed control problems to the warders and the adult community of political prisoners. The young prisoners themselves approached Mgabela, who worked in the prison hospital, "pleading," as he characterizes it, to be circumcised. Conducting this procedure involved risks, since it required that he have access to a knife, perform an operation, and maintain secrecy, all of which violated prison rules and would extend his sentence if discovered. The guards joined in abetting this covert practice once they recognized the adult African politicals could then assist them in reining in untoward behavior. Circumcision would make these unruly young men accountable to the Xhosa elders within the prisoner community. The prison authorities finally learned of Mgabela's practice and asked for a written explanation. He offered this account: "In jail there is only one committee that can discipline the people and that is our own committee. . . . Pretoria will be in trouble [all over the world] when a warder is shooting people on Robben Island. . . . They can't allow the young prisoner to step out of line. But I can secure this danger in time" (2000, 51). The authorities agreed he had provided a service.

Although he was found guilty of possessing a knife, he was not asked to surrender it. He was given a "slap on the wrist" punishment of missing two meals and spending one night in the punishment cells, and transferred to the kitchen.

Overcoming Mortification

The interpersonal exchanges I have been tracing between the prisoners and their warders constituted a vernacular rhetoric for ameliorating the immediacy of life-threatening violence that defined the prison's outlaw culture in the 1960s. Absent legal remedy and physical means of self-defense, the political prisoners determined to use the moment-by-moment exchanges within the prison as a vernacular discourse of power. It interrupted the warders' perception of their capacity to do to the prisoners as they pleased without consequence and of the political prisoners as lacking the resourcefulness for effective resistance. Incrementally, the prisoners eroded the virulent racism of Robben Island's culture and effected new, more felicitous terms of engagement within the prison.

Mortification practices, such as those in place at Robben Island during the 1960s and into the 1970s, help to explain how, in facilities like Robben Island, those with power are able to subject other humans to monstrous forms of brutality so stunning that we can only wonder at their human possibility. As the Nazi death camps make evident, a regime based on inflicting pain requires a system of depersonalization that fits the prisoner's body into narratives of bare life. To overcome the guards' natural resistance to executing barbaric tasks that transgress the moral boundaries for respecting human dignity, the prison must deprive the prisoner of individuality. Bodies are routinely stripped, which is not the way humans present themselves in public. We tend not to congregate with other naked bodies, reserving our nakedness for the restricted space and gaze of privacy. Bodies are assembled en masse. Naked, they appear as herds of animals, not individual persons. Bodies are starved to the point where the prisoners eat like animals, some driven to scavenging for extra morsels of food. Their mere animality is accentuated by shaving their heads and facial hair. Prisoners are stripped of their names, which communicate individual identities with personalities, histories, and agency, and given numbers, which reduce them to ledger entries, or referred to with personal profanations of obscene names, negative attributes, or taunts. They are required to live in their own filth, so that their cells come to resemble pens of livestock unable to keep themselves clean. Prisoners are subjected to forced sodomy or rape. Guards do not engage them in face-to-face interaction, which would require recognizing them as individuals and persons able to be conversational partners. Such tacit recognition of the other's humanity would impose limits making it more difficult later when called upon to administer bodily abuse. Language barriers also serve as a mode of depersonalization, since they make it difficult for prisoners to communicate individual thoughts, feelings, needs, or responses to their warders and reduce them to following set commands, much as animals.

At Robben Island these practices were made life threatening by the unchecked sadism of the guards and the uncontrolled violence of the prison gangs, who were maiming and even murdering other prisoners. Setting boundaries became a form of truthful speech by refusing submission to the norms of violence then in play. It was a form of refutation that spoke a vernacular of resistance and of group solidarity. The total institution of Robben Island depended on its supervisory staff being able to control a large population of inmates. Concerted resistance posed a problem that required attention, and its urgency magnified with the eventual negative publicity about conditions in the prison. At every point where the prisoners were able to call into question prevailing conditions, they asserted agency. At every point where the prison responded with something other than physical brutality, it acknowledged the prisoner as in some measure more than a brute animal, as somebody.

Setting boundaries also opened a space of articulation for the prisoners to respond to their warders as fellow humans. If the vice that permeated Robben Island was racism, the prisoners' acts of caring for the warders' and the common law prisoners' welfare through help with their studies, encouragement to improve themselves for career advancement, and addressing them with interest and concern for their families brought the virtue of hospitality to combat it. Parrhesia served as a structure both for drawing the line on how they would be treated and for bringing those who threatened their physical well-being to see themselves and the prisoners in terms of their common humanity. It this respect, acts of hospitality were vernacular modes of parrhesia through performances of virtue, urgings to warders to stand in truth to their own human dignity, to not allow themselves to be used by the prison system. Practices of hospitality required truth telling in which prisoner ideals and lived commitments became visible markers of their distinctive humanity and eventually a basis for exchanges that highlighted and challenged the invidious racism of their warders.

Practices of truth telling also changed the prison quotidian by providing an expressive idiom in which a strategic politics of resistance focused on the larger struggle for liberation could be practiced.

Reorganizing the Prison and Prison Paideia: The University of Resistance

The rhetorical dimension of parrhesia that I have been stressing allows for and places significant emphasis on action. Living in truth is not a monastic commitment. It is a political/moral commitment and practice in the lived realities of the social world. Accepting the possibility that living in truth may cost dearly, including one's life, does not embrace a foregone conclusion that speaking the truth will be ignored or be inconsequential or fatal. There is always the possibility and hope that it will succeed. In the world of lived politics, where differences of opinion and political ends are a given and where iterative relationships are a defining condition, the telos of parrhesia is personal integrity in a process that can accommodate difference and allows for the possibility of mutually acceptable solutions to common problems. The great success of parrhesia at Robben Island was in moving the warders and prisoners into relationships that, within the limitations and constraints of prison, more nearly resembled the iterative ones of civil society, which included the relationships of the quid pro quo.

These modes of accommodation and civil relationship were primarily directed toward reducing the extreme cruelty and danger that defined prison life on Robben Island. Their success at modifying the overt organization of their lives as prisoners, and thereby reducing its oppressiveness, also served to cover and assist the alternative organizational structure put in place by the prisoners. This is the second story of prison reform on Robben Island, the story of how it became the university of resistance.

The political prisoners came from three main resistance groups: the Pan African Congress (PAC), which was the dominant group in the early 1960s; the ANC, which became the dominant group by the late-1960s and remained so until apartheid ended; and the Black Consciousness Movement (BCM), which began to appear near the mid-1970s. Relations among them often were tense, and cooperation was not universal.[17] This distrust remained at least into the 1980s. Chris Sidlayiya (c. 1994), who arrived at Robben Island in 1983, reports that at that time there were three political organizations in the prison, and they were recruiting members. "They were giving you things to join the organization, like sport shoes, etc. I tell them we are coming from the same place, have the same trial, I'm not going to tell anyone what to do. I have an organization—ANC."

The Rivonia convictions sent the core of ANC leadership to prison—Sisulu, Mbecki, Kathrada, Andrew Mlangeni, Raymond Mhlaba, Elias Motsoaledi, Thomas Mashifane, and Mandela. The government's fear that convicted militant leaders would politicize the common prisoners and its corresponding policy of segregating the political prisoners to prevent their radicalizing rhetoric from being dispersed across the penal system converged to make Robben Island a rich pool of dissident leaders and thinkers of stature. Placing political prisoners in one location allowed the anti-apartheid leadership access to one another and made it possible for the prisoners to organize themselves within the prison in ways that might thwart the government's intent of breaking the resistance movement.

Mandela writes that the primary enemy of the prisoner is the routine of prison life. The ANC leaders, who were in single cells isolated from the rest of the prisoners, quickly realized that the only way to survive in prison was through discipline. They challenged prison routine by bringing their understanding of organization to bear on its own population within the prison. In 1964, the ANC leadership's function was to keep the ANC prisoners in contact with one another. Each of the large common cells, which housed up to eighty men, was divided into small groups, with each group having a leader. This group leader served as its public relations officer and was known to the other public relations officers in the cell. Each cell had a leader whose identity was kept secret from those outside the cell. This person reported to a section leader, who in turn reported to the oversight committee for communication. Given the need for clandestine circulation of information, this structure provided a reliable method for circulating information and maintaining discipline among the ANC prisoners while providing identity security for those responsible for information flow and policy decisions should anyone responsible for maintaining the information flow be discovered (Mhabala 2002).

The leaders also determined that the only way to sustain the resistance movement was to prepare the younger prisoners to assume leadership roles upon release. In addition to the communication committee, they established an umbrella of committees that involved all of the political prisoners, regardless of their affiliation, and reorganized prison time to mirror the civil society to which the ANC aspired. In effect, the daily activities of the prisoners were reorganizing the prison. At the first level, they were engaging in activities of self-defense. At the next, they were engaging in acts of resistance. At a third level, they were engaging in activities that resignified the prison quotidian. The significance of this third level of activity lay in its appropriating power to regulate conduct, within the constraints of being in prison, in ways that projected the relationships of civil society. Each activity was a performance of vernacular rhetoric, inculcating a political vision in the moment-by-moment living of everyday interactions. Insofar as the prison served as a metonym for the racist state, each effective resignification of prison's inward isolation into a community of outward-looking cooperation further empowered their alternative political vision of an inclusively democratic South African state.

The ethos of Mandela and Sisulu allowed them to establish leadership structures. These were overseen by an internal committee, known as the High Organ, which dealt with questions of policy. Leaders were selected from the various political organizations represented in the prison. Raymond Mhabala (2002) reports that in order to preserve the spirit of community, the ANC had to be careful not to exploit its superior numbers by filling all the leadership positions since that likely would stir resistance from PAC prisoners. For example, since his group was small and nonthreatening, he was given a leadership position. Initially, the High Organ consisted of ANC leaders who had been members of its National Executive Committee: Mandela, Mbeki, Mhlaba, and Sisulu. Policy positions were discussed and decided by the group. To maintain consistency, the High Organ often designated a spokesperson or a delegation to represent the group when lodging complaints, making requests, or representing their interests to the authorities. Individual actions were under the guidance of the group. When issues arose, typically involving prison disciplinary charges, committees coached the accused on how to respond to authorities.

The ANC in particular established a committee structure to deal with education (studying, tutoring, and working on course assignments), politics (discussion of issues, thought, and policy), discipline (adhering to group norms and maintaining a spirit of group solidarity), and sports and recreation (sports clubs, cultural activities, and intellectual avocations such as thought societies devoted to pursuits of science, society, and literature). The committees were sites of embodied solidarity and felt *phelia.* They were arenas of discipline and pathos on which the prisoners' survival depended.

The committees also were a technology of sorts, a *techne* or art of translating political theory into praxis. They were a rhetorical technology. They used processes of persuasion in contexts of deliberation and adjudication. They instilled the specific ethos of parrhesia as a core political value. They also inculcated the virtue of accountability. Foucault, writing of the original meaning of *"police,"* notes that it governs "not by law but by a specific, a permanent, and a positive intervention in the behavior of individuals" (1988, 159). It sought to "foster civic respect and public morality" (154). The committees served a similar function. They were self-policing units within the larger organization of the prison's subrosa civil society. They sought to foster a live, active, productive man living with other live, active, productive men, or society. The minutes of the sports and recreation meetings are especially important in this regard. Since they were produced in the context of everyday life on the island for use by the prisoners themselves, and not for an external audience, they offer insight into the prisoners' self-perceptions.

The formal characteristics of the minutes are noteworthy. Individuals are referred to as Mr. They identify specific issues and actions taken. They record disputes over rules and officiating and how they were resolved. They report meetings with the prison administration and their outcomes. They record business conducted according to parliamentary procedure. They reflect how the organization of sports clubs created forums for conducting official business and provided an opportunity for participants to develop their skills at various governance practices that occur in official group meetings—committees and assemblies, primarily, but sometimes adjudicating bodies as well. They are marked by rhetorical norms of civility and decorum expressed in the micropractices of formal address, formal procedures, and formal actions.

The sports clubs provided opportunities for collaborative enterprise. Initially teams were composed along lines of political affiliation. This proved to heighten political rivalries. As sports clubs grew in popularity, teams were formed across organizational lines, leading to integration of political partisans in a common effort. The minutes record the link between the pleasure and prestige associated with sport and accountability. For example, the report of the Referees Union for 1970–71 records that fortnightly lectures were held for the purpose of "studying the laws of the game and current developments in our soccer rules relating to the referee" (Referees Union 1971). Two weeks later, at the soccer league's Executive Committee meeting, Harry Gwala expressed concern about prisoners who wanted to serve as officials at soccer matches but were not attending political lessons. He suggested that priority be given to those who were actively involved in furthering their education ("Minutes" 1971). The minutes also reveal the vulnerability of the community. Buntman observes:

"What comes across in the hundreds of sports club minutes and letters is the fragility of the community—how easily tempers flared, how important sport (and other recreation, including cultural activities) was to maintaining morale and relieving tension, and yet how difficult it was to maintain sporting standards, both in the administration and games themselves" (2004, 68).

Sports clubs also provided opportunity for formal negotiations with the prison administration. For example, Naidoo, who was secretary of the Soccer League, wrote the officer commanding to make a series of requests. The requests are framed around Naidoo's concern over the problem of the growing popularity of the sport and his inability to admit more teams to the league and schedule matches under current space and time limitations. The letter begins and ends with an invitation to the officer commanding to attend a match, which Naidoo assures him will be most entertaining, but that it would be especially so if he were to permit them an additional playing field and three hours instead of ninety minutes for each match. The negotiation was really about increasing the opportunities for prisoner interaction across group lines and for more time spent out of the cells (Naidoo 1968). For prisoners who came later, the functional utility of the sports clubs had become part of Robben Island's political structure. Denmark Tungwane, who came to the island in 1986, points out that since it was the only prisoner structure recognized as legitimate by the authorities, prisoners could use it to argue for other prisoner benefits. "For instance, the whole battle for televisions on the Island came through that structure" (quoted in Buntman 2004, 90).

Many of the prisoners sentenced to the island in the 1970s were young and poorly versed in South African history or Marxist political thought. Nor were they leaders or trained to serve as leaders. Most of these prisoners were sentenced for shorter terms than the ANC leadership convicted in the 1960s, and were likely to be paroled when they were in their thirties. Since they represented a talent pool of potential leaders, specific learning groups were formed to provide the education they would need in economics, history, and political thought as well as in political organization.

Finally, the alternative organization devoted a great deal of thought and effort to acquiring and disseminating information. A critical part of political education and a fundamental component of political emancipation in the prison was the struggle to obtain news. Newspapers especially provided a connection to the outside, to developments in the country, and materials for discussion and debate. Contraband newspapers were at a premium, and the prisoners used a variety of means to acquire them, from retrieving the newspaper pages the warders used to wrap their lunches or bribing common prisoners who had access to newspapers, to extortion, such as that of Maharaj described earlier. Prisoners attended religious services and spoke afterward to the chaplain to gain information. They requested meetings with their attorney on pretext of an urgency, such as to address issues pertaining to a family member's will, which permitted a meeting without a guard present where information could be shared openly. They had family members send bribes to addresses provided by the guards in return for assistance in smuggling information in and out of the prison (Nair 1995). Inside the prison, the kitchen was a nerve center that served as a clandestine postal service. Messages were covered in plastic wrap and hidden in pots used to distribute food throughout the prison. In this way information passed undetected through internal borders. They also used secure places to smuggle written messages from the High Organ to individuals who had access to the rest of the political population, and had networks of dissemination to coordinate prisoner actions, such as the first major hunger strike in 1966. The Disciplinary Committee, which had decided to start a hunger strike the next day, instructed R. B. Ngxiki, sent to the prison in 1964 and who worked in the library, to spread the word. Ngxiki used his freedom to visit cells in order to collect books as cover for instructing prisoners to refrain from taking breakfast the next morning (2000, 84–86).

Since information was shared among the different political organizations in the prison, it also provided a basis for discussion of political events and their meaning for the ongoing struggle and the nation's future. There were sharp differences across and within groups. For nearly a decade, Mandela and Mbeki were at odds over negotiating with the apartheid regime, while the ideological divide over the link (or not) of ANC Marxism to the Communist Party and of whether a post-apartheid South Africa should be a racially inclusive or exclusive state ran deep. Since it was clear that the politicals shared the common enemy of apartheid and that whatever differences they had were about how to shape the future of a country once freed from its oppressive hegemonic structure, norms of tolerance for ideological differences marked their discussions. Sonny Venkatrathnam, a member of the African People's Democratic Union of South Africa who was imprisoned in 1972, offers insight into the discourse ethics of agreeing to disagree that allowed different perspectives to collaborate: "Most of the people on the Island, and in the single cells at least, don't enter into ideological debates. . . . But on other issues we will debate, and if part of our logical standpoints don't convert we will argue and discuss, and we will not allow intolerance. . . . We could talk to each other as equals" (quoted in Buntman 2004, 90).

The activities involved with acquiring and sharing news reinterpreted their relationship to outside conditions of domination they were attempting to reshape. They both challenged the state's edict of isolation and advanced the political activity of intra- and interorganizational structures to obtain, distribute, discuss, and analyze news. Moreover, they furthered the aim of integrating political analysis with the political education of prisoners who were expected to become informed and effective activists when, upon release, they were reinserted into society (Buntman 2004, 252).

The reform at Robben Island provides a model of the civil society that was to follow. The rhetorical mechanism for achieving this reform was vernacular performances of frank speech with prison officials and warders that put their relationship with the prisoners in a light more respectful of their human dignity and opened the space for Robben Island's organizational change. Running a political organization inside the prison that simultaneously was able to have agency for setting the prison's internal climate required establishing inclusive political relations. Against the racist image of the NP, the question foremost within the struggle was whether there would be a South Africa for all South Africans or only for people of color. Against the slave economy of apartheid, the question was whether there would be a South Africa based on Marxist ideals of socialism or some other model. Questions such as these invited the prisoners to engage in rhetorical practices consistent with living in truth.

Eventually, the model of an inclusive South African democracy developed through theoretical deliberation among the various factions within the prison. It was developed in praxis through the organization within the prison, which both conditioned and was performed in daily interactions. These ongoing negotiations over how they would act and interact transformed the prison's inherent political structure from an autocracy to a civil society. It required a vernacular rhetoric of moment-by-moment exchanges that reinforced the dignity of each prisoner, and the ethos of collaboration, and invested the prisoners with agency in a world designed to destroy both. The power of experiencing agency through moment-by-moment acts of resistance, and, in turn, forming political conscience through acts experienced as a rhetoric of hope, is summarized forcefully by Benson Fihla (c. 2000):

> I would say what made us survive at Robben Island, was because of the politicization that was . . . put on us. It helped us a lot to survive you know, because then we started realizing that we are definitely prisoners of hope, there is a hope, there is a future for us. So that, that hardened us in fact in a way, that made us last, that made us even forget that we are serving twenty years, or serving fourteen years, you know, just could—just survive, just much later is a long time, we're going to be here for a long time, because we had this political discussion, regular political discussion, groupings and all that here at the quarry, in the cells, discussion, so that this, that's why they say it was a graduation for politicians, that's why they graduated. It helped them a lot, definitely helped them to survive, because otherwise, the question—what make criminals to be abnormal and inhuman, it's because there is no politicization, do not do, they just think about their own interests, they do not think as a group of the future.

Vernacular Rhetoric, Prison Paideia, and Civil Society

Robben Island is a physical geography located at the margins of South Africa. The NP intended it to be a symbolic geography that located its inmates at the political margins of South African society. This physical reality was subverted by a rhetorical inversion as ancient as the subject itself: appropriating a physical place for use as a symbolic place, using it as an inventional site from which to reread it, and investing it with symbolic significance that transformed its corporeal meaning. When the prisoners appropriated the isolated prison island as a metonym for the state, they transformed it from a representation of the larger society's racial exclusion into a representation of emergent power among the politically disenfranchised. This inversion of part and whole created such centripetal force that eventually it flung the island and its prisoners into the center of South African politics, where a prisoner serving a life sentence was regarded at home and abroad as the moral and political voice of opposition calling for an inclusive South African democracy. His ethos made it impossible for the government to ignore Mandela's political vision.

Locating their struggle to overthrow apartheid at the center of South African politics carried its own transforming implications for the meaning of the prisoner's activity. One lesson of oppression is that you cannot deaden people to the humiliation of their dignity. They may be silent and comply out of fear, but their humiliation stays with them. Sometimes subjects of totalitarian states pretend it doesn't matter, while their humiliation etches itself deeply into their emotional memory only to manifest itself in cynicism absent a positive program for change or in heroics doomed to defeat. The Robben Island story teaches that actively saying "no" can have positive consequences for the oppressed community and for tempering the hand of the oppressor when it foregoes heroics of the grand moment for resistance in daily activity.

Without question, resistance is shaped by material constraints, and a state penitentiary imposes maximum constraints. However, resistance also is shaped by effective rhetoric. Symbolic inducements, whether intended or inadvertent, have the capacity to awaken consciousness and inform conscience. Whether they succeed is an empirical question; the evidence is in the symbolic exchanges that read events differently than how the authorities read these same events. Especially in the case of resistance rhetoric, its inducements are effective insofar as they awaken psychological and moral awareness of a space for rearticulating power relations within the structural limits of place. When that happens, the actors begin to perform more than the drama of opposition, or resisting what is, and advancing affirmations of values and beliefs they espouse. This is a reasonable operational meaning for emancipation—the capacity to advance and affirm political meaning in your own terms.

What binds us morally, Judith Butler argues, is how we are addressed. "[In] the situation of being addressed, the demand . . . comes from elsewhere, sometimes a nameless elsewhere, by which our obligations are articulated and pressed upon us" (2004, 130). Her observation contains an important inversion of the rhetorical situation, usually understood in reference to some perceived condition in the world that must be addressed. By repositioning the rhetorical situation in the experience of being addressed, she reminds us that until we have the experience of being in a rhetorical situation, we cannot engage rhetorically. The experience of being addressed and having an obligation to respond, she says, "comes to me from elsewhere, embedded, and unplanned. In fact, it tends to ruin my plans, and if my plans are ruined, that may well be the sign that something is morally binding upon me" (130). Butler's observation also summarizes the necessity for considering parrhesia as rhetorical speech. Its capacity to address power in a way that not only articulates power's obligations but also presses them upon power in such a way that it ruins power's plans accounts for the possibility of speaking the truth to enjoin others to live in truth.

For the islanders, daily resistance took the form of addressing their warders from their commitment to live in truth. Through every act of parrhesia, they chipped away at the invidious racism the defined the prison's culture. Each act was an assertion of their humanity and also the humanity of their warders. Moment-by-moment exchanges in which they drew boundaries based on commitments to live in truth, showed goodwill to those who had behaved wretchedly toward them, or insisted that the prison and its agents abide by its own rules, constituted a vernacular rhetoric of hospitality and of hope. It addressed warders and administrators with questions that ruined their plans. Men who had never been engaged by people of color found themselves being called on for an answer. An institution that had never been challenged found its rules invoked against it and had to find answers that could rationalize its practices or change them. These forms of address reconstituted the prison's agency as it constituted prisoner agency.

The prisoners' agential force carried forward to the rhetoric enacted in the prison quotidian by participation in an organization outside the regime imposed by the state, by living in a community with discipline and solidarity, and by pursuing realistic alterations to power relations. These vernacular exchanges eventually disrupted the oppressor's monopoly on violence by exerting a gentle violence of its own, as the prisoners' iterative resignifying through daily performance reinforced an alternative political vision.

This was a prison paideia, an education concerned with political formation, with awakening the prisoners to their possibilities as humans and as free citizens capacitated to lead and govern. Their studies had little concern for territory, but great concern for economics, history, politics, and law. These are subjects that focus on how state intervention alters social life. They emphasize how "it wields its power over living as living beings, and its politics, therefore, has to be a biopolitics" (Foucault 1988, 160). Post Robben Island, the politics of hope that Benson Fihla extolled as critical to their survival would be critical to the nation's survival. The prison paideia of Robben Island's civil society was concerned with political rationality by which political choices are structured.

The prisoners had formed a social contract of sorts that permitted rival groups to coexist for the common good. They escaped prison in their minds and in their daily conduct by acting as if they were living in a polity quite other than the apartheid structure then in place. They constructed a parliament of sorts through the counter-public sphere of their group discussions, collective decision making, and disciplined negotiations with authorities. They were setting the terms of collective life insofar as possible within the constraints of being imprisoned.

In these performances, the revolutionaries who were prisoners on Robben Island became exemplary republicans, acting as citizens should in an inclusive democracy. Through the network of groups within their alternative organization of the island they created and influenced public opinion, spoke politics and power, and argued for the reform of the prison in the name of shared—dare we say South African national—values. By protesting, persuading, and voting, they claimed citizens' rights and fulfilled citizens' duties. In other words, they were acting like citizens, performing that which they were never allowed to do in preparation for the time when matters would be different. They were at once a part of South African civil society and excluded from it, performing in a way that projected an inventional possibility while being systematically harassed, surveilled, brutalized, and racially oppressed. Even as they were excluded, these prisoners created an alternative public sphere that projected a vision of an alternative civil society that did not yet fully exist in South Africa but the struggle for which they had dedicated their lives.[18]

Social actors theorize civil society through their rhetoric—in their insistent search for free spaces for rhetorical exchange and in their rhetorical performances in those spaces. Their image of civil society is not that of the state but of the aims of life. Havel has written, "Life in its essence, moves towards plurality, diversity, independent self-constitution and self-organization, in short, towards the fulfillment of its own freedom" (Havel 1986c, 43–44). This was the spirit that marked the resistance of the islanders, it defined the mission of their "university's" curriculum, it emancipated them from the control of their oppressors, and eventually it gave birth to the democracy that continues today.

Apartheid Laws

The Prohibition of Mixed Marriages Act of 1949 prohibited racially mixed marriages, and was later amended to prohibit extramarital sex between racially mixed couples.

The Population Registration Act of 1950 required a record of every person's race.

The Group Areas Act of 1950 forced physical separation of races by creating racially defined residential areas, which led to forced removal of those living in the "wrong" areas.

The Suppression of Communism Act of 1950 outlawed the Communist Party, and defined communism so broadly as to ban any call for radical change.

The Bantu Building Act of 1951 allowed Blacks to be trained in construction trades but restricted their work to areas designated for Blacks and made it a criminal offense for a black person to perform skilled work in any urban area save ones designated for black occupation.

The Separate Representation Act of 1951, together with an amendment in 1956, eliminated Coloreds from the voter rolls.

The Prevention of Illegal Squatting Act of 1951 empowered the minister of Native Affairs to remove Blacks from public or privately owned land and establish resettlement camps for these displaced persons.

The Natives Laws Amendment Act of 1952 narrowed the definition of Blacks who had the right of permanent residency in towns to those who had been born in a town and lived there continuously for not less than fifteen years, or had been employed there continuously for at least fifteen years, or had been employed by the same employer for at least ten years.

The Natives (Abolition of Passes and Co-ordination of Documents) Act of 1952 forced black people to carry documentation with them at all times. No black person could leave a rural or urban area without a permit from the local authorities. Upon arrival in an urban area, a permit to seek work had to be obtained within seventy-two hours.

The Native Labour Act of 1953 made it illegal for Blacks to strike.

The Bantu Education Act of 1953 authorized compiling a curriculum suited to the nature and requirements of black people, while preventing education that would lead to aspirations to positions they were prohibited from holding.

The Reservation of Separate Amenities Act of 1954 forced segregation of all public amenities, public buildings, and public transportation in order to eliminate any contact between whites and other races.

The Natives Resettlement Act of 1954, Group Areas Development Act of 1955, and Natives (Prohibition of Interdicts) Act of 1956 denied Blacks the option of appealing to the courts against forced removals.

The Terrorism Act of 1967 allowed for indefinite detention without trial.

The Bantu Homeland Citizens Act of 1970 compelled all black people to become a citizen of the homeland that corresponded to their ethnic group, regardless of whether they had ever lived there, and removed their South African citizenship (South African History Online n.d.).

Specific Human Rights Concerns in the ICRC Report

Each day the prisoners were searched: They had to strip naked, and bend down, in order to touch the floor. A doctor would then insert his gloved finger into the prisoners' rectum, and twist it (warders would beat them with pick handles if the men did not bend low enough). This search was said to be a "check for hidden items," but it was clearly an act merely in order to humiliate and degrade prisoners.

Another humiliating medical order was that the men had to leap across the yard completely naked. They were ordered to jump up and down.

Prisoners were woken up at 5:30 each morning, if not earlier, and had to be asleep by 8:00 that night.

Prisoners were ordered to hurry, otherwise the warders screamed racist comments like "Kaffir, you are breathing on me."

Over 60 prisoners were crammed into a cell made for 20.

Breakfast consisted of a cup of bitter coffee and cold, lumpy porridge. The men ate squatting on their haunches. Warders were instructed to beat any bottom that touched the floor.

If prisoners were sent to Cape Town for the day to do hard labour, upon arrival they were thrown off the aging Robben Island ferry, making their handcuffed hands a bloody mess. The journey there was horrid: the stench of sweat, faeces and urine dominated the air.

During the day, prisoners were forced to endure hours of hard labour. This resulted in painful blisters forming on their hands, making the work a double nightmare. No first aid kits were provided, so the prisoners had to apply urine to their wounds to sterilize them.

They were made to do pointless jobs, such as spending three weeks digging a mountain of sand in one place, moving it to another place, and then being ordered to transport it to it original position. This took hours of effort, and was a degrading project.

Prisoners were raped and abused by warders.

Coloured, Indian, and African prisoners were all treated differently. The Africans had the least privileges.

Visits from family and friends were severely restricted.[19]

5. *Women of the Small Zone and a Rhetoric of Indirection*

On October 9, 1986, the Soviet Union released Ukrainian poet and dissident Irina Ratushinskaya from the Mordovian labor camp at Barashevo where she was serving a seven-year sentence for her conviction under Article 70 of the KGB criminal code for "Anti-Soviet agitation and propaganda." Her release was unexpected. She had served just three-and-a-half years of her sentence, and was subject to five years exile after her release before she could return to her home in Kiev. With the Reykjavik summit between Mikhail Gorbachev and Ronald Reagan to begin just two days later, speculation was that the two events were connected, perhaps as a pawn to advance negotiations over arms control (*Times,* October 11, 1986). It also attracted public attention to the Soviet camps and the plight of prisoners of conscience (POCs) who were incarcerated there. Two months after her release, Ratushinskaya and her husband and fellow dissident, Igor Gerashchenko, were permitted to leave the Soviet Union, and in 1989 she published her memoir of Barashevo, *Grey Is the Color of Hope.*

The memoir attracted instant attention for the insights it offered into life in the labor camps and human rights issues, reflected in the women's artful maneuvering to survive the camp's systematic attempts to crush their spirits. The women's struggle to maintain solidarity in the face of assaults on human dignity required unwavering commitment to oppositional values. Ratushinskaya's telling of the women's story illustrates how assertions of contested values often occur through more subtle means than direct address. Although parrhesia speaks truth directly to authority, *indirection* can serve as a rhetorical mechanism for speaking the truth, given how it co-opts the discursive rules in play to combat the state's monopoly on violence.

Rhetoric by Indirection

Resistance often relies on the authorities to become unwitting foils. The willingness of those in power to impose their will by force can be framed in ways that expose their mendacity. Nothing is quite as effective at making the point that those in power have little in common with ordinary citizens as actions that ignore citizens' rights and, in fact, abuse them. Resistance depends on establishing a sense of affiliation among ordinary citizens with its opposition to the existing order, even if it cannot achieve consensus on ends. It relies on symbolic means to make sense of the state as a threatening menace and to project its vision of a transformed social order. This is to say that an important part of resistance is the rhetorical project of providing a basis for the political cohesion necessary for concerted acts of opposition.

Anticolonial and civil rights movements of the last century provide ample illustrations of formal resistance rhetoric that were up to the task. Speeches and writings such as Mahatma Gandhi's *Hind Swaraj* (1997), Vaclav Havel's "The Power of the Powerless" (1986), Nelson Mandela's "The Struggle Is My Life" (1961), Frantz Fanon's *The Wretched of the Earth* (1963), and Martin Luther King Jr.'s "I Have a Dream" speech (1963b) were instrumental in reorienting a national consciousness to new perspectives on existing political conditions. Public declarations such as Czechoslovakia's opposition leaders issuing the founding statement of Charter 77 (1977) or South Africa's Congress of the People's "*Freedom Charter*" (1955) provided a platform of beliefs and commitments that allowed ongoing criticism of the government. Even public events that appeared to be acceptable public ceremonies were transformed into statements of opposition when something occurred that reflected widespread support for a cause or a person associated with dissent. At times it appears in public events that are transformed into statements of opposition—for example, the unexpected size of the crowds that spontaneously assembled during the 1979 visit of John Paul II to Poland, at the Czech rock band Plastic People of the Universe's concerts following the Prague Spring, or more recently in the United States at the campaign speeches of Barack Obama in 2008 or, alternatively, at Tea Party rallies in 2009 and 2010. Each embodied deeply held aspirations through exuberant displays of affiliation with an individual or group associated with an alternative set of values to the state's or the ruling political party's. Each, in its own way, manifested the publicity principle (Luban 1996) by showing widespread support for a figure or group that called into question the assumption that representatives on average are wiser or more committed to the common good than the ordinary citizen. Such displays give dissent a public face. They can inspire solidarity among those whose sense of political agency has been compromised. They can alert an external world of readers and viewers to the larger discursive arena where the underlying causes of dissent and resistance are themes of everyday life and encourage their support.

At the same time, they also reflect a particular form of resistance that has the luxury of open expression without yet finding itself in the custody of courts or warders who threaten their freedom and often their lives. By the logic of Georgio Agamben (1998), their performance of their human right to free political expression poses a conundrum. On the one hand, they represent an obstacle to sovereignty that, if left unchallenged, may result in revolution. Yet, by virtue of the magnitude of their following, they cannot be declared *homines sacri*, banned to a state between life and death, without their banishment posing a risk to sovereignty itself.

Who You Talk To Is Not Who You Hope to Reach

In a world of contingencies, imagination can compensate for material constraints on the range of alternatives for displaying power. The rabble-rousing address of a militant leader to an audience of ardent supporters may have inventional virtues, but we still understand it as rabble rousing directly addressed to an audience, however ephemeral, susceptible to the ardor of strong emotions that lead to action. On the other hand, emotional ardor leading to resistance can come from less direct appeals. A public performance seemingly moderate in its tone and addressed to a specific audience also is accessible to others who, in their own ways, can be influenced by what they see and overhear. Sometimes reaching onlookers is the point. Rabble-rousers in jail may intentionally use the declared audience for their invectives as a foil to make a point *about* the foil to an undeclared one. They can engage in frank speech whose purpose is to persuade through *indirection*.

"Indirection" can have a variety of meanings. As I use the concept, it refers to a rhetorical structure that shapes invention of appeals that are constitutive of identity and agency. In the context of POC discourse, it is a rhetorical mechanism that takes the audience to the heart of the rhetor's antagonist, exposes its fraudulence, and in its expression of defiance speaks for the whole community.

One of the more obvious ways indirection functions is to make the antagonist perform in ways that will arouse public ire. A case in point is the way the civil rights movement structured its campaigns in order to attract media attention. In April 1963, the Southern Christian Leadership Conference (SCLC) staged demonstrations in Birmingham, Alabama, to protest segregation of public facilities. The choice of Birmingham was strategic. The SCLC and its leaders—Martin Luther King Jr. in particular—were aware of the importance of the media to the success of their nonviolent protests. Having spent the better part of two years in Albany, Georgia, waging a campaign for voter registration and integration of public facilities, the movement leaders were disappointed that their campaign did not excite strong public pressure for federal intervention. They believed they had been foiled by a savvy police chief who used mass arrests to disrupt the campaign, but without resorting to violence. Without the spectacle of confrontation, which police violence certainly would have produced, the Albany campaign had not attracted the type of media attention that would have made it a national cause célèbre. Birmingham was targeted because it had, among other attributes, a lame-duck commissioner of public safety, Theophilus Eugene "Bull" Connor, who was a noted hothead and racist. Connor dependably would respond to demonstrators with violence (Hubbard 1968, 5). Had King waited until Birmingham's newly elected commissioner had taken office, police responses to the demonstrators likely would have been considerably less brutal (McAdam 2000, 126).

King and his lieutenants had done their homework well. Civil rights demonstrators descended on Birmingham and took to the streets to march for integration of public facilities. Since they had not secured a parade permit, their march was illegal.

After five days of untypical restraint, Connor unloosed police dogs and trained fire hoses on the demonstrators. National media captured images and footage of snarling dogs biting the arms of men who were trying to pull away, and of bodies sent spilling across the streets of Birmingham and slammed into storefronts by the force of fire hoses. Their appearance in newspapers, magazines, and TV news broadcasts across the United States succeeded in generating massive public support for the movement and for federal intervention on its behalf. King's strategy was to use events of direct nonviolent confrontation in Birmingham as a means of reaching his intended audience—the wider national public.

King was arrested for his part in the demonstrations, as he knew he would be, and was placed in solitary confinement in the Birmingham city jail. While there he read an ad in the local newspaper taken out by eight local clergymen calling for restraint by the civil rights activists. His "Letter from Birmingham Jail" (April 16, 1963) was written in reply to a statement issued by the Alabama clergymen, but was published as an open letter, which fitted with the overall strategy of the Birmingham campaign intended to alter national consciousness of racism in the United States. King's letter appears to play by the rules. It sticks to the issues, avoids ad hominem attacks on the clergy as racists, refutes their arguments without injecting his detention as the focal point, adheres to norms of civility and decorum that govern public debate, and so forth. Its most moving passage also seizes the moment's kairotic[1] possibilities with an emotionally charged narration of the costs segregation exacts on his children (Leff 2003). King's appeal was unlikely to persuade his declared audience much less segregationists in the American South. However, abiding by the norms of civility and decorum increased his chances to move an audience of readers not already opposed to integration and following the story of the civil rights protest in Birmingham and his subsequent arrest.

The remarkable civility of King's reply to the Alabama clergymen, given the passion that fuels his rejection of gradualism, provides an apt illustration of civility's rhetorical power. King, in the Birmingham jail, his civil disobedience defying the sovereign right of southern society to impose segregation, finds himself constructed as a *homo sacer* outside society, but writes within the conventions of civil discourse. His letter invokes norms of republican discourse (Hariman 1995, 95–140), thereby challenging his construction by the civil authorities in terms of bare life—a construction made vivid by the images and footage of black bodies under attack by police dogs and hurled as if debris by fire hoses—by exhibiting his political qualifications. He mounts a challenge in the eyes of a nation of onlookers to the legitimacy of a state's sovereign right to impose segregation.

Rhetorical norms of civility that worked to King's advantage in the "Letter" are also available as a potential source of control. Feigning civility is an ever-present possibility lurking at the edges and applying pressure to conform to rules that constrain the rhetorical options for expressing opposition. From the one-down perspective, civility seems to abide by rhetorical mechanisms that normalize existing asymmetries of power (see Hall and Hewitt 1970). To counter this, resisters often advocate and engage in rhetorical practices of incivility as their best hope for disrupting and possibly dislodging the existing order. The drama of deviance—extreme public displays, such as ACT UP using outlandish performances to publicize its political ends, interrupting the New York Stock Exchange, disrupting services in New York's St. Patrick's Cathedral, or staging costumed parades that are marked with barbs aimed at heterosexual onlookers (Brouwer 2001)—makes its point about the practices of targeted "others" to an audience drawn to staged spectacles of protest. As with civility, incivility is a Janus-faced form of parrhesia. It appears to address one audience while another is its actual target. It, too, can be a practice of rhetoric by indirection.

The strategic value of adhering to and violating norms of propriety underscores the performative character of indirection. It relies on a convincing enactment of one set of expectations that provides a credible appearance of addressing its *ostensible* audience in order to reach its *intended* audience. Indirection relies on our understanding the enacted roles and knowing how to read the gestures of sincere address in order to interpret what we see and hear. It relies on the rhetorical situation that calls for a statement to provide the kairotic moment to dramatize conditions calling for redress. Indirection is among the POCs' most potent rhetorical resources.

Invoking Who We Are

Thus far I have relied on an obvious characteristic of indirection as a rhetorical mechanism; namely, that it addresses an apparent audience with the intention of reaching a different target audience of onlookers. When performed by a POC, indirection has as a minimum three additional defining characteristics.[2] First, it is a mechanism in which *the person of the rhetor serves as a metonymic embodiment of the body politic*. The prisoner's personal struggle with the state and with the conditions of custody for survival represents the body politic's struggle to survive the thumb of oppression. The POC makes a special claim on us to understand our own political situation in terms of his or her role as it is being performed under current circumstances. Certainly we can understand roles and situations directly, but in the case of the POC, who may lack access to means of direct appeal, public understanding often must be built through indirection. The POC relies on our capacity to recognize the roles we are witnessing, and then organize our mental map to make sense of what we see and the world in which such events occur. As in a drama, the powerless's confrontation of power can cause the moment of recognition, what Aristotle's *Poetics* refers to as *peripety*, where denaturalizing the assumptions of authority can lead its witnesses to the realization that what is happening to this person or this group is happening to the collective. In tragedy, *peripety's* moment of sudden recognition is accompanied by an equally sudden reversal of fortune. The same is true for indirection. Insofar as it awakens a sense that what is happening to the POC is happening to the body politic, it can undermine the capacity of authority to suppress sentiments of opposition.

Quite apart from any voyeuristic pleasure we may derive from observing the spectacle of conflict, in the case of POCs, *indirection confronts onlookers with a scene that involves them as witnesses to the pain of others*—psychological, physical, political, social, economic, and cultural. The pain of others makes claims beyond compassion. Our bodily experiences help us to empathize with physical and psychological violations of human dignity, agency, human rights, and justice. Although we can imagine and empathize with its anguish, as Michael Ignatieff has argued, the image of a suffering body does not *assert* a moral claim; it can only *instantiate* a moral claim *if* the observers feel under a potential obligation to those who are suffering. As long as we remain fixated by the images and in emotional states of horror and empathy without knowing the root causes for the suffering and humiliation, our compassion unleashed by these emotions risks succumbing to a form of amnesia, a mechanism for forgetting the role of the West in situations that breed political unrest, or to social work for onlookers (Ignatieff et al. 2001, 16). The performative character of indirection can move onlookers past emotional fixation or amnesia of obligations. Insofar as it transforms them into an ensemble of witnesses within a drama of resistance, it can urge them to intercede. Indirection gives onlookers their dramatic role.

The epistemic implications of indirection's performativity suggest how it may lead to an awareness of relationship. What we learn depends on how we learn it. Indirection has its unique way of teaching. Witnessing the pain of a POC is at once intensely personal and public. It requires effort to make sense of what we witness subjectively. As Hanna Arendt has argued, reality requires a public realm of appearance for us to pass beyond a personal meaning to intersubjective meaning (1958, 50–57). Communication with others confirm that others see and share what we see as truthful. Dialogue is the method for forming a common sense of reality. In the process of going beyond personal meaning to intersubjective meaning, we learn something of ourselves. One of the things we learn is how we see ourselves in relation to what we are witnessing; it is a moment of self-discovery. Another thing we learn is how our sense matches up against the public sense being made of the scene, including the public sense of relationship; it is a moment of sociality. These epistemic apperceptions of self and other are themselves acts of involvement brought to consciousness through indirection. The rhetorical power of POCs resisting pain brings us past spectacle, where we observe without involvement, to a self-understanding and awareness of others grounded in relationship. Inclusion in the performativity of indirection mobilizes identification with resisting bodies and with others in the ensemble of witnesses with whom we have a shared response to the scene we are witnessing. In this, the POC initiates collective resistance to bare life.

Unfortunately, the moral sanction against publicly disregarding appeals of pain does not always prevail, as the twentieth century taught us. Ignatieff is right; private responses sometimes play in a different register. Despite impressively exhorting humanity to relieve their suffering, as occurred in Bosnia during the 1990s and as has occurred numerous times in Africa's recent history, sometimes the pleas of bodies in pain, and of political prisoners in particular, are deflected by their perverse power to attract voyeuristic attention, as Foucault's oeuvre chronicles, or by detachment from the scene because it is perceived as lacking self-interest. Involvement of the intended audience as more than passive onlookers to the scene requires rhetorical skill to overcome less noble responses. It challenges the construction of the *homo sacer* as the damned outside society and beyond claim on human empathy, to which each of us is vulnerable.

Indirection may not always take the form of discursive appeal; bodily performances are no less exhortative and no less instantiations of symbolic realities with which we can identify. Without question, a great deal of our response to tortured bodies as metonyms for the body politic is triggered by the pathos they elicit. However, in all of its manifestations the POC's tortured body is also a performance of conscience by indirection. As its third characteristic shared by POCs, indirection's capacity to involve its audience as related to if not part of a body politic *in extremis* reflects a primordial choice of appeal. Making the body politic visible and tangible in his or her person reflects a commitment to a unique way of seeing and living in a world by both the rhetor and those witnessing and participating in the POCs' political performance. In other terms, as Natanson (1965) has astutely observed, *indirection is rhetoric of ethos*. It is an affirmation of *bios*, a qualified political life.

The Todorov Problem

During the period of Soviet rule, a criminal conviction resulted in imprisonment or hard labor in the camps. Applebaum (2003) estimates that over time the USSR's 473 labor camps housed as many as 15 percent of the Russian population. The vast majority of those in the camps were common criminals whose fate seldom received public notice. Matters were different for those who were charged with a political crime. They often were cast in the starring role of a three-act morality play: show trial, verdict, and imprisonment. Their convictions often became a cause célèbre to send the message of the dangers attached to criticism or suspicion of opposition to the party.

The story of life in the gulag is familiar. It entered the imaginary of the West first through Aleksandr Solzhenitsyn's *The Gulag Archipelago* (1974–76), and then via numerous other accounts of life in the camps. For the most part, they are told as a form of public testimony. They offer accounts of human beings who expressed an opinion or were careless about what they had read or whom they had talked to. Few had engaged in deliberate acts to undermine the state, the crime for which most politicals were convicted; they had expressed an opinion. They were torn from loved ones; subjected to physical trauma of cold, hunger, exhaustion, and physical and psychological maltreatment; watched as other humans were worked until they dropped and then left to die; and emerged with an irreparable hole punched in their spirits, their bodies, and their lives. Their accounts are a form of testimony by those who must bear witness to what was done to them. Their assertion is that "by putting my suffering on the public record, everyone will know what the government tried to keep secret. Whether that changes anything is less important for getting on with my life than setting the record straight."

These testimonies often were framed by others, whether officials of state or scholars or media commentators, in the larger political drama of the Cold War. A sterling example is Tzvetan Todorov's account of life in Communist Bulgaria's camps, *Voices from the Gulag* (1999). Todorov reorganized the individual survivor stories to create episodic accounts around themes, which he then stitched together to interpret their horrors in the camps through a Cold War narrative. He transforms testimony given to make a public statement of what happened to the camp survivor into a geopolitical statement through the metonym of the "gulag." The Bulgarian language, interestingly, does not have a term for "gulag"—Todorov's witnesses would have used "camp" —but the West does, and that is the crux of what I call the "*Todorov* problem." It consists of hijacking a person's story from what he or she was attempting to accomplish— in this case, to bear witness—in order to accomplish the political aim of those who transmit their account—say, finding its meaning through the frame of Cold War geopolitics.[3]

Regardless of prevailing geopolitical realities, wrenching the story from its own context and inserting it in a metanarrative strips the survivor's story of a personal human tragedy that has meaning in itself by insisting it can be understood and explained only in terms of something larger than itself. It disrupts the excruciatingly painful plea for us to bear personal witness to another's personal experience by repositioning us in the impersonal relationship of a comprehensive explanation of historical experience.

The "Todorov problem" lurks whenever we are interpreting stories from the camps. One way to avoid it is to focus on the rhetorical features of the story itself, especially its vernacular rhetoric, which is always to some degree an attempt to express power relations from the perspective of those outside power in terms of their mundane particularity. Irina Ratushinskaya's *Grey Is the Color of Hope* illustrates this point through the play of rhetorical indirection that defines the experiences of the women POCs in the camp at Barashevo and that involves the reader in their story and its construction of their humanity.

Indirection and the Small Zone

Irina Ratushinskaya was raised in Odessa. She started writing poetry as a child, but not in earnest until her early twenties, when she was fired from her job at a teacher's training college for refusing to fail Jewish students arbitrarily on entrance exams as a means for meeting the school's strict ethnic quotas. Although she held a master's degree in physics, her passion was poetry. Writing poetry was not necessarily dangerous, but for people living in a culture of suspicion, you could never be too careful. The most innocent comment or careless couplet could lead to arrest and conviction for "propaganda and agitation that called to overturn or undermining of the Soviet power" (CyberUSSR 2002).

Irina was not careful. She was disseminating her poems, along with short stories, in the underground literary magazine *Samizdat*, and distributing her verse in typescript to other writers. This diverse circulation gave her literary production the appearance of dissident expression, which was reinforced by her letters to her husband, Igor, protesting the exile of dissident physicist Andrei Sakharov. She was aware that her letters and poems published in the underground press could lead to trouble, but conscience insisted she continue writing. She was arrested in 1982, and on March 5, 1983, the day after her twenty-ninth birthday, she sat in a Kiev courtroom listening to the charges brought against her. She was convicted of engaging in "anti-Soviet agitation and propaganda" and sentenced to seven years in prison at the hard labor camp at Barashevo, to be followed by five years internal exile. She was released in 1987, the day before the Gorbachev-Reagan talks at Reykjavik commenced, having served less than four years, apparently as a political expediency forced on the Soviet government by the international clamor calling for her release and for its potential positive effects on advancing negotiations with the United States on arms control. Her memoir, *Grey Is the Color of Hope*, is her account of her prison experience.

Irina begins her story at the end, with her being chauffeured in a black Volga through the streets of Kiev. The KGB agent who accompanies her is cordial enough, engaging in small talk—the weather, literature, art. She has been here before, brought to the precipice of release only to be sent back to the camp. She keeps her guard up. Still, this time she is convinced she will be freed, unless they snatch her back at her mother's front door. Their twisted minds make anything possible. She looks at the prison uniform on the seat beside her; its dreary gray contrasts with the colors of fall leaves and the odors of freedom that call to her from Kiev's streets. They arrive at her mother's apartment; the KGB agent brings her to the door. Irina walks down the familiar hallway; her mother appears and is overcome with joy. She is free. And she has nothing to be ashamed of.

The memoir's beginning introduces a woman who appears psychologically and physically exhausted. Still we sense her strength of mind and character. Four years in prison have changed her life, but they have not defeated her. Irina's story will offer an account of human resilience and virtues that allowed her to face her ordeal and remain whole. It is a retrospective on her horrifying experience and an invitation to witness the possibilities of the human spirit to assert its dignity and keep it intact.

Barashevo

Grey constructs Barashevo as the zone of struggle between the prison and a small group of women POCs. Its moral dimensions are introduced as Irina commences her journey there. She describes the claustrophobic oppressive stuffiness of the *stolypin*[4] railway cars, crowded with prisoners and heavy with the stench of a transit prison. She floats above barking dogs, menacing guards with machine guns, and the "welter of female bodies and faces penned up in a wire enclosure measuring three cubic meters" (10).[5] The memory of Igor being ushered out of the courtroom after testifying at her trial and calling, as he looked back, "Hold steady, darling, I love you!" sustains her. She asks, "Tell me dear comrade judges, has anyone ever looked at you like that! Or at you, my warder escort? Or at you, Prison Governor Petrunya? No, of course they haven't. And that is why you cannot understand how I can face the journey to the camp with a smile" (10).

At Barashevo, each prisoner's body is a biopolitical node. If the detention of the common criminal does not make the biopolitics of her body immediately evident, the political prisoner's status corrects that. The politically inscribed body invokes its "person-ality" as an imminent threat to sovereignty. By taking custody of her body, the very act of her exclusion from society includes her in the meaning of the state that has the power to exclude her. Each is decreed to be *homo sacer*, able to be killed but not sacrificed because sacrifice would qualify her life with something symbolic of that which transcended *zoe*, her bare existence as a natural being. When, as was the case for Irina, her exclusion is for a crime of parrhesia, the reduction to bare life is predicated on denying her voice. The lines of struggle around the POC's body are clear: there will be a concerted effort to break her so that she will be permanently silenced, and she will resist to reassert the voice she is being denied. This is the struggle of the women politicals at Barashevo, a struggle for agency.

Their tormentors' oafishness and brutality regularly rip through the surreal world of Irina's new locale, emerging in the restraints of capricious regulations, harsh punishments, and indignities to the women's bodies intended to break their spirits. They gouge their marks on the bark of each prisoner's mind and the collective mind of her readers. These women's refusal to comply poses a direct assertion to their warders of each politicals humanity. It also is a rhetoric of indirection, first to those in the prison who see and hear their reclaiming of voice, and next to her readers who are witnesses not only to their torment but also to the community that allows them to survive.

Resistance Within

By the time Irina reaches Barashevo, she has had indoctrination to being a *zek* (prisoner) by the criminals who share her journey in the *stolypin* and those at the transfer prison at Potma. She learns that common criminals will steal if given the opportunity and lie afterward. They are hardened and often have little sympathy for the plight of others. Still, Irina's sense of kinship with these women is striking. Most of the women at Potma are ordinary felons with whom she has little in common. Yet she reports their openness to her, their interest in her poems, their instruction on *zek* slang, their communication with her "on the pipe,"[6] and their willingness to teach her the ropes so she will survive what lies ahead in the camp. She is impressively self-composed.

Upon arrival at Barashevo Irina is taken to the Small Zone, where the female political prisoners are held. It consists of a small cottage fenced off from the rest of the prison and set on a small plot of land that they use, in part, for a vegetable garden. There are five other women in the Zone when she arrives; their number will swell to a dozen by the time of her release. Most of the women are older; some have served more than one term. They welcome Irina and her poetry to their group in a happy confusion of words and thoughts pulsing with the warm rhythms of domesticity. She finds in this warmth an affirmation of their humanity:

> Here, in our Zone, the inmates are not to be feared . . . simply because they are human beings in the full sense of the word. We may be crammed into a small house, we may be dressed in rags, they can carry out searches and lightening raids in our quarters, but we retain our human dignity. We will not get down on all fours to them, try though they may to make us. We will not carry out demeaning or senseless commands, because we have not surrendered our freedom. Yes, we are behind barbed wire, they have stripped us of everything they could, they have torn us away from our friends and families, but unless we acknowledge this as their right, we remain free. (40)

The consequences of refusing to comply with demeaning demands are severe, especially for the older women whose frailty is ill-suited for the punishment meted out for each refusal. Yet their acts of kindness and support and their solidarity in resistance keep them whole. Among the ways the women engage the prison, three are especially illustrative of their use of indirection: their engagement of the KGB, their appeals to law, and their moral vernacular of human rights.

KGB. Irina first encounters the KGB in the person of the chief officer in charge of the Zone, Senior Lieutenant Podust, who is portrayed as a small-minded megalomaniac. She issues arbitrary orders, insists the women wear name tags pinned on their chests, plants an informant in the Zone, refuses to order medical treatment for the women when it is clear they are ill, denies visitation[7] for trivial reasons, and sends the women to the prison isolation cell (SHIZO) for the slightest infraction and often in contravention of their legal rights.

A critical moment comes when Podust tries to spread the rumor that Edita, a newly arrived political, is syphilitic. The women become irate at Podust's attempt to turn them against one another, and decide to retaliate. They file a lawsuit against Podust for slander, which by indirection sends its own message that they are not entirely without means; they shun her by refusing to acknowledge her presence, and, in another manifestation of indirection, they name Edita their housekeeper, which was a position of responsibility for organizing the domestic activities of the Zone (99–103). Podust's authority is further undermined when their response circulates among the criminal inmates, who consider it a sign that the POCs regard her as irrelevant.

Podust responds with fury. To supplement their vitamin-deficient diet of bread and rotted-fish broth, the women had cultivated a small vegetable garden in the hard ground outside their cottage. Their garden is a human intervention in the boring routine of prison life. It acquires rhetorical life, as word of it spreads. Its rhetorical power rests on indirection. The garden opens an inventional space for establishing human connection with their warders, who slip them seeds and offer admiring comments about their flourishing crop. The criminal section regards the garden as a symbol of self-sufficiency. The prison authorities recognize the garden's dangerous message as a visible sign that instead of being reduced to bare life, the women in the Small Zone are acquiring gravitas. To retaliate, Podust marches a detail of criminal prisoners into the Zone and gives the women a choice: they may keep their garden if they cease their refusal to wear the separate identity tags that mark them as political prisoners; if they persist, their garden will be destroyed. The women persist. Podust orders the criminal prisoners to uproot it.

A scene of silent condemnation ensues in which the women of the Zone stand impassively, refusing to respond as the prisoner detail rips their garden from the ground. Their self-control interrogates the prison's disciplinary capacity, where control of the prisoner's body makes the state's biopolitical statement to the general population, to the prisoners in the camp, and to dissidents in particular. From the prisoners' perspective, in which their bodies were regarded as symbolic weapons to communicate their depth of opposition to KGB assaults on their dignity, demonstrations of self-control were exhortative interventions.

The power of rhetorical indirection is manifest for those observing this political drama unfold. The guards are disturbed by what is taking place; one of them sheds tears. The common prisoners give each other knowing looks: "How about that then? These politicals don't give a damn about Podust!" The operation doesn't work out as Podust had planned. The women's silence speaks a vernacular of dignity that transforms an everyday practice of social control into a significant moment of resistance. Silent self-control in the face of the prison's harsh reprisal for refusing to comply with a stupid order recalibrated an utterly weightless routine of discipline into a morally accountable act of palpable weight: "The unvoiced condemnation of the criminal prisoners became ever more tangible with every passing moment, and finally one of the women flung her hoe to the ground in disgust: put me in SHIZO if you will, but I won't carry on with this!" (106).

Law. Dissidents and oppressed groups commonly share the aspiration for inclusion under constitutional provisions intended to protect the rights of citizens. Consequently, POCs often focus their rhetorical efforts on forcing the state to play by the rules. The prisoner in custody has few options. In an authoritarian state, where physical maltreatment of POCs is known only if their supporters are made aware, family and friends on the outside are relied on to publicize their abuse. Since censorship prohibits politicals from communicating anything that comments on conditions in the prison, they are effectively held *incommunicado*. Apart from smuggling information to the outside, the methods for public resistance rely on the rules in play.

The rules in play in Central and Eastern Europe during the period of Communist rule were the constitution and the legal and penal codes. Although the judiciary and later the prison invoked the pretense of sovereignty to do as it pleased with the prisoner's body, both accused and prisoners in the USSR did their best to mount forensic counteroffensives by waging rhetorical battle over the constitutionality of their treatment.[8]

In this vein, the women of the Zone used the destruction of the garden as grounds for lodging a formal protest by sending a declaration to the Presidium of the Supreme Soviet protesting the requirement that they wear identity tags. Irina wonders: "How is it that we are always going on about Podust this, Podust that? Was it she who thought up the identity tags? Who, then? Whoever it was, let them see what we think of them and not pretend that they are blameless" (107). In an obvious reference to the Nazis requiring Jews to wear identity tags, they write in part: "The enforced wearing of identity tags is an affront to human dignity, a fact which is universally acknowledged and which was affirmed at the Nuremberg Trials. Soviet legislation claims that the administration of punishment is not intended to cause physical suffering or violate human dignity: (Art. 1 of the Corrective Labor Code of the RSFR) (108).

When a physician attempts to administer an injection without disclosing its contents, Ratushinskaya writes the hospital superintendent to point out that covert medication is forbidden by law (192). When they verify, by means of a smuggled thermometer, that the temperature in SCHIZO is below the 16° C required by law, they insist on pencil and paper to write the procurator, which is their legal right (209). Letters insisting that the law be followed are written to the Presidium, the procurator of the camp, the Central Medical Administration, and other bodies.

The authorities either ignore their appeals or say they have looked into the matter and found the charges to be baseless. At one point, after they have been in SCHIZO for seven days under frigid conditions of 9° C (48° F), the deputy procurator paid a "friendly visit" to their cell to see how they were doing. The women say they are not interested in discussing their condition with him; he should get them qualified medical attention. They are, however, prepared to discuss violations of the law.

"By law you cannot discuss other peoples affairs, only your own"
"What about the constitution?"
"Never mind the constitution!" (235)

Apart from the slander suit against Podust, which led to her eventual reassignment, their legal petitions were ineffectual. Getting results was not the point. By putting their complaints on the record, they were able to establish an official record of their treatment. And because they were able to get word of these petitions to those on the outside, official legal appeals engaged an external public on conditions in Barashevo. Their legal appeals increasingly dealt with the camp's failure to provide medical treatment and abide by rules and regulations of the prison system intended to protect the physical and psychological health of prisoners. Through the efforts of Igor, who persisted in getting word of her maltreatment into the samizdat network and to the West, Irina's declining health, and that of the other women, was kept in circulation. Within the reticulate public sphere of human rights discourse, Amnesty International and P.E.N. conducted concerted campaigns for her release based on her declining health. Richard Rodgers, an Anglican minister, decided to forgo a fast in support of imprisoned Orthodox Christian Alexander Ogorodnikov in order to campaign for Ratushinskaya's release to the West for medical treatment (Anonymous n.d.). In the United Kingdom, a contingent of MPs introduced two petitions from their constituents calling on the foreign secretary to work for her release (Hansard 1986). In the United States, thirty-one teachers and writers published a call in the New *York Review of Books* (Hower et al. 1983) for readers to write the Soviet ambassador to the United States, M.A. Dobrynin, expressing their concern. In New York City, twenty writers gathered outside the Soviet mission to read Ratushinskaya's poetry (Anderson and Dunlap 1986).

Set within the frame of judicial norms intended to protect the rights of citizens, the women's treatment conveyed ominous consequences for persisting in their resistance. The camp's overt indifference to their health made clear that if one of them were to die from failing health, it would write her off (224). In the broader context, however, the camp did not have an entirely free hand. The women of Small Zone's insistence on their legal rights exemplifies the way institutionalized norms of civil conduct can be a vehicle of indirection for exposing the state's hypocrisy when contrasted with their embodiment in practice and can bring external pressure to bear.

Human rights. For the general prison population, controlling violence, maintaining order, and enforcing compliance are among the prison's primary concerns. Political prisoners present a different set of needs. They are imprisoned for political commitments that led to "crimes" committed in the name of a cause and consequently do not usually engage in violence toward one another. Their acts of disorder typically are tactical and inventive, with the intent to make a point about the politics of their treatment as politicals. They set behavioral boundaries for their warders and themselves based on ideological and political commitments. Typically, they draw a line whenever their human dignity is challenged or compromised. They may engage the prison authorities on the legality of their treatment to force them to play by the rules, and they may exhibit their disdain for warders who impose petty requirements, but the ultimate consequence of these tactics depends on their capacity to engage the raison d'etre of the camp's biopolitics, which is to reduce the prisoner to bare life. Often this means they are treated as if they are mere animals lacking in self-sufficiency. Ultimately, their bodies become the site of a political struggle. This is an ambiguous locus fraught with rhetorical risks.

The prison can bring prisoners to the point of physical attrition, which can break them. They may sign a paper recanting their prior acts or a loyalty oath to stop the torment, sometimes to protect their family, and sometimes to gain their freedom. This is a difficult step for POCs, who are committed to ideals that make it impossible to cooperate in their own political and moral demise. Often these prisoners are prepared to die rather than accept a Faustian bargain.

On the other hand, it is imprudent for the prison to let matters get that far. A political prisoner's death at the hands of his or her warders can create an international controversy. It can produce economic and political consequences, which pose external constraints on the prison system's administration of inhuman treatment. If institutional control of the prisoner's body authorizes the prison to administer extreme punishment, the prisoner can design tactics to force matters to the edge and call the prison's bluff. For the women in the Zone, their bodies became their ultimate weapon by choice. It was a weapon of vernacularity that allowed them to voice a moral argument for their human rights.

Grey focuses our attention on the women's bodies through the vehicle of their increasing medical needs. As time passes, their sparse diet and the harsh prison regime take their toll. Their declining health is a matter of indifference to the prison, which refuses their requests for medical treatment, even for obvious needs. When the women are sent to the infirmary, the marginal competence of the physicians who treat them is matched by their lack of sympathy. They frequently return the women to the Zone without proper care. Medical problems that could have been resolved escalate into grave illness that requires serious medical intervention, often after permanent damage has occurred.

The women discuss Podust's and the KGB's apparent delight in tormenting them as fundamentally cruel. They consider them absent anything but an occupation that makes it possible to assert their will with force. Their cruelty is carried to the extreme when the KGB and Podust use the punishment of SCHIZO and the hunger strikes they triggered to drive the Zone's women to the edge of death.

Outside SHIZO, we learn of mundane confrontations, small victories, and occasional dramatic episodes, each laced with the struggle between ordinary virtues and vices. Over time, however, the menace of Barashevo's power becomes more ominous.

The moral high ground for making formal objections to violations of constitutional rights and prison regulations, for refusing to comply with petty requests, for supporting each other in their contests with the authorities, had shrunk to a narrow ledge precariously balanced over the abyss of prison life. For some, the ledge gave way as they succumbed to pressure to withdraw support of the others or never again see their loved ones; but the majority persist at the price of an increasing prospect of death. By using any excuse to send them to the punishment cells, Podust and the KGB keep the women in a spiral of declining health. Their pledge to go on a hunger strike when an ill woman was sent to SCHIZO bound them to frequent hunger strikes. Over three years, these solidarity strikes had sapped their strength to the point where every detention in the punishment cells precipitated a hunger strike, meaning the next one could be their last. To those on the outside who were aware of their situation and were transmitting it to the West, their resisting bodies became an eloquent human rights appeal.

Ratushinskaya's accounts of SCHIZO call us to witness the harsh realities of the Small Zone women's torment and the ferocity of their tormentors. Upon entering SCHIZO, they are stripped to a cotton smock and undergarments. They are confined for up to fifteen days in the damp cold of a cell that is small (6 by 7 feet) and never more than 15° C (barely 60° F) and sometimes as frigid as 9° C (below 50° F). Sometimes its small window has a broken pane or a frame not secured to glass, so that wind and snow whip in. The women cling to the cell's water pipe whenever hot water is running to capture its ambient heat. They sleep on wooden or metal pallets. Mice run over their bodies at night. Their reduced rations and hunger strikes, some lasting up to fourteen days, have left them weak and emaciated. Yet in their weakened state, they struggle with their heavy and awkward slop pots every other day, first to remove them from a brace that secures them to the wall and then to push them down a corridor, where their contents are emptied. SCHIZO is a grim statement of the prison's brutal willingness to inflict human suffering.

The women, on the other hand, understand that the prison officials and the KGB always see the Western press lurking in the background; more than anything, they fear publicity. If the women stand up to them, the authorities invariably back off. By enduring the prison's torments, they force the prison's hand. There are limits; causing a prisoner's death would publicize the authorities' mendacity. By retaliating with tactics that actually might lead to their deaths, the women step outside reduction to bare life; they seize control of how the plot will end and give voice to their human identity.

Their most effective way of fighting back was to go on a hunger strike. This point was made clear to them shortly after the uprooting of their garden. The memoir renders a scene of resistance so vivid that it rivets us as voyeurs horrified at what we see, unable to look away, and likely to retain a picture of it for years (114–37).

Following the garden incident, Podust decides their refusal to wear the identity tags must be punished. She singles out two women, Tanya Osipova and Natasha Lazavera, to be sent to SCHIZO for ten and thirteen days, respectively. The weaker Natasha is selected for the longer sentence, perhaps to send a message through the likely consequence that thirteen days in the detention cell will have on her body. The women form a pact: if one is sent to SCHIZO, the rest will refuse to work; if an ill woman is sent there, they will go on a hunger strike. Since Natasha is ill, they will strike for thirteen days.

After the seventh day on strike, Podust arrives to inform the three women Raya, Tatyana, and Irina, they are to be force-fed, as the law requires after seven days. Force-feeding was a practice based more on cruelty than concern for the prisoner's welfare:

> To do this they handcuff you, prise [sic] your jaws apart with an iron lever, which crushes your teeth, shove a tube down your throat and pour two liters of some kind of solution down it. . . . The object of the exercise is not to save the life of a hunger striker; even with force-feeding you will die if you refuse to eat long enough. Force-feeding is aimed at prolonging the agony from two months to a year or eighteen months. (123)

Because publicity is most feared by the prison, the women devise a plan to maximize getting word to the outside. They are in the center of the hospital, adjacent to where women from three camps are brought for treatment. The resident service personnel also go there for treatment. The hospital is full to overflowing, and its patients have contact with the adjacent men's criminal zone. So when brought into the room where force-feeding is to be administered, if they will shout out who they are and what is happening to them, tell the inmates to let the outside know, give the phone number and city of relatives they should call, plead to let the world know, at least 1,000 prisoners will know, some of whom will be up for release. The odds are good that their resistance will get instant notice.

The next day Irina is the first one brought into the room where force-feeding is to be administered. She refuses her consent. Her account provides us with a moral vernacular human rights appeal made more powerful by her use of her body.

> "Ratushinskaya, we are going to force feed you."
>
> That's Podust getting her word in, I am suddenly seized from behind. I push my elbows forward to make it harder for them to handcuff me.
>
> "Everyone! Everyone! Remember this!"
>
> I shout out our names, why we are hunger striking, who's in SHIZO and for how many days, and who is being force-fed. Podust and her accomplices try to pin me down, but I'm in that state in which people can carry safes out of

burning buildings or stop a moving car with their shoulder. I drag them around the room as they all cling to me and yell, yell without ceasing, repeating all the information for the second time now.

"Telephone Kiev 444-33-95! Kiev! Tell Igor everything! 444-33-95! Write it down!"

And again and again. I feel no pain, even though they have my hands twisted behind my back, nor am I conscious of the combined weight of their bodies. I only feel the trembling in a hand which has my shoulder in a viselike grip.

This was not easy for the guards. They were not trained to handle such a situation, they were not expecting such resistance, and were somewhat shaken by the preceding scene. They do not even realize immediately that I am not biting or kicking, but merely twisting out of their hold. Moreover, they are ashamed of what they're doing; unlike Podust they are not in the grip of sadistic pleasure, all they want to do is stop my shouting quickly, quickly, quickly as possible. Finally they realize instead of pinning me down, what they need to do is make me lose my footing. So they lift me as though I were a feather, and throw me—head first against a wooden trestle. Under the circumstance, how could they gauge their strength—the strength of six large men—against my hunger striking weight?

A red ball seems to explode loudly inside my head, and it is only from Tatyana Mikhailovna's accounts that I know what happened next. (127–28)

Irina was rendered unconscious and remained in that state for some time.

Her subsequent narrative indicates she is aware of the consequences of indirection. If she had struck her temple on the trestle, she tells us, or they had used more force and killed her, it would have been impossible to conceal; there would have been an international uproar. Even without direct witnesses, many would have been made witness to her murder during force-feeding. The consequence was they did not force-feed her or any of the other women in the Zone during the rest of her remaining time at Barashevo. The lasting result for Irina has been recurrent pounding headaches from the blow to her head.

Ratushinskaya's account of the women's resistance focuses on their direct encounters with the Soviet hierarchy at Barashevo. We hear little of the guards, who often occupy center stage in POC narratives, or of their relationship with them other than that some are harsher than others. Consequently, the memoir paints the internal scene of a contest over sovereignty. Almost all of the women are strong in living their commitment to free expression and preservation of their humanity. Almost all speak up to the prison's authorities, with Irina regarded as the leader in speaking what cannot be said without permission. In a contest waged directly through parrhesia, Irina is the parrhesiastes of the group.

Their frank speech is not without the residual effect that came from fast-spreading word inside the prison. The criminal prisoners notice how they stand up to the authorities and are impressed by their bravery. Whenever there are opportunities for interactions with the women of the Zone, they show their interest and regard. They are eager to learn more of their treatment, to have Irina share poems, to express their admiration for the Zone and their self-doubt about their own capacity to escape the condition of bare life. More important for the POCs, they rely on the circulation of information about their resistance to get word out of the prison, where Igor can share it with his contacts in the West. Their understanding is clear that publicity will make witnesses of the West, which will lead to pressure for mitigation of their treatment, if not their release.

Ratushinskaya's narrative of resistance fits with the testimony of others who had been in the camps. Its powerful construction of a Manichaean struggle between the women and the prison regime captures how the Zone's women relied on the rhetorical force of indirection in forming their resistance tactics. The relationships born of making others in Barashevo witness to their assertions of agency challenged the camp's systematic efforts to reduce them to bare life. There were alternatives to the self-loathing that allowed the state to regulate the camps as it did. Conducting oneself on principle was always an option. The memoir offers onlookers, those in the prison and in the outside world at that time, and its subsequent readers an alternative to the bare life that the state had institutionalized.

Community

There is another relationship with the women in the Small Zone that develops for the reader of *Grey Is the Color of Hope*. This one centers on its community of women that comes alive for the reader through witnessing how they live with and for one another. It also relies heavily on rhetoric by indirection, but in a way that more centrally features its readers as witnesses constituted through indirection.

The hellish torment of a regime intended to break the political prisoner's will requires that the prisoners devise psychic strategies for survival. Ratushinskaya's memoir is distinguished within this male-dominated genre by providing a distinctive feminine sensitivity to the trials of the camps. Amid the constant battle of wits and will with the KBG and prison officials, the women in the Zone created a world of human values steeped in the joys of feminine bonds and concerns. The Zone was a place of domesticity.

Against the backdrop of Barashevo's savagery, coarseness, bureaucratic blindness, and pedantry, the women of the Zone share startling moments of celebration, hospitality, humanity, and ordinary virtue. They spend months preparing gifts to celebrate birthdays and Christian name days; religious holidays are observed; and because the Eastern rites have different calendars, Christmas and Easter are celebrated twice.

They sew fancy dresses out of remnants of cloth for birthday celebrants, crown the celebrant with a laurel of leaves saved from skimpy rations of broth, and use morsels passed on by kindhearted zeks to make a cake. They spend hours discussing each other's domestic situations and the pain of separation from husband and family, and they worry about their parents' and each other's health. They tease Irina to get her to recite poems, protect the more infirmed and elderly from overexertion, and share the joy of moments that allow spontaneous celebration.

Seasons offer quotidian delights by taking advantage of the summer weather to set a table outdoors and decorate it with wild flowers to give a festive air to a dinner of barely edible mush. The year's end offers the bittersweet comfort that Natasha, who is so ill and weak she cannot lift herself off the floor, and Irina draw from celebrating New Year's in SHIZO by making the outline of a full-size Christmas tree on the floor with a paste of tooth powder and water. "The whole thing came out really well. It was such a happy little tree" (227). One of the memoir's most riotous moments of unrestrained joy is their celebration of the Epiphany in the traditional Ukrainian way. In weather 25° C below freezing, they run naked through the snow to douse themselves with hot water from tubs they have set in snowdrifts. "Halfway [back to the house] I am unable to stop myself from waltzing instead of running. Tanya throws a towel over my shoulders. We do not need to look for reasons to laugh this night" (308–9). Their delight in a ritual that takes them out of the camp to a larger one of religion and community reflects the bond they share as prisoners and as women. Her account has the idyllic feel of joyous female festival akin to the ancient Greek Adonia: exultant in tone, free of bodily inhibition, faithful to the rituals that tie them to a larger culture of faith and beliefs, and joined to one another through their shared reverence for life, their convictions, and a mutual love that is deep and gentle.

The celebrations of birthdays, name days, and religious holidays, and the ritualized ways in which they celebrate them, are signs of community based in reverence. There are many ordinary virtues the women display by their resistance and their mutual support. They are courageous in their performances of frank speech, brave in fearlessly facing the dangers of SHIZO, tenacious in resisting anything that might compromise their human dignity, and steadfast on their pledge to suffer collectively the consequences of resistance. They are loyal to each other, caring in times of need, gentle in their ways of speaking and comforting, generous with emotional support, and respectful of each other in all ways. Each of these are linked by reverence, "a sense that there is something larger than a human being, accompanied by capacity for awe, respect, and shame . . . [that] is often expressed in and reinforced by ceremony" (Woodruff 2001, 63).

The prison treats human life with contempt; the women hold it in awe. The prison is indifferent to human dignity; the women are respectful of each human's inherent dignity. The prison's lack of guiding principles exposes its weakness in quelling their defiance; the women's guiding principles provide them strength. Their linked virtues reflect their commitments—standards that define their community. As Woodruff notes, we might feel the pain of shame were we to be exposed to others as violating community standards, which would not be a virtuous response. "But when reverence is in play, we feel shame when exposed in our own minds to shortcomings vis-à-vis the ideals toward which we stand in awe, and this reaction does belong to virtue" (63).

The story of the Zone's community is part of the story of resistance at Barashevo, existing as an oasis of reverence in the camp's desert of misanthropy. But it involves us differently as a rhetoric of indirection than the focus on their contest with Barashevo's authorities. The women's resistance within Barashevo deploys indirection as a rhetorical mechanism that reminds the authorities of others, presently or within reach, who can observe what they are doing and respond in ways they cannot control. It helps to sets limits on and to temper the severity of their treatment. We are made witness, secondhand, to how others are responding to what they see and overhear. The story of the Small Zone's community, however, positions us in a different relationship to the book. Ratushinskaya's construction of the Zone's sisterhood comes to us as their primary onlookers. It gives a different voice to these women who are finding ways to hang on to their humanity by living life in a certain way that beckons us to witness and understand something remarkable: the power of conscience on the character of community. As we struggle to make sense of the misanthropic impulses of the prison and its world of moral desolation, we are offered the alternative of the emerging women's community of dignity and hope. We are invited to appreciate the values they revere and the power of reverence, a forgotten virtue, to constitute a community of conscience.

A Call to Ethos

The arguments that biopower has become paradigmatic of contemporary politics and that we live in an era of perpetual state of exception seem to have strong empirical support. They alert us to modalities of political relations based on control rather than persuasion, to a politics of bureaucratic administration rather than public deliberation. The POC stands as a reminder that, unlike the original valuing of parrhesia and protection of the parrhesiates from punishment for telling the truth, frank speech has become chancy at best.

Yet dissent does occur, even under the harshest regimes, and although frequently addressed directly to power, the dangers of speaking frankly to power and the prohibitions against speaking truth to partisans often leave little choice but to make strategic incursions with structures of indirection. They perform an interrogation of power that calls an audience of witnesses into being. It invokes both onlookers and those who understand what is being said in public in a different register than its overt meaning. The call is to adhere to the imperatives of conscience that give moral legitimacy to political action.

Subjugation, however subtle its violence, forces a cleavage between whatever identification may have existed between the body politic and the state, and highlights cultural norms of political and legal identity. In this context, the dissident who is arrested and convicted for political crimes can stand by deputy for the oppressed body politic. The identification of Poles with Adam Michnik, Myanmarians with Aung San Suu Kyi, Czechs with Vaclav Havel, Russian Jews with Anatoli Sharansky, Chinese with Wei Jingsheng, Irish nationalists with Bobby Sands, and Russians with the women in the Small Zone testifies to the power of the POC's body in the state's hands as a potent metonym. The prisoner's body becomes the discursive field that stands for what happens to the body politic as a whole. When the state disregards constitutional guarantees, the rules of court, or norms of humane treatment, it reaffirms a statement about its monopoly on violence. When displayed before an audience of onlookers, these abridgements of human rights can transform its witnesses into participants in the moral pageant unfolding in public view. Such events require more than an acknowledgment that they are occurring; they require a public sphere in which their meaning can be considered and passive witnesses can be activated to make a choice.

Rhetoric by indirection assumes sufficient cultural literacy to infer the point being made from what we are seeing. It enters the public sphere of its target audience as something other than a mode of deliberation, and it shapes a public sphere as something other than a forum for deliberation. It is no surprise, therefore, that vernacular discourse plays a key role in its execution. Bodies in pain or prisoners being railroaded make no moral claims on their own. Indirection reflects a rhetorical choice to establish them. By playing out a political drama in which onlookers have a stake, it reflects an alternate world to the lived realities of its times. The POC's pain invites onlookers to see it as a display of conscience, as a sign of each POC's *ethos* and the *ethos* of the people and ideals they represent. In this same regard, vernacular rhetoric, by its very nature, has embedded choices that indirection performs. Indirection's indictment of what is and its beckoning call to choice reference a world of values, actions, and commitments. These characteristics define political relationships we endorse and on which judgment and conduct can be based. It confronts its audience with making its own choice about itself as part of a body politic in extremis. Indirection's vernacular appeals engage an audience of witnesses on terms of its own moral quotidian, which gives it rhetorical salience and power.

These most un-Agamben-like performances are always working in the background. And because they are, they suggest that the moral vernacular of human rights escapes the dystopian vision of the state of exception and bare life Agamben regards as the currently ongoing and universal condition of sovereignty. As long as there is a language outside official power that can speak its own language of power to others who share it, subjugation to bare life is always being contested under the surface.

These contests are constituted by and waged with vernacular rhetorical resources. These moment-by-moment acts of resistance are rhetorical manifestations of the commonly voiced aspiration of dissidents to live in truth.

Finally, the women in the Small Zone teach us that conscience is not a matter of reason and study but of attachments to commitments that cannot be broken without shattering ourselves. Attachments to religious faith or nation or human dignity do not come from an argument but from ties that develop over time. We grow to them through practices; it has a base in history as it is lived. The actor inhabits them and they the actor. These attachments can be shared by others, even if not of the same culture, if they have the capacity to experience those feelings. The reader's role is more than to witness a contest over sovereignty and the consequences of parrhesia; it is to heed a beckoning to ordinary virtues that can awaken our humanity and on which we can build a human world. Their rhetoric of such a world is, by indirection, a call to its reader to choose also to live that way. For that reason, it calls us to ethos.

6. *Passive Aggression of Bodily Sufficiency*
The H-Blocks Hunger Strike of 1981

King: He has chosen death:
Refusing to eat or drink, that he may bring
Disgrace upon me; for there is a custom,
An old foolish custom, that if a man
Be wronged, or think he is wronged, and starve
Upon another's threshold till he die,
The Common People, for all time to come,
Will rise a heavy cry against the threshold,
Even though it be the King's
The King's Threshold, by W. B. Yeats

P ain resists language. It is a personal experience, something privately encountered, something the sufferer grasps with ease, something experienced as real, but something that cannot be shared. Grasping another's pain takes effort; it has to be translated into language, which can only offer a pale representation. In her classic study *The Body in Pain,* Elaine Scarry observes that this utter rigidity of pain makes "its resistance to language . . . not simply one of its incidental or accidental attributes but . . . essential to what it is" (1985, 5). Since the outsider's awareness depends on a report, pain's reality is always in doubt (Arendt 1958, 50–51; Scarry 1985, 4–5).

Despite pain's utter privacy, the pain-wracked body can enter the public realm, where its anguish can be witnessed and its witnesses can be moved to empathy. Despite bodily pain's utter privacy, the public appearance of the suffering body makes a rhetorical plea, an exhortation for humanity's compassion that it might intervene to end its anguish. Sometimes its pleas move audiences to action; sometimes they go unheard; sometimes they are ignored. The very fact that it can be apprehended, however, even if only by report, reminds us that whatever else politics might include, democracy ties it inexorably to our capacity to invent appeals and respond to what has voice, including how political relations are manifest by bodies in pain.

The moral vernacular of bodily pain becomes a potent form of resistance insofar as the body in pain can acquire voice and rhetorical agency. When the prisoner of conscience (POC) uses it by design, it functions as a rhetorical mechanism, as an instantiation of *passive aggression.*[1] Passive aggression is not the same as the maladaptive personality pattern of passive-aggressive behavior, which refers to passivity as resistance in the form of failure to follow through with expectations in interpersonal situations. Passive aggression, in the context of this discussion, refers to the prisoner's use of the body to establish physical relationships that accentuate the power differential with the penal institution, as represented by the warders who enact its policies. The subjugated prisoner uses extreme forms of passivity to induce a state of bodily pain rather than comply with unacceptable prison conditions. Noncompliance that induces bodily pain is aggressive in that it denies the rationality of institutional logics and provokes a response to restore it. When this retaliation is harsh, the bodily insufficiency of the distressed prisoner, helpless and passive before the superior force of the judicial/penal system, acquires superior rhetorical sufficiency.[2]

We can develop this exploration by tracing the interplay of bodily sufficiency and insufficiency as a mode of passive aggression performed by the Provisional Irish Republican Army (IRA) prisoners at Maze prison, Belfast, which culminated in the 1981 Hunger Strike. In defiance of the prison's overwhelming power to reduce the prisoner to animal behavior, the prisoner can respond with bodily performances that are moral assertions of a basic human right to agency, to refuse treatment that, by its degrading character, denies the body's humanity. When this defiance takes the form of self-induced performances of bodily pain, the prisoners' passive aggression inverts the institutional logic of bodily sufficiency and insufficiency. Within the confines of the prison, the moral demands of exaggerated displays of insufficiency are fragile because they depend on the sensibilities of the authorities to respond to assertions that deny the organizational logic of the prison. When this inversion is publicized, it moves the prison's institutional logic into the moral ecology of civil society where justice and human rights set the parameters for a sustainable balance among resources of bodily sufficiency and insufficiency. The moral vernacular of bodily sufficiency and insufficiency, once publicized, threatens to expose the moral compass of the penal authorities and the state, and thereby how they use their power to control the juridical/penological ecology. This is an exposé of ordinary vices, at once difficult to contain and damning. Finally, there are political consequences of passive aggression with respect to the paradigm of IRA resistance, the moral vernacular of the prisoner's body used as a *topos* for public moral argument, and the acquisition of a moral vernacular that centers, sometimes unwittingly, on political pain.

Bodily Pain, Bodily Insufficiency

The body in pain is a rhetorical site. From Homer on, storytellers have used corporeal reference to convey strong emotions. In Book 5 of *The Iliad*, for example, Homer structures his narrative of a world in chaos through the anatomical destruction wrought by spear, arrow, and club during full-scale combat before Troy's gate. His graphic depiction of Achaeans and Trojans meeting their demise made each individual body's destruction synecdochic for the devastation war had visited upon Attica and Troy. Homer's battlefield scene bound the physical piercing of flesh and breaking of bone to the devastation each death visited on that warrior's family and its world. On the larger stage of the Western tradition, Homer initiated the fusion of bodily pain with cultural pain. In antiquity, this fusion was exploited in the oratory of the courts, assemblies, and civic ceremonies, where audiences were brought to heightened emotion by depictions of physical suffering, emotional anguish, and extravagant displays of grief.[3]

In modern times, the connection of embodied pain to cultural themes assumed broader scope, when the political[4] was wedded to issues of individual and cultural pain. At the dawn of the twentieth century, for example, Sigmund Freud's theory of psychopathology established the pleasure principle as the basic motivation for individual conduct, thereby inexorably wedding the body's struggle with psychic pain to the formation of subjectivity and to an explanatory mechanism for human action. Since the mid-1960s, a flood of work has addressed the body as a discursive formation and field of social political and identity conflict. Most prominently, feminist intellectuals, such as Hélène Cixous, who challenges women to write from their bodies (1976); poststructuralists, such as Michel Foucault, whose oeuvre explores the other as object of desire for the discursive formation of knowledge and power (1973, 1975, 1977, 1980); and political philosophers, such as Georgio Agamben, who grounds sovereignty in the authority to banish the *homo sacer* to a bare life of mere biological existence (1998, 2005), situate biopolitical control of the body in its discursive formation.

Collectively, such works disclose myriad incongruities in how we experience our bodies. The privacy of our sensations, the personal awareness derived from physical acts, and the joys and pleasures aroused through intimate contact with other bodies teach us profound lessons about our personal identity and self-sufficiency (see Sennett 1994, 16–21). We each experience our own body in ways that are unavailable to the inspection of others. Our pain is not alone in its privacy as a personal experience. Our ecstasy also is our own and known only secondhand to those with whom we share its secrets.

Still, our bodies are in the world, where they must struggle for agency and voice. There we encounter strange and unlike things, and our engagement of them is scrutinized by a larger authority of church, society, institutions, or the state that gives them meaning. Like Adam and Eve after the fall, our innocence is lost, and we experience shame in our nakedness. Beyond the gates of our privacy, we become aware of our flaws and experience rebuke for our personal insufficiency. We can be disciplined; we can even be reduced to bare life.

These reflections bear directly on the relation between bodily pain and the rhetorical mechanism of passive aggression. Rebuke is an important reality of prison experience. Prisoners are denied human identity: their names are erased, in their place they are given a number; they are confined to spaces where their movement is monitored and controlled; they are rewarded or punished based on conformity or nonconformity to a logic of obedience. Their identity is defined in terms of its corporeality and rebuffed for its insufficiency. However, our biological status is at once meaningful in both its corporeal characteristics and its openness to numerous forms of signification. Even considered as a mere biological organism or in medicalized terms of its anatomical parts and their functions, it is still regarded in a *particular* respect. Its meaning can only be asserted from a point of view that, once seen in that particular way, makes an assertion. Stripping the body of any qualifications except its mere animal existence, *eo ipso* strips it of subjectivity as an individuated human being. It makes an assertion of power by considering the body as utterly without self-sufficiency; it reduces it to an object of control.

The regime of the prison is a struggle over bodily sufficiency whereby the prison disciplines bodies that are, by its definition, unruly, while each act of prisoner resistance asserts a personal identity and subjectivity. Both grapple with the body as an ambiguous signifier and rely on the visual impact of bodies to advance assertions of belief, solidarity, control, and dissent. Because they are embodied assertions, we can witness them and testify with confidence to their presence. Bodily display can assert the prisoner's submission to a regime of discipline or defiance of an imposed authority. Both are captured by the use of the term "demonstration": one as a proof of authority by bodies under control, the other as a proof of agency by mass gatherings of protest. Both double as an extension of *demonstrative* rhetoric (as Roman rhetoricians labeled epideictic discourse) and the self-evidence of a *demonstrative* proof.

Of course, bodies are never hopelessly ambiguous because they are never stripped completely of rhetorical resources. The materiality of form and treatment may attract attention, and we may impose an interpretation on them. With nothing beyond unvarnished bodily display, however, the meaning we attribute is not necessarily the assertion being advanced. Insofar as a body may make a public statement, it requires a context and significant symbols (most typically words) to explain its actions. Absent context and significant symbols, the body's declarations remain largely inchoate. Claim making, in short, requires *framing* for a body to appeal in ways that may, at the very least, elicit empathy and, in the case of the political relationships inherent to disciplining it, establish identification that makes the prisoner's corporeal pain one with our political pain, or, more removed, invoke the conscience of its public and move it to exert pressure on official bodies authorized to act.

An apt, if tragic, illustration of the body's ability to make claims is contained in the recent and still unfolding history of the Balkans. When trouble hit Kosovo, North Atlantic Treaty Organization (NATO) forces engaged in air attacks on the Serb Republic of Yugoslavia to force it to abandon its program of genocide against Kosovo's ethnic Albanians. Photographs of slain Kosovar civilians and video footage of Albanian Kosovars fleeing their province into Albania, Macedonia, and Monte-negro served as evidence to refute Serbian denials that they were embarked on a cam-paign of ethnic cleansing. Viewers were aware of how to interpret these images not just because a reporter told them what they were seeing. Perspective made a differ-ence. For Serbs, these images were seen as necessary casualties from reclaiming terri-tory that was rightly theirs; for Kosovars, they were depictions of genocide. Bodies of a certain sort made partisan assertions their opponent could not abide. The very exis-tence of Albanian Kosovar bodies, Muslim bodies, signified an alternative historicity to Serbia's, with an ethnic majority whose bloodlines were tied to Kosovo's soil in ways that contested Serbia's narrative of the province's holy status as the historic site of its own ethnic redemption cycle.[5] Kosovar bodies in space and time asserted their reality and, further, laid claim to basic legal and human rights that are protected by statute and international agreement. For Slobodan Miloševic's regime, they were in-surgents attempting to steal territory that was not rightly theirs to claim. Serbian jus-tification for its military actions on eschatological grounds had little traction for an international audience that neither understood its frame nor shared it. Reports of sys-tematic annihilation of Muslim Kosovars and purging of their birth, marriage, and property records seemed irrefutable evidence of ethnic cleansing. Airbrushing from Kosovo's history ethnic Albanians and their claims to indigenous and majority status effectively erased their claim to historicity. With no bodies in its physical territory and no evidence of their existence on Kosovo's public records, Albanian Kosovars would have crossed a river of forgetfulness that had no bridges back to public memory.

If history is a guide, however, the attempt to regulate the body by obliterating its dialogical possibilities is itself problematic, especially when it comes to political pris-oners. Dissidence grounded in claims to identity dies a hard death. As we have seen, political powers have difficulty silencing the POC who, before all else, speaks an alter-native political identity through the signifying power of a body that must be radically disciplined by removal from public life. A state that claims it is intent on "protecting" the larger body politic is countered, sometimes extremely so, by its inability to com-pletely silence the politicized bodies it regulates. As long as a public is engaged by their existence, whether through their supporters' agitation or letters and reports smuggled out of the prison, they practice their own rhetoric of the body politic.

Removal and control of the dissident's physical body may be a regime's intended therapy administered to restore the body politic's health, but it underestimates the body's testifying potency. Using the courts to put political troublemakers in jail re-bukes the dissident's self-sufficiency in a material fashion that creates tension for the state's own self-sufficiency. Removing the opposition by forcibly controlling its body is an admission that dissident ideas cannot be refuted, thereby bestowing a hyper-rhetorical presence on the political prisoner's body. This is another way of saying that POCs, having lost control of their bodies by choosing incarceration as preferable to the state's Faustian bargain for freedom, have their bodies transformed into a resource for subverting their oppressors. When other, more conventional rhetorical means have failed, it becomes their last but most potent resource. Following self-immolation, the most graphic form of this transformation in bodily sufficiency and insufficiency is the hunger strike.

Passive Aggression by Fasting to Death

Self-starvation is inexplicable without a frame.[6] Although the person with anorexia may capture our attention by the sheer spectacle of a body wasting away, we require an explanatory context to tell us whether we are watching a religious fast, an involuntary famine, a manifestation of cultural psychosis, a hunger strike, or some other form of human behavior. The hunger strike particularly is tied to an explanatory frame. It is undertaken as a form of protest directed against a superior power with the intent of subverting it by intentionally reducing the body to helplessness while placing its helplessness in that power's hands. It requires a contextualized event and a discourse to frame it; otherwise the point of the fast remains mysterious.

The authorities, mindful of how fundamental words are to its meaning, attempt to control the hunger striker's voice by banning it from the public realm (Ellmann 1993). However, the hunger striker's body, even if muted, is part of a political discourse about grievance and right; it still manages to speak. Fasting to death at least implicitly recognizes a hierarchy of political power and performs its self-consumption within this frame. By placing their lives in the hands of a more powerful authority, hunger strikers use the body's physical powerlessness to overwhelm their oppressor's political power; it forces power to either bend or be exposed for its callous disregard of the lives it could save. This is a rhetorical performance that mobilizes the topos of magnification, of argument from more and less, for an ironic display of intertextual reversals in which bodily insufficiency grows into symbolic superiority and, through this performance of strength, diminishes the reigning political power by exposing its symbolic insufficiency.

In these reversals, the materiality of the striker's pain shares the degraded body's capacity to join opposites: sufficiency/insufficieny, abnegation/acquisition, passivity/assertiveness. Corporeal pain expanded into rhetorical potency rests on a performance of passive aggression, which, in turn, is mobilized as a rhetorical mechanism through publicity. The body in pain requires an audience to witness its suffering and to judge authority's resistance to its plea and reluctance to end its agony. The spectacle of the striker's starvation offers a moral dilemma to the state: either acknowledge the legitimacy of my complaint to save my life or, by continuing your refusal, stand publicly condemned for your moral insensitivity to my death.

In itself, wordless and wasting, the fasting body cannot force the state to cave, but its public display of anorexic helplessness before a superior power presents itself as paradigmatic for the society's *moral ecology*: its culture of values and commitments that provides moral reasons for action; it is a form of practical reason by which a society constitutes a meaningful world that promotes human dignity, solidarity, and the common good, and by which it averts the "remorseless working of things" that is the tragedy of the commons (Hardin 1968). Through a pageant that plainly portrays the state's authority to end the striker's death march should it choose, the hunger strike focuses attention on seemingly misguided values that would allow a person to perish rather than negotiate his or her complaint. By appealing to the state's power to act, the hunger striker's body advances a powerful, if ironic, argument about the striker as a mirror of a society capable of self-control, personal sacrifice, solidarity, and readiness to pursue the common good. It implies that legitimation can only rest on the authority's capacity to share these commitments. The spectacle of the striker's disintegrating body thus becomes a performance of passive aggression subverting the superior power of an intransigent foe by making it morally culpable before the larger community of witnesses.

The striker's body becomes a corporeal manifestation of his or her grievance. It drives a wedge (Johnstone 1990) that decouples state action from an expression of national values. By denaturalizing the synthesis of national identity with the state's exercise of authority, the striker's body opens a rhetorical space to invite critical reflection on the taken-for-granted fusion of power with the persona of the state's leader. Witnessing the body's self-consumption simultaneously fixes our gaze on the authority's display of intransigence in the face of appeals for moral recognition and civil accommodation. The back and forth of prisoner bodies in pain and the penal system's quest to restore order is a performance of magnification. As the physical body diminishes, its rhetorical incarnation grows, touching the conscience of ever-enlarging circles of society. Sometimes, as in the cases of Gandhi in India, Andrei Sakharov and Nathan Sharansky in the former Soviet Union, and Bobby Sands in Northern Ireland, its rhetorical presence crosses national borders and even spans oceans to elicit a common urging that the authority be responsive to larger demands of civility and morality. The starving body is mobilized as a rhetorical form by its embodiment of passive aggression. Through its material performance of the topos of more and less words magnify the wasting body's moral weight, enlarge its mass through publicity, and transform its powerless physical form into a powerful moral evocation that advances the striker's demands while questioning the legitimacy of rulers unwilling to compromise. Through the pressure its helplessness elicits from external groups, it becomes a subversive threat to its oppressor's superior power. Finally, as the body declines into death, its corporeal frailty conquers its physical master by acquiring transcendent rhetorical life as a martyr. In death it robustly survives, drawing life from words that memorialize past grievances and give meaning and force to a cause of opposition.

The suffering body's march from personal pain to public symbol requires voices to spread news of its anguish. They must publicize its gradual demise by linking the body's ordeal to a cause and its opposition. The inevitable selectivity of the press in reporting the striker's decline and how the custodians of its fate responded encourages the attending public to perceive self-inflicted suffering as emblematic of a decayed body politic or as political blackmail. Framing matters greatly for reinforcing existing prejudices that can sway the uncommitted.

The hunger striker as a signifying body whose personal pain becomes public testimony also reminds us of the fragility of bodily argument without an attendant discourse to protect its ambiguous message from alternative and confounding readings.[7] The incongruity between private experience of personal awareness and public experience of the body as an object of discourse, between private awareness of self-sufficiency and public rebuke for personal insufficiency, between private freedom of personal expression and public regulation of bodily expression, is a play of the body's capacity for dialogical performances. These contrasting modalities of bodies in pain suggest their inherent interrogation of and by political, social, and cultural texts about them. When the privacy of bodily pain is transformed into public discourse on its pain, its intertextuality makes it both a site and source of public deliberation.

These claims are manifest in the rhetorical power exerted by Provisional IRA[8] inmates in Northern Ireland's Maze prison at Long Kesh during the late 1970s and early 1980s. The more than 400 IRA prisoners in H-Blocks engaged in continuous protest through rhetorical displays of their bodies for over four years to have their "special status" as de facto political prisoners restored. Their grievance culminated in the 1981 fast-to-death by Bobby Sands and nine other IRA inmates before the strike was terminated.

The Struggle for Political Status at Long Kesh

On March 1, 1981, Bobby Sands began a hunger strike as the last-ditch effort of Republican prisoners at Long Kesh to have special status restored. The prisoners in H-Blocks had been using their bodies for over four years protesting criminalization of their deeds in what they considered paramilitary actions. Their protest began with their refusal to wear prison uniforms assigned to criminal offenders. Rather than go naked, the prisoners covered themselves with the blankets in their cells. This practice was soon widespread among incoming Republican prisoners and became known as the "blanket protest." It was followed by a "no-wash protest," the "dirty protest," and an ill-fated hunger strike at the end of 1980 that ended when the prisoners, mistakenly believing the state had agreed to conditions that would restore their special status as political prisoners, called it off. Each stage in their escalating confrontation had required the "Blanketmen," as they came to be known, to make increasingly dramatic use of their bodies to escalate their resistance. The final hunger strike had an aura of inevitability as the next logical and only remaining corporeal act of resistance in the

Provo prisoners' arsenal.[9] It was a culminating statement of commitment to principles worth the ultimate sacrifice.

Bobby Sands was an IRA activist and agitator who was among the leaders of the Republican prisoners. He was serving a fourteen-year sentence for possession of firearms and had spent half of his young life in detention for IRA activities, though none of his offenses involved taking human life. Sands organized the final hunger strike to secure five demands, which were rights associated with political prisoners: the right to wear their own clothes; to refrain from industrial prison work; to associate freely with one another; to receive one parcel, letter, or visit per week; to organize their own recreational and educational activities; and to have lost remission time restored. Initially, four inmates were to begin fasts at regular intervals. Should they die, other prisoners were prepared to take their place, each vowing to fast until death unless the British government met their terms.

Sands died sixty-six days later, on May 5, 1981, having just turned twenty-seven and been elected a member of Parliament while fasting. His hunger strike received international press coverage and focused world opinion and anger on Prime Minister Margaret Thatcher and the British government. His death was reported on the front page of newspapers in every major American city and most cities around the world. The papers condemning Thatcher included *Le Monde, Izvestia,* the *Hindustan Times,* the *Hong Kong Standard, Noticias* (the semiofficial paper of Mozambique), and the *Sowetan* (South Africa's mainly black newspaper). Anti-British demonstrations occurred in Antwerp, Athens, Brisbane, Chicago, Ghent, Milan, Oslo, and Paris, among other cities. The New Jersey state legislature passed a resolution honoring Sands's "courage and commitment." Teheran announced the Iranian government would send a representative to the funeral. The Indian parliament split as the Opposition stood for a minute of silence in Sands's memory, while members of Indira Gandhi's ruling party refused to join in. World leaders, such as Lech Walesa, paid Sands tribute as a "great man who sacrificed his life for his struggle." British targets were bombed in Lisbon, Milan, and Toulouse (Beresford 1987, 98–99; O'Malley 1990, 4).

The Long Kesh hunger strike itself lasted for a total of 217 days and claimed the lives of ten men. It was called off after it became clear that the strikers' families were going to intervene and authorize intravenous feeding to save their lives. None of the prisoners' demands were met, which led hard-liners in Ulster and London to claim victory from showing the prisoners who was in charge. More was involved in this hunger strike, however, than the prisoners' five demands. This hunger strike, intended to raise consciousness of the issues involved in the struggle between Republicans and the British over the future of Ireland, also further polarized Northern Ireland, forced deep divisions within the Catholic Church, challenged the morality of the British government in the court of world opinion, and thereby raised questions about the moral ecology that regulates the self-organizing activities of the Irish body politic.

The Irish Culture of the Hunger Strike

The Long Kesh hunger strike may have been the last scene in the prisoners' four-year struggle for restoration of special status, but in the broader scheme of Irish Republican politics it was the latest scene in Ireland's 800-year struggle with the British. Sands and his compatriots chose an ancestral means to perform their grievance. That a people possessed of legendary gifts for winsome expression should have a tradition of the body passing from speech to express the ultimate gravity of a complaint is at least ironic. It also can prove to be a stroke of rhetorical genius or stupidity. The spectacle of the body's voluntary death march can be a powerfully eloquent statement of conviction and an inventional moment that generates public discourse whose urgency and moral intensity grow while its inspiring source fades before our very eyes. However, without the necessary publicity to establish an audience with a sense of obligation to intervene, it can be discredited as emotional blackmail, or worse, it can be ignored.

The cultural significance of the hunger strike in Ireland traces back to the Middle Ages when it was invoked as a strategy to resolve a dispute by forcing one's adversary to negotiate. Its roots draw from Irish religious and civil traditions to make this tactic of last resort a resonant expression of a conviction so deeply held that it is worth sacrificing your life. In Ireland's Christian tradition, for example, legend holds that St. Patrick engaged in several fasts to protest divine rulings, with God always relenting. On the civil side, its status actually was formalized. In medieval Ireland fasting against a person to rectify an injustice had a place in the civil code. Thus, it was both a form of direct appeal by one disputant to another, such as a peasant who wanted to lodge a grievance against the lord of the manor, and a public maneuver, since the grievant would fast on the adversary's doorstep to recover a debt or right a wrong, thereby placing his or her life quite literally in the other party's hands in a way that the community could witness. The striker sought to bring about a negotiation by shaming the opponent. The faster assumed the adversary had an informed moral conscience that would lead him or her to negotiate rather than be publicly disgraced by letting another human perish over a quarrel. This practice was taken so seriously that should the grievant die, the party being struck would be held legally culpable and required to compensate the deceased's family for their loss.

The cultural efficacy of mediating disputes by fasting to death was politicized during Ireland's twentieth-century struggles for independence. Irish insurgents transformed the hunger strike from a culturally legitimated practice with legal status into a display of political conscience. Its union with the struggle for political independence positioned the striker's dying body as a metonym of an oppressed body politic.

Although there were few fantasies that it would force the British to negotiate their independence, its connection to the political psychology of the oppressed assured it
would have a radicalizing effect on Irish partisans. There were hunger strikes following
the Easter Rising in 1916 and the partitioning of Ireland in 1921. During this period
there also was a celebrated fast by Terence MacSwiney, Lord Mayor of Cork, who died
in October 24, 1920, after seventy-three days without food. On his inauguration as
mayor, he proclaimed, "It is not those who can inflict the most, but those who can suffer the most who will conquer." His words became the slogan for Irish Republicanism
and placed fasting to death in the nonviolent tradition of passive resistance.

Republican hunger strikes occurred periodically thereafter in Ireland as a mode of
political protest. Patrick McGrath, a veteran of the 1916 Easter Rising, began a fast
upon being imprisoned in 1939. The public outcry forced the government to release
him after forty-three days. The next year, when two other IRA men, Tony D'Arcy
and Jack McNeela, commenced a strike, the government of Eamon de Velera showed
it understood the rhetorical potentialities of a protest fast. Government censors restricted press coverage to diminish the strike's impact on the public.

After a twenty-five-year hiatus, hunger striking resumed in the 1970s. The IRA
engaged in hunger strikes in 1972 to gain prisoner of war (POW) status in Long
Kesh prison, and IRA prisoners were granted special status. Later in the 1970s,
Doloures and Marian Price, along with two men sentenced with them for a London
car bombing, fasted for return to Ireland to serve their sentences. They were force-
fed, and their strike lasted for 200 days. Eventually, they were repatriated; however,
their force-feeding was a source of great controversy and led the British government
to adopt a policy banning intervention to feed a fasting prisoner against his or her
will. In the fall of 1980, prisoners again invoked the hunger strike to force negotiation and reinstatement of special status.

The failure of that strike did not deter the Long Kesh prisoners. On March 1,
1981, Bobby Sands led the Republican prisoners on the fateful strike whose national
significance, now rooted in Irish politics as well as culture, spoke to the people of Ireland and the world with conflicted images of a society seemingly bereft of civility
wedded to the IRA's political cause. The image was conflicted because it juxtaposed
the passivity of nonviolent resistance to men convicted of terrorist crimes in a performative rhetoric of passive aggression. It called its witnesses to shed indifference to
the tortured act of self-extermination by those who had embarked upon violence
to achieve political ends. Whereas the means of the faster and terrorist place them at
opposite polls on the spectrum of political resistance, in the Irish culture of the
hunger strike, they were rhetorical comrades.

"A nobler call, in a holier cause"

The starving body's search for meaning finds expression in the responses of those who
witness its torments. Their reactions to what they see and to the interpretations of

others constitute the rhetorical salience of the starving body by the terms they choose to make this act discursively accessible. Acts of terrorism are no less needy than the anorexic body for words to give them meaning. Their accounts must do more than explain why violent acts have been committed because paramilitary violence and self-starvation to death speak beyond themselves to remind the world of grievances and to issue calls for the reorganization of society. Their rhetorical efficacy works within the moral ecology of the publics they constitute but also is constrained by the moral ecology of the enemy with whom they must interact.

If the politics of British-Irish relations has bequeathed a legacy of violence and oppressions, we are cautioned by the vampire-like dependence of self-starvation and terrorism on words not to dismiss them as forms of antirhetoric. The physical acts of the Provisional IRA acquire meaning through rhetorical acts that identify them with their agents. Without these rhetorical acts, the IRA would have no identity as an agent seeking to alter Irish political relations. In a most fundamental sense, the IRA itself is a rhetorical construction. Nonetheless, the IRA cannot make its material performances mean whatever its chooses. It asserts claims about itself and the world within ever-widening cultural frames that have been negotiated for centuries. During *the Troubles*, an appellation whose understatement underscores this historical moment's deadliness, the IRA's rhetoricality was locked within the irreconcilable cultural frames of Ireland and England considered both apart and, paradoxically, as inseparably joined. Its words, therefore, also were performances of cultural understandings that were beyond its power to control.

Differences between the national experiences of Ireland and England provide fertile soil for intense hostility by Irish Republicans. Although the unrest associated with Northern Ireland often is portrayed along sectarian lines, the grievance of Republicans is not with Protestants but with England. The Protestant majority in Northern Ireland is a product of historical actions by the British Crown dating from the sixteenth century. At that time, England began to confiscate lands in Ireland to establish plantations. What started as a minor practice escalated to mass confiscations of property primarily owned by Catholics. The Irish Rebellion, 1641–53, attempted to regain the land. The rebels eventually were defeated by Oliver Cromwell, who made these confiscations official during the 1650s when he sent thousands of parliamentary soldiers to settle in Ireland and imported thousands of Protestant settlers to live on the plantations (Wheeler 1999). This policy radically changed the demography of Ireland by creating substantial settlements with largely Protestant inhabitants and, importantly, a cultural frame for understanding resistance by the predominantly Catholic indigenous Irish to the Crown's confiscation of their property along sectarian lines. This historical grievance continued to play out through exploitative colonial policies and practices that deepened Irish enmity toward the British and periodic risings that attempted but failed to remove British rule (Lyons 1985/1963).

The depth of Irish antipathy for the British is captured by the "Proclamation of the Republic" issued at the commencement of the Easter Rising in 1916. It begins with the benediction of God and dead descendants authorizing its call to join Ireland's historical struggle. "IRISHMEN AND IRISHWOMEN: In the name of God and of dead generations from which she receives her old tradition of nationhood, Ireland, through us, summons her children to her flag and strikes for her freedom" (Clarke et al. 1990/1916, 1). The rising lasted only a few days before Padraic Pearse, president of the insurgent Irish Republic, surrendered unconditionally. Its leaders were court-martialed, convicted of treason, and executed by firing squad at Dublin's Kilmainham prison. The manner of their executions, conducted without regard for the emotional trauma suffered by the surviving loved ones and often marked by gratuitous acts of cruelty in the hours before they were shot, only exacerbated Republican loathing (Lyons 1985; O'Sullivan 2007; Stevenson 1996).

This contempt is cemented in public memory by the trial and execution of James Connolly, commandant-general of the Dublin Division and one of the nine signatories of the "Proclamation." Connolly had been mortally wounded in the fighting at the city's post office, where the Dublin Division was making its stand. Despite the surgeon's report that Connolly was dying of his wounds, he was court-martialed at a military hospital in Dublin and sentenced to death. His statement to the court-martial echoed the "Proclamation" by aligning the Easter Rising with a holy cause:

> We went out to break the connection between this country and the British Empire, and to establish an Irish Republic. We believe that the call we then issued to the people of Ireland was a nobler call, in a holier cause, than any call issued to them during this war [World War I]. . . . We succeeded in proving that Irishmen are ready to die endeavoring to win for Ireland those national rights which the British government has been asking them to die to win for Belgium. As long as that remains the case, the cause of Irish freedom is safe. . . . I personally thank God that I have lived to see the day when thousands of Irish men and boys, and hundreds of Irish women and girls, were ready to affirm that truth, and to attest it with their lives if need be. (Connolly 1990/1916, 188–89)

Primo Levi reminds us of the ordinary virtue that should govern the last moments of the condemned: "For people condemned to die, tradition prescribes an austere ceremony, calculated to emphasize that all passions and anger have died down, and the act of justice represents only a sad duty towards society which moves even the executioner to pity for the victim" (1959, 5). The British were to have none of this spirit as far as the Irish insurgents were concerned. Since Connolly's wounds made it impossible for him to walk or stand for his execution, he was taken by military ambulance to Kilmainham Jail where, on May 12, 1916, in a stunning display of insensitivity and political ineptitude, he was carried on a stretcher into the inner courtyard, tied to a chair, and shot. Along with other executed rebels, his body was put into a mass grave with no coffin. The manner of his execution, coupled with the fact that he would have died in a matter of days, especially angered the Irish, many of whom previously had not been engaged by the Easter Rising. His execution became (and for the IRA prisoners in the H-Blocks remained) a symbol of British cruelty toward Irish nationalists.

During the Troubles, which began with sectarian clashes in January 1969 and lasted until the Stormont, or Good Friday, Agreement in April 1998, Irish Catholicism's antipathy toward English Protestantism as a source of suppression was reinforced by reciprocal acts of violence that parsed along sectarian lines. Against staunch insistence on affiliation with London by the North, Ireland's then third-world economy stood in stark contrast to England's status as one of the big seven economic powers of the world. Nor did Republican eyes see Irish poverty as completely divorced from its colonial status within the dominion of the United Kingdom.

The political economy of relations with England had produced a legacy of subjugation on which the IRA drew to situate it actions in line with past patriots who had struggled for Irish independence. For many nationalists, particularly those aligned with Sinn Fein, the sacrifice, suffering, and death of fathers and daughters, mothers and husbands, relatives and girlfriends or boyfriends, neighbors and ancestors still finds meaning as freedom fighters dedicated to the continuing struggle against colonization by Westminster. During the Troubles, the union of Northern Ireland with Great Britain presented itself as an extension of an Irish body politic tortured and in pain from British occupation of Irish land. This union framed the Irish nation as at war with Great Britain and the paramilitary arm of the Northern Unionists, who supported ties with the United Kingdom. Even when denounced as extreme and dangerous because it resorted to violence, an Irish understanding of the political economy of the North gave credence to Sinn Fein's exhortations that define violence within the frame of British domination. Its call was resonant with patriotic opposition that helped even the wariest Irish nationalist make sense of otherwise seemingly senseless killing. But the IRA itself was not a large force, and the efficacy of its tactics depended upon its ability to force concessions from the British.

England portrays the history of Irish relations as distorted by the Irish's exaggerated or inaccurate claims of suppression and exploitation. Whereas Irish political understandings have historically supported a rhetoric that configures violence directed at the British presence in the North into paramilitary performances—albeit, for most, misguided performances—of patriotism, for England and the Protestant North, these acts support a counterrhetoric that constructs them as performances of anarchy and criminal acts by a terrorist band. When the United Irishmen movement, which banded together Catholics and dissenting Protestants, mostly Presbyterians, started at the end of the eighteenth century, its effort to emancipate Catholics and grant wider representation in the Irish Parliament were frustrated by the British and ended with the quashed rebellion of 1803 (Cronin 1980). By British lights, this is exemplary of the IRA's spurning political alternatives in favor of violence intended to coerce into submission those it opposes, and shows the IRA's utter disregard for civilian life, civic virtues, and democratic principles.[10]

The hunger strike itself instantiates a further cultural difference. The tactical value of fasting to death requires that your opponent's moral conscience regards life as to be cherished above all else. It aids negotiation when a culture regards it as shameful to allow a person with whom you have a grievance to deteriorate and die on your doorstep. Its tactical force evaporates when your opponent views your action through a different lens and would be glad to be rid of you. It folds, as well, when it is outside a cultural frame that assigns moral culpability for refusing to negotiate and therefore obviates cultural identification with the faster. Situations such as these suggest that the moral ecology of the hunger strike is directly related to its efficacy in managing rhetorical resources. What is the meaning of a hunger strike when the foe refuses to acknowledge the self-definition of the contested acts as resistance by the body politic? What is its meaning when the adversary denies the legitimacy of your grievance, views your action to seek redress as itself criminal, and reduces your act of protest to a definitional question that is irrelevant and meaningless in light of the deaths and mayhem your violence caused?

What is its meaning when the opponent not only refuses to acknowledge the starving body as an expression of the body politic but, in treating it as an individual act, invokes an alternative moral frame that insists on your autonomy to starve to death as an ultimate expression of freedom that it cannot abridge without violating your absolute authority over your own body, and so refrains from force-feeding because it is equivalent to rape (Dooley-Clarke 1981)? In short, the rhetorical character of the hunger strike is not completely within the faster's control. When the state denies the legitimacy of the striker's claims and then respects the striker's wish by allowing the fast to reach its inevitable conclusion, it raises questions about the strike's own moral ecology. Starvation to death is translated into public imagination through competing moral vernaculars that not only are incommensurate and to some degree are unintelligible to the opponents, but also, from the other's perspective, are inflammatory. Such a confrontation between a fast-to-death and an unresponsive authority eventually intensifies to a spectacular fusion of antagonists in a death lock that sculpts the meaning of a civil(ized) society. Thus, we arrive at the rhetorical construction of the struggle at Long Kesh for political status.

"You must be joking me"

The Provisional IRA tied the body inescapably to political choice manifest in strategies of visibility and invisibility. As a paramilitary organization, its effectiveness required that its bodies strike and disappear. Their invisibility threatened ever-present mayhem to other bodies for ignoring their claim to political rights, rendering their victims' visible instantiations of the political chaos Ireland experienced by partition.

They knew that if they were caught, their own bodies would be subjected to pain for refusing, as they must, to cooperate with their jailers, and thereby perform political pain through perceptible bodily pain.

The body's political role would continue in prison, where the penal administration places visibility at the center of its optic regime. An administration based on optics uses prison garb to appropriate the prisoner's bodily space by disciplining it into conformity with the institutional space of the prison. The prison uniform makes an overt statement about criminal status, loss of personal identity, and subjugation to a higher authority. Controlling the body's spatiality for visual conformity extends the space of the prison itself to maximize its optic possibilities for viewing prisoners. In prison, the body is clothed in garb that signifies its criminal status. Its spatial confinement and spatial assignment for performance of menial labor facilitate surveillance and signify a status outside society. For this reason, political prisoners seek identity apart from the criminal prison population; they regard themselves as prisoners of war. Whereas criminals commit crimes of personal motivation, political prisoners are incarcerated for acts of conscience. The political conscience that underwrites their deeds is therefore importantly marked by the covering and spatial construction of their bodies: garbed in their own clothes, segregated from ordinary criminals, and not required to perform industrial labor. These considerations weave through the sequence of events leading up to the 1981 Hunger Strike at Long Kesh.

Following 1969, the surge of guerrilla activity that accompanied the insurgence in Belfast led Westminster to subordinate the primacy of law to the exigencies of politics. In 1971, Westminster authorized detention without trial for those arrested for committing terrorist acts. This policy, known as "Internment," was established under provisions of Northern Ireland's Special Powers Act, which had been in place since partition and allowed the government to enact draconian state-of-emergency measures. Although both Republicans and Unionists committed terrorist acts, enforcement was one-sided, since no Protestants were detained. The politicization of this law enforcement strategy made it unpopular and undercut any possibility it may have had for juridical legitimacy in Republican eyes. Moreover, unlike its past collaborative efforts with the Irish Republic to bring increased terrorist activity under control, the North acted unilaterally, which roused the Irish Republic to protest vigorously that it had not been consulted or informed and to worry about the implications of unilateral action for Republican sympathizers. Additionally, there was considerable backlash when revelation of the "in-depth" interrogation methods used on a dozen IRA suspects made these tactics appear to cross the line into torture (Taylor 1997, 112–21).

Under Internment, the government rounded up 342 Republican suspects and placed them at a number of facilities, including the Long Kesh military camp, also known as Maze prison. Internees and their supporters vigorously protested their detention with what the prisoner administration referred to as "Ordinary Decent Criminals" (ODC). In 1972, as a response to this agitation, the Whitelaw Report recommended that prisoners who were members of the Provisional IRA and other groups with Irish Republican sentiments be awarded special status, which allowed them to be treated as political prisoners. They were segregated from the criminal population and housed in separate cells, called "the Cages"; allowed to wear their own clothes; not required to engage in the industrial work of the prison; allowed to congregate among themselves; and permitted to conduct their own educational programs.

At the end of 1972, the Diplock Committee, commissioned to investigate ways to deal with terrorist activity occurring in Northern Ireland, recommended "extrajudicial" processes for bringing paramilitary offenders to trial. Its recommendations were adopted, and special courts, called Diplock courts, were established. They were an alternative to the highly politicized "extrajudicial" practice of Internment; however, they circumvented normal legal procedures with a number of changes in how suspected terrorists were treated. Diplock courts dispensed with juries as a solution to the problem of terrorist intimidation that had made witnesses unwilling to testify and convictions hard to obtain. In addition, the new procedures authorized enhanced powers of arrest and interrogation (warrantless arrest in some instances and "enhanced" interrogation, which occupied an ambiguous border with torture), and new rules concerning admissible evidence (involuntary confessions as long as not extracted as a result of "torture" or "inhuman or degrading treatment" as defined by the report) (State of Northern Ireland 1972, 7 j). It switched the burden of proof to the defendant in all cases involving firearms and explosives, and denied bail except by the High Court, and then under restrictive guidelines.

The Diplock courts established conveyor belt justice that sent significant numbers of people accused of paramilitary offenses to prison. By 1975, there were 1,119 Special Category prisoners along with 535 detainees in Northern Ireland's prisons (Coogan 1997, 70). The vast majority were at the decommissioned Royal Air Force airfield at Long Kesh, where the number of prisoners had outstripped the capacity of its Nissan huts to house them and the warders to control them. In October 1974, the Special Category prisoners set fire to the prison camp. According to former IRA prisoner Jim McCann (2009), Republican POWs took action in response to what they perceived to be constant harassment by the prison authorities. Hundreds of POWs took part in burning the cages and taking over the camp. The British army was deployed, and, after two days of intense fighting, the insurrection was quelled. Hundreds of prisoners were seriously injured by rubber bullets fired at point-blank range and by batons. More seriously, as the battle intensified, the prisoners had been driven onto the prison's playing field, where they were attacked with gas dropped from helicopters hovering over the yard. In 2005, the *Observer* published an investigative article (Morrison and Bright 2005) that reported the gas involved was highly toxic CR, which induces nausea, irritation to the eyes, and intense pain to exposed skin. According to McCann, "There were grown men screaming for their mothers. . . . We'd all had experience with CS gas (used for riot control), which was easy to avoid, but you couldn't get away from it [CR]. I felt like I was on fire. They just decided to experiment on us. We were guinea pigs" (Morrison and Bright 2005).

When the prison camp was repaired, its new construction reflected the hard-line attitude toward paramilitary detainees that would be in place shortly. Long Kesh is an enormous site, measuring 145 hectares (358 acres). Its expanse made it possible to design an unusual space of confinement. When Long Kesh became a detention center, the Nissan huts, originally constructed to house the airmen, were used as detention units. Each hut held large numbers of prisoners, as many as 600 in each cage, which facilitated congregation among them (one of the rights that accompanied special status). The new prison structure would have a different spatial arrangement designed to segregate the prisoners and hold them in individual cells. Although its formal name, Maze, was coincidentally related to its shape, it was an apt description for the reconstructed prison's labyrinthine design. The prison's H-Blocks consisted of eight H-shaped buildings. Its repetitive design had a disorienting effect on those who passed through its gates, and, once inside, those unfamiliar with it could lose their bearings. The repetitive design was consistent with the architectural rationality of the prison, which was built as a technologically enhanced penopticon to provide maximum security and systematic isolation of the prisoners. Inside the prison, just behind the perimeter wall, were wide, 4.5-meter areas called "*Inertias.*" The Inertias were divided into thirty-six numbered sections and had floor-level motion sensors, enabling the guards to pinpoint quickly the location of anyone trying to escape. There were only two gates leading to the prison core. The gates opened onto a network of roads, each of which could be closed at any time and thereby seal off a section of the prison if needed. Each H-block had ninety-six cells measuring 5 meters square. The shape and penoptic design, intended to isolate the IRA convicts who were now to be treated as ordinary felons, also repeated in microcosm the conflict being waged on the outside, as a physical/political labyrinth in which Republicans and loyalists were to be locked up face-to-face.

In 1976, England revoked its policy of Internment when it criminalized terrorist acts and discontinued "Special Category" as a penal status. Criminalization effectively abolished political motivation from the moral ecology of the British penal system. Men convicted of Republican terrorist acts after March 1, 1976, were to be incarcerated in the H-Blocks, were no longer to be segregated from the ODC population, would be required to wear prison attire, would be assigned to the normal work details with the other prisoners, and would be denied freedom of congregation and freedom to conduct their own educational programs.

Criminalization proved to be inflammatory among Republican prisoners and their supporters on the outside. More than a legal policy, it was a political statement that denied the centuries-long Republican belief that they were engaged in a political war of resistance to force Britain's colonial presence from Irish soil. The moral value of Republican acts was directly attacked in a British propaganda campaign that deployed the vernacular of organized crime to redefine Republicans as "terrorists." It de-romanticized their self-understanding as freedom fighters and patriots by referring to the IRA as "thugs," "godfathers," and "gangs." Politically motivated violations of law were defined outside the moral properties of civilized society and, therefore, civil society. This change in the moral vocabulary redefined Republican militant behavior from warfare to criminal violations. For the prisoners, whose paramilitary behavior was narrated with the moral vernacular of resistance, the government's countermove upped the rhetorical ante. The prison performed a body rhetoric of its own by placing Provo bodies in criminal cells. However, its (re)classification of their imprisoned bodies also made them metonyms of an imprisoned body politic. The political consequences for which of these conflicting rhetorics prevailed were huge. Their contrasting frames for the relationship paramilitary bodies bore to the body politic guaranteed resistance within Long Kesh.

After the criminalization policy was announced, the Provos determined to refuse its conditions, which would first be challenged by refusing to wear prison garb. Their tactic was directed at more than regaining special status; it was to bring about the "total destruction of the juridical/penological facades that masked the actual politicization of the courts and prison" (Feldmann 1991, 148).

On August 18,1976, Ciaran Nugent, convicted of hijacking a van for IRA-related activity, was the first Provo prisoner processed into Long Kesh under the new rules. When he was asked his clothes size so he could be given a prison uniform, he replied, "You must be joking me," and he refused to wear anything but a blanket. By September, Nugent's defiance had sparked a blanket protest among Republican inmates. By refusing to dress, the prisoners effectively refused the prison's most conspicuous and pervasive resource for establishing criminal status as the state had defined it. Refusing compulsory visibility made their bodies both the site of their political struggle and their main weapon of opposition. The authorities responded by treating the prisoners' naked bodies as a sign of mere animality. As long as their nakedness was concealed only by their prison blankets, these prisoners would be caged in their cells, could not participate in industrial work with the other inmates or enjoy visitation privileges, which effectively segregated them, like animals, from other human contact, and would lose remission of their sentences for their failure to be cooperative. The concerted action of the blanket protest defied institutional definitions of the Republicans' bodies; the prison's response intensified its reduction of their human bodies to mere biological existence.

The Blanketmen remained confined to their cells except to use the showers and for visitations, when they wore uniforms rather than forego the visit. For use of the showers, the prisoners had been issued two towels, one to wrap around their waists and the other to dry themselves. In November 1976, the prison tried to enforce a "single towel" rule. With only a single towel, they would have to expose themselves to the guards, who habitually engaged in crude jeering at the naked men. Strenuous protest led the authorities to relent. By late 1977, however, the single-towel rule was reimposed, and by late 1978 mirror and˙strip searches were initiated. Prisons use the mirror search is used to detect concealed items. This concern had foundation in the case of Provo prisoners, who regularly smuggled messages out of and contraband into Maze Prison concealed in the body's orifices. However, they also were demeaning invasions of the body, which the H-Blocks' warders intensified through needless searches and rough treatment of the prisoners. On March 17, 1978, the prisoners refused to leave their cells in protest of the single towel rule and the now routine mirror and strip searches. The next day the "dirty protest" began.

By refusing to visit the washrooms, the prisoners had no way to empty their own slop pots. Their warders refused to empty them and administered beatings instead. The prisoners retaliated by emptying their contents through the spyholes and out the windows of their cells. The prison responded by sealing the spyholes and windows. The prisoners refused to end their protest and instead disposed of their excreta by smearing it on the walls and ceilings of their cells.

The dirty protest required the prisoner to sublimate the self to the body's value as a political instrument. By using their bodies as political weapons, they had reversed the prison's dehumanizing treatment and its erasure of their political identity. If the prison was going to insist their clothed bodies give them the visible appearance of a common criminal, they would erase the discernable identity inherent to clothing by going naked. If the prison was going to humiliate their bodies by surveilling their interiors as if they were merely containers of contraband, they would retaliate by making their interior contents an external and visible sign of political alterity. The dirty protest used a biological idiom, a vernacular of human refuse, a passivity reinvented as startling agency in a performance of the purely biological. The defilement of their cells, without the frame of resistance, would seem to be an antirhetoric, a disgusting display of humans living like animals in their own waste. Within a resistance frame, the moral vernacular of living in their own filth made an assertion about political relations that would compel humans to live this way and about the moral compass of authorities who would permit it to continue without seeking a solution.

The dirty protest's tactical use of the biological idiom challenged the rationality of the prison's administrative practices and, in fact, forced the entire H-Blocks population to "speak" it. The defilement of the cells and the mirror searches were biological homologies. The warders spoke the biological idiom in an attempt to restore penal rationality. The prisoners spoke this idiom to assert a human right that decoupled the prison regime from rationality. They used it as a moral vernacular whose inventive possibilities threw the prison's administrative norms into crisis. To restore order Maze's administration had to respatialize the prison. The Provos compelled the prison to perform wing shifts to clean the cells and perform forced washings to clean the prisoners. These were acts of reciprocal violence structured by and repeated because of the prisoners' bodily performances. Their vernacular invention to inscribe resistance required erasure in return, and the assertions, once erased, had to be reinscribed.

Who Sets the Agenda?

The dirty protestors' vile living conditions were impossible to contain within Long Kesh. They became a major topic of discussion linked to the policy of criminalization but, more important, to the larger issue of political identity that was at stake. Once conditions inside Long Kesh were known, their dramatic assault on human sensibilities toward inhuman treatment gave events inside the prison increasing power to set the agenda for Republican politics. First, women prisoners at Armaugh joined them in the dirty protest. Although major newspapers, in particular British and unionist news outlets, expunged women from the gendered story of active Republican resistance (Aretxaga 1997) and did not report the activities of the IRA women in Armaugh, references to their solidarity with the dirty protesters were common in the radical Republican newspaper *An Phoblacht/Republican News*. Their joining the men in a solidarity strike was an unusual display of agency in that it broke with the past tight control over how the Armaugh women displayed resistance.[11] This was a display choreographed by the women from within the prison. The *Republican News* also kept a steady stream of articles on the Blanketmen before its readers, often urging citizen action. Although to a lesser degree, the *Belfast Telegraph* offered periodic editorial opinion and commentary about the blanket strike and dirty protest, especially by editorialist Chris Ryder, who interpreted events in the prison and responses of support or concern over their degrading conditions as linked and offering soft support for terrorist attacks. Conditions in the prison were noted by the International Committee of the Red Cross (ICRC), which is charged with monitoring the humane treatment of political prisoners and POWs; the Catholic Church regularly issued pleas to the government to address the way the prisoners were being treated; and members of Ireland's House of Representatives (Dáil Éireann) occasionally expressed concern. On the other side, when the question of the prison conditions for the Blanketmen was raised in Parliament, the government representative would defend the prison as among the finest penal facilities in the world and emphasize that the prisoners, who were murders, arsonists, saboteurs, and gunrunners, were making a choice.[12] Rev. Ian Paisley and editorials in the *News Letter*, a newspaper with extreme loyalist bias, used polemical attacks to fuse the blanket and dirty strikes to the political agenda of Republicans in general.[13]

Widespread attention to events in Long Kesh and the links on all fronts to Republican issues and deeds signaled that an important rhetorical shift was occurring. Prisoners living in their own filth exceeded even the conditions of penned livestock. As their story riveted public attention to conditions in the H-Blocks, their distressed bodies made the prison the dominant topos for discussing British treatment of Republican bodies and positioned the prisoners on the discussion's leading edge. To Republican eyes, the prison provided a new way to think about British oppression and resistance. It reconceptualized the struggle from street violence to passive aggression. If the degradation of their cells also subjected their bodies to degradation, was this not equally a statement of the degradation to the body politic Republicans suffered at British hands?

In the contested moral environment of a civilized, and therefore civil, society, the prisoners used their bodies as a form of *refutatio*, a section in the Republican discourse of indentity intended to refute British claims to civility. For the government and the loyalist community more generally, these acts were dismissed as worthless denials of their criminal status. These prisoners were regarded as convicted murderers, bombers, and arsonists who were not entitled to special treatment. However alarming their degradation seemed, the fact remained that for prison officials and the government, it was self-imposed. Regardless, rhetorical capital is a condition of the audience addressed, and if the authorities' lack of sympathy made the prisoner's protest futile within Long Kesh, the moral question of fundamental human rights and the prisoners insistence on their political identity soon found an external voice able to give the state of their bodies public meaning. To a world of observers whose passions were less inflamed by partisan sentiments, it provided a disturbing interrogation of Britain's juridical/penological moral compass.

In July 1978, national publicity of the prisoners' debased state and their protest for special status intensified when Cardinal Thomas O'Fiaich visited the squalor of Long Kesh. Afterward, he wrote a public letter in which he issued a stinging indictment of British policies that had led to these vile conditions. He asserted that the men's refusal to wear a prison uniform did not entitle the prison administration to deny them rights to physical exercise, freedom of association, and outside contact. In his view, these were "basic human needs for physical and mental health, not privileges to be granted or withheld as rewards or punishments" (in Beresford 1987, 139–40). He concluded with passionate insistence on a political identity that framed their imprisonment and their voluntary acts of debasement as meaningful claims against the legitimacy of the state:

> The authorities refuse to admit that these prisoners are in a different category from the ordinary, yet everything about their trials and family background indicates that they are different. They were sentenced by special courts without juries. The vast majority were convicted on allegedly voluntary confessions which are now placed under grave suspicion by the recent report of Amnesty International. Many are very youthful and come from families which had never been in trouble with the law, though they lived in areas which suffered discrimination in housing and jobs. How can one explain the jump in the

prison population of Northern Ireland from 500 to 3,000 unless a new type of prisoner has emerged?

The severity of O'Fiaich's contention that the treatment of the prisoners' bodies was debasing and a flagrant abuse of their fundamental human rights was met by the Northern Ireland Office with equal ferocity. It responded by describing the prisoners as felons convicted by the due processes of Northern Ireland. Their crimes were heinous: murder and mutilation of over 600 of their own people. The official statement concluded with the admonition that "no one who is convicted of a crime carried out after 1 March 1976—and that includes those involved in the 'dirty' protest —will be given any form of special status. As soon as this decision is understood and accepted, conditions in the cell blocks can return to normal" (Beresford 1987, 141).

The dirty protest failed to move the authorities; special status was not restored, and the debasement of living in filth was left to the prisoners themselves to resolve. Yet the rhetorical claims of the physical body, extended by Cardinal O'Fiaich's letter to the body politic, asserted an alternative set of claims to those of the British for the organization of society. Whereas the British insisted on the blindness of the law to the political motivations of transgressors, O'Fiaich insisted that a civilized society organized itself on the moral requirement to respect "basic human needs for physical and mental health." A civilized society was marked by the ordinary virtue of aligning its treatment of all humans, regardless of status, with respect for their fundamental human dignity; even its prisoners had claim to basic civil treatment accorded to all human beings. It positioned the suffering body of these political dissidents as a reflection of a suffering body politic opposed to British presence on Irish soil and the division of the north from Ireland. It further set the stage for the traditional Irish rhetorical performance of last resort enacted in the hunger strike at Long Kesh in 1980 and 1981.

"I am a political prisoner": Bobby Sands as the Body Politic

After two-and-a-half years on the dirty protest, the Republican prisoners were in poor shape physically and mentally. The prisoners at Long Kesh had embarked on a hunger strike in the final months of 1980 in an attempt to secure concessions on the question of their political status. They voluntarily ended that strike when the government led them to believe a compromise was possible on certain conditions that would de facto restore special status. When that belief subsequently proved erroneous, the Provo OC,[14] Bobby Sands, argued that the dire conditions within the prison were certain to break the morale and solidarity of Republican prisoners unless they were remedied.

The prisoners in H-Blocks had come to think of their living conditions as something other than a protest. To withstand the wretchedness of their confinement, they had developed support mechanisms that intensified solidarity. For example, Sands was fluent in Gaelic and believed one way to increase solidarity among the men and connect them emotionally with Irish history was to teach them the language. He and three others conducted tutorials in their respective wings of the prison. Within a year they had succeeded. After the guards retired from the wing, men with strong voices shouted ideas, commands, encouragement, and the like. Speaking the national vernacular is always already a rhetorical performance of political identity. Speaking it in prison is also a choice of that identity, an enactment that makes the prisoner one with it. It also allowed the men to speak a language their warders did not understand. In addition to learning Gaelic, the prisoners organized tutorials on politics and history, engaged in discussions about important social and political topics, and devised tactics for dealing with the political use of their bodies.

For the Blanketmen, their prison situation was a way of life. Here is how one of the Provos expressed their awareness to Feldman (1991, prisoner excerpt 5.6, 164–65):

> That is what's frustrating about the H-Blocks—that people to this day don't understand what was going on in the H-Blocks. They don't even start to understand. We recognize ourselves that nobody who's not actually been there cannot know what it was like. When people ask me, I find I am at a loss for words, to find words to portray what I really felt. I remember telling people who were always talking about the "protest" we were in, "Hold on a minute. This was more than a fuckin' 'protest!' This was a way of life for us!" It was no longer a protest with a visible end to it. That's how we experienced it at the time. This was our life-style for two, three, four, five years. It had become an alternative life-style for us and not one we wanted by choice like.

As this prisoner's recollection reflects, they also were struggling with the possibility that this may be how they lived out the rest of their lives. The failed 1980 Hunger Strike heightened this dread.

Sands insisted the hunger strike resume. Sinn Fein's leadership reluctantly consented, and Sands announced he would be commencing a hunger strike on March 1, 1981, the fifth anniversary of the withdrawal of political status. Three other inmates would follow him on the strike at regular intervals. Each would fast to death, with his place taken by a fellow inmate who would continue the strike until the prisoners' five demands were met. The decision to subject their bodies to pain, debasement, and even death and their hopes for success were captured by their adoption of Terence MacSwiney's aphorism as their motto: "It is not those who can inflict the most, but those who can suffer the most who will conquer."

From Bodily Insufficiency to Rhetorical Sufficiency

The strike began with Sands agreeing to write a diary of his experience, the British authorities refusing to negotiate in order to avoid binding themselves to any alterations to the prison's rules, and the outside world relatively unconcerned about Sands's impending ordeal and possible death. Prisoners sent notes to Sands offering him best wishes and support.[15] They had no illusion that the Thatcher government would relent of its own accord to prevent their deaths. They calculated that the rhetorical force of their dying bodies would persuade external bodies to insist England intervene in a way that would produce a settlement.

Sands wrote a long note to offer an account of his life. Sinn Fein marked the beginning of the strike with a march through West Belfast to a rally, where a crowd estimated to be between 2,000 and 4,000 assembled. This was a considerably smaller gathering than the 10,000 who had rallied in October the year before at the start of the 1980 strike. The diminished numbers reflected the loss of enthusiasm following the 1980 hunger strike's disappointing failure to gain concessions from the government. The organizers read a statement from the prisoners expressing the grievances at the heart of their protest:

> We have asserted we are political prisoners and everything about our country, our interrogation, trials and prison conditions show that we are politically motivated and not motivated by selfish reasons for selfish ends. As further demonstration of our selflessness and the justice of our cause, a number of our comrades, beginning today with Bobby Sands, will hunger-strike to the death unless the British Governments [*sic*] abandons its criminalization policy and meets our demands. (in Beresford 1987, 61)

Passive aggression reaches the press. The initial stages of the strike received relatively light coverage in the *Irish Times,* the *London Times,* and the *Belfast Telegraph.* Still, from its inception each reported starkly contrasting versions of events that were predictably Republican or Unionist in their emphasis. The *Irish Times* marked the onset of the strike with articles on the activities of supporters and the response by the British government. It reported the comparatively small number of supporters mustered by an IRA rally in Belfast, 4,000 versus 10,000 in the fall, to mark the strike's beginning. It speculated that the suspension of the 1980 strike had dampened public enthusiasm for supporting a tactic unlikely to succeed. The British government was portrayed as steadfast in ignoring the strike. When secretary of state for Northern Ireland, Humphrey Atkins, repeated to Commons the government's determination never to concede special status, Martin Cowley's front-page story in the *Irish Times* of March 3 reported that he was greeted with applause. No mention was made of the hue and cry his account raised in Parliament, which was the focus of *London Times* reporting on that date. Instead, Cowley noted that several MPs "made it clear that they did not want frequent statements," and that Atkins "reciprocated with the strong hint" that he had no intention of making them. This Republican perspective framed Sands's body as in callously indifferent hands.

The *London Times* ("Government Unmoved") coverage, by contrast, appeared on page 8 and reported the actual exchanges in Parliament during which MPs on both sides upbraided Atkins to stop making such statements as "we shall not give way on the issue of political status" and "the Maze prison is one of the most modern in the

United Kingdom and . . . compares favorably with any prison anywhere in the world," since they only publicized the IRA's cause. As Atkins's rebuke for talking about these matters attests, the rhetorical potency of Sands's body was not lost on the British. From a loyalist perspective, in which Sands's body personified criminal terrorism and was undeserving of public discussion, the policy of not emphasizing the strike itself could only be sustained by ignoring Sands. To talk about him went beyond enumerating the government's reasons for rejecting his claims to political status, or reiterating that he was a convicted felon. It meant one also had to address the fact that the government had his body on its hands, along with the insurmountable pathos his dying frame would soon evoke for some form of accommodation.

The *Belfast Telegraph*, a conservative daily that has Northern Ireland's largest circulation, was content to bury the story on page 7, under the headline "Family Backs Hunger Striker." The story offers a synopsis of Sands's criminal activity and reports the scant crowd of "several thousand" who "paraded down the Falls Road." His mother and sister were quoted as supporting his hunger strike. Subsequently, Sands's strike disappeared from the *Tribune's* pages until April.

Britain's rhetorical denial of Sands's corporal body was an extension of its political denial of the national body he claimed to symbolize. By maintaining silence, the meaning of this strike remained elusive to anyone outside the culture of Irish Republican sentiment. To speak about the strike would give it a public voice, ask for an interpretation, and invite rejoinder. The more words offered to account for Sands's strike, the less mysterious it would become, enhancing its call on Irish cultural tradition and its chances for gaining widespread sympathy.

Silence seemed to be working, as public outcry over the strike was minimal. When mention was made, the public narrative portrayed Sands as volitionally starving to death in order to wear his own clothes. To outsiders who questioned whether the government's intractable stance was severe, the government could reply that there was justice in treating common criminals in a common way, and Sands was, after all, a criminal convicted under British law. Equally, what sense could be made of a person starving himself to death in order to wear his own clothes? Surely the magnitude of his demand was incommensurate with taking his own life. As long as Sands was isolated in public imagination as a convicted terrorist, the moral equation requiring punishment for his crimes would outweigh the ostensible claims of his protest.

Passive aggression goes to Parliament. However, Sands was striking for more than the prisoners' five demands. The demands amounted to an ultimatum that Britain concede the political nature of IRA violence, and therefore acknowledge the legitimacy of Republican sentiment and action within the body politic. On March 9, 1981, Sands wrote a communiqué stating: "As you should know I don't care much to entering any discussion the topic of 'negotiations' or for that matter 'settlements.'. . . I've told Bik [McFarlane, OC PIRA, H-Blocks] to let me or anyone else die before submitting to a play like that [a last-minute agreement in order to save the hunger striker in the last stage before death]" (Beresford 1987, 65). Sands was aware that gaining concession of political status would constitute a reversal of Britain's centuries-old refusal to acknowledge an Irish body politic. That meant the Republicans had to control the final narrative, which must include more than the five demands or an eleventh-hour agreement reached to save the strikers' lives.

If his hunger strike was symbolic of Republicans' national aspirations, its representative mass grew exponentially on March 15 when Francis Hughes joined him, and then again on March 22 when they were joined by Raymond McCreesh and Patsy O'Hara. The material increase of those committed to bring about their own physical decline into a void of death presaged the dramatic insertion of the strike into the political body they aspired to represent.

On March 5, Frank Maguire, MP from Fermanaugh-South Tyrone, died suddenly of a heart attack, thus requiring a special election. The constituency of Fermanaugh-South Tyrone included a sizable Catholic population, and the district itself was the site of conflict that reversed the normal power equations associated with the North. During the 1970s, more than sixty people had met violent deaths in Fermanaugh alone, most of them Protestants who were part-time members of the Royal Ulster Constabulary (RUC) and the Ulster Defense Regiment, which heightened tensions between Protestants and Catholics and lent credence to the Protestant claim that the IRA was embarked on a campaign of genocide. Since the murdered men were mostly the younger sons of elderly Protestant farmers, their deaths meant their fathers could no longer work the fields and were forced to sell. Catholics purchased their farms. As Padraig O'Malley observes, "Land was changing tribes, and hence political allegiance. The frontier was being pushed back" (1990, 58). With a Catholic majority of 5,000 voters, a Protestant candidate could win an election only if the Catholic vote was split.

Although Maguire was a Catholic, his political acumen centered more on the needs of his district than on the radical agenda of Republicanism. Fermanaugh-South Tyrone had a record of supporting such radical views; in recent history, it had sent Bernadette Devlin as its representatives to Parliament. Although public speculation centered on the likelihood that Maguire's younger brother Noel would stand for his seat, and that Bernadette Devlin McAliskey would attempt to regain her former seat, the sudden death of Maguire presented the opportunity for Sinn Fein to make Sands's fast a matter of public referendum. Three weeks after Maguire's death, with the press still ignoring Sands's strike, Sinn Fein's Executive Committee, in tacit recognition that the prison was now setting the Republican political agenda, declared that Sands would stand for the vacant seat. Four days later, on March 30, Noel Maguire, who had already filed papers, formally withdrew from the election with a statement that echoed the Irish cultural meaning of a hunger strike: "It has now become a question of conscience with me. I have been told the only way of saving Bobby Sands's life is by letting him go forward in the elections. I just cannot have the life of another man on my hands. I am calling my supporters to throw their weight behind Bobby Sands" (in Beresford 1987, 79). Rev. Ian Paisley's Democratic Unionist Party elected not to field a candidate rather than face embarrassing defeat in a Republican stronghold. The election came down to a two-man contest between Sands and Harry West, the official Unionist candidate. Sands's candidacy was presented as a referendum on the H-Blocks; a vote for him was not support for IRA violence but for bringing an end to the inhuman living conditions of the Republicans at Maze Prison.

By the end of March, Sands's body had wasted considerably. At the start of the strike his weight was 64 kg (151 lbs). By the seventeenth day his weight was down to 57.5 kg (127 lbs), and he no longer could sustain the effort of keeping his diary. On the twenty-third day, with his throat sore and his body pained by the sensation of shocks from the slightest touch, he had been removed to the prison infirmary. Positioning his body, now showing the signs of self-consumption, in the by-election put an end to the government's tactic of ignoring his strike.

Sands's local political campaign received international press coverage, while being relatively ignored in the *Belfast Telegraph* until days before the election. Its first coverage in April appeared on the 6th, buried on page 8. Its next article appeared on Election Day, April 9, under the banner "By-election voters face stark choice" in a bordered 2-by-11 rectangle at the top of page 1. Its ominous tone was repeated in the next day's edition, before the outcome was determined, with a lead story headlined "Big Poll Sparks Unionist Jitters." Jitters turned to gloom in the April 11 edition announcing Sands's victory.

As one might expect, nationalists had a remarkably different response, as they found themselves energized by Sands's campaign. The election brought an influx of Republicans from all parts of Ireland. The mobilized Republican body politic drove through small towns with their convoys openly flying tricolors and playing Republican songs from loudspeakers. As Sands's emaciation deepened, his body gained rhetorical weight through the increasing volume of discourse that identified popular support for his failing body by claiming their unity with it. Publicizing his helpless body, left to devour itself by an administration impervious to its plight, provided rhetorical nourishment to the public construction of Sands as a representative victim of British political oppression in Northern Ireland.

Those outside the Republican frame remained fixated on the ostensible reason for the strike—to gain five privileges that went with special status in the prison— as Sands's motivation to continue his fast. The strangeness of starving yourself to death for the right to wear your own clothes was processed as a violent act to redefine the Republicans' status in prison (*Belfast Tribune*, "No room for doubt," 1981, 1). Within the Republican moral vernacular, it was clear that Sands was prepared to die for the larger goal of destroying the legitimacy of British authority in the North. Inserted into the by-election, the hunger strike appeared more as an expression of power than a demand for power. By fasting to death, Sands was not destroying the hierarchy but working within it; he was not denying the hierarchy but exposing it. He begins his diary by declaring that he has no choice in the matter. His strike "has been forced upon me and my comrades by four-and-a-half years of stark inhumanity": "I am a political prisoner. I am a political prisoner because I am a casualty of a perennial war that is being fought between the oppressed Irish people and an alien, oppressive, unwanted regime that refuses to withdraw from this land" (1983, 219).

The claims of Bobby Sands's body did not go unanswered. British authorities responded to his candidacy by reiterating that he was not a prisoner of war; he was a criminal. Don Concannon, Labor spokesman on Northern Ireland in the House of Commons, proclaimed, "A vote for Sands is a vote for the perpetrators of the LaMon massacre, the murder of Lord Montbatten and the latest brutal inhuman killing of Mrs. Mathers" (Beresford 1987, 83). British authorities denied the legitimacy of Provisional IRA claims to waging a patriotic war of liberation. Assertions that they were continuing a centuries-old struggle to drive the British from Irish soil were countered by British portrayals of Sands and the IRA as distinctly unrepresentative of the Irish people. Britain launched a rhetorical campaign that blamed the Troubles on a small gang of thugs who did not enjoy community support.

On April 9, Sands defeated Harry West by a vote of 30,492 to 29,046. Although Margaret Thatcher remained implacable in responding, "A crime is a crime is a crime. It is not political, it is a crime" (Beresford 1987, 86), Sands's victory nonetheless required the government to address the strike and the issues it had raised. Public endorsement of Sands gave his body official status in Fermanaugh/South Tyrone's body politic as its representative. Sands's victory publicly refuted the thesis of Britain's campaign to portray the prisoners' political aspirations as lacking community support. Although the British wanted to dismiss his election as a propaganda victory for the IRA, the *Washington Post* of April 11 (A21) cited Republicans who maintained, "This result has finally proved through the ballot box how deep the support is for the Republican prisoners." It also fixed international attention on Britain's seeming indifference to negotiate an accommodation that would save Sands's life. Britain now had to appear to be doing everything reasonable to end the strike short of meeting the demands.

The reversals of bare life by the Provos stand as an unlikely expression of biopower. The uses of bodily and institutional spaces for moral vernacular performances of passive aggression suggest the political possibilities when the subjugated body and the space of imprisonment become the inventional topoi for resistance. At the very least they show how they function within the rhetorical mechanism of passive aggression: radical performances of bodily insufficiency provoke inept displays of bodily sufficiency in response. These, in turn, maximize the rhetorical sufficiency of the body in pain. The structural components of the prison and its handling of prisoners become a heuristic for thinking about oppression in the larger society, just as the prisoners' embodied performances of passive aggression do the same for thinking about resistance. It would be an error, however, to conclude that the meaning of the hunger striker's body could be resolved, even by such a dramatic and seemingly clarifying event as Sands's election to Parliament.

By fusing Sands's dying body with the Republican construction of Northern Ireland's body politic, the election effectively mobilized passive aggression in the public deliberation over prison reform in the H-Blocks and, by extension, the Republican movement itself. Coverage by the *Irish Times* lent credence to this interpretation. Two days after the election, a *Times* article by Thomas Ó Cathoar (5) normalized the election results by recounting past instances in which a jailed political dissident had been elected to Parliament from Fermanaugh/South Tyrone and other counties in Ireland. Five days later, on April 16, another article ("Sands," 8) analyzing the election made the same point and further argued that close scrutiny of election results in the counties where jailed Republicans had been elected in the past showed that voters also had a record of defeating Republicans. According to the article, this indicated that the Sands vote did not reflect a blind Catholic-Nationalist sentiment. Instead, it was "a vote for the specific policy Sands put forward, political status for the prisoners in the H Blocks and Armaugh." The article concluded with a note indicating that much of its material came from a file in the Northern Ireland Public Record Office that had been closed to the public and asked, "Is this because of the rather embarrassing story it reveals?"

The frame of prison reform, not support of terrorism, was buttressed in news reporting of related incidents in which Sands's supporters were confronted by the RUC. For example, a 3,000-person demonstration by the Trade Union Sub-Committee of the Anti-H-Block Campaign found its April 15 march to the center of Belfast blocked by a large contingent of the RUC and British soldiers: "When they were stopped in College Square North, on the edge of the city centre, they sat down in the street for half an hour in the bright sunshine to listen to a number of speakers, all of whom emphasized that there should be no confrontation with the security forces." Stewards then made sure the marchers dispersed peacefully back along Falls Road, the only route left open to them after rows of RUC Land Rovers and armored cars had sealed off all other routes to the city center. The only trouble was a little desultory stoning and the burning of a van by a group of youths outside Divis Flats (*Irish Times,* "3,000 stopped," 8).

The depiction of peaceful marchers with responsible leaders sitting in the sun while surrounded by the menacing force of the RUC and the British army whose Land Rovers and armored cars sealed off their access to the city center offered a metonymic representation of the Republican version of Sands's strike and the relationship of his frail body to the British authorities with whom they claimed his fate rested. Without compromise by the British, the spectacle of Sands's self-consumption became a corporeal manifestation of his grievance.

Opinion in Northern Ireland's newspapers tended to provide a loyalist account. They did not refute Sands's politicized body as representative of a Republican body politic; instead, they decried it. The *Belfast Telegraph* regarded the election as shameful, although it counseled against expelling him from a seat he would never fill ("Verdict stands," 1981, 1). The *Orange Torch* decried it as "Choosing Barabbas" ("Choosing Barabbas," 1981, 1), and "one of the most disgusting spectacles of all time" ("The Sands of Time," 1981, 4). And the *News Letter* considered it "A vote for violence" ("A vote for violence," 1981, 1). Editorial debate in the *Belfast* Telegraph quickly shifted to whether felons should be barred from holding elective office and mounting concerns over violence ("Ball bounces," 1981, 7; "Atkins rejects," 1981, 1; "End the nightmare," 1981, 1).

Coverage in the *London Times* laid its stress more on the foregone conclusion that Sands would be elected, given the Catholic majority of Fermanaugh/South Tyrone, and that this would be a propaganda victory for the IRA. After the election it focused on deliberations within the government and among members of Parliament over whether to unseat Sands and how to interpret the election. Following Sands's victory, London *Times* articles commonly began with "Mr. Robert Sands, Provisional IRA gunman." Having inscribed him as a felon and terrorist, and therefore unfit to serve, the implications of Sands's body seated in the House of Commons were seen as grave. The vote for him was depicted both as a blow to moderate Roman Catholic opinion in the Social Democrat and Labor Party (SDLP) and as Catholics laughing at the gravesite of a slain loyalist. Was it a vote for the IRA? Against union? For a gunman? For the H-Blocks issue? Although the *Times's* focus was decidedly on dampening the propaganda value of his election, these accounts were confronted with the indisputable fact that the voters in Fermanaugh/ South Tyrone, who had been reported as going to their polling places out of fear and intimidation, could have spoiled their ballots but chose not to. The voters had made Sands representative of their political aspiration in a way that gave it and him official status. Sands entered the discussion with a pointed interpretation of the election's meaning and strong admonition to Westminster against unseating him. Peter Arnlis, writing in the *An Phoblacht/Republican News* (April 18, 1981, 5), quotes Sands as stating:

> No matter what moves are made, Ireland and the rest of the world will continue to recognize the democratic decision of the people even if the British parliament can not abide by the very tenets which it professes to uphold.
>
> A decision to unseat me will have grave implications for the British people and their democratic processes and is a further whittling away of civil liberties spilling over from the war in Ireland. . . .
>
> [I say to people of influence in Britain and those British politicians] with a conscience [to recognize that] it is not republican hunger striker Bobby Sands, MP, that is the problem, but it is Britain's failed policy of attempting to brand

Irish political prisoners as criminal which has your government scurrying for
legal procedures to unseat a dying man and which, if you allow, will shame you
in the eyes of the world.

The British government might construe his election in ways that diminished its IRA
mandate, but Westminster could no longer ignore him. It had to discuss Sands and
the claims for which he stood.

The credibility of Sands's insistence on the need for reform in the H-Blocks was
supported, as postelection press coverage steadily became a deathwatch. His deterio-
rating body increasingly appeared paradigmatic of Anglo-Irish relations in the North.
Following the election, the international press carried the continuing story of his
steady physical decline, including appeals by his supporters who spoke of Long Kesh
as a "concentration camp" and excoriated the colonial practices of England as at the
root of Sands's protest and "the troubles" of the North (*Washington Post*, April 21,
1981, C3).

Passive aggression on the death watch. On April 21, the *Irish Times* began counting the
number of days Sands had been fasting and reporting medical accounts of his deteri-
orating condition. Although it quoted some local voices dissenting from the publicity being given to Sands's hunger strike in comparison to that accorded victims of IRA
terrorism, *Times* reporting more typically fused his dying body with the issue of
political status. Its coverage framed Sands's strike in terms of the prison reform issue.
In that context, British refusal to accommodate Sands appeared heartlessly stubborn.
Over the following two weeks it also reported a steady stream of visits by world leaders, representatives of the International Commission for Human Rights, a papal nun-
cio, a contingent of three representatives from the European Parliament, local clergy,
and public figures such as Ramsey Clark and Fr. Joseph Berrigan, who issued statements denouncing terrorism while urging Great Britain to find a reasonable accommodation to the long-standing dispute in the H-Blocks. Despite Thatcher's point
that Sands could save his own life by calling off the strike, Sands's claim that his cause
was just and reasonable, as England's was not, received legitimation from press framing of the election as a mandate for prison reform and as an international concern
directed to the NIO and Thatcher for humanitarian response.

Press coverage in Northern Ireland saw this flurry of activity through a different
lens. Members of the European Parliament were denounced as opportunists more
interested in the political capital to be gained from such a visit than in doing some
good to remedy the situation. The Catholic clergy and papal emissaries were attacked
as hypocritical for not condemning Sands, who was committing the mortal sin of
suicide, rather than making entreaties to Sands and Thatcher to reach a settlement
(*Combat*, "Political chicanery," c. May 1981, 41; *Belfast Telegraph*, "Political Choice
in the Maze," April 21, 1981, 1).

As death neared, Sands's body, frail and wasted, grew in its capacity to provoke heated exchange as a source of competing political interpretation between the British and Republican Irish moral ecologies. Starting on April 16, one week after he was elected and immediately after Westminster determined not to unseat him, through May 8, when Sands was buried, the *London Times* ran fifteen articles reporting violence or fear of violence precipitated by Sands's fast to death. A comparable number appeared in the *Belfast Telegraph*. For the *London Times* reader, Sands's dying body was not framed as the exemplar of an Irish body politic but of a terrorist group that brought only strife, bloodshed, and grief to Ulster. For example, the *London Times* of May 2 reported that Secretary of State Atkins accused the IRA of planning to provoke sectarian warfare in the event of Sands's death, including evacuation of a section of Belfast so they could burn the houses and then blame it on Protestant parliamentarians. This was met with ridicule by those in the neighborhood in question, who, Catholics all and involved with the IRA, marveled at being suspected of plotting to burn their own houses.[16] And in a May 20 letter to the editor (*London Times*, 15), General Sir John Hackett obliterated Ireland as a geopolitical identity as he wondered, "When was Ireland in any real sense ever united, even before the cruel liquidation of native Catholic Irish in Ulster, its most recalcitrant kingdom, and their replacement by Protestant lowland Scots? . . . 'Ireland' has long been little more than a geographical expression, a name on what happens to be an island."

For his supporters, the symbiosis of Bobby Sands's body with the body politic expressed their struggle for Irish self-determination. For the British, Sands was a convicted felon whose body had no meaning beyond his individual person. To Republicans, he was struggling for the Irish right to self-organization. For the British, he relinquished that right when he engaged in criminal acts. To spare him amounted to legitimizing this claim and relinquishing the state's authority over his body as a convicted criminal. The rhetoric of Sands's hunger strike advanced a politics of absolutes: absolute helplessness, absolute power to spare another's life, absolute adherence to the law, nonnegotiable principles of political right, nonnegotiable principles of human rights, nonnegotiable principles of control. Passive aggression leaves no middle ground for compromise positions. It creates a victim and a victimizer and demands a moral choice. The best response for those in power is to unmask the victim as a threat to sovereignty so that his murder—both symbolic and literal, if necessary—may be justified.

Without compromise, the spectacle of Sands's self-consumption became a corporeal manifestation of his grievance. Regardless of what the British might say in response, Sands's body fixed the world's gaze on Britain's unyielding stance in the face of a clamor for civil accommodations. The swells of sentiment for the government to end the crisis reflected Britain's inability to silence Sands's emaciated and dying body or deflect its claim that its fate lay in British hands. Thus, as his body diminished, its rhetorical incarnation grew, touching the conscience of ever-enlarging circles of society and crossing national boundaries until its plea for justice became colossal. Sands's body had become a literal manifestation of the rhetorical topos of magnification; as words increased his wasting body's moral weight and enlarged its mass to span continents, its frail physical form metamorphosed into a mighty moral invocation that advanced his demands while questioning the legitimacy of masters unwilling to compromise.

Finally, as Bobby Sands's body sank into death, *Irish Times* (May 8, 1981, 1, 8) coverage constructed a narrative of his corporeal frailty conquering his physical master's domination by acquiring transcendent rhetorical life. In death, his body was claimed by the IRA and given a military funeral. Thousands of mourners were reported to line the three-mile route from the church to the graveyard, while thousands more paraded behind the cortege. His coffin was draped with the tricolors and a barrette and glove symbolic of a slain soldier. A piper playing an H-block song led the funeral procession:

> But I'll wear no convict's uniform
> Nor meekly serve my time
> That Britain may call Ireland's fight
> Eight hundred years of crime.

At one point the procession stopped while IRA soldiers in military dress fired three rifle volleys in salute. At the graveside, Owen Curron, Sands's election agent, eulogized him as "a hero in the struggle that will drive the British out of our country for once and for all." In death Sands's body survived with rhetorical robustness that drew life from words memorializing past grievances and that gave meaning and force to a cause of opposition. He was now the paradigm for the Republican cause. He had become a martyr; he had become immortal.

Passive Aggression and the Thick Moral Vernacular of Political Agency as a Human Right

Feldman has argued that the 1981 Hunger Strike, analyzed within the cognitive and symbolic systems of the paramilitary culture, "should be viewed as a political technology of the body connected to the paramilitary practice both inside and outside the prison. As such, the 1981 Hunger Strike must be analyzed within the general framework of the cultural construction of violence in Northern Ireland" (1991, 22). Using the body as a biopolitical counter to the violence of the state offers compelling insight into the political and rhetorical valences that make POC bodies their most powerful weapon against the overwhelming administrative and policing resources of the state. However, the hunger strike's efficacy lies in its invocation of conscience with a moral vernacular—an argument that expresses moral commitments, relations, and imperatives within the moral understanding and with a moral language indigenous to those most immediately addressed—that proscribes refusing to respond to the starving body. At the same time that it issues this proscription it sustains ambiguity between moral demands and political goals.

In the 1981 Hunger Strike, the link between starving bodies of the Long Kesh Provos and the IRA violence in the streets was blurred. The deeds for which they were in prison were undeniable, but the motivation behind them created an ambiguous criminal/political divide. Even among those voices outside the Sinn Fein and IRA community, the predominance of arguments that both condemned paramilitary violence and called on Prime Minister Thatcher to negotiate in order to save a life is remarkable: the pope, clergy of many denominations, U.S. senators, international humanitarian organizations, members of the European Parliament, internationally renowned leaders, and more made such appeals. The moral vernacular of Irish culture capacitating the hunger striker to confront the more powerful in a way that mitigates a power differential and makes it possible to settle a difference does not travel well. At the same time, the sight of a starving body voluntarily moving toward death speaks an international vernacular of the human right to agency and an understandable summons to interrogate those who seem impervious to the urgency of this body's corporeal state. The technology of the body has little efficacy without witnesses who can testify to the moral dimensions of what they have seen.

The body rhetoric at Maze prison indicates the way passive aggression can function as a rhetorical mechanism. The first decade of the Troubles had been played out through violence in the streets. The bodily sufficiency of nationalists was performed through violent acts of aggression against those who were either representative of or agents responsible for British enforcement of partitioning Ireland or were acts of retribution for violence committed against them. Bodily sufficiency was constituted by the IRA's capacity to impose and evade pain. Political status was an extension of this logic. POW status both confirmed IRA identity as waging a political war and allowed captive bodies to act in ways that granted bodily freedoms denied ordinary convicts. When special status was rescinded, their bodies were banished from the political realm to reappear under the depersonalizing regimes of the prison.

The blanket and dirty protests were acts of retaliation against their reduction to mere animality, to *homines sacri* banished from the political realm. More specifically, they were acts of passive aggression forcing a response from the power that banished them to bare life. The prison lost control of the prisoners' bodies as soon as they used their apparent helplessness as a means to violate the expectation that passivity would lead to compliance. The refusal to wear clothes or to use the washroom or to conform to norms of personal hygiene forced the prison off script. It forced the prison, which orchestrates prison actions calculated to maintain control, to act on the prisoners in unanticipated ways, to administer violence through forced public exposure by denying two towels, violating the interior of their bodies with mirror searches, imposing policies that forced the prisoners to live in their own filth, moving the prisoners to vacant wings where they were forcibly cleaned, and various forms of social interaction that performed the violence of subjecting their nakedness to their warders' gaze and jeers and their degraded bodily state to taunts.

The prisoners transformed their sheer animality into a performance of political agency through a reversed performance of vituperative rhetoric in which their warders were provoked to morally blameworthy acts. Their passivity exerted aggression by subjecting those who had them under control to the gaze of an unsympathetic audience. The ghastly display of prisoners living in their own filth was both riveting and invoked moral condemnation of those who seemed unsympathetic to their degrading conditions. The prisoners reversed the logic of control through performances of bodily insufficiency that were homologous with their defilement by the prison. The homology, in turn, became retaliation through body rhetoric that reversed sufficiency and insufficiency, agent and patient. The materiality of the dirty protest exceeded boundaries of sheer animality by moving resistance from the prison into the public realm where norms of civility hold sway. This represented a paradigm shift, as Feldmann (1991) has argued, for confronting the British. More generally, it suggests the inventive possibilities of the subjugated body to invent collective actions that, once publicized, become extremely potent rhetorical weapons.

Bodily sufficiency, by definition, includes structural relationship between the individual body and its environment and marks each both symbolically and rhetorically. This relationship is most commonly at play under social conditions, where the environmental relationship is with other bodies and the environmental concern of its rhetorical ecology is power. The attempted coercion of prisoners to correct deviant behavior appears to transgress the boundaries of rhetoric. Brutality is not an attempt to influence through persuasion; it seeks forced compliance. Torture is not rhetoric. At the same time, however, brutalized treatment of another human is an attempted, if misbegotten, performance of power,[17] an attempt to impose, maintain, or restore system rationally by a demonstrative display of control. It is called for by the absence or loss (real or threatened) of control. In the H-Blocks, the prison lost institutional control when the prisoners refused to abandon the blanket and dirty protests. Warders and prisoners were structurally joined such that they were always in relations of reciprocity, the materiality of their encounters—the spatiality of the prison, the visual appearance of the prisoner, the condition and treatment of prisoner bodies, and so forth—were always encounters over control of the prison performed through human constructions. They were, in that sense, performances with undetermined outcomes, each capable of exerting influence through its capacity to induce attitude and response and each open to interpretations and reactions beyond their respective control. Each was a rhetoric of its own materiality manifested in bodily performances of agency that were mutual refutations of the other's.

As in the case of the IRA prisoners in the H-Blocks, the passivity of insufficiency, when taken to the extreme of total withdrawal from an imposed regime of subjugation, can induce responses that reverse power and make passivity itself a mode of attack. However, it also requires an outside audience to publicize its mode of resistance before it can deny the sovereign's control. It relies on the affective response it invites from a public that, confronted with the radical alterity of the degraded and suffering body, insists civilized boundaries of bodily treatment be restored. At the same time, we must remember that when the prisoners embarked on the dirty protest, they had not anticipated it would continue for three years. The powerful rhetorical agency of passive aggression can unloose implications beyond the control of the subjugated body or its subjugator.

The gross differences in newspaper accounts of Sands's hunger strike are evidence that the ambiguity of the body in pain can be framed in dialectically opposing ways. Its multiple framings across the divided Anglo/Irish ideological spectrum gave it starkly different readings. Sands fully anticipated this, hence his explicit statements that he did not expect Thatcher to negotiate an end to the strike of her own volition and restore special status; he fully expected to die. However, he was counting on the negative reaction of the international community to an assembly line of "stiffs." And he was counting on that negative reaction not so much to pressure the Thatcher government to negotiate but that the assembly line of dead men would interrupt a British narrative of Irish identity. His bodily insufficiency would become rhetorical sufficiency.

The hunger strike was an antidote to the localization of the IRA prisoners as criminals. The prisoners used it as a rhetorical means for reasserting a political identity that transcended the particular place of a criminal act by resituating their bodies in the cultural space of a historical resistance movement. Each hunger strike makes a human rights appeal. It makes a thick moral vernacular statement about the human right to agency; it is an agential performance that sacrifices the last strong form of agency at its command in order to regain agential autonomy. In many instances, a hunger strike is undertaken to address specific issues confined by their temporality. For example, the hunger strikes at Robben Island were undertaken by the prisoners to deal with specific issues, such as the quality of food. At times it is undertaken for a specific period of time to make a political statement, such as Yelena Bonner's and Andrei Sakharov's hunger strike in the former USSR to protest denial of an exit visa to their daughter-in-law, Elizaveta Alekseyeva, to join her husband, Aleksei Semionov, in the United States. At times it is undertaken as a show of solidarity with others who are facing the extremes imposed by an authoritarian structure, such as those by the women in the Small Zone at the Barashevo prison camp who fasted whenever an ill member of their group was placed in solitary confinement.

The cultural role of the hunger strike for the Irish gives it a different status in that it uniquely connects the striker with Irish history and culture. The 1981 Hunger Strike was a historical interpolation, a material interruption of a British narrative of Irish identity that was physically, psychologically, geographically, and administratively present in the H-Blocks. Its evocation of Irish cultural history disrupted the force of a hegemonic account encoded in the prison by recasting the prison's codes as emblematic of the nation. Sands succeeded in dramatizing the relationship between conditions in the H-Blocks and the body politic through his body's metonymic representation of the condition of prison imposed on Republicans in Northern Ireland. Through the play of bodily sufficiency in insufficiency, replete with biological breakdowns, subversions of institutional regimes of visuality, temporality, and spatiality, the hunger strike interrupted the British narrative that held Northern Ireland as distinct from Ireland; it aborted the government's administrative time of a political arrangement with a temporal urgency that put biological time into the epochal frame of Irish historicity. The hunger strike took the conditions at Long Kesh situated *in time* and placed them in another frame that is always unfolding *through time*. It joined the specific issues of its place and time with the arc of Irish history and its aspiration for a unified nation.

7. *Display Rhetoric and the Fantasia of Demonstrative Displays*
The Dissident Rhetoric of Prisoner 885/63

T he prison memoir poses tricky rhetorical problems. The author's identity matters. Irina Ratushinskaya had a public identity as a poet, and her identity attracted sufficient public notice of her sentence and incarceration in Barashevo Prison camp that her treatment there could intrude on plans for the Reykjavik summit between Presidents Gorbachev of the USSR and Reagan of the United States. Nelson Mandela's international celebrity linked his sentence at Robben Island with continuing resistance to South Africa's policy of apartheid. Throughout his time in prison, from 1962 to 1990, his words were kept before the public, as various collections of his speeches, writings smuggled from prison, and posters announcing "Free Mandela" received international circulation. Authors such as these attract instant attention.

The accessibility of the prison memoir's narrative is significant. As time puts distance between the memoir and the events it records, the urgency of the prisoners' distress fades. Even the sturdiest accounts take on a new meaning with time. Bonhoeffer's *Letters and Papers from Prison*, first published in English in 1953, is still in print. It is of less interest today as an account of life in a Nazi prison than for his thoughtful reflections on theology, virtue, and leading a life in which conscience matters. Even Primo Levi's memoirs, which are still compelling for the insights they offer into the Nazi camps, are prized equally for their insights into the human condition.

The line between local and universal is not easy to negotiate. The importance of capturing the scene can make trials of life at a particular place diminish over time in their call to conscience due to their emphasis on locality. Universal themes that give us insight into the mind of oppression or, more difficult still, that make forgiveness possible, require uncommon vision. Mandela envisions a world of truth and reconciliation; the Soviet authorities remain untrustworthy and incorrigible in Ratushinskaya's account.

These qualifications notwithstanding, the prison memoir is first and foremost a rhetorical document. Its author is writing to the present, not to posterity, with the mission of practicing, in the words of Thomas Farrell, "the art, the fine and useful art, of making things matter" (2008, 470). Under its circumstances, negotiating the rhetorical problems of the genre requires trade-offs. The author, now freed from prison, has a calling, often mandated by those left behind bars, to spread the word about the struggle within the prison. Celebrity may not be available. The conditions in prison, moreover, often have an immediacy that places constraints on the memoir's level of reflection about universal themes, such as recognition and acknowledgment (Garlough 2008), forgiveness and reconciliation. Revolution usually is more single-minded in its call to replace the existing order.

At the same time, prison memoirs can bring us into a foreboding place where, in the darkness of its disregard for the human identity of its prisoners, we see responses that illumine the human capacity to affirm life. And they can engage readers in ways that, through their capacity to bring them into the world of the prison, which is to say into the local, call our conscience, even at a distance, to reject one world and affirm another on moral demands of the prisoners' humanity. When considering how those without power are able to engage in human rights rhetoric, writings such as these are an important source of insight into its thick moral vernacular. I want to return to Robben Island and a humble prisoner memoir, where these considerations define the horizon of its rhetorical project in search of the insights it can provide into the thick moral vernacular rhetoric practiced by prisoners of conscience (POCs).

As discussed in chapter 4, many factors accounted for Robben Island's prison reform from the inside. My endeavor here is to explore one facet that contributed to this success by initiating a changed consciousness within the prison of the political prisoners' identity: *demonstrative* aspects of political conscience in the political prisoners' *displays* of dissent. Display's rhetorical power has deep historical roots, with classical Greek and Roman rhetoricians providing conceptually rich discussions. In part, this is due to the ancient's emphasis on forensic oratory, which afforded ample opportunity and demand to bring the scene before the judge's eyes. There is a suggestive lead in Quintilian's *Institutio Oratoria* that links the rhetorical character of display to demonstration. The prison is an ironically potent rhetorical site in which resistance is enacted through performances of moral vernacular rhetoric, and the most potent of these vernacular resources is the political prisoner's body, which becomes the locus of a deadly biopolitical struggle with the state. Within prison, and to those observing from outside, displays of resistance function as a vernacular mode of epideictic in which "showing" may acquire the demonstrative power of "irrefutable proof." Such public performances interrogate power in a way that denaturalizes equations imposed by prison warders and induces in those who observe them, as it does in those who read about them, a fantasia, an imagined visualization, of political conscience. Their bodily resistance, in short, serves as an inventional locus. It frames the terms of affiliation through graphic displays that transform the political prisoner's identity into a POC and demonstrate political commitments that conscience beseeches its attending public not to abandon. The evidentiary basis for these considerations is Indres Naidoo's memoir of his incarceration as a political prisoner in South Africa's facility on Robben Island, *Island in Chains* (1982).

Demonstrative Rhetoric and the *Fantasia* of Display

In *Institutio Oratoria* (1958), Book VI, Quintilian takes up the topic of emotional appeals. In candor, he observes, a great many pleaders are capable at discovering arguments adequate to prove their points. While he does not "despise" such adequate arguments, he allows that their true function is to instruct pleaders of genuine eloquence in the facts of the case. The real work of the orator, and the place where a person earns distinction, is arousing the judges' emotions. Making strong proofs, he admits, will incline judges to think our case superior to our opponent's, but when we arouse their emotions, they will want it to be better. "And what they wish, they will also believe" (VI.ii.5).[1] By this line, Quintilian is led to conclude that emotions more than reason lie at the heart of eloquence. "For it is in its power over the emotions that the life and soul of oratory is to be found" (VI.ii.7).

In Quintilian's opinion, the first requirement for stirring emotions in others is to feel them personally. We cannot counterfeit grief, anger, or indignation. These and other emotions arise from a certain disposition evoked when we suffer events of personal magnitude and consequence. How else, he wonders, can we explain the eloquence of mourners expressing their grief or the fluency of an unlettered person stirred to anger? These are sincere expressions of feelings, and they are powerfully moving. Consequently, if we want to give our words the appearance of sincerity and move the judges to share them, we must first adapt ourselves to the emotional state of those whose emotions are genuinely felt.

We achieve this emotional simulacrum by a special experience, which the Greeks called φαντασιαι (fantasia). Fantasia occurs when we imagine the absent persons and events so vividly that we respond as if they were before our very eyes.

> Shall I not bring before my eyes all the circumstances which it is reasonable to imagine must have occurred in such a connexion? Shall I not see the assassin burst suddenly from his hiding-place, the victim tremble, cry for help, beg for mercy, or turn to run? Shall I not see the fatal blow delivered and the stricken body fall? Will not the blood, the deathly pallor, the groan of agony, the death-rattle, be indelibly impressed upon my mind? (VI.ii.31)

This remarkable passage, juxtaposed against the orthodoxy of legitimating public judgment through reasoned argument, resituates the force of rhetoric in emotions and our emotions in the undeniable evidence of what we see. And what do we see? Quintilian offers us a sensuous image of the embodied orator whose corporeal experience is authenticated by its individuated immediacy. It is authenticated by the orator's verbal display of the physical scene and by a response of strong emotions.

More than this, fantasia, as a state that stirs emotions likely to impel a person toward a certain outcome, relies on verbal display as a uniquely rhetorical mechanism to evoke its audience's expectations and beliefs. Display provides a structure for the rhetorical choices that are the concern of performing rhetoric: inventing appeals that constitute identity and agency while making something matter to others.

Effective rhetorical display requires the rhetor also be able to imagine the scene. Quintilian counsels that those who are most sensitive to these passing impressions of lush imaginative representation will achieve the state of ενεργεια (*enargeia*). In this state we seem not to narrate, he says, but to exhibit. Our words acquire the immediacy of an eyewitness whose emotions are so actively stirred as to leave the audience with an indelible impression. "For oratory fails of its full effect, and does not assert itself as it should, if its appeal is merely to the hearing, and if the judge merely feels that the facts on which he has to give his decision are being narrated to him, and not displayed in their living truth to the eyes of the mind." (VIII.ii.62)

Enargeia is the source of sincere emotional expression, which, Quintilian insists, the orator is duty bound to perform on behalf of his client whose interests are at stake.

The emotional state (*enargeia*) induced by witnessing the scene (*fantasia*) is complemented by the stylistic quality that captures the energetic action of the scene, or what the Greeks called ενεργεια (energeia). In Book VIII, Quintilian adds his voice to those of other leading Greek and Roman rhetoricians who held that energetic action "finds its peculiar function in securing that nothing that we say is tame" (VIII.iii.89). The audience experiences powerful feelings not just by being told what took place, but by seeing in its details actions in agreement with nature. For this reason, the orator must strive for stylistic qualities in his depiction of the scene that capture energy or vigor through action that an actual observer would witness. "Fix your eyes on nature and follow her," he advises. "All eloquence is concerned with the activities of life, while every man applies to himself what he hears from others, and the mind is always readiest to accept what it recognizes as true to nature" (VIII.111.71).

The Roman rhetorical handbooks, which join *verba* and *actio* as inseparable, were exquisitely sensitive to the fact that action requires engagement of situated deeds and that audiences become engaged by these deeds when they raise issues that touch their lives. Life-engaging decisions, such as those enacted in the law courts and the forum, necessarily involved emotions. While an audience convulsed with emotion would be a public menace, sound judgment on practical conduct requires an ability to experience the pleasures and agonies occasioned by public and private relationships. The classical tradition's rendition of rhetoric as an architectonic productive art couples emotional and rational engagement as tandem necessities for sound public judgment. Quintilian's reference to the orator's duty suggests he thought emotional engagement was essential for a judge to ponder proportion between acts and consequences so that prudence might prevail. He thought such engagement required verbal display.

Quintilian's concern with display emphasized in his discussion of emotional engagement was not confined to matters of style. Roman rhetoricians also accorded it paramount importance in their discussions of epideictic oratory, in which they captured display aspects of this genre when they changed its name from "epideictic" to "demonstrative." This switch, seemingly reliant on a different sense of display than in the passages above, ultimately returns to its energizing/actional features in a way that is both informative of display's rhetorical power (δύναμις *dunamis*) and bears on the evocative power of rhetorical displays by political prisoners.

Harry Caplan expresses the traditional interpretation of this shift from "epideictic" to "demonstrative" in his translation of *Rhetorica ad Herennium* (1964). In a note on epideictic, Caplan states: "The Greek term 'epideictic' did not primarily emphasize the speaker's virtuosity, nor was the Latin equivalent *demonstrativum* intended to imply logical demonstration. Whereas in both deliberative and judicial causes the speaker seeks to persuade his hearers to a course of action, in epideictic his primary purpose is by means of his art to impress his ideas upon them, without action as a goal" (note b, 172–73).

Even if the Romans did not mean to imply that demonstrative oratory was logical demonstration, Richard McKeon (1969, 37–92 passim) makes the important point that the transformation of Greek philosophical method into a rhetorical form was nonetheless a significant change of focus on what counted as proof. Caplan's point about not confusing the shift from "epideictic" to "demonstrative" with scientific demonstration is well taken, but it also reminds us that the Romans considered "display oratory" as a special mode of proof.[2]

A transformative spirit is at work in two additional and related aspects of Roman rhetoric relevant to this discussion: the primacy of the audience's criteria over the foundational ones of metaphysics or epistemology as the standards for judgment, and the relationship of performance to rhetorical invention. These tandem innovations are illustrated by Cicero's permutation of Greek philosophical categories, particularly Aristotle's, in his consideration of loci as an extension of Aristotle's topical theory.

Aristotle developed his theory of dialectical discourse, set forth primarily in his *Topica* and *Categories*, on an a priori system of first principles to which all possible meaningful statements had to conform (Stump 1978, 159–78). Cicero's appropriation of Aristotle's theory replaced its metaphysical foundations with the primacy of rhetorical experience. Cicero regarded rhetorical experience as culminating in the audience's determination of a claim's truth status based on whether it withstood the test of argumentation (Buckley 1970). His *Topica* transformed Aristotle's dialectical system of topoi into a rhetoricized system of loci suited to analyze the needs of practical affairs, or the conduct of public business that sought audience assent.[3]

By replacing metaphysical assumptions with the rhetorical act of gaining audience assent as the basis for knowledge and truth, Cicero captured the importance of loci for rhetorical invention in practical affairs and in philosophical systems. By this shift, Cicero also linked the inventional moment to enacted performance conducted in concert with the audience (*actio*), as well as to prior preparation.[4]

Cicero's emphasis on the primacy of the audience's judgment brings us back to Quintilian on emotions. The demonstrative speech was concerned with honor, a public virtue exhibited by deeds worthy of praise and emulation. Praise always pursues a double objective: to recognize the personal virtue of the extolled, which commands the honor that is their due, and to impart the civic lessons their lives exemplify to a public called upon to witness the honor being bestowed upon them (Hauser 1999a). The rhetor's challenge was to awaken the community's desire to live its public life in ways that endorsed the values for which the extolled stood, if not to emulate this person's exemplary qualities. The orator did not inspire admiration and emulation by *reasoning* about past deeds but by *exhibiting* them. The same means that Quintilian argued were necessary to make the judges *believe* were equally the rhetorical means deployed to *exhibit* public virtue and, thereby, to offer a rhetorical form of demonstration. But there is more.

Quintilian's account attributes the invention of the most powerful appeals to an internal state of *fantasia*. *Fantasia* operates equally as an audience's inventional prompt in discourse that relies on the mechanism of displaying honorable deeds to support claims of praise and offer instruction on how to live a virtuous public life. As Nicole Loraux's (1986) study of funeral orations shows, Athenians' understanding of their city was a rhetorical invention, a fantasy of the social imaginary constructed through the epideictic form. Depictions of deeds extolled and condemned move us beyond abstractions. They teach us how to live our lives by bringing the scene before our mind's eye; they make us witnesses in our imaginations to acts that require our affirmation or condemnation for them to live in collective memory as concrete realities. The community teaches its citizens that courage is a virtue through the rhetorically constructed fantasy of seeing brave deeds performed. Such displays demonstrate through their imagined showing both what we mean by bravery and that the honored citizen was brave. Our collective understanding of the praiseworthy deeds and their call for a common response is evoked by the fantasy of our collective seeing. By this simulacrum in the collective imaginary we also witness a demonstration of sorts that has the force of rhetorical certainty—a symbolically constituted reality.

The rhetorical inflection that moves demonstration from a claim of knowledge to one of understanding cuts across the grain of general scholarly usage. The academy's perspective is predisposed to understand "demonstration" as referring to mathematical, logical, or scientific arguments that purportedly prove conclusions to a level of certainty that defies reasoned refutation. The history of science and of logic is replete with exceptions to that view. To take a famous example, the Holy Office of the Inquisition's response to Galileo's *Dialogue*, printed in 1632, shows that the logical derivation of purportedly evident claims to knowledge can be challenged by changing the axioms on which demonstrations of the claims' truth must rest. Even among scientists, one scholar's demonstration has been grist for another's refutation. René Descartes, for example, writing in the same century as Galileo, used a geometric model of deductive reasoning to establish his philosophical system as a basis of certain knowledge and scientific method, only to have it refuted by the empiricists, most notably Sir Isaac Newton, who turned his system on its head to establish a new observational basis for scientific proof.[5] In either case, the linkage of "demonstration" with display of logical or observational grounds for "proving" displaced all association of the concept with *rhetorical* displays that called upon audiences to imagine and thereby witness actions that exhibited incontestable qualities of virtuous conduct that, in turn, bound them together in civic community.

The instability of demonstration as a concept and a reasoning practice is underscored further by the street rhetoric that became a staple for dissident displays of political disaffection during the twentieth century. Mesmerizing performances of pageants and spectacles, and displays of mass demonstration, so much a part of contemporary mass-mediated culture, are not unique to our time. The ubiquity of mass media representations has simply made us more conscious of, if not more critically reflective about, iconic representations and the vernacular rhetoric of street-level displays occurring beyond the halls of power. Such displays of political sentiment transform the ancient rhetorical practice of *exhibiting* communal values through *demonstrative oratory* to *political demonstrations* that carry the aura of *self-evidence*. The bridge from the Roman transformation of a rhetorical genre into a special mode of proving to political demonstrations in the street telescopes the long history of rhetorical performance based on the *fantasia* of "seeing is believing." As Graham Nash exhorted Americans through song during the tumult of the celebrated Chicago Seven trial, they could "change the world, rearrange the world" if they would simply "come to Chicago" (Nash 1970; see also McKeon 1969).

These performances, enacted as if they conveyed social truths, underscore important conclusions about demonstrative rhetoric and the *fantasia* of display that are relevant to the discourse and action of dissident rhetoric. First, the demonstrations of rhetorical performances parallel qualities inherent in the demonstrations of logical and scientific "proving." Both purportedly are grounded, as Quintilian noted, "in the nature of the object with which they are concerned." Both also induce commitment through "showing" or "exhibiting": the rhetorical demonstration exhibits in discourse or action virtuous or vicious qualities of conduct that invite communal recognition and judgment; in comparison, the logical demonstration exhibits all the proof's elements that, in turn, inescapably yield the conclusion, and the scientific demonstration exhibits the necessary procedural elements that, in turn, foster reliable observation. Finally, both also make claims that follow from purportedly irrefutable premises: rhetorical demonstrations possess an air of moral certainty that parallels the logical certainty inherent to proofs that work consistently from accepted premises to claims in accord with formal rules of reasoning, as well as the scientific certainty inherent in the presumption that whatever one is trained to observe and see is empirically real.

Second, rhetorical displays also demonstrate in one or both of two ways. Rhetorical performance can be enacted before an immediate audience with all the added persuasive power implied by the presumption that "seeing is believing." Often, however, rhetorical performances must be reenactments of actions or events that the audience did not immediately witness. In that case, rhetorical displays must marshal verbal and formal resources that induce the audience to undergo the *fantasia* of imagined seeing. The *fantasia* of visual presence to the action, in which the audience is brought into the emotional ambit of eyewitnesses, then carries the demonstrative force of self-evident, valid proving.

These considerations are especially relevant to dissident rhetoric. As numerous demonstrations protesting wars, denial of civil rights, policies contributing to degradation of the planet's ecology, and the like illustrate, displays of dissent arguably are as influential as official rhetoric in shaping public opinion, informing social judgment, and consolidating social will (Hauser 1999b). For these rhetorical performances to exercise influence, they must organize social knowledge within a dialectic between official authority and moral conviction that makes displays of values and aspirations, as well as their disparity with lived realities, appear self-evident. At the same time, the reality of power differentials also requires that rhetorical displays of dissidence serve as a wedge to open the possibility of negotiation with the adversary (Doxtader 2000). Within the prison, the political prisoner's need for the wedge of display not only calls upon the persuasive powers of demonstration to lodge dissent but also requires a distinctive type of rhetorical locus to generate rhetorical displays that can do so.

The Political Prisoner as a Locus of Political Conscience

In myriad ways political prisoners declare their oppositional identity through individual and collective displays of dissent, including overt confrontation between the individual and the overwhelming power of the state. Consequently, the prisoners become the site—the place—of biopolitical struggle, as they attempt to express their dissonant voices while the authorities use all available means to mute them. They are the particular place, as it were, where the contest occurs, and, as such, their sense of themselves as a material and relational manifestation of resistance precedes and creates the more abstract sense of space in which events occur. As a place, their resisting bodies also double as loci (sometimes their most potent loci) for inventing displays of conscience that otherwise would remain silent and concealed from view.

These displays, as the prisoners' writings themselves, are dialogical, creating tensions and relationships with their warders and readers. Their dialogue arises out of social circumstances in which displays of resistance typically and overtly interrogate and challenge—in Bakhtinean terms, dialogize[6]—the state's authority to police their bodies (Foucault 2008, 1–50). Often they do so less through the rhetoric of political manifesto than by recounting the biopolitical struggle over bare life that takes place between the POC and the authorities and warders within the prison. They indict the state through rhetorically constructed displays of its agents' ignorance, insensitivity, and disregard for basic human dignity, and by their own displays of an alternative political conscience. A central mode of this interrogation is the prisoner's use of the body as an inventional locus for enacting displays of conscience.

The particular case I want to examine in light of the foregoing is the memoir of Indres Naidoo recounting his prison experiences. Naidoo was one of the first volunteers for the armed wing of the African National Congress (ANC), *Umkhonto we Sizwe* (Spear of the Nation). He fell victim to a trap in which he was caught bombing a railroad signal box on the outskirts of Johannesburg. He was tried and convicted of sabotage in 1963 and sentenced to a ten-year term to be served at Robben Island.

After he completed his sentence, Naidoo was banned from further involvement in South African politics; he was under house arrest weekends and evenings and forbidden to have contact with ANC members or to make public statements regarding his imprisonment. Still he used word of mouth to spread information about conditions on Robben Island and the continued resistance of the political prisoners there. These stories linked ongoing events, such as the uprisings in Soweto, to the larger political movement that Robben Island's political prisoners were struggling to keep alive. He finally determined, however, that he had to leave South Africa in order to give greater publicity to the ANC cause and the resistance occurring on Robben Island. With the help of Albie Sachs, herself a noted dissident and prison writer banned from South Africa, Naidoo (1982) tells his story as prisoner 883/63 in his book *Island in Chains*.[7]

Naidoo's rhetorical burden was imposed by the leaders among the ANC prisoners, who charged released prisoners to publicize conditions at Robben Island so that others in South Africa and beyond would learn of its prevailing brutality and of the prisoners' continued resistance. He keeps faith with those still in the prison by providing a first-person account of his treatment. On the surface, the memoir seems reportorial, even anecdotal, by contrast to the writing of noted resistance leaders who faced the rhetorical challenge of explaining their movement's political agenda or of overtly confronting the state it opposed. Consequently, his memoir lacks Dietrich Bonhoeffer's (1967a) analytical incision, Martin Luther King Jr.'s (1963a) argumentative dexterity, Adam Michnick's (1985a) eye for political irony, Fleeta Drumgo's (1971) unrestrained political invective, Jacobo Timerman's (1981) skill at constructing an etiology of torture, Irina Ratushinskaya's (1989) dialogical facility, Nelson Mandela's (1994) political vision, Zhang Xianliang's eye for moral tension (1995), or Vaclav Havel's (1989) capacity to reflect on the deeper significance of his warders' ordinary acts of dehumanization.

If *Island in Chains* is not marked by closely reasoned argument, neither is it mere reportage. Its serial displays of confrontation between sadistic practices that deny human worth and resistance that affirms human dignity construct an emotionally evocative *presentiment* (see Sennett 1979, chapter 6). Naidoo brings his readers into the prison's world of moral and mortal political struggle during the decade from 1963 to 1973—a time of horrific treatment that the prisoners managed eventually to reverse by making them eyewitnesses to its concrete, phenomenological manifestations. Even seemingly quotidian episodes in which prisoners exchange contraband, hide and circulate newspapers, or seek medical assistance for ailing comrades become displays of resistance and assertions of self-worth. At its heart, however, stands the prisoner's body as a contested rhetorical locus that the prison authorities attempt to control and mute, and from which prisoners struggle to enact rhetorical displays of self-worth through defiant acts of civility and deception.

Prison and the Struggle for Rhetorical Place

The prison system arranges space and time in ways that suppress opportunities to enact rhetorical displays of political conscience. Naidoo's narrative captures this oppression through its episodic structure designed to immerse the reader in the POC's struggle with powerful obstacles to enacting political conscience.

The book is organized into three parts: the trip to the island; the island, which is itself divided into two phases of chains bound and chains loosened; and the trip from the island. The first and third parts are organized as coherent stories. The trip to the island tells of his crime and arrest, horrific treatment by the police, trial and conviction, and journey across South Africa to the penal facility on Robben Island. Each of its episodes bears narratival relationship to what preceded and follows. The trip from the island details his final appearance before the parole board, the conditions of his release, the boat trip from the island, and reunion with his family.

The island itself, which forms the center of the book and is the defining space for Naidoo's account of his time in prison, is organized differently. The book consists of a series of disconnected episodes. Each is self-contained, and, in most instances, its order of appearance could be altered without discernable consequence to the narratival integrity of the whole. There is no apparent plot that organizes episodes or informs characters. There is no sense of temporal progression with a past or future, or with a time frame that brackets episodes. Dates simply are not mentioned; calendar time is irrelevant. Its episodes are vignettes, illumining in themselves as stories of conflict with unreasonable authorities and ignorant warders, of repetitive and meaningless activity, and of small acts to sustain community among the damned. At the same time, these small acts that inform us about the political prisoners' daily realities acquire added meaning as they are fitted into an account of resistance. Each is a rhetorical act, an evocative expression of the prison's vernacular that appeals in ways other than the discourse of official forums but grasped and internalized by a people sympathetic to the individuation of each prisoner's pain. On their own each quotidian act might be regarded as a form of "gentle violence" (Bourdieu 1990, 127) in its insistence on solidarity from the other prisoners to resist the reign of terror inside the prison. Within the frame of bodies under assault, however, their *dunamis* is anything but gentle. Each encounter with the warders becomes a condensed expression of the national struggle, a synecdoche that, by concentrating a people's struggle in the besieged prisoner's body, releases uncommonly energetic action (*energeia*).

Naidoo's account exhibits the depersonalizing modes of treatment by Robben Island's warders and equally how the resisting bodies of Robben Island's prisoners reframe their warders' behavior. For those who had been leaders in the struggle, vulnerability was a central concern. Writing of vulnerability to those who have power over them, Judith Butler observes, "We cannot, however, will away this vulnerability. We must attend to it, even abide by it, as we begin to think about what politics might be implied by staying with the thought of corporeal vulnerability itself, a situation in which we can be vanquished or lose to others" (2004, 29).

Against the prison's overwhelming biopower, the prisoners' bodies became a corporeal means for inverting power vectors within the prison. In circumstances that precluded debating political ideals, their physical treatment became an extension of the dialectic between the political prisoners and a racist regime's fantasy of mastery. Their political identity framed their bodies as *bios*, so that each physical interaction became to some measure a statement of an alternative vision of the body politic. Their resisting bodies were, in this sense, a rhetorical locus from which to assert their personhood in the face of dehumanizing and depersonalizing treatment. Each mistreatment intended as a display of the prison's power could be read as a self-indictment of its own venality, preying on captive bodies to sustain its own state of *fantasia*. We should linger a moment on the first part of Naidoo's story, then, because it alerts us to the commitments of the Afrikaner state that led to a regime of terror inside the prison. It also marks the start of Naidoo's journey from a political prisoner fearful for his life to a POC determined to resist his oppressors.

The interrogation. Naidoo's account of his arrest and interrogation is a horrific and graphic display of physical and psychological torture that begins with his being taken into custody (15–26). The police had been informed of the attempted midnight sabotage of a railroad signal box and captured Naidoo and two compatriots in the act of committing their crime. Naidoo was shot attempting to flee, but this did not stop the police from striking him with their rifle butts. After receiving medical attention to remove the bullet, the doctor ordered that he be hospitalized, but the police refused. Instead, they took him to the interrogation center. He recounts hearing his comrades' screams of agony and cries for mercy as he waited to be questioned. As they emerge from the interrogation room with faces disfigured beyond recognition, he is fixated with heightened dread, knowing he will be next.

He remembers being led into the interrogation room, where he counted twelve to fifteen police officers. Naidoo and his accomplices had concluded that Gammat Jardien—the person who had trained them, suggested the target, and supplied the dynamite—had laid their trap. When the interrogator asks who was in charge of the operation, he gives them Jardien. He describes how the police fall on him, punching and kicking until he cries with pain. When asked if he is going to make a statement, he keeps repeating, "Ask Jardien, he knows everything."

People come and go. Naidoo loses track of who is in the room. The torture continues, but, to assure the reader that these were not rogue cops, he notes that the authorities in charge knew what was going on. Since they did not put a stop to it, apparently they approved.

Next a wet canvas bag is placed over his head, and his tormentors started squeezing its knot and choking him.[8] "I gasped for air, and every time I breathed in, the canvas hit me in the face. I was choking, my nostrils and mouth were blocked by the wet canvas; the harder I tried to get air into my lungs, the tighter the bag clamped over me, cutting off the air, preventing my lungs from working." The police laugh and tell him that today he is going to die. He recalls struggling and thrashing on the verge of unconsciousness from suffocation. There is more police laughter. "The bag was released and I swallowed air desperately, but then the canvas slapped into my mouth and once more I started to choke, my body in a total panic." After nearly suffocating him, they remove his shoes and beat the soles of his feet with a rubber baton. He loses sense of time in the shock waves screaming up his legs. Then they pin him down and attach wires to his body. He recalls seeing the wires leading from his body to a dry-cell battery, the wires being attached, "and as they attached the lead to the battery I felt a dreadful shock pass into my body. My whole being seemed to be in shock—I learned afterwards that it was only for a few seconds, but at the time it seemed like five or ten minutes." All the while he screams, "It's Gammat Jardien. . . . Ask Gammat Jardien. Gammat Jardien knows everything." But the shock torture continues, convulsing every particle of his body. "I kept on screaming to them, begging, pleading with them to stop, but the more I cried the more they went on applying the shocks."

Finally, the torture ends. As an exercise of power, torture has value only if it produces a confession that serves a larger political purpose. Killing Naidoo without securing his betrayal of the African National Congress (ANC) movement would turn him into a martyr. It also would expose the cause of his death to public scrutiny in the wider courts of opinion and the judiciary. Having failed to crack his body, Naidoo tells us they went to work on his mind.

He says the police tell him the others have given a full statement, his comrades have sold him out, he is a fool to resist. Then Lt. Steenkamp, head of the Natal Security Branch, interrogates him and offers Naidoo a deal for his cooperation:

> "Listen, man," he said confidently, "we can get you off if you cooperate; you know the maximum penalty for sabotage is death, and the prosecution will ask for the death sentence in this case—you were caught red-handed. I'm a personal friend of Balthazar, I play golf with him every Wednesday"—he was referring to Vorster [then head of the prison system]—"We can send you anywhere in

the country, give you money, buy you a car, buy you a house—you're a young man, twenty-six, you've still got a long way to go; we can send you out of the country, we have many friends overseas. What do you say?"

Without overtly depicting his effort as heroic or his body as politically inscribed, Naidoo's account of his arrest and interrogation brings his reader to a very dark place in the human psyche. He makes us witnesses to willing acts of dehumanization that are self-incriminations of the regime's moral ecology while simultaneously under-scoring his manifest threat to the Afrikaner order, to its way of life, to its power. Meanwhile, Naidoo does not present himself as posing a threat but as a victim of monstrously cruel acts who is struggling for survival. Since we are not told whether he knew more than the identity of his betrayer, we have only his palpable, consum-ing terror in the face of his torment by which to judge his responses. His ordeal reminds us not be judgmental of those who surrender. In Tzvetan Todorov's words, "each victim stands alone and thus powerless before an infinitely superior force" (1996, 130). It also italicizes the prisoner's body as a contested site and source of political meaning with implications for the rhetoric of display.

Since his body is no longer under his own control, the torture inscribes his person as more than embodied; it is a *public place*: a contested place, a biopolitical place, with multilocalities (the location of his body is many different places at the same time) and multivocalities (in each place we may hear many different voices) of empowerment and disempowerment—of the state, the police, the ANC, *Umkhonto we Sizwe*, South Africa, and Naidoo himself. Its concreteness as a place opens his embodied person to interpretation as a rhetorical construction. More important for Naidoo's story, these ontological conditions of place provide an enriched sense of his embodied person as a rhetorical place, a locus of inventional possibility.

Naidoo's account of his physical and psychological torture thus prefigures Robben Island and the larger struggle in which he is engaged: the dialectic of the state's raw power pitted against the frailties of the individual prisoner. This dialectic is particu-larized in the spatialization of the prison as an institution and in the body of the political prisoner. His opening depiction of himself as defenseless, isolated, outnum-bered, and overwhelmed leaves us without a strong sense of him as a challenger of the Afrikaner regime. We wonder how he will be able to survive what lies ahead and remain true to his political convictions. Immediately after his sentencing our ques-tion is answered, as he joins the struggle for his body as the place of battle and a locus for political conscience.

The Trip to Robben Island

The brutal conditions of South Africa's prisons made them a regime of kairotic moments to display white supremacy and conscious choice. Each opened the possi-bility of decisive change for both the prisoners and the prison. Each concrete episode, complete unto itself, was a revelation of the warders' menace and the prisoners' resistance. The meaning of resistance did not come from publicists outside the prison—there was little opportunity to reach the outside[9]—but from bodily expressions of conscious commitments performed before other prisoners and the guards themselves.

Upon arrival at their first installation on the way to Robben Island, a prison outside Johannesburg called the Fort, Naidoo details how the prisoners were marched into the prison yard and ordered to strip. The guards mocked their naked bodies; prodded them with their batons; flicked their straps in the prisoners' faces, coming as close to their eyes as possible; and hurled racial insults at them. They were then given the command "*Tausa!*" ("Dance!"). The guards were ordering the naked prisoner to leap in the air and spin while opening his legs and clapping his hands overhead. He was to land making a clicking sound with his mouth, legs apart and body bent forward to expose an open rectum to the warder's inspection (Naidoo, 31).[10] Naidoo recounts this initiating moment as a line the political prisoners were unwilling to cross.

The prisoner performing the "tausa" became an obligatory participant in his own ritualized humiliation, enacted in public before affirming witnesses who saw it as an assertion of their superiority. The "tausa" also was an inventional place for demonstrative performance of honor and dishonor, which the prisoners seized when they refused the command. The seriousness of resisting bodies as a locus for enacting political conscience became apparent when the guards then escalated the prisoners' act of conscience into a carnival chase.

> The white warders moved away, leaving us to the mercy of the black warders, saying that we were the ones who had tried to blow up a train of black workers. *Kierekops* (sticks with heavy round knots at the top) flashed around us as the black warders chased us from one part of the yard to the other, threatening to beat the life out of us. We just ran and ran, exhausted and humiliated, knowing that our sentence had just begun. (31)

The humiliation of the first day was repeated in countless ways as the prisoners were moved across the country on their journey to Robben Island. Naidoo recounts how the authorities gave them ripped clothes that did not fit, put them into frigid cells without sufficient blankets to retain body heat, shaved their heads, insulted them, poked them with their batons and tripped them as they ran during periods of forced exercise, served meager portions of inedible and unnourishing food or denied them food out of caprice, subjected them to physically exhausting labor and beat them when they showed signs of fatigue, and each afternoon upon returning to the prison yard from their work detail subjected them to a strip search:

> We were running naked, our clothes in our arms: a thousand of us streaming across a yard to place the clothes in a pigeon-hole, then racing, the cold air beating against our skins, to a door containing a metal detector, leaping

through the doorway one after the other, and then grabbing the first set of clothes we saw in a pigeon-hole on the other side, irrespective of who had worn it the previous day, dressing as we ran, ducking blows and hearing insults as we sped towards the kitchen, grabbing a plate of food from prisoners handing out the evening meal—worried that if we missed we would go without food. (45)

Naidoo's story continues episodically without any apparent organizing plot. In the penal system's lifeworld, it seems, there are only experiences. Each experience, however, contains competing displays of energizing action: the warders using the spectacle of overt violence to control the prisoners' bodies as a demonstration of white supremacy; the prisoners responding with the gentle violence of mundane acts of resistance as a demonstration of their human dignity. The journey to Robben Island fades as Naidoo's organizing device, as the *energeia* of the prisoners' experiences is translated into the *fantasia* of apartheid in the prison system's cyclorama of visual displays. Naidoo's account brings his suffering before our eyes, brings us to a state of *enargeia* that an eyewitness to torture might experience. We witness encounters that demonstrate how the ideology of white supremacy controls the penal system's attack on the prisoners' human dignity, how it reduces them to bare life and a proof of the state's sovereignty. The penal system's logic, in which space is constricted to maximize control and temporal progression is replaced by episodic moments of humiliation, does not beckon heroic deeds; it dictates calculating each act for its survival value.

Rhetorical Display and the Timely Enactment of Political Conscience

Finally Naidoo reaches Robben Island. He tells us that upon arrival the new prisoners were taken to the yard where they were forced to stand spread-eagle while the white warders subjected them to a humiliating hand frisk. The prisoners' objectification contined when the guards insisted they be addressed only in Afrikaans. Insisting on Afrikaans was part of the mortification process to strip the prisoner of his sense of self. The language divide between warder and prisoner marked the initiate prisoner as lacking an essential human capacity to communicate. When Naidoo addressed a young guard in English, protesting he did not speak Afrikaans, the guard ridiculed his use of English (which the guard could not speak). Mocking treatment of the initiate's English further marked him as a barbarian, not a person. When Naidoo continued to correct the guard for referring to the prisoners as "coolies" while referring to him as "Sir," the head warden was called to set Naidoo straight: "If you know what's fucking good for you [said the head warden], you will learn to speak Afrikaans bloody fast. Most of my warders don't speak English and what's more you must remember to address them as *Baas*. There's no 'Sir' on the Island, only '*Baas*'" (66).

The warders' insistence on being called Baas (boss) was particularly demeaning because it inscribed the prisoner as a slave subject to the power of his masters. If the depersonalized prisoner was only a slave, then what was to prevent his masters from treating him as an animal?

Naidoo's resistance to his treatment was performed initially in the politics of language—refusing to code switch,[11] the substitution of formal address ("Sir" for "Baas"), the use of civil language in contrast to the guards' crudeness, his respectful talk as a counter to the warders' deliberate attempts at humiliation are remarkable performances of resistance to violence. The imperative to break political prisoners seeks fulfillment in resignation, subservience, or unmitigated terror at the consequences, in the case of Robben Island, for not acknowledging white supremacy.[12] Grief and melancholy would seem to be more likely emotions under the circumstances. The contrast between civility in the face of intimidation was a show of self-possession that the politicals treated as a mandate for survival on Robben Island. For Naidoo's readers outside the Afrikaner's lifeworld, whom he says are his primary audience, he displays linguistic skill that, by its civility, confounds the biopolitics of managing his body. For readers, it reverses positions of power by redefining it. Although they have custody of his body, he retains his dignity by disclosing the limited horizon of his guards and demonstrating a conscience that insisted on being treated as a human being.

There is power of another sort present in this exchange, the power of gentle violence to transform overt violence. Repeated acts of civility toward the guards were a strategy to transform the riot of Robben Island Prison into a facility that respected the humanity of the prisoners. As a first step toward this transformation, the ANC prisoners insisted on maintaining civility in their forms of address and response to the guards and insisted, insofar as possible, that the guards do the same. Initially, polite speech may have been received as antagonistic, but over time its interrogation of the guards' limited horizons, it was hoped, would calm their lust for inflicting pain.

After recounting this initiating exchange, the next day finds Naidoo commencing his sentence of forced labor at the lime quarry. He was to spend the next ten years of his life in the meaningless activity of crushing rocks. He recounts more beatings, more strip searches, the stench and mess of overflowing slop pots that make every confining moment in their cells a debasing misery, systematic degradation such as a prisoner buried up to his neck in the scorching sun for complaining about the extremity of that day's labor and later having his warder urinate on his face while taunting his thirst,[13] medical neglect, refusal to acknowledge any communication not expressed in Afrikaans, and unrelenting insults to bodies wracked with psychological and physical pain.

Naidoo's relentless display of the prison quotidian defines torture and terror through vignettes featuring language, oppressive work conditions, unreasonable orders, unnourishing food, physical and psychological abuse, and more, magnified by the conditions of repetition and idleness that, at the same time, fuel the counter chronotope of resistance. As time condenses to fit the confined and confining space of Robben Island, days, months, years flow together with no temporal referent beyond the vignettes themselves. Each brings out the pointless cruelty of a world constructed to discipline and punish bodies that were neither difficult to handle nor overtly challenging the prison's authority.

Naidoo's account also displays a different organizational principle than the panoptic chronotope of discipline and punish. Public spaces dominated by a regime that enforces its rule by armed guards are ill-suited to deliberation over prevailing conditions. As James Scott (1990) argues, under these conditions the subjugated use the hidden transcript of resistance constructed offstage to counter the public transcript recording who is in charge and the rules in play. In prison, where the idleness of prison time intensifies small things, clandestine conversations, private expressions of resentment, pilfering, sharing contraband, disseminating information, violating small rules, songs of identity and protest, speaking in one's native tongue, and so forth, find their place—their inventional loci—in the larger context of political objectives. Every day on Robben Island provided its kairotic moments to exert the responding gentle violence of such mundane resistance. On a daily basis, conduct in the prison's public places may have been guided by the wisdom of public deference to those whose treatment you loathed; however, the cumulative indignities suffered in silence and recorded in the hidden transcript deepened commitments of resistance. Eventually they would surface as a display of political agency.

Through a miscellany of such episodes, *Island in Chains* constructs Naidoo as a specific person for his readers. He is not particularly heroic, but a fundamentally decent man. He has the ordinary virtues of caring for the pain of others, bravery in the face of attempts to humiliate him, and friendship toward the other prisoners. He has engaging thoughts, feelings, values, and political convictions. His organizing principle is not the prison but his own body. True, Robben Island is the site where his prison experiences occur. However, the experiences themselves are developed through displays of physical and psychological resistance. In a world in which warders respond to arguments with logical absurdities, his body becomes his most effective means for making statements and counterstatements that cannot be ignored. Consequently, when his body resists the injustices of his warders, it is not merely bodily display that we witness. This is a person known to us; his identity is fused with his political values. This fusion gives his body uncommon inventional power built through a *fantasia* of political conscience.

Fantasia and the Performance of Dignity

Naidoo's writing is doubly inscribed, reporting the episodes to which prisoners and prison personnel actually present were witness and presenting these scenes to us as readers. The treatment of prisoners is never fully visual in the sense of being open to documentation and sight. This is especially true of political prisoners, whose treatment often is fabricated in prison documents that deny their complaints or forge accounts of their treatment and that control the perceptions of external observers by steering them from the arenas of harsh treatment. Naidoo's account brings us into this world in a way that we might read as a report of what took place. It also brings the scene before our eyes in a way that invents Robben Island as a locale of incarceration and as a domain of conflict between political ideals. The *fantasia* of presence is most pronounced at moments in which the prison's capacity for cruelty overwhelm the rhetorical power of gentle violence to offer the POCs protection, including moments of political spectacle.

Perhaps the most poignant of these, and illustrative of this double inscription, is Naidoo's response to being publicly whipped (120–26). He tells us the prisoners had been ordered to enter barefoot a stagnant pool of water polluted with slime and dead seagulls and whose bottom consisted of jagged stone. Naidoo refused and, at his hearing, defended his action with a reasoned argument based on the necessary conditions for an order to be valid. He was told his reason had no place in Robben Island's world. His only course was to follow orders blindly, and he was found guilty of insubordination. His punishment was to receive four lashes with a bamboo cane.

Whippings were ritualized events at Robben Island. They took place in the hospital courtyard every Tuesday and Thursday. Naidoo's account offers a moving visualization of his ordeal and demonstration of political conscience. He tells us that as he was brought into the courtyard he noticed the warder who was to whip him holding a six-foot-long bamboo cane, the hospital physician, three or four prison officials, and twenty or thirty guards. "I heard the burly chief warder saying . . . that he was going to kill me that day, and that I would have scars for the rest of my life. He kept boasting about how efficient he was . . . and the other warders egged him on, almost hysterical with excitement." He tells us he was stripped naked and strapped to a wooden frame called the "whipping Mary." His buttocks were framed by strips of foam rubber secured to his lower back and thighs.

> I heard the whistle of the cane. Next moment it felt as though a sharp knife had cut across my backside. There was no pain immediately but suddenly, my whole body felt as though it had been given an electric shock. I grabbed hold of the Mary with both hands and clung tightly to it.
>
> The chief warder commented sarcastically, "*Oj, die koolie wil nie huil nie—* the coolie doesn't want to cry," and all the warders joined in the chorus.

The next two strokes missed their mark, but the final one hit the same spot as the first. "The stroke was so painful that after it I could hardly see in front of me. I was dazed and strange shapes appeared in front of my eyes. I grabbed hold of the Mary and hung on to it as I tried to regain control of myself." Naidoo did not speak or groan. He was untied and told to return to his cell. His pain was so great he could not put on his pants and held his shirt up so its tail would not brush against his wound. He moved unsteadily across the yard to his cell, determined not to show signs of weakening. As he entered his cell, he noticed "for some reason or other, the prisoners had not been sent out to work that day. As I staggered inside there was absolute silence and the prisoners waited for me to say something. Then, in the midst of my comrades, with no warders around to see, I collapsed."

Naidoo's whipping was intended to inflict humiliation through a performance of mortification before his peers. Had he cried like a wounded animal, it would be a sign he had succumbed to pain and a statement to the other prisoners that, in breaking him, their warders had once more asserted their superiority. His public caning was intended as one more proof that he and they were objects in the lifeworld of apartheid and the prisoners' status as among the banished. In addition, this also was a display of mortification before an assembly of prison guards; it was intended to reinforce the social order.

Such displays also risk defeat, should the intended victim somehow prevail. The sovereign's willingness to banish the *homo sacer* but not sacrifice him or her is calculated to avoid creating a martyr, since the martyr represents a threat to sovereignty. The intended victim undermines the sovereign's identity through an act of resistance that asserts a thick moral vernacular of his or her individuation as a human and his or her human right to be treated with dignity. The public display of Naidoo's mortification violates the edict against sacrificing the *homo sacer*. By not succumbing, Naidoo gained the momentary victory of silencing his warders and of seizing an opportunity for solidarity of conscience among the other political prisoners. The guards may have wanted the prisoners to see him break, but the prisoners most assuredly did not. In fulfilling the other prisoners' desires, is it not conceivable the *energeia* of his silence defied victimage, acquired an alternative symbolic value of a thick moral vernacular that moved the prisoners to believe they also might prevail?

At the same time, the *enargeia* of Naidoo's visualization of his corporeal political performance constitutes the *fantasia* of presence to a demonstration of the principle at stake. It is one thing to invent arguments against a political system and a representation of civil society that might replace it, and another to arouse an emotional response that brings an audience to both condemn one practice and endorse another. Similarly, it is one thing to arouse emotional responses to actions by portraying them in a scene brought before the audience and another to arouse emotional responses to principles by bringing them before a reader's eyes. The latter requires a fusion of language and idea in a way that is iconic, as occurs with Naidoo's bodily performance that is decidedly not stripped of individuating human qualities, but a participant in the *bios politikos* of apartheid's biopolitics. His body functions as a rhetorical place, a heuristic for inventing resistance now manifested as rhetorical display through his bodily performance of resistance.

Naidoo's embodied resistance provides his readers with material evidence that displays of warder violence had ceased to be the defining vernacular of Robben Island. His body was a metonym for a power struggle over the terms of engagement between the guards and political prisoners. The prisoners' resistance was more than bodies fighting back to protect themselves; it was an act of conscience performed out of a fidelitous commitment to the inviolability of their human dignity.

The demonstrative force of Naidoo's bodily display during the whipping funsctions as a material analog to reasoned argument. It is a proof laced with Hegelian irony. Naidoo's broken body ruptures the prison's surface of brutal authority. Silencing the chorus of jeering guards demonstrates the moral superiority of his brokenness to a penal order based on brute force and renders his bodily display of self-possession an act of war. His silent assertion of human dignity is an aggression of spirit that reframes internal affairs between these prisoners and their warders as a power struggle in which the prisoners are not lacking resources.

Reading such deep consequences into Naidoo's refusal to break during the public caning is warranted by his narrative, which continues to develop a story of prisoner solidarity that leads to victories, however ephemeral, in the prisoners' struggle to realign the power vectors within the prison. It also suggests the need to revise my earlier characterization of *Island in Chains* as apparently lacking plot. Examining Naidoo's memoir in terms of its display rhetoric as a *fantasia* of political conscience discloses how its seemingly disjointed episodic structure and potpourri of dramatic moments and mundane acts are unified by the underlying manifestation of the power struggle at Robben Island. It defined the prison experience as advancing the ANC's cause to overthrow apartheid and establish South African democracy on the trajectory of recognition and acknowledgment; of not only grasping the humaneness of people of color but also expressing care for how they were treated (see Garlough 2007).

As the memoir continues, we note prisoner solidarity in a hunger strike that achieved concessions from the prison authorities, warders' gradually lessening of racial slurs and increased address by name, and warders speaking to prisoners in English and in some cases engaging in lengthy conversations. We also learn that the prison department agreed to permit them to study and that the prisoners, many of whom were well educated, acted as tutors to guards who were struggling to pass their own college courses. We learn of improved medical treatment, of access to outside observers from the International Committee of the Red Cross (ICRC) and the South African parliament to discuss conditions in the prison, of the formation of cultural clubs and activities that are either approved or permitted if not officially sanctioned. We learn of the formation of a soccer league and mini-Olympics that were organized and administered by the political prisoners. Finally, we learn of Naidoo's high esteem among the prisoners, as reflected in his numerous leadership positions. In short, the prisoners' spatialization of political conscience constructed an alternative political reality to the official chronotope of South Africa's penal system, projecting a multiracial civil society that was the antithesis of apartheid.

The visual possibilities of Naidoo's narrative, then, go beyond metaphoric reasoning, which portrays apparent differences as assimilated into a unity, and irony, which portrays apparent unities as distanced from one another. It situates us in a story through the point of view of his voice, which, not incidentally, transports us to the scene through his bodily experiences. They have taken us from his paralysis with fear over survival during the torture of his initial police interrogation to acts of political resistance that seek realignment of power within the prison. The *as if* quality of what we see is not just Naidoo's body in pain, but a body fused with a political cause; what it does and what it suffers are iconic with the very principles for which it stands. If we *hold as true* what as readers we imagine *as if* present from Naidoo's point of view, we have experienced the state of belief Quintilian situated at the heart of eloquence. If we respond to his body in pain with the belief we would accord an eloquent demonstration, *as if* to a fusion of suffering and truth, it is the result of the emotional state of *fantasia*. *Island in Chains* has brought us to this state through the rhetorical mechanism of display to guide and structure rhetorical inventions that constitute the "hallucination of presence" (Ricoeur 1990, 186). The *enargeia* of his memoir moves us beyond responding *as if* to a narrated story and to a state where we now respond *as if* present to its scene and participating in it.

Display Rhetoric, *Fantasia*, and the Thick Moral Vernacular Rhetoric of a Civil Society

Note, then, the demonstrative possibilities inherent to display rhetoric: how the *enargeia* of display rhetoric can engage our emotions *as if* we were witnessing the scene, how the *fantasia* of witnessing can be so powerful as to induce a sense of certainty that compels assent, how bodily display can function as an inventional place or locus while simultaneously serving as a place of political contest, and how narratives of embodied performances of subjugation and resistance can acquire demonstrative force. These considerations have been particularized in demonstrations of political conscience performed through bodily displays by Robben Island Prison's political prisoners who contested the prison's disciplining of their bodies with their own bodily resistance.

My argument has recognized that the public arena of the prison yard is not an agora. In the agora, the public nature of community truths requires they be spoken. Politics requires that public realities be seen and heard; it cannot be practiced as a private monologue about personal convictions. Political prisoners, on the other hand, are denied voice. Without open political congress, POCs must find alternative means to occupy a public arena in which to contest the way things are. Their resistance publicizes otherwise internal realities.

POCs, by definition, behave as public persons. Consequently, even public spaces constructed to serve as sites of humiliation and capitulation become opportunities to display commitments of conscience through the energetic actions of imprisoned bodies and the correlative *enargeia* of narratives alive with verbal displays. These displays constitute a thick moral vernacular of resistance and human rights. Whereas the prisoner in prison time leaves the faint trace of a record–offense, sentence, time and place served, official actions—the POC leaves abundant traces in the minds of prisoners, if witnessed and represented, and with an external public, if published, through the thick moral vernacular of acts that interrogate the biopolitics of the prison and can influence the minds and actions of witnesses. Their bodies speak the common language of defiance, and their defiance creates dialogizing friction between assertions of personal identity and the depersonalizing system logic of the prison. This friction, in turn, can be explained by the *fantasia* of presence that constitutes the identity and agency of their political conscience through the inventional character of bodily performance.

Given the urgency of the prisoners' personal and political situation, I have argued that displays of bodily resistance are often the only but also the most effective means for inventing displays of conscience. They open a negotiation of sorts—with enemies, other prisoners, and possibly an external public—that counters the sentence's arbitrary boundaries of space and time, and the muteness it enforces, with the concrete place and time of their embodied political conscience. Within this negotiation, the evocative power of the prisoner's body can reach beyond immediate witnesses to distant readers by bringing the prisoner's dialogue with terror before their eyes. Presenting this confrontation with *enargeia*-inducing displays offers a form of argument that is difficult to refute.

Dorrinda Outram, writing of the French Revolution, argues that bodies contesting the rights of the aristocracy "possessed the power, which the competing linguistic discourses obviously did not, to focus dignity and legitimacy in incontestable, because nonverbal, ways on the bodies of known individuals who acted as personifications of value systems" (1989, 4). Similarly, for sympathetic viewers and readers, bodily displays by political prisoners function demonstratively as irrefutable proof of the existing order's moral culpability. Even allowing that many of these prisoners had committed illegal and possibly life-threatening acts, the reader still is confronted with a basic moral question about limits to disciplining the body of another human and responses to defiance. The *fantasia* of manhandling compels the conclusion that these limits have been transgressed.

Depictions of the body in pain are, in the larger scope of ongoing political struggle, inventional loci. For the prison writer who has not been lionized, his rhetorical problem often is to dissociate his person from a perception of his deeds as criminal so that he can emphasize his identity as a prisoner with political status. Naidoo addressed this problem in an instructive way. Through episodic engagements that invented a political ethos, he dissociated his person from a perception of his deeds as criminal so that he could emphasize his political identity. This invented image, constructed through verbal displays of his engagements with oppression, engulfed the state's best efforts at framing and organizing the meaning of his incarcerations in criminal terms. At the center of his story was the place of his body, whose struggles served to strengthen an already formed dissident character while indicting the habitude of the regime he opposed and that held him prisoner for acting on his beliefs. Bringing these displays before our eyes offered a *fantasia* of terror and resistance. It also evoked a further *fantasia* of civil society born of the contrast between an Afrikaner regime that constructed political prisoners as animals to be dominated by cruelty and the prisoners' ongoing acts of refusal aimed at creating a space for negotiating conditions in the prison.

ANC leader and former Robben Island prisoner Neville Alexander has written, "What happens in a prison is a reflection of what happens in the surrounding society" (1994, 50). The prisoners in Robben Island organized themselves as a sub-rosa civil society in which they conducted serious negotiations among the leadership of the various factions in the struggle for what the future society would look like, and they provided continuing education to the inmates in the political skills necessary to bring about political reform. The rhetorical character of a prison memoir can bring this struggle and its attendant political vision to society outside the prison. If we read the manhandling of political prisoners as indicative of a society with flagrant disregard for the human dignity of those who advance alternatives to the ruling social vision, surely Naidoo's memoir of his embodied experience serves as an antidote inventing an alternative vision of civil(ized) society for readers on the outside in South Africa beyond.

The contrasting images of society projected in his account of the prison's disciplining of politicized bodies and the prisoners' bodily displays of resistance exhibit the recurring irony of the rhetorical domain occupied by POCs. Symbolic resources in this domain are inherently entwined with witnessed, represented, and discussed dissident bodies, transforming their apparent subjugation into (sometimes) potent rhetorical weapons against the powers that control them. For readers engulfed by descriptive prose that juxtaposes their treatment with their resistance, rhetorical displays of pain interrogate state rhetoric by reversing the official and unofficial language of political appeal. It shows its readers how the prison regime attempted to break the political spine of anti-apartheid militants and the creative imagination driving their resistance. The mistreated body driven to extremes, including the possibility of self-annihilation, over each principle it seeks to negotiate appears to us as a political consciousness that will not permit the prisoners to cave. Made visible, concrete, corporeal, and personal, this *fantasia* of consciousness overtakes the prisoners' criminal status with its display of the far darker evil of treatment insensitive to their humanity.

Such bodily displays are demonstrative acts. They communicate a certainty about their oppositional stands analogous to logical force. By interrogating the state with performances embodying, as Outram puts it, "incontestable" premises, they expose opposing premises as demonstrably bankrupt and weak. The words and deeds of wardens and warders, who represent the state, are crudely indecent in their intransigence and indifference before human pain. They seem unable to get beyond slang expressions of power lacking in historical consciousness or learned insight. Their performances reduce official speech to a parody of itself, uttering clichés as substitutes for analysis.

Naidoo's memoir offers the body as a rhetorical place, a source of inventing new expressions of political relations through kairotic insertions of pain to steer its negotiation with power. It confronts its reading public with the monstrosity of a government that condones such acts out of refusal to recognize that this disciplined body is also a human being. For a public situated in the *fantasia* of the resister's body, inflicting torture and abuse thus becomes a perverse self-interrogation by the regime of its own lack of conscience. Self-interrogated, self-indicted, entrenched power explodes in its dialectic with the dissident movement.

Being situated in the prisoner's body has theoretical significance in another way. The persuasive power of particularity has been a staple of rhetorical thought since antiquity and of moral life in the biblical tradition. The culture of Western modernity, on the other hand, has contrary impulses to stress the universal over the particular, to diminish the significance of the vernacular, and to favor the disengaged and anonymous over the drama of personal engagement. This bent deflects us from those aspects of rhetoric that have the greatest power to win the judges' hearts and thereby, as Quintilian assessed matters, gain their assent. The edifice of objectivity and detachment encounters heavy weather whenever our eyes are directed toward those very facets modernity tends to discount.

Narratives of particular persons, as the Western tradition has recorded since Homer's *Iliad*, are more than their individually embodied stories. Each person's story, by the very fact that it is shared, means that this embodied being also inhabits a public place. It occupies a specific historical locale shared with other particular persons who have their own stories, each of which interacts in some way with the others. For this reason, human engagements with place are always political and therefore concerned with power; the rhetoric of their narratives is always constitutive of an *as if* reality occupied by some people's stories and not others. Against abstract and disembodied space, the specificity of place involves the dialectic between these narratives and their environment (Sheldrake 2001,1). The demonstrative consequence of this dialectic over power, in *fantasia*'s thrall over this prisoner's bodily place, compels a reader's assent to a particular history with an identifiable human pursuing a specific political pilgrimage toward an alternative destiny to what now exists.

The dialectic situated in the body as a place or locale of resistance also suggests how the contested body functions as a rhetorical place or locus and, moreover, the dialectical character of rhetorical loci. Extrapolating from the body as a place from which we invent, we may speculate that loci generally are conditioned by and interactive with the context of inventing. As we move from conceptualizing *place* as an *abstract heuristic category* to *place* as an *inventional standpoint,* loci become particular, concrete places that cannot avoid engaging their indigenous multivocalities and multilocalities and whose meanings are interpretations of the dialectic occurring there.

Finally, contrary to the early Foucauldian characterization of oppressed bodies as objects or symbols manifesting existing power relations, the demonstrative force of biopolitics on Robben Island suggests resisting bodies may be active creators of new power relations that sustain individuals in their confrontation with systems of power. Political conscience, enacted through bodily performances that resisted denial of their human worth, constructed dignified individual bodies that became a source of authority among the other prisoners and a public resource for their complaints. Within its counter-*fantasia* to the state's totalizing myth of power, displays of pain can be more than an individual's anguish; each suffering body can become a metonymic representation of an alternative body politic capable of affirming an independent identity. The rhetorically constructed body in pain writes its appeal at the sensuous level of individual experience. Sensuous experience bypasses the a priori epistemology that buttresses official rhetoric with the immediacy of identification that grows out of each reader (as each prisoner) having a personal body. Over and against a discourse of power, which deciphers the criminal body with the abstractions of the existing social and political order that subjugates it, the body in pain produces its own knowledge through concrete sensory experience of the individual, which, transformed into abstractions, can transcend their temporal constraints to speak uncontested truths. Such bodily displays act as a demonstrative rhetoric exhibiting with irrefutable force where matters stand.

8.   *Quo Vadis America*

National Conscience in Framing Prisoner Bodies at Abu Ghraib

O n January 10, 2008, the U.S. Army threw out the conviction of the only officer court-martialed in the Abu Ghraib prisoner abuse scandal, Col. Steven L.
Jordan. Jordan, who had previously been acquitted of charges that he failed to super-
vise the eleven lower-ranked soldiers convicted for their roles in the abuse of Iraqi
prisoners, had been found guilty of disobeying an order not to talk about the investigation. The jury recommended a criminal reprimand, the lightest possible sentence.
However, the presiding judge cleared Jordan of any criminal wrongdoing and instead
gave him an administrative reprimand. His being cleared of any criminal wrongdoing meant that within the army's judicial system, barring some unexpected disclosure,
accountability up the chain of command has stopped at the rank of staff sergeant; no
officer or civilian official will be held criminally responsible for the prisoner abuse at
Abu Ghraib prison.

Abu Ghraib encapsulates the vexed nature of the war on terrorism declared by
President George W. Bush following the attacks on the World Trade Center and the
Pentagon by Muslim extremists on September 11, 2001. It has come to stand for the
treatment by the U.S. military and Central Intelligence Agency (CIA) of detainees
who are suspected of ties with the al Qaeda terrorist network, U.S. policy on the
rights of enemy detainees with respect to the Geneva and other conventions to which
the United States is a signatory regarding torture and prisoner of war (POW) rights,
the unpreparedness of leaders and soldiers for waging an unconventional war where
the terms of engagement are no longer along a symmetrical front line and the means
of combat involve terrorist tactics that include suicide bombers using the civilian
population for cover, and confusion among American citizens over the rationale for
the war in Iraq. More significant, Abu Ghraib continues to stand as a symbol of a
neoconservative (aka neocon) theory of the supremacy of executive power, the *unitary executive*, which vests the U.S. president, as commander in chief, with absolute
authority to act as he or she sees fit in the service of national defense (Yoo 2006).
Finally, it captures the role of new media in defining public understanding of war and
sustaining or eroding its public support.

Unlike the previous cases considered in this book, the prisoners at Abu Ghraib, for the most part, were not themselves active agents engaged in resistance. The vast majority of prisoners suspected of terrorist activity there and at Guantánamo were detained after sweep arrests. They were in the wrong place at the wrong time, were victims of false information, or were suspected based on translator errors. Further, prisoner conscience was never a central factor shaping the significant body of rhetoric addressed to what was done there. And for good reason: the vast majority of prisoners were not politicals. However, their images became intensely politicized in the human rights debate that raged once they were made public. That debate was less about the prisoners themselves than the actions of the U.S. forces in charge of them.

I have argued that prisoners of conscience (POCs) are doubly so, that in addition to the state that incarcerates them for their beliefs, their conscience holds them prisoner to act in certain ways. Abu Ghraib presents us with a significant event in which the centrality of conscience to moral traditions and honor was evoked beyond the prison by what happened in the prison. In cases like this, might we not also extend the reach of conscience to those to whom it calls? I want to explore the possibility that the Abu Ghraib images issued a call of conscience to the United States. These photographs, once in circulation, raised the question of whether America's citizens and leaders still adhered to the nation's traditional moral commitments. This moral question could only be answered by the everyday responses of ordinary citizens response to the acts these images captured. The intersection of the war frame developed by the Bush adminstration following the September 11 terrorist attacks and the images circulating in public deflected national reflection from adminstration policies. Rather than clearly exhibiting signs they were prisoners of their own conscience, Americans acted instead to put the matter behind them, leaving us to wonder quo vadis America?

These images shocked America's rhetorical landscape. Barbara Ehrenreich (2004) lamented that, as a feminist, the behavior of the women soldiers captured in the Abu Ghraib images broke her heart and destroyed her illusions that women somehow were different than men when it came to sexual violence, illusions that saw "men as the perpetual perpetrators, women as the perpetual victims and male sexual violence against women as the root of all injustice." The lesson Ehenreich drew from Abu Ghraib was "a uterus is not a substitute for a conscience." Scholars such as psychologist Ed Tejirian (2005) and clergy such as Rabbi Harold M. Schulweis (2008) linked responses of officials with the famous P. G. Zimbardo (1975) study of prison violence. Some, including President Bush, denied that the images depicted torture, which allowed him to evade questions of conscience, whereas others, among them Vice President Cheney, were perfectly willing to face the question head on by defending the torture of detainees as required by conscience in order to serve the higher good of protecting the nation. Sgt. Joe Darby, the whistleblower on Abu Ghraib, told

GQ (Hylton 2006) that slipping the disk of photographs to the army investigation team was an act of conscience.

More important, the photographs were framed by the national and international media as speaking to the conscience and character of the nation (Milam 2004). Karen J. Greenberg (2006), the executive director of the Center on Law and Security at the New York University School of Law, called for congressional investigation to clarify basic questions about the American character raised by the photographs that would remain hidden behind the screen of secrecy until testimony was taken. Conservative columnist William F. Buckley, writing in the *National Review* online, found the dishonorable conduct of the few involved in the debasing treatment of prisoners at Abu Ghraib was refuted by public response: "the vindication of American honor came in the corporate feeling of revulsion over what was done" (2004). Former vice president Al Gore, on the other hand, thought Abu Ghraib brought humiliation to the United States in the eyes of the world, and laid blame for this directly on President Bush (2004). Nearly two years after the revelations, questions of character and honor seemed unresolved, and author and playwright Roger Pulvers (2006), writing in the *Japan Times*, wondered whether, at a deeper level, they ever could be in light of how Americans see themselves and their country: "The images of the tortured prisoners of Abu Ghraib should, by all rights, haunt the American conscience. But that conscience is so permeated with aggressive self-righteousness that there is no room for reflection or remorse."

National reflection on basic tenets of American identity, most especially those associated with honor, was not eagerly sought or encouraged by a government fighting two wars of waning popularity. The military had already established policies regulating embedded reporters to control the flow of information and shape public perceptions by limiting where reporters were permitted to go and what they were permitted to report (Kurtz 2003). The military also was keenly aware of the political power carried by visual images. It had, for example, banned pictures of the caskets of soldiers who were killed in battle from being televised or printed in newspapers as they were returned to U.S. soil because images of war dead were believed to erode public sentiment in support of the wars in Afghanistan and Iraq (Milbank 2003; Carter 2004; Barrett 2004; Stolberg 2004; National Security Archive 2005).

More to the point, the Bush adminstration had achieved stunning success in conflating its war on terror, which was framed as a response to the September 11 attacks, with its invasion of Iraq, ostensibly to remove Sadam Hussein's stash of weapons of mass destruction (WMD). As shown in a study published by the Program in International Policy Attitudes, a joint program of the Center on Policy Attitudes and the Center for International and Security Studies at the University of Maryland, this conflation had such deep roots that a sizable segment of Bush supporters persisted in holding to it even in the face of the Duelfer (2004) and the 9/11 Commission

(National Commission 2004) reports, widely covered in the press, which had arrived at contrary conclusions. In fact, when asked about these reports, a majority of Bush supporters asserted the conclusions of these reports were opposite to what they had actually found. According to the center's study:

> A large majority of Bush supporters believe that before the war Iraq had weapons of mass destruction or a major program for building them. A substantial majority of Bush supporters assume that most experts believe Iraq had WMD, and that this was the conclusion of the recently released report by Charles Duelfer. A large majority of Bush supporters believes that Iraq was providing substantial support to al Qaeda and that clear evidence of this support has been found. A large majority believes that most experts also have this view, and a substantial majority believes that this was the conclusion of the 9/11 Commission. (Kull 2004, 3)

In the case of Abu Ghraib, however, the viral nature of new media proved beyond the reach of governmental control as images from the prison, already in circulation within networks of enlistees, spread instantaneously and globally after a *60 Minutes II* broadcast accelerated them to national consciousness. Their circulation undercut the apparent success of the president's public rhetoric by reframing military actions theretofore successfully portrayed as noble in the administration's prosecution of the war on terror.

The Abu Ghraib images showed military personnel engaged in actions that sent viewers scrambling to make sense of them. The official story was that the treatment of prisoners at Abu Ghraib, which included rape, torture, sexual humiliation, and homicide, was the result of a few soldiers who had acted on their own and did not represent official U.S. policy for treatment of enemy detainees. However, photographs of MPs leering at naked detainees in sexualized poses, of prisoners in stress positions, or with female underpants on their heads, or being manhandled, were so askew with national understanding of how its military conducts itself and the humanity of those who were being treated in this way that they raised questions about the circumstances that prompted soldiers to administer harsh treatment and whether they were, in fact, acting on their own. Amid reports of renditions of enemy detainees to sites where they were being tortured, photographs of prisoners at Guantánamo Bay's Camp Delta in stress positions and legal battles over the habeas corpus rights of enemy detainees lent credence to wider claims that the military and the CIA were torturing enemy prisoners. Their slideshow of abuse horrified many in the United States, embarrassed the Bush adminstration, and inflamed the Muslim world.

Consider the competing frames of Bush adminstration rhetoric and the Abu Ghraib images regarding military conduct and the rights of those under military control and how the rhetorical mechanism of framing can control issues by quieting or raising questions of conscience that ultimately have to be addressed by those whose gaze is being directed. The specific frames examined here are those provided by the memos written by the Office of Legal Counsel (OLC) and Department of Justice (DOJ) attorneys regarding the treatment of enemy detainees and by the Abu Ghraib images. Others have examined these images for what they might tell us about soldier conduct and about the photographers who took them. Although relevant to this discussion, my ultimate concern is with the American citizens and how these frames invited them to participate in the war on terror and ultimately heed or deflect the call of conscience.

Rhetorical Frames

The idea that words matter for shaping public understanding and action has been part of recorded thought on Western rhetoric since the fifth century BCE. Regardless of tradition, framing has always been an abiding concern of rhetoricians and rhetors. In its contemporary sense, the idea of a frame was introduced by Erving Goffman, who was initially concerned with impression management as an explanation for complex human performances (Goffman 1959). He advanced a dramaturgical approach that emphasized how the context of interaction—the environment and audience–shaped an actor's performance of a role in order to influence audience perceptions. The objective of impression management was to direct audience perceptions in ways consistent with the actor's goals. Goffman extended this analysis when he developed the idea of frames to label "schemata of interpretation" used by individuals or groups "to locate, perceive, identify, and label" events and occurrences (Goffman 1974, 21). Frames render events and occurrences meaningful, and guide action in response to them by organizing how audiences experience them. They are intrinsically related to rhetoric because they direct ordinary citizens on how to think about and understand public problems (Nelson and Kinder 1996).

As a series of mental and emotional filters that guide thought and behavior, frames frequently involve public discourse. Most commonly this is understood as an interface between media discourse, such as news reporting, and interpersonal interactions, such as occur when people discuss what's in the news (Iyengar 1991). It also extends to movement mobilization, as those affiliated with a cause are activated to respond to events and groups that bear on their goals, such as opposition from authorities or countermovements, and to consciousness raising that often accompanies collective action (McAdam, McCarthy, and Zald 1996; Snow and Benford 1988).

The need for a conceptual frame that can select and give salience to certain aspects of perceived reality is indicative of how problematic events, situations, and actions can either ignite schemes and stereotypes that destabilize otherwise quiescent clusters of meaning (*concentration*), which direct how we understand dimensions and/or relationships within our social world, or accelerate (*speed*) the disruptive potential of elements that are inherently unstable within select host frames. For example, most societies regard the welfare of children to be a societal concern. The state therefore

guarantees certain social benefits to all children and considers them its wards to ensure their access to health care and education, and protection from parental abuse.
The flow of undocumented immigrants into the United States, however, destabilizes
this understanding with respect to their children when their presence is perceived as
a consequence of a foreign nation's social problems and the cause of new social problems in the host nation. Rather than framing them within the quiescent understanding of the state's commitment to protect the welfare of children, they are perceived as
problematic in terms of economic and other costs. A case in point was California's
Proposition 187, approved overwhelmingly in 1994 by voters (59 to 41 percent),
which, among other things, explicitly denied tuition-free K–12 education to children
in the United States without authorization, that is, the children of undocumented
aliens. More recently, framing these youths as aliens prevailed over framing them as
social assets, leading to the 2010 Senate defeat of the Dream Act, which would have
given them citizenship if they attended college or joined the armed services. Equally,
partner relationships among gay and lesbian couples are inherently unstable within
the frame of social policy defined in terms of heteronormativity, as witnessed by the
widespread, albeit not nationally divisive, debate in the United States over partner
benefits. Although militant groups, such as ACT UP, have engaged in social protest,
as Daniel Brouwer (1998, 2001, 2004) has shown, they more extensively have acted
within the official public sphere of legislative bodies to gain legal rights. When gays
and lesbians extended their agitation for partner rights to marriage, however, it precipitated a much more volatile debate in institutional and preinstitutional public
spheres over the definition of marriage and protected rights, even leading to a pro-
posal by President George W. Bush of a constitutional amendment restricting marriage to a union between a man and a woman.

Not all frames are created equal. Their chance of catching on and enduring
depends in part on how they comport with what we know about the world or how
they resonate with frames we are used to and regularly employ to make sense of our
experiences. Their capacity to direct our perceptions depends on their *phenomenological resonance*, or relevance to the life world of their audience. When a frame has a
good fit with events in the world, its rhetorical potency gives it *empirical credibility*.
When it squares with the audience's experience, it acquires *experiential commensura-
bility* (Snow and Benford 1988). Even if individuals cannot directly relate a frame to
their personal experiences, empirical credibility—the fit between a frame and real
world events—plays a major role in its acceptance (D'Anjou 1996, 56).

This credibility must not be interpreted as "objective" empirical adequacy. Rather,
it denotes the ease with which audiences reconcile a frame with what they consider
their (possibly mediated) experiences, which can even be derived from mass media
discourses. For example, concern for the visibility of risks attending off-shore drilling
can be managed in multiple frames—economic viability, sufficiency to meet market
demand, environmental consequences, worker safety, and so forth. However, the BP

Deep Water Horizon explosion in 2010 in the Gulf of Mexico rendered the risk frame more credible in its immediate aftermath than others, even with those audiences not directly affected by the disaster.

A rhetorically potent frame also resonates with existing cultural narratives. Its congruence with the life experience of its addressees gives it one of its most important viability attributes: *narrative fidelity* (Snow and Benford 1988; Gamson and Modigliani 1989, 5; Oberschall 1996, 99). For instance, inner-city residents faced with smog will easily pick up on the notion that industrial development is threatening the "natural" balance of the ecosystem. In contrast, invisible risks such as radioactivity require a more elaborate mediation of the same framework, as they cannot be directly observed and play practically no role in the everyday life of most people.

Importantly, frames are communicated to ordinary citizens through the media. The citizenry relies on these frames to help organize and provide lucidity to the all-too-little time and attention the news media devote to intricate social issues. However, such reliance can come at a price. A frame may limit the considerations an audience perceives as bearing on the issue as well as confine debate (Nelson, Oxley, and Clawson 1997). In their analysis of the frames employed in the media coverage of Susan Smith's trial for the murder of her two children, for example, Hasian and Flores (2000) found the frame of "bad mother" crowded out the possibility for discussion of various other relevant discourses, including child abuse, incest, divorce, and racism. Gamson et al. (1992), however, emphasize that frames are vulnerable, and this fragility makes them a "locus of potential struggle."

As the research on media frames shows, words alone are not the only source of frames. Images are especially potent sources, in that they provide an inherent frame through what they include and what they exclude. Each image offers a glimpse of life, but a selective glimpse that is a product of poses, spontaneous action, editing, and time and space that direct our gaze and thus gives an interpretation by the person who made it and guides the interpretation of the viewer.[1]

Bodily Frames

In *The Human Condition*, Hannah Arendt makes an argument for differentiating a world of personal experiences that are privately encountered and therefore real to no one but the individual who has them, and those that are commonly encountered and therefore worldly realities for all who share them. To make this distinction concrete, she points to the utterly undeniable but equally unsharable personal experience of pain. Arendt reminds us that great bodily pain is both the most intense of human feelings and "at the same time the most private and least communicable of all." Intense pain drives us into an interior world where our agony severs contact with reality beyond the body's walls. Locked in our interior, we are left sharing nothing that might represent this private reality and allow us to communicate the altered world we now inhabit. Yet agony so excruciating that it can deprive us of our ability to feel reality beyond the exclusiveness of pain's interiority can succumb to its own ineffability. Once relieved, it can be forgotten instantly. "Pain, in other words, truly a borderline experience between life as 'being among men' (*inter homines esse*) and death, is so subjective and removed from the world of things and men that it cannot assume an appearance at all" (Arendt 1958, 50–51).

Arendt's formulation of pain's utter privacy is unassailable so long as we restrict pain to the actual suffering experienced by the body in distress. Witnessing its agony is a more complicated matter. Because we have a corporeal body, we can identify with the body in pain, imagine its anguish, and empathize with it. How we respond, however, is conditioned by our sense of relationship to that body. The image of a suffering body does not *assert* a moral claim; it can only *instantiate* a moral claim *if* the observers feel under a potential obligation to those who are suffering (Ignatieff 1997, 11–12). Without a sense of potential obligation to those who are suffering, we can become fixated by the images of bodily pain and experience emotional states of horror and empathy without knowing the root causes for the suffering and humiliation or how these may implicate us. Our stare without a sense of obligation reduces the torment to a terrifying spectacle that holds us in mesmerized thrall, wherein we experience what Edmund Burke referred to as "astonishment . . . in which all [the soul's] motions are suspended with some degree of terror" (1909/1757, 88), while ignoring the suffering body's implicit plea to make its torture stop.

Plato recognized this power of the body in pain to fascinate a viewer detached from its suffering. In *The Republic*, Book IV, while setting forth his tripartite theory of the psyche, Plato describes how reason may be overwhelmed by base passion in a way that causes the self to become angry with a part of its nature. He has Socrates relate the story he has heard about Leontius, son of Aglaion, reluctantly yielding to a repulsive attraction:

> Coming up one day from the Piraeus, under the north wall on the outside, he observed some dead bodies lying on the ground at the place of public execution. He felt a desire to see them, and also a dread and aversion to them; for a time he struggled and covered his eyes, but at length the desire got the better of him; and forcing them open, he ran up to the dead bodies, saying Look, ye wretches, take your fill of the fair sight. (439e)

Commenting on this passage, Susan Sontag observes, "Plato appears to take it for granted that we . . . have an appetite for sights of degradation and pain and mutilation" (2003, 97).

The spectacle of disciplining the body publicly and the many forms it has taken confirms Plato's assessment that humans experience both dread and pleasure from witnessing the pain of others. Whether this is a sign of generalized psychosis, others may debate. I am more interested in the rhetorical potency that bodies in pain, a tragic constant of the public realm, can exert. The conflicted appetite of dread and pleasure is excited and gratified when the rhetorical work of framing clarifies the humanity of these bodies. It connects us to them as humans and makes a call to our conscience. Or, just as significant, rhetoric can frame them as nonhuman and therefore deny obligation to relieve their pain. In line with my argument on the capacity of displays of pain to move their viewers, when these frames are visual, they can acquire the evidentiary force of demonstration.

The rhetoric of human rights acknowledges this power by, for example, attempting to mobilize public pressure with accounts of torture to dissident bodies. The resisting bodies of political prisoners are mobilized in frames of abuse and torture to form identification through an attending audience's empathy for the sufferer's anguish. Yet the moral sanction against publicly disregarding such appeals does not always prevail, as the twentieth century taught us. Private responses sometimes play in a different register. Despite impressively exhorting humanity to relieve their suffering, sometimes the pleas of bodies in pain are deflected by their even greater power of attraction. Rather than evoking identification, they draw an audience compelled to look while resolving whatever conflict suffering may arouse by choosing to do nothing. That was the case for the prisoners at Abu Ghraib, whose repulsive treatment by their guards was photographed by their tormentors and then discovered and circulated to an international audience. Without attempting to make a moral plea, images of their tortured bodies came to an international public, especially an American one, as a rhetorical frame that carried a moral claim of obligation to the sufferer.

Image and Interpretation

Thus far my examination of POC rhetoric has focused on their letters, memoirs, testimonies, legal pleas, and the like as an entrée into the world of the prison and the way their bodies are disciplined by the state. In memoirs especially, the narrative form provides a phenomenology of suffering. Their authors are not always people of international acclaim, such as Vaclav Havel, or leaders of liberation movements, such as Nelson Mandela. Often they are persons whose notoriety comes from the stories they tell. The narratives of Irina Ratushinskaya and Indres Naidoo are more than long and sustained howls of torture. They include accounts of their activities, life in the prison, treatment by the guards, relations with other prisoners, strategies they adopt for coping with the torture of unremitting pain, sadness over separation from their families and loved ones, and reflections on a political vision that explains why they are not breaking. Still, these narratives also provide accounts of how their bodies have been manhandled and humiliated, and through our reading we become participants in the scenes of their horror. They bring us into the place Plato described in Book IV of *The Republic,* where we find ourselves made witness to the pain of others and must confront the questions their pain raises of us. Accounts of arrests leading to brutal interrogations, of torture to get information that often is of a nonspecific kind, of the psychological pressure to break and of the struggle to keep sane, offer graphic images—*visiones*—in which the *fantasia* of presence invites the reader into the torture chamber and into the terror and agony of a body in distress. Through *ekphrasis*, these writers create visualizations that, while lacking the visual facticity of photographic images, provide the first-person voice of a narrator who shares the personal experience of being subjected to physical brutality.

This is to say that the memoir is a product of rhetorical design. Its author is able to speak of an interior response to physical brutality. He or she creates a narrative that interprets ideas, people, and events in ways that encourage the reader's disposition to respond. For the prison writer, *visiones* is a product of rhetorical invention that is a deliberate attempt to position the reader with a specific end in mind. When the visual field of physical brutality is literally brought into play, as in photographs of World War I battlefields, of Ku Klux Klan lynchings, of the Nazi camps and lagers, and most recently of Iraqi prisoners at Abu Ghraib, the images contain greater ambiguity. Images become permanent markers of important events. They are significantly attached to events, and their interpretation is connected to the details of the narrative that we have of the event. They both frame and are framed, with the possibility of becoming demonstrative proof (see McKeon 1966).

Sontag long maintained that photographs, unlike words, are other than interpretations of the world. "What can be read about the world is frankly an interpretation, as are older kinds of flat-surface visual statements, like paintings and drawings. Photographed images do not seem to be statements about the world so much as pieces of it: miniatures of reality that anyone can make or acquire" (1973). They may be able to move us in the moment, but that is because they are inserted within an existing political consciousness. On their own, in her view, they lack narrative coherence.

Judith Butler has challenged Sontag's position. Butler argues that "while narrative coherence might be a standard for some sorts of interpretation, it is surely not so for all. Indeed, if the notion of a 'visual interpretation' is not to become oxymoronic, it seems important to acknowledge that, in framing reality, the photograph has already determined what will count within the frame—and this act of determination is surely interpretive, as are potentially, the various effects of angle, focus, light, etc." (2009, 67). Daniel Okrent supports Butler's view. Commenting on famed fashion and portrait photographer Richard Avedon's view that "there is no such thing as inaccuracy in a photograph. All photographs are accurate. None of them is the truth," Okrent (2005) reminds us that a photographer points the camera and shoots, moves the lens three inches and shoots again—different picture, different reality. Robert Hariman and John Lucaites refine this point when they observe that "a fundamental property of still photography reinforces the idea that the image represents a condition rather than a moment in an unfolding story. The corresponding idea that completes the image dramatically is that any response to and change in that condition must come from outside the frame" (2007, 60).

The importance of a visual frame for shaping public understanding is especially evident in the way wars are now reported. Embedded reporters travel with military units stationed in war zones. In return for access to military brass and battlefield conditions, they agree to restrictions on what they will write and photographs they will publish. As Butler writes: "In the case of the recent and current wars, the visual perspective that the U.S. Department of Defense permitted to the media actively structured our cognitive apprehension of the war. And although restricting how or what we see is not exactly the same as dictating a storyline, it is a way of interpreting in advance what will and will not be included in the field of perception" (2009, 66). Embedding gives perspective—it is an interpretation ahead of time that ensures the war we see is the war the Department of Defense (DOD) wants civilians see.

The Abu Ghraib images' capacity to frame events and perceptions of them came into conflict with the war frame the Bush adminstration had been assiduously constructing since 9/11. It produced a dissonant dialogue of sorts over the treatment of enemy bodies. While not completely satisfying as an explanation for what was done, the way the circulating images were read encouraged a national response satisfying enough to permit the dissonance to be resolved, or at least reduced to the point where the nation could put the incident behind it.

The War on Terrorism

Following the al Qaeda terrorist attack of September 11, 2001, President George W. Bush faced the decision of how to respond. Past terrorist attacks on U.S. soil had been handled as criminal offenses under the jurisdiction of the DOJ. The truck-bombing in the North Tower of the World Trade Center in New York City on February 26, 1993, and the truck-bombing of the Alfred P. Murrah Federal Building in Oklahoma City, Oklahoma, on April 19, 1995, are notorious examples. In the World Trade Center case, the DOJ brought ten defendants to trial and gained convictions for seditious conspiracy. The Oklahoma City bombing was the deadliest terrorist attack on U.S. soil prior to the September 11 attack and resulted in the deaths of 168 people. The Federal Bureau of Investigation (FBI) investigation led to the arrest of Timothy McVeigh, who was found guilty of murder and executed for his crime.

The president framed the September 11 attack differently. He briefly addressed the nation on the evening of the event and declared, "We will make no distinction between the terrorists who committed these acts and those who harbor them" (2001a). Given that the only way to hold foreign governments responsible is either through some form of pressure, such as sanctions, or through force, the president signaled that his thinking had gone beyond the American judicial system. The immediate effects of these massive suicide bombings were felt nationally, and the adminstration's rhetorical construction of its response outside the frame of past precedents seemed appropriate to most Americans. Unlike past terrorist attacks on

U.S. soil, this one caused national havoc. Air traffic was grounded for two days. Wall Street closed, and the Dow Jones industrial average plummeted by 504 points when the stock exchange reopened the following week. Nearly 3,000 casualties resulted, the vast majority of whom were civilians, including 2,605 in New York City and citizens from more than ninety countries. 24/7 news coverage included the video loop containing dramatic footage of planes slamming into the World Trade Center towers; people jumping to their deaths; the collapse of the North and South towers; and accounts of heroic performance by the New York City Police Department, the New York City Fire Department, and civilians in the burning buildings who led others to safe exit or, tragically, died while remaining behind trying to assist others unable to escape the blazing inferno unaided. Stories of those who died in the plane crashes were not only heart wrenching but, in the case of United Airlines 093, mythologized passengers who rushed the hijackers and through their heroic efforts crashed the plane into the Pennsylvania countryside, thereby aborting the hijackers' attempt to attack the nation's capital again. While no more tragic than the bombing of the Murrah office building, the magnitude of this catastrophe; the fact that it was perpetrated by a terrorist network from without the United States; the clear intent of coordinated assaults to disrupt commerce and assassinate government officials, possibly including the president; the ripple effects felt in transportation and the stock market; and the compelling optics that accompanied nonstop coverage of the disaster, replete with frequent replays of planes detonating on impact with the World Trade Center, encouraged a national siege mentality and general support for the president's position that the attack was an act of war.

From the adminstration's perspective, declaring the attacks a criminal offense would place investigation and prosecution under DOJ jurisdiction and require abiding by the rules of the U.S. criminal justice system, which offer protections to the accused on presumption of innocence and impose standards of evidence for convictions much greater than exist under conditions of war. The president consulted the OLC about his constitutional powers for mounting a response, while making his personal conviction evident with a declaration of a national state of emergency on September 14 and authorization for the Pentagon to call up 50,000 National Guard reservists to active duty for homeland defense and recovery missions. That same day, speaking to rescuers working at ground zero in New York, he responded to their chants of "USA, USA" by pledging, "I can hear you. The rest of the world hears you. And the people who knocked these buildings down will hear all of us soon" (CNN .COM 2001). His promise was featured on TV and print news outlets.

Bush's framing of the attacks as an act of war was reinforced to the nation the following week in his address to a joint session of Congress on September 20, 2001. He declared: "On September the eleventh, enemies of freedom committed an act of war against our country" (Bush 2001e). Five days later this view was sanctioned by an OLC opinion signed by John Yoo that concluded "a foreign attack had occurred on

September 11, the United States was at war, and President Bush had the power 'not only to retaliate against any person, organization, or state suspected of involvement in terrorist attacks on the United States, but also against foreign states suspected of harboring or supporting such organizations.'" The opinion continued to affirm the presidential power "to deploy military force preemptively against terrorist organizations" (Yoo 2006, 10).

Framing the September 11 attack as an act of war was significant because it provided justification for several important policies adopted by the Bush adminstration. First, it shifted authority for finding and prosecuting terrorists from the DOJ to the DOD. This shift meant the rules for detention, interrogation, and prisoner rights were those of the military set forth in military codes rather than the criminal justice system of civilian codes. Second, it provided the pretext for advancing, under the theory of the unitary executive, the president's absolute power as commander in chief to act unilaterally in order to prosecute the war. The Bush adminstration argued that Article II of the Constitution gave the president, as part of his executive powers, control over foreign policy, including the power to sign and enforce treaties. Under the president's war power, this became critical once the authorization of harsh interrogation measures for enemy detainees, which the adminstration argued were necessary to protect national security, came into conflict with international accords, such as the Geneva Conventions. Third, as commander in chief, the president had the authority to determine how enemy detainees were to be treated, including sending them to black sites[2] or to other countries through extraordinary rendition[3] for interrogation, denying them access to legal counsel and *habeas corpus* rights, authorizing harsh interrogation, and trying them in military tribunals rather than military or federal courts. Fourth, under conditions of war, the president also claimed his executive authority permitted him to conduct surveillance on anyone at anytime in order to detect possible terrorist plans and thereby avert another attack on U.S. soil.

The absolute power of the president was formalized by executive orders and congressional action. On September 18, 2001, Congress passed as a joint resolution the Authorization for Use of Military Force Against Terrorists (Pub.L. 107–40, 115 Stat. 224). Commonly known as AUMF, it was one of two such resolutions (the other passed in 2002 authorizing military force against Iraq) that were invoked in support of actions that claimed unitary executive justification. The 2001 AUMF authorized the president "to use all necessary and appropriate force against those nations, organizations, or persons he determines planned, authorized, committed, or aided the terrorist attacks that occurred on September 11, 2001, or harbored such organizations or persons, in order to prevent any future acts of international terrorism against the United States by such nations, organizations or persons." This resolution was invoked by the adminstration to legitimate military commissions to try prisoners held at Guantánamo Bay and warrantless electronic surveillance, which had been prohibited by the Foreign Intelligence Surveillance Act of 1978. Next, in his September 20 speech to a joint session of Congress, as noted above, Bush stated that as a matter of policy the U.S. government would not distinguish between terrorist organizations and nations or governments that gave them safe harbor. Within this frame, the Afghani offer to try Osama bin Laden in an Afghan court was rejected as harboring the enemy. On October 6, Bush ordered the invasion of Afghanistan to destroy the al Qaeda network.

On October 26, the president signed into law the Uniting and Strengthening America by Providing Appropriate Tools Required to Intercept and Obstruct Terrorism Act of 2001 (USA PATRIOT Act, aka Patriot Act). The Patriot Act radically reduced restrictions on law enforcement agencies regarding their ability to search telephone and email communications and financial, medical, and other records, and regarding their ability to gather foreign intelligence within the United States, while it expanded the secretary of the treasury's authority to regulate financial transactions, especially those involving foreign individuals and entities, and of the various federal agencies that deal with detaining and deporting immigrants suspected of terrorist acts. Section 802 of the Patriot Act also expanded the powers of law enforcement agencies for dealing with domestic terrorism, including expanding its definition to include any act dangerous to human life that violates federal or state criminal laws and appears to be intended to intimidate or coerce a civilian population, influence the policy of a government by intimidation or coercion, or affect the conduct of a government by mass destruction, assassination, or kidnapping, and is committed within the territorial jurisdiction of the United States (H.R. 3162 2001). Finally, on November 13 the president signed an executive order in which he found that it was "not practicable" to try enemy detainees in military courts and instead ordered they be tried by military tribunals, which have less stringent rules of evidence and a lower threshold of probability for determining guilt. It also placed enemy detainees under the jurisdiction of the secretary of defense, whom he authorized to determine the "appropriate location for their detention" and to issue necessary orders and regulations for the military commissions to function. Bush asserted these measures were necessary based on his determination that "an extraordinary emergency exists for national defense purposes, that the emergency constitutes an urgent and compelling government interest, and that issuance of this order is necessary to meet this emergency" (Bush 2001f, 25–28).

Positioning the president's powers firmly within a war frame had the advantage for the adminstration of accentuating its interpretation of the unitary executive. In his memo of September 25, 2001, answering Bush's question on the scope of the president's authority to take military action in response to the terrorist attacks, Yoo concluded the Constitution vests the president with "plenary authority as Commander in Chief." Indeed, "the power of the President is at its zenith under the Constitution [*sic*] when the President is directing military operations of the armed forces, because the power of Commander in Chief is assigned solely to the

President" (5). In this and subsequent memos (see Yoo's memos in Greenberg and Dratel 2005), Yoo set forth a theory of executive war power that made the president's word law on any matter he deemed related to the war effort and, further, regarded any attempt by Congress to limit it as unconstitutional, because it would violate his plenary powers as commander in chief, and any interference by the courts as overreaching their authority by interfering with the executive's conduct of warfare.

Since the United States was in a state of war, the next issue was to sort out the executive's authority to determine the disposition of enemy prisoners under control of the military or government agencies, such as the CIA. At first the issue was confined to enemy combatants captured during Operation Enduring Freedom waged to destroy the al Qaeda network. Most of those who were captured in the Afghanistan conflict were sent to the Camp Delta prison facility located at Guantánamo Bay. However, some who were suspected of having valuable information were sent to black sites, where they were interrogated by members of the U.S. intelligence community, or rendered to other nations, whose interrogation techniques were known to include torture.

The president asked the OLC to provide him with an opinion on whether the detainees were protected by the Geneva Conventions. This raised the related concern over whether there were limits on how the detainees could be treated. In a series of memos from various officials in the OLC, DOJ, and White House, the adminstration's war frame portrayed al Qaeda and Taliban warriors as not entitled to Geneva protection. Given the nature of the Geneva Conventions, the exclusion was more than a legal technicality; it amounted to an exclusion of captive bodies from protection against inhuman treatment.

The Geneva Conventions were drafted in 1949 in order to address the abuses of POWs that had occurred during World War II. Its purpose was to ensure that combatants were treated humanely. Its overriding concern is neither political nor military but with the rights of each soldier and civilian as a person. The primacy of personality is evident in the document itself and in the commentaries of those who were major forces in shaping them, especially the International Committee of the Red Cross (ICRC). Thus, when it came time to craft a final version of Common Article 3, which appears in each of the four conventions, the phrase "contracting parties" was deleted so that the emphasis was placed on the person of the combatant held by the enemy. Although the initial impulse for drafting Article 3 was to address the conditions that occurred in civil war, the ambiguous phrase "armed conflict not of an international character occurring in the territory of one of the High Contracting Parties" has come to be interpreted as applying to individuals who are *hors de combat* in the territory of a signatory to the conventions.

The U.S. Supreme Court reiterated this interpretation, which reflects a shift in international law from an emphasis on states to an emphasis on human rights, in Hamdan v. Rumsfeld. Justice John Paul Stevens, writing for the Court, concluded:

"Common Article 3 . . . affords some minimal protection, falling short of full protection under the Conventions, to individuals associated with neither a signatory nor even a nonsignatory who are involved in a conflict 'in the territory of a signatory.' The latter kind of conflict does not involve a clash between nations (whether signatories or not)" (2006, 6–7). Concern for the person of each individual, as reflected in Justice Stevens's opinion, is set forth most explicitly in Article 2 of the United Nations (U.N.) Convention Against Torture (1984):

> Each State Party shall take effective legislative, administrative, judicial or other measures to prevent acts of torture in any territory under its jurisdiction.
>
> No exceptional circumstances whatsoever, whether a state of war or a threat of war, internal political instability or any other public emergency, may be invoked as a justification of torture.
>
> An order from a superior officer or a public authority may not be invoked as a justification of torture.

The values expressed in these documents regarding the person of each detainee establish the norms for their treatment in the thin moral vernacular of human rights documents and court decisions, which stand as guides and interpretations for state policy. It requires humane treatment of persons taking no active part in hostilities, whether they be civilians or detainees since removed from combat; the prohibition of violence to life and person, such as murder or torture; the prohibition of "outrages upon personal dignity," including "humiliating and degrading treatment"; and the requirement of proper care for the wounded and sick.

The administration's lawyers saw matters differently. They argued consistently and with great imagination (Bybee 2002a, 2002b, 2002c; Gonzales 2002; Philbin 2002; Philbin and Yoo 2001; Yoo 2002; Yoo and Delahunty 2002) that the September 11 attack introduced a new paradigm of war in which the considerations of person emphasized by the human rights frame were, in the words of then White House counsel Alberto Gonzalez, "obsolete" (2002). From the White House's perspective, national security trumped all other considerations. With a state of war firmly established as its frame for thinking and communicating about the al Qaeda and Taliban prisoners taken in Afghanistan, the several memos written concerning treatment of detainees emphasized their lack of rights and the president's executive power to prosecute the war as he saw fit (Bush 2001d).

The war frame proved to have unusual rhetorical elasticity, as it accommodated two powerful lines of argument: one religious, the other legal. On the religious side, the recurrent theme of American Zion, which stretches back to the time of colonial settlement, echoed in the president's proclamation of September 14 at a National Day of Prayer and Remembrance for the Victims of the Terrorist Attacks (Bush 2001c) and through his depiction of the attack as an act of evil that called the United

States to its historical responsibility to avenge evil by bringing the evildoers to justice (Bush 2001a):

> Civilized people around the world denounce the evildoers who devised and executed these terrible attacks. Justice demands that those who helped or harbored the terrorists be punished—and punished severely. The enormity of their evil demands it. We will use all the resources of the United States and our cooperating friends and allies to pursue those responsible for this evil, until justice is done.

These sentiments were echoed during the National Prayer Meeting in Washington, D.C. In his moving remarks (Bush 2001b), the president first commented on the individual lives of those who died, noting that their names were just now becoming known and mentioning representative last words and deeds that epitomized their courage and the grief of their loved ones at the tragedy of their loss. He offered them comfort with these words of faith: "As we've been assured, neither death nor life nor angels nor principalities, nor powers nor things present nor things to come nor height nor depth can separate us from God's love." If Osama bin Laden's (2001) published characterization of the victims as infidels and the attack as the work of God reflected a jihadist's commitment to a holy calling, his sentiments only echoed Bush's wedding of the frame of war to religion when he dedicated the nation to revenge their deaths with words that made war against terror a historic responsibility and a holy cause:

> Just three days removed from these events, Americans do not yet have the distance of history, but our responsibility to history is already clear: to answer these attacks and rid the world of evil.
>
> War has been waged against us by stealth and deceit and murder.
>
> This nation is peaceful, but fierce when stirred to anger. This conflict was begun on the timing and terms of others; it will end in a way and at an hour of our choosing. (Bush 2001b)

The biblical tone of these remarks garnered initial support, as they gave moral justification for aggression against perpetrators who were the ethnic/religious Other from a land that was little known by most Americans, apart from its notoriety for drug trafficking and its subjugation of women alternately under the rule of Taliban fundamentalists and the domination of warlords. For most Americans, Afghanistan was a mysterious land of the ethnic Other who had murdered nearly 3,000 Americans in the September 11 attack. Despite the adminstration's explicit attempts to separate Islamic extremists of al Qaeda and the Taliban from Islam itself, and the invited presence of Imam Muzammil H. Siddiqi, whose prayer at the National Cathedral ceremony was that we might repel evil with good, Bush's joining of war with religion provided a powerful frame for sanctioning extreme violence against a foe defined as an enemy of Christianity, Judaism, and Western culture.

Dehumanizing the Enemy Body

On the legal side, the adminstration translated Americans' anger into policy for the treatment of enemy detainees. Already armed with state of emergency Proclamation 7463, which authorized the Pentagon to call up thousands of reservists; the AUMF resolution granting Bush war powers; and the OLC opinion that he had full power to prosecute military operations as he saw fit, the president issued his Military Order (MO) of November 13, 2001 (Bush 2001f), in which he reiterated that because "an extraordinary emergency exists for national defense purposes," he was ordering that enemy detainees who were not citizens of the United States—that is, anyone who was suspected to be a member of al Qaeda, or to have engaged in terrorist activity, or to have aided and abetted or conspired to commit an act of terrorism, or had threatened to act in ways that would cause harm on any aspect of the United States, or who knowingly harbored anyone who fit this description—shall be turned over to the control of the secretary of defense. The secretary in turn would determine the location of their detention, the conditions of their treatment, and whether they would be tried. If tried, it would be before a military commission, with the commissioners sitting as triers of both fact and law. Since it is not practicable to apply the rules of evidence used in criminal cases tried in U.S. district courts, the presiding judge would determine the admissibility of evidence based on its probative value. Conviction and sentencing would require a two-thirds vote, with no possibility of appeal to a civilian court. Only the secretary or the president was authorized to review decisions.

Although not mentioned in Bush's MO, John Yoo writes that in the weeks after September 11, lawyers at state, defense, justice, and the White House formed an interagency task force to study the issues related to detention and trial of al Qaeda members. "The one thing we all agreed on was that any detention facility should be located outside the United States. . . . We researched whether the courts would have jurisdiction over the facility, and concluded that if federal courts took jurisdiction over POW camps, they might start to run them by their own lights, substituting familiar peacetime prison standards for military needs and standards" (2006, 142). They also reasoned, based on the practice of the first Bush and Clinton adminstrations to hold at Guantánamo Bay Haitian refugees who attempted to enter the United States illegally, that the courts "wouldn't consider Gitmo [Guantánamo Bay] as falling within their habeas jurisdiction" (142). This meant that as a matter of policy enemy detainees who were not U.S. citizens could be held indefinitely without legal recourse to determine whether they were being detained for probable cause, without charge, without rights to a trial, and, if tried and found guilty, without appeal to a neutral court.

Denial of habeas corpus rights was particularly relevant to the government, which had less interest in convictions than in culling information about terrorist networks and imminent threats. Within the war frame, national security superseded questions of justice. The majority of prisoners picked up in sweep arrests or handed over to

U.S. troops for a bounty of up to $5,000 had no information to share (Reid 2010). They were farmers or merchants who happened to be in the wrong place at the wrong time, or who happened to fall victim to a personal enemy offered the opportunity to gain revenge at a profit. Early on, a *Los Angeles Times* article (Miller 2002) estimated 10 percent of the prisoners were innocent. Later it became evident that the number of detainees of no intelligence value was far greater. In a signed declaration supporting a law suit by a Guantánamo detainee, Col. Lawrence Wilkerson, a top aide to former secretary of state Colin Powell, alleged that Vice President Dick Cheney and Secretary of Defense Donald Rumsfeld knew very early that the majority of the original 742 detainees were innocent but believed its was "politically impossible to release them" (Reid 2010). As with all the detainees, their human value was diminished as they were stripped of all legal rights, they faced the prospect of being detained in harsh conditions for the foreseeable future, and their bodies were now subject to whatever treatment their captors thought might best serve their captors' own military ends. Just as civilians killed in an air strike on an enemy location, their bodies were considered collateral damage.

The Torture Memos

As interrogation proceeded, the U.S. military sought guidance on how far it could go when questioning detainees. The military was especially concerned about treatment of those believed to have valuable information, and who had become resistant to standard interrogation techniques. Gen. Michael Dunleavy, in charge of interrogations at Guantánamo, concluded more aggressive techniques were needed and charged his staff judge advocate, Lt. Col. Diane Beaver, to prepare a legal review of options. Beaver, who had no experience with international law, led some brainstorming sessions with the objective of gathering new interrogation techniques. CIA and Defense Intelligence Agency (DIA) operatives at Guantánamo Bay participated, and ideas came from a variety of sources, perhaps the most surprising being "24"—a popular drama series broadcast by the Fox television network. Its lead character, Jack Bauer, relentlessly pursued terrorists, and his tactics prevented many attacks on the United States by getting the terrorist to disclose the location of the "ticking bomb" before it exploded. Rules didn't apply to Bauer, who did what he wanted when he wanted in order to force terrorists to talk. When Philippe Sands interviewed her, Beaver provided a life-imitates-art moment when she allowed that those in the brainstorming sessions "had already seen the first series [sic] (of "24"), it was hugely popular," and "he gave people lots of ideas" (Sands 2008, 62).

On October 11, 2002, Lt. Col. Jerald Phifer sent a memo to Dunleavy requesting approval of three categories of interrogation techniques, and Beaver sent an accompanying legal brief recommending their approval. The recommendations (in Hynes 2002) included use of stress positions, such as standing for four hours, use of twenty-hour interrogations (without specifying the length of time between sessions), forcing the detainee to go naked, forced grooming such as shaving facial hair (which would be a violation of Muslim detainees' religious beliefs), and exposure to phobias (such as fear of dogs) to induce stress. Category III techniques included threats of pain to the detainee or his family, exposure to cold, and waterboarding.

The legal reasoning of Beaver is impressively revealing of how detainee bodies were understood. With respect to inflicting pain, she argued, based on Supreme Court decisions dealing with the Eighth Amendment's prohibition of cruel and unusual punishment, that "analysis is based primarily on whether the government had a good faith legitimate governmental interest, and did not act maliciously and sadistically for the very purpose of causing harm." Thus, techniques such as waterboarding or exposure to the elements, she reasoned, were legal: "So long as the force used could plausibly have been thought necessary in a particular situation to achieve a legitimate governmental objective, and it was applied in a good faith effort and not maliciously or sadistically for the very purpose of causing harm, the proposed techniques are likely to pass constitutional muster." And in cases where there might be a violation of the Uniform Code of Military Justice, such as threatening a detainee with death, "it would be advisable to have permission or immunity in advance from the convening authority, for military members utilizing these methods" (Beaver 2002, 232–34). Beaver's legal analysis concedes no rights to the detainees and is exclusively concerned with avoiding interrogator culpability for using harsh techniques. As long as they could make a defense that they did not intend to cause pain or injury, even though that would be the result, then they could do anything they wanted to detainee bodies. In cases where they were in doubt, getting prior approval would also allow them to do as they wished and not face legal consequences. Although the president's February 7 order stating that while the detainees did not have Geneva protection they were to be treated as if they did, its caveat of "to the extent appropriate and consistent with military necessity" was foremost in Beaver's reasoning that insisted Geneva did not apply.

Phifer's request for permission to use the three categories of techniques and Beaver's legal opinion recommending their approval were forwarded to the Defense Department, where they were reviewed by the secretary's general counsel, William J. Haynes II, who consulted Deputy Secretary Doug Feith and Gen. Richard Myers, chairman of the Joint Chiefs of Staff. Haynes recommended use of Categories I and II and only the use of mild, noninjurious contact from Category III. Importantly, Haynes (2002) observed that while he did not believe Category III techniques were required at that time, he regarded them as "legally available." Rumsfeld approved the recommendation on December 6, 2002, with the handwritten note at the bottom, "However, I stand for 8–10 hours a day. Why is standing limited to 4 hours?" (Greenberg and Dratel 2005, 225–39).[4]

The paper trail that put techniques of interrogation into the frame of conducting the war made these legal opinions and the policy decision appear as originating outside the adminstration and its actions as a response to the military's request. Unbeknownst to Beaver, as she crafted an opinion that many knowledgeable in international law find to violate it (Sands 2008; Luban 2005; Mayer 2008), the torture issue had been addressed by the OLC and DOJ in memoranda known as the "torture memos."[5] They specifically address the legality of harsh (aka "enhanced") interrogation techniques that had been under discussion. The most notorious of these was the torture memo from Assistant Attorney General Jay Bybee to White House Counsel Alberto Gonzales dated August 1, 2002. In it, Bybee argues that for treatment to reach the level of torture, its precise objective must be to inflict severe pain and suffering. If that was not its precise intent, then the interrogator would have a legal defense that he or she had not committed torture. Second, the result of the treatment had to be so severe as to produce pain "equivalent in intensity to the pain accompanying serious physical injury, such as organ failure, impairment of bodily function, or even death" (2002c, 172). Equally, for psychological treatment to reach the level of torture, the mental pain caused must result in prolonged mental harm, lasting for months or even for years. Not finding the key terms—"prolonged mental harm" and "disrupt profoundly the senses or personality"—in the 1996 War Crimes Act (WCA) Sec. 2340, in the medical literature, or elsewhere in U.S. law, Bybee proceeds to define their meaning from the *Oxford English Dictionary* and to offer examples that would, in most cases, require institutionalization: drug-induced dementia, deterioration of language function, impaired ability to execute simple motor activities, brief onset of psychotic disorder such as dillusions, hallucinations, or even a catatonic state (181). Moreover, it must be the interrogator's intent to cause prolonged mental harm. The single-minded concern over whether the act was prosecutable in court made incidental the being of the person suffering the physical and mental anguish inflicted to gather information. Next, Bybee argues that even if a method might cross the line drawn in WCA Sec. 2340, application of the statute would be an infringement on the president's commander in chief authority. In other words, in a state of war, the president may do as he or she sees fit in prosecuting the war. There is no check on his or her executive authority as commander in chief. Finally, if for some reason a court should bring charges against a member of the military or a government agency for crossing the line and engaging in torture, the defendant has the ready defenses of "necessity" and "self-defense." Under the "ticking bomb" scenario, "the more certain that government officials are that a particular individual has information needed to prevent an attack, the more necessary interrogation will be. Second, the more likely it appears to be that a terrorist attack is likely to occur, and the greater the amount of damage expected from such an attack, the more that an interrogation to get information would become necessary" (209). Self-defense also could be invoked as a defense since the government agent is acting in defense of the nation.

Collectively, the torture memos provided a web of legal interpretations that invested the president with authority to do as he pleased with prisoner bodies in conducting the war on terror and legal cover for those who were acting within the framework of his executive orders to gather information from enemy detainees. Unlike Agamben's *homo sacer*, who is placed outside the law and whose treatment is at the edict of a sovereign who has suspended the law, the torture memos sought to provide a legal basis founded in the U.S. Constitution for the president's right to do as he pleased. By their reasoning, presidential decisions on prisoner treatment were not political decisions, except when the decision was to adhere to calls for humane treatment by treaties that did not apply. Harsh treatment was a legal prerogative of the president in his capacity as commander in chief. As such, it placed the bodies of suspected terrorist prisoners within the law, made harsh treatment legal, and provided legal cover for those who administered it.

The memos amount to deciding which lives have value. They place the detainees' lives in a frame that diminishes their humanity and therefore their protection from being subjected to pain. Whereas the rhetoric of human rights and of the Geneva Conventions and WCA invokes the primacy of personhood, the frame of the torture memos gives primacy to national defense, and denies, on technical grounds, equality of personhood between the ethnic other who has been placed in the category of suspected terrorist and the U.S. citizen who is to be protected from terrorist attack.

In the war frame, we are invited to accept uncritically that subjecting another to harsh treatment protects the nation and is essential for waging war. We are invited to hold those who commit these acts as innocent of a human rights violation, as not legally culpable because they have acted in our defense. We are asked to consider the context of the interrogator's actions as justification for his or her acts and as authorizing an interpretation of laws as not applicable or as meaning something other than what they seem to state explicitly.

The torture memos argue, contrary to human rights accords, that under conditions of war, some lives are more precious than others, and therefore are more deserving of protection than others. More than this, the precariousness of these lives derives from translating the moral definition of them as evil, and therefore less grievable (Butler 2009), into the legal definition of their status, which denies them personality with inherent protections from harm to body and mind, and therefore as less valuable. The war frame offers moral and legal grounds for treating them in whatever way the president authorizes in the name of national defense. For citizens who learn that they have been made to bear the burden of harsh treatment and been audience to the convoluted rhetoric that defines this treatment as not meeting the threshold of torture, the war frame also invites a perception of the material reality of their treatment as within norms of propriety.

Emerging doubt. Earlier I argued that the state often asserted sovereignty by treating POCs as mere animals. Judith Butler maintains that in the case of detainees suspected of terrorism, however, the treatment of their bodies "is not the same as 'bare life,' since the lives in question are not cast outside the polis in a state of radical exposure, but bound and constrained by power relations in a situation of forcible exposure." They feel the effects of "the exercise of state power freed from the constraints of all law" (2009, 29).

As the adminstration's lawyers were compiling legal opinions to justify the president taking whatever action he deemed appropriate to pursuing the wars in Afghanistan and Iraq, and offering advice to interrogators on how to immunize themselves from prosecution, others were taking a different view of the U.S. treatment of its enemy detainees. Critics of the war on terrorism focused mainly on concerns about the implications of the president's directive of November 13, 2002, specifying the treatment of enemy detainees, the consequences for civil liberties of the Patriot Act, and the wisdom of the war in Iraq.

The November 13 directive brought a response from Human Rights Watch (HRW), which sent a letter to Secretary of Defense Rumsfeld during the week of May 25, 2002. It was troubled by the plans outlined by Bush for prosecuting and even holding detainees indefinitely without trial. HRW executive director Kenneth Roth objected, "The Bush Administration cannot hold people indefinitely without charge or send them to countries where they might be tortured. . . . As time goes by and the number of detainees grows, so does the pressure on the U.S. government to act" (2002). Roth continued to point out the United States' legal obligation to determine the detainees' status, in accordance with the Geneva Conventions, and called for the use of criminal proceedings where warranted. The urgency of determining the detainees' legal status was underscored by noting the rise in prisoner population immanent at Guantánamo with the soon-to-be-completed new block of 150 cells and transfer of detainees that would bring its population to exceed 500. Roth warned the United States about its responsibility not to transfer or repatriate prisoners to countries where they would be at risk of torture.

Legal scholar David Cole (2003) wrote similarly about the double standard for treatment of aliens who were detained on suspicion of having terrorist ties. Contrary to the unitary executive theory advanced by lawyers in the OLC and DOJ, Cole's analysis challenged the constitutionality of the president's policies. William Schultz (2003), director of Amnesty International, challenged the legality of Attorney General John Ashcroft's use of existing immigration laws for lengthy internments of aliens, even after they had been ordered deported or had agreed to leave. And contrary to the adminstration's claims, the public sphere was beginning to have a discussion about the denial of habeas corpus rights not being confined to enemy aliens but also to suspected terrorists who were American citizens and being held in judicial limbo—Yasser Hamdi and Jose Padilla being prime examples.

Warnings also were being raised about the danger of the Patriot Act leading to adminstration abuses. Issues of warrantless wiretaps; detention without charge for seven days, which could be extended to six months if the attorney general deemed the person might represent a risk to national security; and monitoring detainee-attorney conversations if the DOJ determined that such conversations might facilitate terrorist activity by passing on instructions or information, were among the newly authorized powers of the government that were being contested. Legal scholar Ronald Dworkin, among others, argued that these were measures we associate with lawless totalitarian dictatorships. "If any American were tried by a foreign government in that way, even for a minor offense, let alone a capital crime, we would denounce that government as itself criminal" (2002, 44).

The resilience of WMD rhetoric within the war frame. Despite these objections to adminstration measures, as the nation's attention turned to Iraq and its alleged role in supporting al Qaeda activity and allegedly developing an arsenal of WMD that represented an immanent threat to national security, the war frame continued to provide effective cover for U.S. treatment of enemy detainees. The rhetorical fusion of Saddam Hussein with al Qaeda and the September 11 attacks proved a potent mix. Allegations that Hussein had WMD and would use them for offensive purposes were credible. He had used chemical weapons before in the Iran-Iraq War, with 50,000 Iranian casualties estimated during the eight-year conflict (1980–88) and another 100,000 suffering long-term effects, and against Kurds living in Iran during the Halabja poison gas attack, which took place on March 16, 1988, during the closing months of the Iran-Iraq War. That attack took 5,000 lives and injured 11,000 more, mostly civilians. It is regarded as an act of genocide and the largest chemical weapons attack in history directed against a civilian-populated area.

Notwithstanding the twelve-year embargo on Iraq following the Persian Gulf War (aka Operation Desert Storm, August 2, 1990–February 28, 1991), these images were resuscitated after the September 11 attack. In his August 26, 2002, speech at the Veterans of Foreign Wars (VFW) National Convention, Vice President Cheney (2002) warned, "Simply stated, there is no doubt that Saddam Hussein now has weapons of mass destruction." The next month, in his speech to the U.N. General Assembly, Bush (2002) stated, "Right now, Iraq is expanding and improving facilities that were used for the production of biological weapons." At his December 2 press briefing, White Hourse Press Secretary Ari Fleischer (2002) dismissed Hussein's denial that Iraq had WMD. "If he declares he has none, then we will know that Saddam Hussein is once again misleading the world." A month later Fleischer (2003) informed the press corps, "We know for a fact that there are weapons there." Then, in his State of the Union address, Bush (2003a) told the nation, "Our intelligence officials estimate that Saddam Hussein had the materials to produce as much as 500 tons of sarin, mustard and VX nerve agent." A week later, on February 5, Secretary of State Colin Powell (2003a), perhaps the most respected U.S. voice on these matters, asserted to the U.N. Security Council, "We know that Saddam Hussein is determined to keep his weapons of mass destruction, is determined to make more." That weekend, the president (Bush 2003b) used his radio address to affirm, "We have sources that tell us that Saddam Hussein recently authorized Iraqi field commanders to use chemical weapons—the very weapons the dictator tells [the] U.S. he does not have." On February 28, with the president having given Hussein a deadline to surrender his WMD and with the specter of war looming, Powell (2003b) told a Radio France interviewer, "If Iraq had disarmed itself, gotten rid of its weapons of mass destruction over the past 12 years, or over the last several months since (U.N. Resolution) 1441 was enacted, we would not be facing the crisis that we now have before us. . . . But the suggestion that we are doing this because we want to go to every country in the Middle East and rearrange all of its pieces is not correct." The next week, Powell (2003c) raised and answered this question in his remarks to the U.N. Security Council, "So has the strategic decision been made to disarm Iraq of its weapons of mass destruction by the leadership in Baghdad? . . . I think our judgment has to be clearly not." Finally, in his 2003 address to the nation, Bush (2003c) asserted, "Intelligence gathered by this and other governments leaves no doubt that the Iraq regime continues to possess and conceal some of the most lethal weapons ever devised."

The war frame accommodated an Iraq-WMD-terrorism coupling with palpable effect on American sentiment. In the Gallup Poll of January 11–14, 2002, 77 percent favored military action against Iraq as part of the war on terrorism, up from 74 percent in the November 26–27, 2001, poll.[6] After a decline, the June 17–19, 2002, poll saw 47 percent of Americans saying that removing Saddam Hussein from power should be a very important foreign policy goal, while less than one in six Americans thought this should not be an important goal. Core support for removing Hussein from power remained steady up to the March 2003 invasion. The March 3–5 Gallup Poll reported 59 percent favored attempting to remove Hussein from power, while 37 percent opposed.[7] Support for the war effort remained strong into 2004, as a spring Gallup Poll reported 55 percent of Americans were very/somewhat satisfied with the way things were going for the United States in the war on terrorism. The administration's rhetoric that conflated conditions in Iraq with terrorist organizations and the danger they represented to the United States was working. It tapped into a patriotic fervor born from the September 11 attack and extended it to support a policy of military action with the objective of regime change. It also kept objections to how it treated enemy detainees largely confined to, in the words of John Yoo, "pundits and professors" (2006, *passim*).

The war frame used to justify the extraordinary actions taken by the administration at home and in the Middle East while at the same time denying POW rights to detainees was equally successful. A September 2003 Washington Post–ABC News poll asked: "Do you support or oppose the federal government holding suspected terrorists without trial at the U.S. military prison in Guantánamo Bay, Cuba?" The responses were: Support–65 percent; Oppose–28 percent; No opinion–7 percent (abcnews 2006, 3). Inventive legal interpretations supporting the nonapplicability of treaties, U.S. law, and the U.S. legal code at Guantánamo Bay rendered the detainees into "illegal enemy combatants" deemed not to qualify for protections such as habeas corpus rights and determination by a qualified court of whether they were being held legally. In short, there was a war on terror, but detainees who were on the other side—terrorists rendered stateless since they were not soldiers fighting in the military of a nation—were not POWs. Arguably, the war on terror was a war when it suited the adminstration's purposes. Then came the revelations about Abu Ghraib. The images denormalized the legal arguments by placing the acts in a different frame, a different arrangement of space and time that invited outrage at the interrogators rather than our admiration and gratitude.

Abu Ghraib and the Call of Conscience

The story of what occurred at Abu Ghraib is by now well known, although its meaning remains deeply contested. That contest is largely a function of competing frames that depicted the treatment of Iraqi detainees as the actions of a few rogue soldiers insufficiently controlled by a weak command structure or as the result of explicit orders that trace back to the MO of November 13, 2001, and the president's memorandum of February 7, 2002. The interpretations of what took place were and remain interpolated by the images of prisoner treatment circulating in the public sphere.

Who's in Charge?

The prison at Abu Ghraib was built in the 1960s by British contractors. It was a huge facility, occupying 280 acres with over 4 kilometers of security perimeter and twenty-four guard towers. During Hussein's regime, it had five sections. The political section included a closed wing, which housed only Shi'ites, and the open wing, which held all types of real and suspected activists. Those in the closed wing were denied visitors and contact with the outside world. They were housed in cells measuring 4 by 4 meters that were crammed with as many as forty prisoners. By 2001, it housed as many as 15,000 prisoners, which included hundreds of Kurds and other citizens of Iranian origin who were captured during the Iran-Iraq War and had been held incommunicado and without charges under harsh conditions for close to two decades. This population also included many who had been subjected to Iraq's outlawed experimental chemical and biological warfare programs. Then, in 2002, Hussein declared an amnesty to thank the Iraqi people for a referendum that extended his reign for seven years and released all prisoners with the exception of convicted murderers. An estimated 13,000 prisoners were set free from Abu Ghraib, and it was deserted when American forces occupied it in 2003.

The use of Abu Ghraib as a detention facility for POWs was compromised from the outset by ambiguity over the command function of Military Police (MP) and Military Intelligence (MI) within the prison. The Pentagon decoupled the MP and MI command structures, which had different missions and levels of access to decision makers. While MI had a direct line to the Pentagon, Maj. Gen. Janice Karpinski, commanding officer of the prison facility and within the MP chain of command, found herself out of the intelligence loop that went directly to Rumsfeld's office and, consequently, both uninformed about interrogation tactics and excluded from important decisions about what went on in the prison under her command. Matters were further complicated when the Pentagon, dissatisfied with the intelligence it was receiving from detainees at Abu Ghraib, sent Maj. Gen. Geoffrey Miller, who had been in charge of MI at Guantánamo Bay and, as we saw earlier, had initiated the Beaver memo that led to Rumsfeld's approval of harsh interrogation techniques, to tour the facility and make recommendations. According to the *Los Angeles Times*, Miller's recommendations for overhauling detention and interrogation procedures in Iraq included his advice that "it was time to 'Gitmo-ize' Abu Ghraib by introducing the kind of aggressive techniques used to grill suspects in Guantánamo" (McDonnell 2004). Under orders to get results, many of the MI personnel, often untrained in interrogation techniques and/or acting in disregard of military procedures for interrogation, ordered MPs to give prisoners slated for interrogation a "hard time" the night before. The MPs, also untrained in interrogation procedures, instead of clearing orders with their superiors, acted inappropriately by improvising ways to "soften up" detainees. Finally, commanding officers had not reprimanded their subordinates for violations nor had they taken action to prevent them from recurring. Not the least of these was women soldiers assigned to administrative duties spending evenings fraternizing with MPs in the criminal wing (Taguba 2004; Schlesinger 2004; Jones and Fay 2004).

The abuse of prisoners was not unknown to the prison command structure. The ICRC had filed a report with the Coalition Forces (CF) in February 2004, in which it described the main violations at CF facilities as including:

> Brutality against protected persons upon capture and initial custody, sometimes causing death or serious injury
>
> Absence at notification of arrest of persons deprived of their liberty to their families causing distress among persons deprived of their liberty and their families
>
> Physical or psychological coercion during interrogation to secure information
> Prolonged solitary confinement in cells devoid of daylight, and
> Excessive and disproportionate use of force against persons deprived of their liberty resulting in death or injury during their period of internment. (3)

The report's section on Abu Ghraib discusses specific abuses observed there during the ICRC's mid-October 2003 inspection. It had observed interrogations conducted by military intelligence officers in Unit 1A, the "isolation section" of Abu Ghraib Correctional Facility. The observers witnessed and/or documented harsh treatment during arrest; beatings, some causing death and with fabricated cause of death indicated on death certificates; prisoners with hands secured behind their backs with flexicuffs, hooded, and made to sit on a hot surface thought to be the hood of a vehicle; lesions and burns consistent with prisoners' allegations of how they were treated; hematoma consistent with repeated whipping or beating; threats, insults, verbal violence, sleep deprivation caused by piping loud music or by constant light in cells devoid of windows; completely naked prisoners in totally empty concrete cells and in total darkness, allegedly for several consecutive days; and prisoners being made to walk in the corridors handcuffed and naked, or with women's underwear on the head, or being handcuffed either dressed or naked to the bed bars or the cell door. "Upon witnessing such cases, the ICRC interrupted its visits and requested an explanation from the authorities. The military intelligence officer in charge of the interrogation explained that this practice was 'part of the process'" (International Committee of the Red Cross 2004, 13).

The report continues to note that the ICRC's medical delegate examined prisoners who presented "signs of concentration difficulties, memory problems, verbal expression difficulties, incoherent speech, acute anxiety reactions, abnormal behaviour and suicidal tendencies. These symptoms appeared to have been caused by the methods and duration of interrogation. One person held in isolation that the ICRC examined, was unresponsive to verbal and painful stimuli. His heart rate was 120 beats per minute and his respiratory rate 18 per minute. He was diagnosed as suffering from somatoform (mental) disorder, specifically a conversion disorder, most likely due to the ill-treatment he was subjected to during interrogation" (13).

Finally, prisoners alleged they had not been informed of the reason for their arrest, and could not ask questions or seek clarification in this regard. Families were not notified, as required by the Geneva Conventions. This allegation was particularly alarming in light of the report by a CF military intelligence officer to the ICRC that 70 to 90 percent of detainees in Iraq were arrested by mistake.

The ICRC and HRW objections apparently caught the attention of Lt. Gen. Ricardo Sanchez, senior officer in Iraq, who opened an AR 15–6 investigation into the conduct of the 800th MP Brigade in charge of the Abu Ghraib facility. In addition to detainee abuse, Sanchez noted reports of detainee escapes and accountability lapses between November 1, 2003, and the present as the focus of the investigation, and placed Maj. Gen. Antonio Taguba in charge. In January 2004, Spc. Joseph Darby, an MP at Abu Ghraib, slid an envelope under the door of the army's Criminal Investigation Division. The package contained compact discs of hundreds of digital photographs, many depicting abuse, that Cpl. Charles Graner had nonchalantly shared with Darby. These provided prima facie evidence, in the Taguba Report's words:

> that between October and December 2003, at the Abu Ghraib Confinement
> Facility (BCCF), numerous incidents of sadistic, blatant, and wanton criminal

abuses were inflicted on several detainees. This systemic and illegal abuse of detainees was intentionally perpetrated by several members of the military police guard force (372nd Military Police Company, 320th Military Police Battalion, 800th MP Brigade), in Tier (section) 1-A of the Abu Ghraib Prison (BCCF). The allegations of abuse were substantiated by detailed witness statements (ANNEX 26) and the discovery of extremely graphic photographic evidence. (Taguba 2004, 416)

Although the Taguba Report was classified, CBS acquired a copy, along with some of the photographic evidence, and aired the report's findings and several of the damning images on its April 28, 2004, broadcast of *60 Minutes II*. A week later Seymour Hersh published an article in the *New Yorker* going into more detail about the sexual humiliation of the detainees, the physical beatings, stress positions, and the murky role of MI operatives in the prisoner mistreatment. These reports, along with the photographic evidence, had the potential to reframe the war on terrorism. The 60 Minutes II broadcast ignited an international outcry. Americans originally saw slightly more than a dozen images, which featured scenes of prisoners cowering before attack dogs, being sexually humiliated, assembled naked in human pyramids, being beaten by their guards, and in poses that suggested they were subjected to at least the threat of electrical shocks. Hersh's more analytical article gave greater detail about the extent of savagery by commenting on the full range of abuses depicted in the photographs, only a fraction of which had been aired.

See What We Are Doing: Images of War

The American public had been introduced into a visual economy of the Iraq War through the images provided by embedded reporters. In return for access to battlefield and occupation sites, they had agreed to limit their reporting to approved sites. After the famed "mission accomplished" announcement by President Bush six weeks after the invasion of Iraq began,[8] the battle line became asymmetrical. American television was awash with nightly reports of insurgent attacks, mostly by suicide bombers, roadside bombs, and long-range missiles that made the notion of "front lines" obsolete and the distinction between combat and noncombat military roles difficult to sustain. Practically speaking, an unconventional war with an asymmetrical battle line offers support troops and local inhabitants no protection from combat. Thus, Americans witnessed military personnel and civilians being targeted regardless of whether they occupied what are designated "direct ground combat positions."

Nightly scenes of suicide bombings were balanced by stories of military valor, as U.S. soldiers faced a shadowy enemy who could be anyone and strike from anywhere at anytime. Nonetheless, a year later support for the war remained close to what it had been at the time of the Iraq invasion (59 percent at its inception versus 55 percent in early 2004), as images and video footage of bombing scenes kept the threat of terrorist attacks fresh in the public's eye, while the costs of the war in lives lost were visually absent because of the aforementioned adminstration ban on photographing the caskets of military casualties when they returned to the United States.

The photographs from Abu Ghraib interrupted this economy. For some, such as the *New Yorker's* Seymour Hersh (2004), "The photographs tell it all." The images of naked Iraqis appearing in humiliating poses, their defenseless bodies threatened by attack dogs, chained in painful positions, placed in human pyramids, hooded and attached to wires while balancing on a box on end, posed to appear as if performing oral sex, offer the spectacle of, to quote the Taguba Report (2004, part 1), "sadistic, blatant, and wanton criminal abuse." The meaning of these photographs, however, relied less on an official report than how they circulated publicly. What these images tell us of prisoner treatment and military conduct at Abu Ghraib, however, remains an open question, especially when we focus less on what they mean through the lens of a critic's sensibilities and more on the responses these photographs evoked from Americans and, more important, why they responded as they did. That concern leads us to consider how the moral vernacular of their visual rhetoric interrogates the official rhetoric of the Bush adminstration on the treatment of enemy detainees.

At the time the Abu Ghraib incident became an international story, there were a small number of images in circulation. In the six-month period immediately following the *60 Minutes II* airing and publication of the Hersh article, when the Abu Ghraib story was at its zenith, I was able to locate twenty-eight images of torture at the prison.[9] There were, of course, many more than this on the CDs turned in by Darby and found on the memory cards of the MPs implicated in the scandal. These included photographs and videos of soldiers having sex and images of naked Iraqi female prisoners, which were reported widely in the press. Since the end of 2004, many more have entered the public domain, although many remain classified as the Obama adminstration reversed its position ordering release of the photographs on grounds that they would inflame passion in the Middle East and place U.S. soldiers at increased risk.

However, the images that circulated initially were few in number. These were not only available on the Internet but were the photographs most commonly discussed in the news media. Of these twenty-eight, five involve dogs, six depict human pyramids, five are of men placed in stress positions, one depicts prisoners simulating fellatio, four are of a dead man, four involve Pfc. Lynndie England, one involves Cpl. Grener punching one among a pile of manacled detainees, three involve Spc. Sabrina Harman. Principal among these was the iconic image of a hooded Iraqi detainee standing on a box on end with wires attached to his body (image 1), photographs of England in sexualized poses with a man on a leash (image 2) or leering at a naked prisoner who is holding his penis (although the shading of his genitalia on the image circulating on the Internet made it appear he was masturbating) (image 3), and photographs of naked prisoners stacked on top of one another to form a human

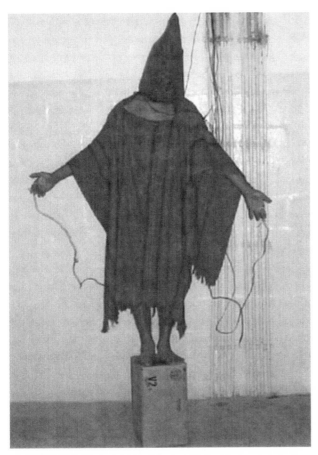

Image 1

pyramid (image 4). There were two additional images available on the Internet—one from the outset (image 5) and another that was released by Australia's Special Broadcasting Service TV on February 26, 2006, and posted the next day on Antiwar.com (image 6).

Image 1 captures a man hooded and wearing a poncho with arms outstretched, standing on a box with electric wires attached to his fingers. The prisoner's name is Satar Jabar, referred to by the Abu Ghraib MPs as "Gilligan." At her trial, Sabrina Harman testified that she attached the wires to his fingers and "joked" with him that if he fell off he would be electrocuted. This became the iconic image of Abu Ghraib, with the figure of the hooded "Gilligan" evoking interpretations most commonly linked to Christ on the cross and the Ku Klux Klan. In the uncropped version of this photograph, Sgt. Chip Frederick is seen standing in the foreground on the right side of the frame looking intently at the screen on his camera, perhaps scanning photographs he had taken. The juxtaposition of utter detachment from the unfolding scene and infliction of psychological terror captured by the uncropped photograph is a self-critique of the degree to which the MPs had become desensitized to the gratuitous pain they were inflicting on their detainees. The cropped version, however, took on an interpretive life of its own.

The image has an aesthetic quality that engages our imagination. Viewers did not know who was under the hood. There is no self-evident reading. It was appropriated on the web and in graphic art as a crucifixion scene (Eisenman 2007; Klein 2010; Sentilles 2008; Tanzer 2008). As Stephen F. Eisenman has pointed out, the image of Christ's crucifixion has a long history of aestheticization in Western history, such as "Christ on the Cross" by Diego Velasquez, Phillippe Champaigne, Albrecht Dürer, and Peter Rubens. What these images have in common, is "in each case excruciating pain and destruction [are] represented as beautiful, and even erotic . . . [Therefore,] Christ at the moment of his crucifixion is often depicted as intensely beautiful, even sexually aroused" (Eisenman 2007, 61, 63).

For Eisenman, the image's instantiation of the "ancient pathos formula of beautiful suffering—the introversion of subordination"—is evidence it has reemerged in "the minds, eyes and bodies of men and women serving in the U.S. military in Iraq . . ." (2007, 111). Modernized, he calls it the "Abu Ghraib effect," a moral blindness which allows [the U.S. public and the amateur photographers at Abu Ghraib] to ignore, or even to justify, however partially or provisionally the facts of degradation and brutality manifest in the pictures" (9).

Without gainsaying the validity of the aesthetic producing a voyeuristic effect in which brutality to others becomes a source of visual fascination, the ambiguity of the image is complicated by the obvious irony of the Christ crucified image appearing in the hood and robe reminiscent of the Ku Klux Klan. It crowns the sacrificed victim with the most notorious and vilest image of U.S. moral failure now being sacrificed by Americans acting on similarly racist impulses.

In this same register, the photograph is distinctive among those initially made public in that it the denies the Muslim body identity. By covering it, the image shrouds "person-ality" and the individual's human right to freedom of action, association, and thought. It focuses our attention on a submissive figure, apparently put in this pose with a warning of dire consequences, possibly execution, if he moves.

These associations—the aesthetic reading of the crucifixion and its association with trophy photographs of black lynchings, the denial of "person-ality" and human rights—does not give the prisoner, or the guards who committed the deeds, a human face. However, it does point to the soldiers who had taken the snapshots and focused public anger on them.

As widely circulated as was the "Gilligan" image, the sexualized poses in images 2 and 3 provided a dominant frame for the abuses at Abu Ghraib. Together they established a narrative that did not direct the most pertinent questions of responsibility up

Image 2

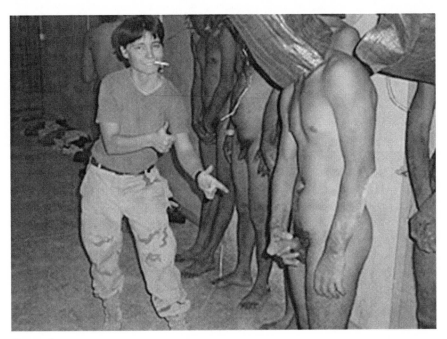

Image 3

the chain of command. In fact, as we know, the circulation of these disturbing photographs of sexualized humiliation gave public meaning to U.S. military complicity through the dominant image of Pfc. Lynndie England. In one (image 2), England has a collared Iraqi prisoner, cowering on the floor, attached to her leash as she strikes a dominatrix pose. In another (image 3), she strikes a jaunty pose with a cigarette dangling from her lips and giving the thumbs-up sign while offering the camera a leering grin as she points to the genitals of a young Iraqi. In a third (image 4), England stands arm in arm with Cpl. Graner behind a pyramid of perhaps seven naked Iraqi prisoners while grinning into the camera and giving the thumbs-up sign.

Hersh's initial assessment that the pictures spoke for themselves was challenged when the storyline destabilized soon after the images, apparently taken as private souvenirs, became public. They intersected the discussion of prisoner treatment at

Image 4

Guantánamo then circulating in the public sphere. At issue were such matters as American citizens being detained while their rights to habeas corpus were denied and publicized photographs of Taliban prisoners in shackles and painful postures that lent credibility to rumors of harsh treatment. In the context of the Guantánamo discussion, outrage over the sexualized humiliation of the Iraqi prisoners initially focused on the chain of command. The soldiers alleged they were acting under orders. Verifying or refuting that required inquiry up the chain for who might have issued orders to treat prisoners in violation of the Geneva Conventions. That line of investigation quickly ended when the nation's attention was redirected toward England, the unlikely administrator of torture. Instead of constituting citizens as critical judges of whether this sexual humiliation was authorized, they were encouraged to assume the role of spectators of Pvt. England—petite, young, already demoted in rank, and, as we soon learned, a "fallen woman"—as lead character in an embarrassing and sexualized barracks scandal.

Some tried to dismiss the pictures as a release of stress under the trying conditions confronting an occupying force.[10] On his May 3, 2004, show, Rush Limbaugh concluded that the women among American troops who mistreated Iraqi prisoners of war were "babes" and that pictures of the alleged abuse were no worse than "anything you'd see Madonna, or Britney Spears do on stage."

> And these American prisoners of war—have you people noticed who the torturers are? Women! The babes! The babes are meting out the torture. . . .
>
> You know, if you look at—if you, really, if you look at these pictures, I mean, I don't know if it's just me, but it looks just like anything you'd see Madonna, or Britney Spears do on stage. Maybe I'm—yeah. And get an NEA grant for something like this. I mean, this is something that you can see on stage at Lincoln Center from an NEA grant, maybe on Sex in the City—the movie. I mean, I don't—it's just me.

The next day, as President Bush prepared to address the Arab world to condemn the abuse of Iraqi prisoners by U.S. military personnel, Limbaugh continued his "kids will be kids" storyline when he justified the U.S. guards' mistreatment as young people letting off a little steam.

> CALLER: It was like a college fraternity prank that stacked up naked men.
> LIMBAUGH: Exactly. Exactly my point! This is no different than what happens at the Skull and Bones initiation and we're going to ruin people's lives over it and we're going to hamper our military effort, and then we are going to really hammer them because they had a good time. You know, these people are being fired at every day. I'm talking about people having a good time, these people, you ever heard of emotional release? You ever heard of need to blow some steam off? (2004)

The idea that this was a prank fed into the developing focus on the young woman who became the instant poster girl for the prisoners' abuse. On CBS's *60 Minutes II*, Al-Schweiri, an Abu Ghraib prisoner, offered this explanation of U.S. abuse: "They were trying to humiliate us. . . . They wanted us to feel as though we were women, the way women feel and this is the worst insult, to feel like a woman" (in Mascirotte 2004). The coherence of that interpretation with media depictions of England res-onated in the American cultural imaginary as well. The picture of "leash man," with England in a dominatrix pose against the backdrop of stark cinder block walls and cell bars sporting an untidy adornment of towels and laundry, catapulted the viewer into the male prison culture where the stronger make the weaker their "bitches." England, depicted in the S&M pose of dominatrix, meanwhile performed the alter-nate "bitch" role of overpowering woman. For some, such as ICeman posting on om _blog, England was a sexual fantasy incarnate. "Men, that girl really turns me on! I hope she puts ME on a leash."[11] For others, she became the source of inspiration to do the same. The September 2, 2004, NCBuy (2004) carried a wireless flash under the headline: "LONDON (Wireless Flash)—There's a new craze sweeping the Internet and it's called 'The Lynndie.'" The article began, "Across the globe, camera-toting mischief-makers are snapping shots of themselves mimicking the finger-pointing pose of alleged Iraqi prison scandal perpetrator Lynndie England."

England's persona took an unexpected turn when her identity changed from Pvt. Lynndie England to "fallen" and pregnant Lynndie England, and we learned, in addi-tion, that the father was Spc. Charles Grener, also already demoted in rank, to whom she reported. In a fashion redolent with nineteenth-century definitions of woman-hood, media accounts framed England's military competence with patriarchal images of women that subordinate their suitability for military roles to feminine stereotypes (Hauser and Sanprie 2007). Her body's condition became a refutation that she could have been ordered to perform the humiliations, as she alleged, or proof that she was twisted.

On May 14, W. Thomas Smith Jr., a former Marine paratrooper writing for the *National Review* online, framed his assessment of England's account that she was following orders by observing: "Perhaps England was ordered to pose for seamy photographs: One with a cigarette dangling from her smiling lips as she points to a naked prisoner's genitals, the other as she holds an animal leash attached to a collar on another prisoner. But how could a 21-year-old mother-to-be (England is five-months pregnant) deemed responsible enough to work in an enemy prisoner facility in a war zone obey such an order? And then act is if she's enjoying it?" (Smith 2004).

The question for Smith is clearly one of feminine character, and one senses from the tone of incredulity that there is an implied "unfit" before the "mother-to-be" depiction of England's participation in the pornographic humiliation of Iraqi men. The association of England's role with her pregnancy had as much relevance to the question of responsibility for torture at Abu Ghraib as Hillary Clinton's hair to the

Whitewater scandal. But it fitted with the way depictions of bodies in pain were being recast as a story of a bad ("bad") woman acting out her sexual fantasies by projecting the torture through the lens of the perpetrator's body.

The *National Review* was not alone in focusing on England's pregnancy. As the charges levied against her worked their way through the military courts, press coverage made reference to her pregnancy, her body as "visibly pregnant," and, where her body was not mentioned, photographs accompanied the story showing her to be "visibly pregnant." Richard Goldstein (2004), writing in *Village Voice* online under the headline: "Bitch Bites Man! Why Lynndie England Is the Public Face of Torturegate," observed: "But then, England is no maiden, as the media duly noted by reporting that she'd been knocked up by her military boyfriend Charles Graner. He's also been named in the torture case, and many stories about him mentioned that he had been accused of abusing his former wife. But when a dude acts out, it's dog bites man. When a babe misbehaves, it's bitch bites man—and unfortunately that's a story."

The "sad but true" excuse for the sex angle that had captivated press coverage may explain why news coverage featured her so prominently, but it ignores the consequences for political relations resulting from how the images of tortured bodies were being framed. With England firmly established as the poster girl for Abu Ghraib, public attention and outrage remained focused on the troops captured in the images. As long as that remained the focus of attention, the military's claim that this was the action of a few rogue MPs and that it did not reflect troops acting under orders from above remained plausible cover. Thus, the report of former defense secretary James Schlesinger (2004), which notes adminstration policies such as the August 1, 2002, DOJ opinion that redefined torture as pain "equivalent in intensity to the pain accompanying serious physical injury such as organ failure, impairment of bodily function, or even death," fails to evaluate whether the policies played a role in contributing to the abuses. Equally, the 171-page Fay Report (Jones and Fay 2004) cites more than two-dozen military intelligence officers, along with several military contractors. It details some forty-four incidents, including the stripping, hooding, and sodomizing of detainees; subjecting them to temperature extremes; leading them around naked on leashes; and attaching electrical wires to their genitals. In one case, two naked youths were terrorized by snarling, unmuzzled military dogs held by military personnel who competed to try to make the teenagers defecate. Yet it fails to address the obvious question: what role did official government policies play in bringing about the horrendous abuses? Although news outlets reported the soldiers' claims that they were acting under orders, there was little apparent enthusiasm by the news media either to ferret out facts that supported or refuted their allegations. In the absence of corroborating or refuting evidence, citizens were left with a "that's what they say" impression of the MPs' defense that they were scapegoats.

Might things have been different were other photographs given wide circulation? We will never have a definitive answer to that question. However, there are different

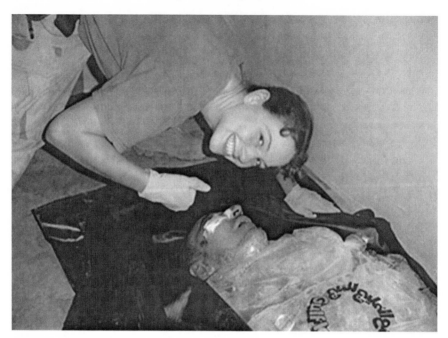

Image 5

frames provided by two other photographs that are part of the Abu Ghraib collection: one available from the outset (image 5) and one that became publicly available two years later (image 6).

Image 5 contains a dead man in a body bag with Spc. Harman kneeling next to his head looking up into the camera with a smile and giving the thumbs-up sign. Harman, who was convicted by a court-martial for her conduct at Abu Ghraib, sat for nine hours of interviews with Errol Morris for his movie *Standard Operating Procedure* dealing with abuses at the prison. She said she began taking pictures almost immediately.

> ERROL MORRIS: Why did you have this urge right from the beginning? Because it was so weird, or . . . ?
> SABRINA HARMAN: I don't know, it's just—It's kind of hard to believe if I come up to you and I'm like, "Hey, this is going on," you probably wouldn't believe me unless I had something to show you. So if I say, "Hey, this is going on. Look, I have proof," you can't deny it, I guess (Magazine 2008).

The impulse to document what was happening may have been her initial motivation, but the numerous scenes of degradation, such as human pyramids and Graner suturing dog bite wounds of detainees, in which Harman grins into the camera while giving the thumbs-up sign, indicate she was as much participant as recorder of documentary evidence to demonstrate some truth about prisoner treatment.

The corpse in image 5 is Manadel al-Jamadi, referred to as Detainee-28 in the Fay Report, an Iraqi man who had been detained by the CIA. Al-Jamadi had been captured by a Navy Seal team, which suspected him of involvement in an attack against the ICRC. According to the Fay Report, "He was reportedly resisting arrest, and a SEAL Team member butt-stroked him on the side of the head to suppress the threat he posed" (Jones and Fay 2004, 76). He was bought to the prison between 4:30 and 5:30 on the morning of November 4, apparently in good health, but without notification of the Joint Interrogation and Debriefing Center (JIDC), and removed to a shower in tier 1b. He was restrained in a position known as the Palestinian hanging, in which the arms are secured behind the person and then hoisted above the person's head. An army specialist was summoned to the shower stall and found al-Jamadi was dead. Al-Jamadi was a ghost detainee, meaning his identity had not been recorded. Had it been recorded, a report on the incident would have been required, and there may well have been a formal investigation. Since he was a ghost prisoner, however, the Other Government Agency (OGA, aka CIA) instructed he be packed in ice and kept in a room until the next day. To remove him from prison, he was placed on a gurney with an IV in his arm, to make it appear as if he were ill in order to avoid agitating the prisoners. Once removed, his body was disposed of. There was good reason to avoid calling his death to the attention of the prisoners, since they had rioted the night before over poor conditions in the prison, which was crowded, filthy, and dangerous. There had been considerable violence in the effort to reestablish order, which provided convenient cover in the report on the riot that listed al-Jimadi as one of three prisoners killed in suppressing it.

Later, on November 4, Harman and Graner came upon the closed room where his body was stored on ice in a body bag awaiting removal from the prison. They asked the MI guarding the room for permission to look at al-Jamadi's body. Their viewing is recorded in twenty-six images, including image 5 in which Harman grins as she poses alongside al-Jamadi's corpse. She is wearing army fatigues; her hair is pulled back in a pony tail. She is grinning into the camera and giving the thumbs-up sign. Harman's appearance mutes her gender, does not frame her as a sexual predator, and does not depict sexual humiliation of the Muslim body.

This photograph did not receive wide press circulation, perhaps out of respect for the dead. At the same time, it asks for a different response from its viewer than images 1–4. From one perspective, it can be seen as a desecration of al-Jimadi's corpse, oblivious to its history as a human and reduced to an object of ghoulish curiosity. Even discounting that it is framed by the collection of twenty-six images, the majority taken of the corpse's head and body from different angles, the photograph's disturbing lack of propriety is evident. Harman grinning into the camera and giving the thumbs-up sign, as if this were a victory, another of the bad guys who no longer can cause trouble, belies her earlier claim that she wanted to document what was happening. Her grin and gesture are oblivious to the fact that she is witness to a homicide, or that the deceased man had not yet been proven to be a bad guy and may have been as innocent as the majority of political prisoners at Abu Ghraib who, in overwhelming numbers, had done nothing wrong. Harman looking up from the corpse, while grinning and giving the thumbs-up sign, suggests that her interest was less to record this death than her own curiosity and even celebration of what military personnel at the prison were able to do to those in their charge. The image is predatory, neither protecting the dead man's identity nor concealing the power of those in charge to victimize and even slay those under their control. This image is a celebration of raw power.

From a second perspective, the photograph raises questions about the corpse: Who is he? What has he done? What happened to him? Who is responsible? Who ordered his death? These questions lead away from Harman. Was it the CIA? Did it act as Graner alleged in an April 2005 statement to the army Criminal Investigation Command (CID): "You know these guys can kill people. . . . The OGA guys do whatever they want. They don't exist" (in Scherer and Benjamin 2006). Was Harman's expression of disbelief accurate in pointing to where national concern should be focused?

> They tried to charge me with destruction of government property, which I don't understand. And then maltreatment, of taking the photos of a dead guy. But he's dead, I don't know how that's maltreatment. And altering evidence, for taking a bandage from his eye to take a photo of it? And then I placed it back. When he died, they cleaned him all up and then stuck the bandages on. So it's not really altering evidence, they had already done that for me. In order to make the other charges stick, they were going to have to bring in the photos. Which they didn't want—to bring up the dead guy at all, [or] the OGA, because obviously they covered up a murder and that would just make them look bad. So they dropped all the charges pertaining to the OGA and the shower. (in Lasage 2009)

That trail likely would have led to CIA interrogator Mark Swanner and contract translator "Clint C.," who were prime suspects for al-Jamadi's murder. That, in turn, would have led to inquiry into the treatment of prisoners, the approval of interrogation techniques by Rumsfeld, and the OLC and DOJ memos that provided their legal warrant. However, Clint C. got immunity from criminal prosecution for his testimony, and Swanner has never been charged (Lasage 2009).

When the image of Harman kneeling over al-Jamadi's corpse became public, his status as a ghost prisoner evaporated. In a fitting reversal of positive and negative that was an inherent part of photography before the digital camera, the public photograph reversed his erasure, gave him a physical identity. It defeated the ghost the army tried to create. He could never be recalled to life, but the photographs made him a part of our collective lives. What remained was what we would do with the questions raised by the images of his corpse, turned into an object for curiosity seekers: Why was nobody held accountable for his death? Why had the general in charge or her superiors up the chain of command to the secretary of defense, and quite possibly the president, done nothing?

So far I have examined photographs that display ordinary vices, the failings of soldiers and the military that show their venality and suggest as much about their superiors. We have seen how those photographs that were in circulation were appropriated in ways that led to the soldiers' failings while deflecting attention from their superiors. We also saw how the Harman image with the corpse of al-Jamadi asks a different set of questions that begins to interrogate the official discourse of the Bush adminstration to justify treatment of enemy bodies reduced to bare life. I now want to consider image 6, which was not placed in circulation until 2006—two years after the scandal broke—and which has not received widespread circulation on the Internet.

Image 6 captures a naked man standing against a wall. He is the solitary figure in the photograph. It is shot at an eye-of-god angle from above. The man's left hand is holding his forehead, and his right arm is positioned across his torso, holding his body. There is light coming from above that falls on his head and left shoulder. The dispersal of shadows suggests the space is without natural lighting, and the shadows and lighting contrast across the man's body. Elements of framing, contrasting lighting, and body position give the image an aesthetic quality. We don't know whether the man was posed for this picture. He is standing erect against the wall. There is symmetry to this picture. We can linger on it. We find ourselves asking many questions.

If we did not know this was a photograph in prison, we might consider it as possibly a picture of a man deep in contemplation. However, there are elements that suggest there is more to it. Although his posture suggests he is deep in thought, the fact that he is standing naked and ramrod straight against an institutional wall and that he is being observed makes us suspect there is more than contemplation at play. Who is observing him? Why is he being observed? Why is he in an institution? What is the institution? Perhaps the man is not just contemplating but also trying to comfort himself, perhaps from torment. If that is so, why is he tormented? There is no visible cause; he is a subject withdrawn to an interior space where he must find consolation through his own devices.

Knowing it is an image from Abu Ghraib changes this picture. We know who administered his pain, and surely we can target our emotions at the cause. However, we also have information that implicates us as citizens, or that implicates the U.S. government and its policies. Our focus can go elsewhere than rogue soldiers. Is that because there isn't a visible abuser? Is that because there isn't an obvious act of abuse? The erasure of the tormentor also erases the obvious target of blame. The photographs of

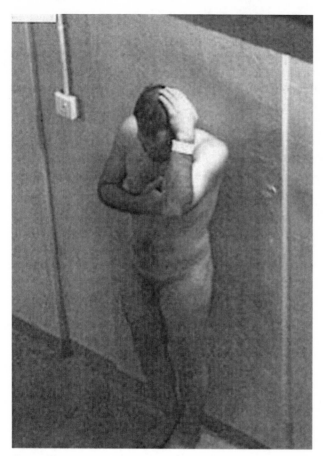

Image 6

England administering sexual humiliation or the MPs striking posed smiles akin to tourists while standing behind pyramids of naked Iraqi detainees are shocking. Our shock is not just from the pain to which we are eyewitnesses but from the expressions of pleasure on the MPs faces, who seem to be experiencing a rush from the pain of others. Our shock also serves as a form of emotional deflection. We look; we feel shame; we feel anger; we know whom to blame because we have photographic evidence. We can salve our conscience; we are innocent. The personalized response also does not interrogate the policy that stands behind the treatment. The naked man standing against the wall is not a photograph that shocks.

The photographs in which we see the MPs administering abuse make their viewers eyewitnesses to scenes in which the scene itself serves as a form of inartistic proof, a testimony that calls on us to recognize that abuse has taken place. And yet their reception indicates their call was not clearly heard; some not only failed to recognize them as images of abuse but also appropriated them into cultural narratives that had little, if anything, to do with the scenes they captured. For those who did hear their call, the extreme treatment of naked, hooded, handcuffed, defenseless men being manhandled and humiliated by MPs is so far beyond what an American public was prepared to associate with its military, much less to be made eyewitnesses, that the perpetrators of cruelty, caught on camera, were easy targets for blame.

The man standing naked against the Abu Ghraib wall places us in a different relationship to the prisoner body. To suffer is one thing; it is quite another to live with the photographed images of suffering, which does not necessarily strengthen conscience and the ability to be compassionate (Sontag 1973). It can also corrupt them. Once we have seen such images, we have started down the road of seeing more—and more. Repeated viewing of the Abu Ghraib photographs, as with all shocking images, can transfix and anesthetize. But after repeated exposure, these images also become less real. The shock of photographed atrocities wears off. The sense of taboo that makes us indignant and sorrowful is easily satisfied by accepting our eyewitness role. We need not become actively engaged because the images speak for themselves, and our shock, once registered at the behavior of American troops, has relieved us of the need to do more.

The Iraqi prisoner photograph is open-ended, and that is its value. It does not provide answers to questions of what was going on in the prison or the complex politics of prisoner treatment in the war on terrorism that we may not quite understand. It does not tell us what to feel, as, albeit unwittingly, do the photographs that feature explicit acts of degradation. It makes us go beyond its frame to search for missing pieces that can explain his desolation. Its ambiguity provides a starting point for discovering its connection to events outside the frame and even outside the prison that can help us understand and, finally, form our own judgment rather than have one conveniently provided. The solitary man demands that we encounter him as an individual, precisely what the most circulated images denied.

If we are to make sense of this man's bodily display, we must actively interrogate the circumstances of his inward withdrawal. The photograph does not do the work for us, does not leave us off the hook by giving us an easy interpretation. Instead, it opens an inventional space in which we must actively interrogate its circumstances. We must fit it into a frame of other pictures that have constituted our understanding of Abu Ghraib. And because only the invisible photographer is present in this scene, there is greater latitude for locating the cause of his inner pain. This photograph involves its viewer in an active way that blurs the line between testimony asking for recognition of what took place and a more active sense of witnessing that asks the viewer to bear witness to a wrong that has been committed (see Oliver 2004; Peters 2005).

It is not true that Americans sanctioned torture. In fact, a careful analysis of poll data between the 9/11 attack and the election of 2008 shows that quite the opposite is the case (Rejali and Gronke 2009). It's that Americans were shielded from it, and so believed it was not happening. And when it did appear, we were seduced into a frame that gave us the perpetrators, defined their offense in lesser terms, and diverted us from considerations that would have begged a cause. Of twenty-eight letters commenting on the Abu Ghraib scandal published in *nytonline.com* between May 4 and 14, 2004, only two called for a thorough investigation up the chain of command. Most focus on their embarrassment and on the need to bring those responsible (the MIs and MPs at Abu Ghraib) to justice. Mary Bell, one of only two letter writers asking that those at higher places be held responsible, asked: "Who put an inept female reservist in charge of Abu Ghraib, and why were so few trained in interrogation? These responsibilities ultimately go to the commander in chief and his cabinet, especially to the secretary of defense and the Joint Chiefs of Staff" (nytonline 2004).

Instead of that concern as the centerpiece of public discussion, with Sabrina Harman as the image of the scandal or the image of the solitary man withdrawn in his search for consolation, we received images of Lynndie England, the most ubiquitous of which have been those of her pointing to an Iraqi man's penis and of "leash man." Why did England become the face of torturegate? As the foregoing suggests, England fits into cultural narratives about women, about expectant mothers, about sexual fantasies, and quite possibly about sexual aversions. She fits into a journalism of titillation in which we are shown just enough flesh to rivet our attention, while blurring those parts of the prisoners' bodies as a signal of what we need to repress. Putting an image before the public of a woman with her kitten-with-a-whip grin as she humiliates male bodies also allays the military's homophobic fears while tapping into permissible sexual fantasies. Rather than forging identification with humiliated bodies that invoke a sense of moral obligation to them and inspire an external expectation of investigation into accountability up the chain of command, the sexualized aesthetic of a woman's body as centerfold of the scandal directed American attention inward to its sense of how this soldier acted.

Quo Vadis America?

Immediately after the terrorist attack of September 11, 2001, until the end of George W. Bush's presidency, the legal voices of his adminstration created a frame of war that offered legal cover to the military and the CIA for harsh treatment of enemy detainees. Without fear of judicial action, prisoners held at Guantánamo Bay, Abu Ghraib, and other facilities were subjected to abusive treatment that, to many, seemed to cross the line into torture. Within the war frame, however, there was little opposition to this treatment outside of academic circles and a handful of political commentators. For the most part, it went unchallenged. When the treatment of prisoners at Abu Ghraib became a public scandal, the kairotic moment to challenge the Bush adminstration's construction of the enemy body was at hand. The photographic evidence was demonstrative proof of abuse, a display of crossing the line of honor and respect into the nether regions where the human body is reduced to its sheer animality. The images were an interrogation of the adminstration's policies and potentially reframed the treatment of enemy prisoners in terms of their human right to be protected from torture.

And yet they seemed to lead elsewhere. These photographs were not simply documentation of what took place. They are the genesis of a project of illicit gaze that implicates its viewers while simultaneously offering them the chance to hold its makers accountable. If the torture memos represent an attempt to extend executive privilege over the detained bodies of suspected enemies to the point where they have no rights, the images from Abu Ghraib represent its material manifestation in prisoner treatment. Harman's claim that she took photographs to record what was taking place, that she was akin to a diarist recording her observations as her reality, is belied by the energy of a smile that speaks of her inner experience of excitement from active participation in what was taking place. And what was taking place? What was authentic? The simulated sex acts? The prisoner's terror? The guards' participation in their prisoners' humiliation? Their glee at being part of the scene? Their cruelty recorded on digital images that can and did have a viral existence on the web? The images' power to create a planet of witnesses who are simultaneously invited to be voyeurs and judges? Beyond what Butler (2009) has argued regarding the invitation of the Abu Ghraib images to interrogate the photographers who made these images, the images and their production pull us into their scenes.

Regrettably, the story of the pictures became less about the tortured bodies than about us. If there is a moral plea in this, it bears greater resemblance to the self-regarding pain of mortification over the behavior of the prison personnel who represent us than the public plea of compassion for dehumanized bodies. Fixation on the sexualized bodies of the Iraqi detainees and of Pvt. England positioned Americans to respond as a mass of self-mortified Dimmsdales, moral weaklings salving our conscience through pity of the victims, which performs a version of mass social work (Ignatieff et al. 2001, 16). It allows us to misuse the humiliated bodies to serve our own interests as onlookers, forcing them to serve as a means to nourish our own self-esteem through denunciation and to control our own fears.

These images serve a subversive function by creating a dialectical tension between their literality and reality by inviting us into an aesthetic, ideological, and political interpretation of what occurred at Abu Ghraib and in other U.S.-controlled facilities where Taliban, al Qaeda, and Iraqi detainees were held. They frame events that require us to make a connection to them in order to make sense of them. Are they literally what they appear to be—soldiers abusing their prisoners? Or are they reflections of a reality we can only grasp if we dial back the noise of these images' literality? But in order to dial back their noise, to get past the immediacy of the story each tells, we must get rid of everything that covers up the manifestation of a silent evidence each contains. We must become as anthropologists examining the images for their vernacular meanings.

Baudrillard (2000) has written: "Instead of lamenting the relinquishing of the real to superficial images, one would do well to challenge the surrender of the image to the real. The power of the image can only be restored by liberating the image from reality. By giving back to the image its specificity (its 'stupidity' according to Clement Rosset), the real itself can rediscover its true image." In the Abu Ghraib photographs, images of prisoner humiliation and of guard cruelty give way to the real. However, it is a different reality than the staged photograph. It is the reality that stands behind the staging, also captured in snapshots that document the real and provide meaning to the staged that exceeds the staged moment, illustrated, I have argued, by the solitary man standing naked against the prison wall.

Antigone asks Creon, who has forbidden the burial of her slain brother, Polynices, "whose words stand behind these laws?" So we are invited to ask, in the same vein, "whose words stand behind these deeds?" This is the question that gets asked if you dial back the noise, and that question led somewhere Americans chose not to go.

9. *The Moral Vernacular of Political Agency*

The concepts of civilization and barbarism ride in tandem throughout Western history. Walter Benjamin observed, "There is no document of civilization that is not at the same time a document of barbarism" (1969, 256). The rhetoric of political prisoners asserts in reply, "That is because what appears as civilization often is barbarism all the way down." The state's responses to those who are imprisoned for acts of dissent are reflections of what is happening in the larger society, and if barbarity is the staple of treatment meted out to prisoners of conscience (POCs), it most assuredly is a sign that civilization in the larger society is being constructed on a base of repression.

Although those imprisoned for political commitments often speak of and against a national barbarism that is the wellspring from which dissidence flows, the outside world does not always hear. News of repression may travel fast among those in jeopardy, but the repressive state can make it difficult to disclose the extent of its abuse to the outside world. Consequently, dissent and the consequences for dissidents often go unnoticed and unremembered beyond their national borders. When word does get out, events in places like Rwanda, Somalia, or Burundi can seem remote to Western audiences and without clear relation to their national interests. When the former Yugoslavia was flying apart, former secretary of state James Baker famously observed, "We have no dog in this fight." His words summarize a more general response in an international context to brutalities committed in remote places.

Internecine conflict in the far corners of Africa or the backwaters of the Caucuses do seem far removed from narrowly construed Western national interests. The desire not to spill native blood and waste national treasure for someone else's troubles offers a strong incentive against involvement. When savage unrest is called to our attention, it is easier for government officials to claim the moral high ground of denunciation than the more difficult task of denying political and economic complicity in the tragedies of others. Complicity, after all, carries a moral responsibility to do something. It is easier, when our attention is called to such scenes, to say in chorus with Baker's successor, Warren Christopher, this is "a humanitarian crisis a long way from home" that "does not involve our vital interests," state our abhorrence, and ignore the voices of POCs.

And yet, and yet . . . as we have seen, those who have gone through violent up-heavals have much to tell us. They have faced extermination, starvation, torture, prison, and physical and psychological mistreatment. They have often been reduced to an animal's existence and still kept records; written secret diaries; smuggled infor-mation into, within, and out of prison; persisted in resisting when all hope seemed lost; and accepted brutalization and even death rather than sacrifice their conscience. They have beseeched us to stop the crimes committed against them and urged their fellow citizens to sustain the struggle. They provide a link across generations and nations to the human quest for freedom. Without their voices, we sink into the black hole of forgetfulness where we become blind to who is being pushed past the edges of civilization and humanity and suffer our own loss of conscience. The question is whether we will listen.

Therein lies the problem. The victims of war in Rwanda, Somalia, Sudan, Biafra, Uganda, Liberia, Columbia, Sierra Leone, and Congo come to us through televised images that show us human misery beyond comprehension. They provide us with humanitarian appeals that are disjointed from the political and economic conditions in which they are embedded. It is true that in the world of jihadists, boy soldiers, and paramilitary armies exercising their will in failed states, acts of violence do not ap-pear to serve evident political aims and, in fact, seem defined by their absence. Where substantive causes can be located, they often are in culture—religion, traditional family structures, and centuries-old ethnic antagonisms. Furthermore, as in Robert Mugabe's Zimbabwe or Omar al-Bashir's Sudan, there are reigns of terror where the only agenda seems to be retaining the political and economic spoils that accompany naked power. They commit violence against the persons of the enemy group because of who they are or for coercing their cooperation with the personal aggrandizement of a ruthless dictator.

This is not to say that there are no political and economic causes for such calamities, but that they are neither the theme of resistance, such as was the case in the dissident movements of Central and Eastern Europe during the Cold War, or the anti-apartheidists of South Africa, or the nationalists of Northern Ireland, or the socialist Sandinistas of Nicaragua. Unlike those cases, reports of human carnage today focus on the violence rather than its underlying causes, and images of postmodern conflicts further confusion because they defy Enlightenment values pervasive in the West; story and picture show us mayhem without reason.

Images of broken bodies and ruined lives beckon us to solidarity but from a frame whose irrationality makes solidarity difficult because we cannot think of the reality our unity might share. The vernacular means of political resistance exerted by POCs offer an avenue for reconsidering the bleakness of this account and for finding soli-darity in a reality we all share. I believe we can find this avenue by working backward from the considerations of conscience I explored arising from the Abu Ghraib photo-graphs of prisoner abuse.

There is a widely held view, advanced most prominently by Susan Sontag, that photographs can present us with scenes of moral calamity but can do nothing to explain their histories or causes because they lack narrative. Although photographs of human destruction shock us, this idea holds that through repeated viewing, our shock wears off. We become desensitized to the victims' devastation and are left with deadened consciences that reduce us to moral dullards (Sontag 1990, 20–21). Sontag's rationalistic insistence that we need a narrative to account for what we are seeing locates meaning in the mind and is wary of the place of emotions, which photographic images are extremely efficient at exciting, precisely because they lead reason astray.

Documentary photography's capacity to provide powerful images of violence and suffering also has led some to argue that it is morally wrong to view them. These critics charge that such images are pornographic and induce desensitizing voyeurism, which is sometimes a source of pleasure from the anguish of others or even a reproduction of the violence already committed (Kleinman and Kleinman 1997; Sontag 2003).

On the other hand, photographs of this sort considered seriously as rhetorical phenomena defy the reason/emotion dichotomy. When we engage them in terms of how they make things matter, or as rhetorical in some fundamental way, the dichotomy breaks down. An adequate account of a photograph's capacity to establish politically and morally salient meaning cannot avoid addressing the attachment people feel to the persons, places, and events in the photograph's frame. They are presented directly rather than through symbolic means, and because we have bodies, because we have families, because we have human attachments, we can imagine what these people have gone through and recognize that something wrong has been done to them. The intersection of the interests, values, and motives of viewers and those whose plight is frozen in the image is basic to caring and can evoke emotional responses that are integral to forming moral judgments.

Our capacity for empathy, moreover, provides the basis for refuting the charge that such images are pornographic. Susie Linfield (2010) has argued brilliantly that since the violence committed has taken the person's life in many cases, and left him or her broken beyond repair in many others, nothing we do by looking can possibly approach what has already been suffered." Ultimately," she writes, "pious denouncements of the 'pornographic' photograph reveal something that is, I think, fairly simple: a desire to not look at the world's cruelest moments and remain, therefore, unsullied" (45). She continues, "In fact, the desensitizing argument is exactly wrong. For most of history most people have known little, and cared less, about suffering of those who are unknown or alien" (46). For Linfield, "The important question, when we think about photography and human rights, is not how many images we see, or how brutal or explicit or 'pornographic' they are. . . . The real issue is how we *use* images of cruelty. Can they help us make meaning of the present and the past? If so, what meanings do we make, and how do we act upon them? The ultimate answers to such questions reside not in the pictures but in ourselves" (60).

Linfield's formulation of the question suggests that these images speak an international moral language. Certainly not everyone who sees them responds to their call, but a failure to respond does not mean a failure to understand what is being seen. Some may recognize and not be moved because their ideological commitments have hardened them to the pain of others. Nazi Heinrich Jöst photographing Jews in the Warsaw ghetto did not see them as human but as disgusting, nor did his moral compass produce a sense that he needed to do something to stop their abuse (see Linfield, 64–87, *passim*). Perhaps for that reason, Linfield speculates, his photographs are unsparing images of the state of Jews quarantined there. And because of their remorselessness, these images have the capacity to raise conscience across national and cultural borders in those who are neither ideologically insulated nor emotionally detached from the hideous conditions they present.

Still, the photographs alone offer a general form of solidarity. They speak a vernacular of human rights in terms that make us aware of how rhetorically vacuous, beyond the audiences of diplomats, international courts, and NGOs, the thin moral vernacular of human rights covenants sometimes can be. It is surely important to articulate basic principles of human worth and human rights. Looking at photographs of those who have been stripped of everything human reminds us, however, that while the thin moral vernacular of human rights provides a language for NGOs, petitioning states, and international courts to champion those whose lives have been shattered, the only person who needs to make a human rights appeal is this one whose life is no longer perceptibly human. At the same time, the solidarity we may feel with these victims is initiated through the eye of a photographer who has captured human suffering in a way that makes a thick moral vernacular appeal for their human rights. In fact, images of refugees whose treatment has stripped them of everything recognizably human remind us that in the eyes of some, their very humanity has been questioned and possibly denied. Obviously those who desecrated them did not treat them as human. Their eyes were blind to their victims as possessing human rights that entitled them to respect and protection. If "human" is an assigned trait (Howard 1992), then what sense can be made of a claim to *human* rights by those who, at the extreme, suffer the atrocities inflicted on them for political views and practices proscribed by the state? Disturbing photographs of those whose rights have been denied may evoke empathy and compassion, but are they not also a thick moral vernacular expression of political agency? For that answer, we must turn to the political prisoner.

The political prisoner's response of conscience to the rhetoric of the state is a discourse constructed upon a discourse. The first is a discourse of hegemonic power subjugating those who bear a sign of beliefs, race, religion, or ethnicity that marks them as alien and therefore a threat that must be controlled. It is a discourse of essence. The political prisoner's response is a discourse of process. It destabilizes the assumptions on which hegemonic power rests and, by defying its foundations, raises a series of questions and answers that sketch a moral vernacular of political agency. Their verbal and bodily appeals call our attention to the instability of political agency—the prisoner's and the state's.

Within the frame of the nation-state, each political subject makes a claim to a specific political identity. The Romans expressed the relevant question of political identity under the rule of law: "Who are you?" Now, as for the Romans, the most desired response is "a citizen." A citizen assumes certain duties, has specific rights, and is entitled to general protection against harm to his or her person and property. John Kennedy (1963), speaking during the Cold War to beleaguered citizens of West Berlin, referred to this response—whether "Civis Romanus sum" or "Ich bin ein Berliner"—as a citizen's "proudest boast."

Under the state of emergency, a transformation occurs in the classification of subjects. Those who are considered a threat to the state are stripped of their citizenship and treated in ways that denies them *personality*. The question of identity changes from determining civil status—"Who are you?" (for example, "Civis Romanus sum")—to determining human/subhuman status—"What are you?" (for example, "a Hutu"). This new question reflects a state of exception in which the classification of subjects becomes an essential expression of sovereignty. It expresses the sovereign's power to inscribe a political essense on the native, the Jew, the gypsy, the ethnic Other, and the refugee by shifting the question of essence—the question of the being's defining characteristic—from a civic identity (citizen) grounded in personality to a biological status (bare life) grounded in animality. Stripping them of citizenship places them outside rubrics that proscribe certain types of treatment based on their "humanness."

Along lines Foucault assigns to the penitentiary (1977), the modern repressive state places its subjects under surveillance; their movement, residence, and employment are regulated on grounds of protecting national interests. Zones of exclusion, given material form through pass laws or a dividing line between the colonial settlers' city and the native quarter or the refugee camp or now, more commonly, security zones, are initiated to make surveillance and control of outcast bodies easier. Whenever a state of emergency defines the political order, we may rest assured that the established terms of engagement between that state and its subjects will be based on a panoptic model in which those who are designated as Other have no protection from surveillance or cruelty. The divide between *Who are you* and *What are you* has heuristic value for sketching the political and moral significance "humanness" has to a person. It is especially provocative with respect to the question of how the politically damned acquire political agency.

With respect for the political outcast who has engaged in resistance against an authoritarian regime and been convicted of unlawful acts, there are three questions of identity and agency that grow from the distinction between human and animal. The first two are favored by the state in dealing with the offender: *What have you done?* and *What are you?* The answer to the first is "I have broken the law," "I have committed this specific offense." Under the state's juridical logic, this answer transforms concern for the person's political subjectivity (Who are you?) into one of biopolitical objectification (What are you?).

The second question, What are you?, seeks identifying marks that permit classification. In the state of exception, this question places the individual outside the law and the protection citizens enjoy. These questions are explicitly raised in the official rhetoric of laws and the judicial/penal code. The answers, in turn, are assumed in official rhetoric, and embodied in practices and performances by the state and by the prisoner.

The POC constructs a contradictory discourse by erecting counterclaims that require the official discourse to be spoken while being independent and resistant of it. It reframes the original questions and gives them new meaning. This reframing also poses a third question, a transformation of a transformation, by reverting back to the original question of citizenship: *Who are you?* The POC's answer specifies a person's qualifications and agency.

To the first question—What have you done?—the state provides its own answer: you have broken the law. In the case of political offenders, the state's answer may include harsher measures beyond loss of freedom and disciplining the criminal body to obey the state's power. It may administer forms of treatment intended to break their will to resist and reduce them to subservience, even after release. The criminal classification inscribed on the political prisoner's body carries over to the POC within the judicial/penal system through the state's answer to question two—What are you? —by imposing regulations specific to the outcast's objectification through a penological classification that denies his or her personality. When a person is not communicated with in a language he or she understands or not permitted to speak his or her own language, that person loses the basic defining condition of humanness: the ability to speak. The register of meaningful transactions migrates into the body, where harsh treatment places him or her outside the shelter that rule of law provides for the citizen subject.

Outside prison, citizenship and the rights and protections that accompany it are ways in which personality—the fundamental assumption in the Universal Declaration of Human Rights (UDHR) about what is to be protected—is granted to some while denied to the subjugated Other. For oppressed subjects, laws restricting residence, assembly, work, marriage, education, and congregation with those who are protected as human come into play. They allow the state to segregate subjects who are outside civilization and vulnerable to barbarism.

These same subjects acting from conscience reply with a discourse of resistance. In the streets and fields, factories and mines of Algiers's Kasbah, Prague, Belfast's west side, Soweto, Warsaw's ghetto, Gdansk, Guatemala's Zacapa, and Yangon, natives have attempted and continue attempting to undermine oppressive practices of governmentality predicated on the question of "What are you?" Transforming the "what" question to one of "who" that is less focused on citizenship than identity challenges the human/subhuman divide underlying governmentality (see Foucault 2008). It is an exercise of human identity through an act of resistance that manifests conscious design—a human characteristic.

This challenge carries over to the judicial/penal system, which bases its treatment of prisoners on the classification of their crime. The prisoner acting out of conscience transforms the system's question, "What have you done?" into "Who are you?" It is not what they have done, which is evidently to have broken the law, that brings them as specific persons to prison, but how they have broken it: in a way that shattered the state's typology by which lawbreakers are classified and given meaning.

Here an important distinction arises. The earlier question of "Who" was tied to political identity. It conferred citizenship, which provided a basis for claims to rights and liberties as norms of humanness. Its recognition of rights and of humanness are political constructions.

By contrast, the transformed question of the POC moves from the political order to the moral, reverses the relationship of citizen and human by grounding rights in personality, which lays claim to norms that accompany human and political status. The former essentializes humanness in a secondary characteristic of political identity, the latter emphasizes the emergence of norms from an apriori identity as a person.

By insisting on the first order formulation of the "who" question to define the prisoner within the judicial/penal system, the POC presents a confounding reality. The acts of the POC cannot be explained by the motivations for crime regulated through the penal code. The code does not account for political desire, which makes the POC strange within the jurisdiction of a juridical/penological administration of punishment intended as a corrective to produce a social good, namely, a law-abiding citizen. Nor does the code account for an assertion of agency, which is explicitly proscribed by the political prisoner's classification within the biopolitics of the state's laws and policies but equally explicitly present in the act of political resistance. Once the typology is shattered, the question becomes one of identity; it requires a new classification of the prisoner.

The answer to the reframed question "Who are you?" stands as a refutation of the system itself, which then becomes a trigger for measures designed to restore order to the prison. It intensifies the prison's efforts to reduce the prisoner to mere animality.

This second discourse, the POC's response, intersects the state's essentializing discourse of power, with a processual discourse of recognition. It relocates the spatial dialectic of penal confinement to a social space that reproduces relations of identity and difference. This relocation of essence to process enters the midst of political life in ways that cannot be denied within the prison, although it may not always be confirmed on the outside. It may occur through official rhetoric (such as petitions to authority), but more commonly is performed in the vernacular rhetoric of everyday prison life. The refusal of South Africa's political prisoners at Robben Island to submit to demeaning acts, such as calling their warder's "Baas," and using the rules in the penal code to force the prison officials to comply with the law, or the extreme acts of resistance by the Blanketmen in Maze prison that forced an international furor over their subhuman treatment, appropriated the language of agency in a vernacular of moment-by-moment human interactions and appearances—a vernacular of personality that is moral in character.

In the process of refusing and then changing the state's question, the prisoners meet themselves as a part of a larger public, as engaged by issues that go beyond the immediacy of personal survival to experience and recognize their shared identity as injured. Butler has observed, "To be injured means that one has a chance to reflect upon injury, to find out the mechanisms of its distribution, to find out who else suffers from permeable borders, unexpected violence, dispossession, and fear, and in what ways" (2004, xii). The process of self-discovery in meeting themselves as a human and then political reality occurs through a thick moral vernacular—a moral language of speech and performance that is constituted by their common experience, their public appearance as in a particular state-of-being in relationship to one another and to themselves, which, in turn, defines their relationship to the state and its agents.

The thick moral vernaculars I have been discussing have a dimension beyond resistance. They often responded to their prison conditions with act of ordinary virtues. They extended hospitality to the warders by acts of kindness, openness to helping them, engaging them in conversation, and explaining why they were engaged in resistance. They showed reverence for persons and moments that evoked a sense of something larger than themselves, by their "capacity for awe, respect, and shame," and by their finding ways to commemorate these personas and moments (Woodruff 2001, 63). They displayed loyalty by acts of sharing and support that often came at personal cost. They appealed to justice in defense of one another and to activate an ethos of bearing witness to the inhuman treatment of others. Responding to their warders and to each other with defiance and forgiveness, kindness and candor were forms of recognizing the other's humanity and acknowledging the other's need for care. In that way, acts of ordinary virtue became expressions of the remnants of their humanity, moral vernacular expressions of human rights and resonant expressions of political agency.

To have voice is to have certainty of your agency and therefore of your humanity. Among political prisoners, the vernacular rhetoric of agency empowers a moral discourse that proscribes certain forms of treatment. For them, it is a parrhesiastic performance of truth. For contested authorities, on the other hand, the POC's voice is often an invitation to retribution. The Soviet commissars who established the camps' barbaric rules for treatment of political prisoners certainly were not swayed by Nathan Sharansky's or Irina Ratushinskaya's performances of thought and deed; they felt no urgency to mitigate the harsh treatment that had stripped these prisoners of their health and driven them to the brink of physical collapse.

To observers outside the juridical/penal system's administrative structure—sometimes their warders, sometimes other prisoners, sometimes an observation team of the International Committee of the Red Cross (ICRC), sometimes a national audience, sometimes the world community—the POCs' voice can be emblematic of their humanness. Its performance of political agency can capacitate us as testifying witnesses to their humanity. We can recognize that their rights as humans have been abused, and acknowledge their call for care. Their mistreatment brings out the way in which suffering is a pure undergoing, something experienced in the prisoners passivity and endured. It brings the unknowable pain of the prisoner—unknowable because it is an embodied experience of another—to others as suffering that is recognizable as an evil. Unlike the photographic image of suffering, the performative dimension of the POC's suffering contextualizes it, offers contrast, and exhibits an alternative ethos of ordinary virtue that is understood through juridical/penal excess that is the evil they suffer. Suffering signifies not only the suffer's humanity but the violation of their humanity and, in that, their human right to protection from violence against their person and personality.

The prisoners' suffering calls to us as an evil inflicted on them by the state. It places us in the situation where, as Butler has described it, we are addressed by a moral demand that articulates our obligations and presses them upon us. "What is morally binding . . . does not proceed from my autonomy or my reflexivity. It comes to me from elsewhere, unbidden, unexpected, and unplanned. In fact, it tends to ruin my plans, and if my plans are ruined, that may well be the sign that something is morally binding upon me" (Butler 2004, 130). The prisoners' suffering interrupts the rationality of the state's presentation of punishment as necessary for the criminals' expiation. The POC's passivity is a performance of agency that undermines the rationality of inflicting pain by confronting a totalizing display of force with human vulnerability in suffering. It is a call to conscience that brings the prisoners, as well as witnesses on the outside, to recognize themselves as a public thrust into a situation demanding an ethical response where we accept our responsibility to and for each other.

Unlike the images of human mayhem that cause consternation over the carnage being suffered in faraway places while asking us to act on a vague sense of connection to the victims, POC resistance employs a thick moral vernacular of human rights. It is thick in that it entails a set of perceptions that connect bodily treatment to political aims. It is thick in that it constitutes human rights through experiences rather than quasi-legal or judicial precepts. It is thick in that it uses a language of political agency that is at least resonant with the prisoners' native culture and possibly with wider publics who are given pause when aspirations for self-determination are met with bone-crushing assaults that fail to recognize any boundaries on abusive treatment. It is thick in that it evidences ordinary virtues that are definitively human.

These everyday assertions of identity and rights impose themselves upon a juridical/penological discourse in which the prisoner is given a criminal identity through a judicial sentence. The sentence takes away rights, confines movement, dictates behavior, severs connection to an outside world, denies freedoms of speech and assembly, imposes discipline, and administers punishment for failure to comply. The discourse of the sentence is, officially, about justice. It constitutes the criminal as a threat who must be confined for society's welfare and provides its own rationale for treating inmates as it does by virtue of ensuring that justice is served. The state depicts opposition as an attempt to undermine the nation. Framed in this way, the political prisoner represents a particularly lethal threat to the general population, for which harsh measures are warranted to protect the nation's safety. The juridical/penological discourse of crime and punishment is appropriated by the discourse of sovereignty in which power, not justice, is the central concern. Giving political prisoners a criminal identity while insisting on treating them as a threat to the state transforms legal into political discourse. However, as structured within the judicial/penal system, the patina of justice lingers, authorizing treatment of prisoners that is less concerned with their rehabilitation than with destroying their will to fight back.

The process of moment-by-moment engagement by the POC with this official discourse of crime and punishment, encapsulated by the sentence, exposes the state's political motivations; it redefines the overt relationship between the state and the POC from criminal to political. Here I mean more than that it brings into play the struggle on the outside. In addition to that, it turns relations within the prison toward a new, political direction, in which there is ongoing negotiation over how prisoners and warders will act and interact. In this negotiation, power is contested with unusual rhetorical means that can subvert the overwhelming imbalance of material power represented not least by the fact that the warders have guns and prisoners do not. This internal political contest, in turn, projects the prison into the larger society as a discursive interrogation of existing conditions and the locus of political agency.

Within the confines of the prison, the moral vernacular rhetoric of political acts exists outside of and coexists with the official discourse of the sentence. These two discourses intersect and interact in ways not entirely within the prison's control. Rhetorical mechanisms such as parrhesia, indirection, passive aggression, display, and framing structure rhetorical performances and have the capacity, in turn, to structure responses. These structures, while neither exhaustive of those used by POCs nor exclusive to resistance rhetoric, have exceptional salience in the prison environment. Although it would be an overstatement to claim that they cause a specific response from the prison authorities, it is not overreaching to claim that they narrow the prison's options. They change the prison's rhetorical dynamic by manifesting the prisoner's capacity to make choices and act. They throw open the meaning of the prisoner's sentence, the meaning of the prisoner's treatment, and the question of who is in charge. Because the prisoners do not accept the terms of the sentence, and negotiate their own treatment, they require the prison to act within boundaries not of its own choosing. Forcing the prison to abide by the penal code in respecting the prisoner's person, bringing charges against warders for violating the law, calling public attention to conditions in the prison that are inhuman, staging resistance in ways that expose the venality of an institution insistent on breaking the prisoners' will through mean and degrading treatment, using the prison's public places as quasi-public spheres for vernacular displays of an alternative identity, reaching agreements on tradeoffs that make the authorities dependent on the prisoners in order to retain order, and refusing to participate in one's own degradation are a few of the ways we have seen where POCs put the prison in a position where it was made accountable for its actions.

Here we come full circle to considerations we entertained at the beginning of this exploration of human rights and moral vernacular rhetoric. I also have argued that the shift from discussing human rights abuses based on nonnegotiable first principles of natural law or cultural identity to using human rights accords as a moral vernacular marked a shift from a rhetoric of imputation to a rhetoric of accountability. In the thin moral vernacular of human rights talk, this shift moves the human rights discussion from moral debate to political deliberation and negotiation over the conditions and consequences of action and responsibility.

Similarly, the POC's thick moral vernacular of human rights focuses on concrete situations in which actions give these rights meaning. Whereas human rights talk addresses the practices of human rights abusers in terms of institutional relations, which may have to do with reciprocity arrangements touching on matters of economics, education, culture, or even defense, the POC's thick moral vernacular deals with exposing the rights withholder's practices to shame. By exposing the ordinary vices of racism and malice at Robben Island, cruelty and treachery in Barashevo's Small Zone, deceit and hypocrisy at Long Kesh, and brutality at Abu Ghraib, the thick moral vernacular becomes a normative discourse.

The rhetorical mechanisms that were so effective in triggering responses that changed the prison dynamic of power and control also contrasted the venality of the state's attempts to quash resistance with the prisoners' ordinary virtues. The caring of Robben Island's inmates toward their warders and their courage in insisting that their human dignity not be compromised, the reverence for each other and steadfastness in the mutual pledges shared among the women of the Small Zone, and the tenacity and courage of the Blanketmen at Long Kesh each counteracted the normalizing of monstrous treatment at the hands of an unsympathetic state. Sometimes the contrast brought about transformation in the prison culture, as at Robben Island; sometimes it sparked solidarity and respect among the prison population, as at Barashevo; sometimes it called an international public into being to pressure a rights-withholding state to reform, as at Maze prison; and sometimes it produced a discourse that, while sympathetic to the abused, had its disgust deflected from offices and persons who were arguably responsible, as at Abu Ghraib.

Although the normative content of accountability is difficult to translate into objective standards for evaluating the behavior of public actors, the stark contrasts between treatment of prisoners and their expressions of agency brings juridical/penalogical behavior into a public forum where there are consequences. Unlike accountability rhetoric in civil society, the abusing state has no interest in informing the public about its conduct, and, except for the rare case brought before the International Criminal Court, there is no official body to interrogate the legitimacy of its conduct. However, the thick moral vernacular of human rights, whether spoken to a guard or performed before an international audience, constitutes an arena in which the issue is between the prisoners' assertion of "personality" and the institutional measures that deny it. This is a clash that invites judgment, whether it is the warder's decision to cease subjecting the prisoner to barbarism or the condemnation of the world community of rights withholders for denying the personality of the POC whose actions are clearly human and deserving of humane treatment. To repeat the observation by Dorrinda Outram noted earlier concerning the French insurgents challenging the rights of the French aristocracy, their contesting bodies "possessed the power, which the competing linguistic discourses obviously did not, to focus dignity and legitimacy in incontestable, because nonverbal, ways on the bodies of known individuals who acted as personifications of value systems" (1989, 4).

The speed of history is very fast; the speed of progress is slow. The POC lives at a particular time and under circumstances that often seem, in retrospect, to have passed relatively quickly. Twenty or thirty or even forty years is a short span considered against the arc of national history. As one struggle passes, perhaps resolved in ways that foster democracy, there is another to take its place. This does not mean the struggle for freedom and self-determination is futile or that we are excused from considering our role in its causes, listening to the way those in peril express their right to a life worth living, and responding to their pleas for freedom and safety. Time is neither homogeneous nor futile. It keeps alive the hope that the struggle for human rights will eventually prevail, if not in our lifetime, then perhaps the next generation's. In his "Theses on the Philosophy of History," Benjamin has written, "there is a secret agreement between past generations and the present one. Our coming was expected on earth. Like every generation that preceded us, we have been endowed with a *weak* Messianic power, a power to which the past has a claim" (1969, 258). Using our *weak* power to keep the door of justice open is our pledge to continue striving toward a world of amity and hope.

Notes

Chapter 1. Reclaiming Voice

1. The unitary executive theory holds that the president controls the entire executive branch and therefore may interpret laws as he or she sees fit, especially on matters of national security.

2. The Washington Post–ABC News Poll of January 21, 2009, reported that Americans supported President Obama's order banning torture. Those who were opposed to using torture under any circumstance outweighed those in favor under certain circumstances by the wide margin of 58 to 40 percent (http://voices.washingtonpost.com/behind-the-numbers/ 2009/01/on_torture.html?wprss=behind-the-numbers). Respondents favored the president's order to close the prison facility on Guantánamo housing enemy combatant detainees by a margin of 53 to 42 percent (http://voices.washingtonpost.com/behind-the-numbers/2009/01/ wapo-abc_poll_on_gitmo.html?wprss=behind-the-numbers).

3. The Office of Legal Council is a small, elite office of two-dozen lawyers within the Justice Department that offers legal advice to the entire executive branch of the government. It is inconspicuous, and many of its opinions remain secret, although custom treats them as binding on federal agencies (see Luban 2007, 37).

4. I develop the ideas of thin and thick moral vernaculars in chapters 2 and 3.

5. Peter Beneson coined the label "prisoner of conscience" in his article "The Forgotten Prisoners" (1961). Beneson wrote: "Any person who is physically restrained (by imprisonment or otherwise) from expressing (in any form of words or symbols) any opinion which he honestly holds and which does not advocate or condone personal violence. We also exclude those people who have conspired with a foreign government to overthrow their own." This definition, which has been adopted by human rights organizations such as Amnesty International, is broad and can refer to anyone imprisoned based on their belief, religion, race, color, language, lifestyle, or sexual orientation so long as they have not advocated or engaged in violence.

6. See Mandela (1994), Michnik (1985a), Soyinka (1972), and Timerman (1981) for a sampling of POCs who make explicit professions of the personal costs they were prepared to pay to retain an authentic political voice. It is important to note that human frailty sometimes overcomes heroic determination; Soyinka and Timerman eventually were broken by their tormentors.

7. Agamben's emphasis on control of the body does not gainsay the importance of citizenship with respect to how the alien body is treated. As Arendt (1968, 262–302) has argued, since the First World War the stateless person and the refugee have become a growing class of persons who pose a significant problem for the states that control their bodies. Without citizenship, they are denied classification as human and a claim to human rights.

8. Some scholars argue that the term possibly comes from the *muselmann's* inability to stand for any time due to the loss of leg muscle, thus spending much of the time in a prone position, recalling the position of the Mussulman (Muslim) during prayers.

9. Agamben argues that even democracy exhibits this trait, and must in order to establish its sovereignty. His discussion of the history of the state of exception makes an arguable case for this claim by tracing its presence in Europe and the United States. Closer examination of the universality of the state of exception is beyond the scope of this project. However, as will be evident in later chapters, treatment of political prisoners by the British and American governments lends credence to his claim. See Agamben (2005, 11–22).

10. For an account of the relationship of the confession to the sovereign's face, which is often at the heart of the demand for personal repentance, see Lizhi (2011a). Lizhi's (2011b) 1989 letter to Deng Xiaoping offers an example of a "confession" intended to save the sovereign's face.

11. Michael Hyde has written about the call to conscience in his well-regarded book *The Call of Conscience* (2001). Hyde is working within a different tradition than the one I am following in this project.

12. "Prague Spring" refers to the experiment in "socialism with a human face" that swept across Czechoslovakia in 1968. Alexander Dubcek, leader of the Czechoslovak Communist Party, introduced liberalizing reforms allowing freedom of assembly and speech. The experiment ended when Warsaw Pact troops invaded the country and seized control of the government.

13. The "Todorov problem" refers to a mode of argumentation employed by Tzvetan Todorov in *Voices from the Gulag* (1999). Todorov uses the narratives of camp survivors, who are providing testimony to witness what took place, in order to make an anti-Communist argument suited to Western Cold War ideology. It is doubtful his anti-Communist intent was that of the storytellers. The term "gulag" is not used by Bulgarians; they refer to "camps." The survivors' stories are excerpted and edited into a different narrative intended to make a political indictment of the regime. The problem refers to the rhetorical strategy of appropriating testimony offered for one purpose in order to serve a different ideological end. I am indebted to Nadia Kaneva, whose seminar discussion of Todorov's book and whose native insights into Bulgarian camp survivors helped in formulating the "problem." Kaneva (2007) offers a detailed discussion of Bulgarian camp narratives. For Havel's critique of Western misunderstanding of the Czech moral vernacular, in addition to "Power of the Powerless," see "Politics and Conscience" and "An Anatomy of Reticence" in *Living in Truth* (1986). I elaborate on the Todorov problem in chapter 5.

Chapter 2. Human Rights and Human Rights Talk

1. See Rousseau, *Of the Social Contract*, book 1, chapter 7: "Hence for the social compact not to be an empty formula, it tacitly includes the following engagement which alone can give force the rest, that whosoever refuses to obey the general will shall be constrained to do so by the entire body: which means nothing other than that he shall be forced to be free" (55).

2. The Human Rights Commission, which Roosevelt chaired, had originally planed to present a covenant document along with the UDHR that would contain provisions for its enforcement. Agreement on its terms proved exceedingly difficult, as representatives either followed instructions from their governments or their governments indicated they would not

ratify the document. As a result, the UDHR acquired the status of *customary international law*, which is based on the belief that its principles are universal and indisputable, or are expressions of natural law. However, not all nations interpret these principles in the same way. The U.N. subsequently did adopt two covenants intended to provide for enforcement, the International Covenant on Civil and Political Rights and the International Covenant on Economic, Social and Rights. However, these are nonbinding, although the U.N. regards them as carrying the moral force of binding obligations on the international community. See Clark (2000).

3. I use the UDHR as my exemplar for human rights covenants in general, such as the Geneva Accords or the U.N. Convention on the Rights of the Child. Although each convention and set of accords has its own specific concern, my argument about human rights rhetoric applies generally.

4. Estimates of genocide during the twentieth century include 800,000 Armenians by the Turks at the beginning of the century, five million Jews at Hitler's hand, two million Cambodians during Pol Pot's four-year reign, 100,000 Kurds gassed and executed by Hussein, 800,000 Tutsi Rwandans executed by Hutu Rwandans in 100 days, 200,000 Bosnians, and at least 100,000 Albanian men unaccounted for and presumed killed under Milosevic's orders, in addition to the loss of approximately twenty million Chinese slaughtered by the Japanese Empire and tens of millions more in the Soviet gulag. These figures are cited in Power (2002), xix–xx, 9, and Newman (1995), 167–68.

5. Since its founding, the U.N. has approved only two military actions: authorization for the United States to intervene on behalf of its ally South Korea to push back the North Korean forces and action against Iraq after it invaded Kuwait.

6. The Bush administration and U.S. military quickly diverted public attention from their complicity in the treatment of detainees by focusing blame on the soldiers taking and appearing in the photographs. I develop this point further in chapter 8.

7. Aristotle set forth three ends of rhetoric corresponding to the three genres that comprise public life: deliberative oratory particular to the legislative assembly that aims at useful measures to resolve public problems, forensic or judicial oratory particular to law courts that seeks justice in punishment and reward, and epideictic or demonstrative oratory particular to ceremonial occasions that aims at praise or blame of honorable or dishonorable deeds. See Kennedy (2007).

8. A rhetoric of imputation demands that the opponent justify his or her position or stand guilty of irrational behavior. It is a demand also open to insistence that an opponent justify his or her assumptions. A call for rational justification, as Bartley (1962) showed, leads to an infinite regress resulting in a futile attempt to resolve a moral dispute. At some point the regression of justifications reaches the point of ultimate commitments that one holds as axioms of the good life. They cannot be proven or justified, they simply are. At this point, the accuser's position is subject to a *tu quoque* objection as being equally irrational. The justificationist position is defeasible (McKeon 1954; Weimer 1977) because it seeks maxims and rules of action to justify conduct without attention to the problems of accountability of persons and groups who do not share its starting premises.

9. Since the articles of the UDHR do not rest on shared *a priori* assumptions, the validity of each with respect to particular behaviors becomes a function of mutual agreement. This has consequences for the efficacy of assailing the validity of opposing claims that rest on

assumptions outside one's own *a priori* frame, such as Western revulsion at amputation of a limb for the crime of theft. See note 5. See also Hauser and Cushman (1973) and McKeon (1954, 1960).

10. See Hauser (1999b) for a discussion of multiple public spheres and their rhetorical characteristics.

11. Aristotle developed the idea of *phainomena* as appearances in *Nichomachean Ethics*. See Nussbaum (1986, 290–317) and Farrell (1993, 28–33) for explication of his doctrine and its relevance to rhetoric.

12. In *Between Past and Future* (1977), Hanna Arendt asserts: "The more people's standpoints I have present in my mind while I am pondering a given issue, and the better I can imagine how I would feel and think if I were in their place, the stronger will be my capacity for representational thinking and the more valid my final conclusions, my opinion" (241). In political relations, Arendt intimates that representative thinking is not the product of inner debate or the spectatorship or retrospection of storytellers or historians, but is related to excellence, which requires the presence of others. Insofar as judgment refers to prudential conduct, the excellence in question is the judgment that thus and so is the proper course of action (1958).

Chapter 3. Thick Moral Vernacular and Human Rights

1. The extent of this shift is reflected in the proliferation of such scholarly work as movement studies alone, which number well over 300 in the rhetoric literature since the publication of Leland Griffin's *Quarterly Journal of Speech* (1952) article calling for the study of historical movements.

2. Peter Simonson pointed me in the direction of intellectual foment about rhetoric that began in the 1930s as prelude to current theorizing of vernacular rhetoric.

3. Geertz borrows the concept of "deep play" from Bentham's *The Theory of Legislation* (1931/1789). Bentham argued that deep play is a form of irrational behavior that occurs when the stakes are so high that a player has more to lose than to gain.

4. The idea of antivernacular was prompted by Felix Girke and developed further through discussion among students enrolled in my graduate seminar in vernacular rhetoric at the University of Colorado during the spring of 2007. I am indebted to both.

5. John William Yettaw, an American, swam across a lake to Suu Kyi's villa, where he stayed for two days pleading exhaustion from the one-mile swim. The reasons for his actions remained murky, but provided authorities with a pretext for charging Suu Kyi with violation of the restrictions imposed by her house arrest. Suu Kyi was sentenced to three years in prison for the violation, which was later commuted to eighteen months house arrest. At the time, she had already been confined under house arrest for seven years and was nearing the date for her confinement to end. Despite strong protest from NGOs (see, for example, Amnesty International 2007), she was detained under house arrest for fifteen years before her release on November 10, 2010.

6. The publicity principle holds that there are reasons to doubt that representatives, on average, are wiser or more committed to the common good than the ordinary citizen. Luban explains as follows: "The empirical validity of the publicity principle turns not on whether the Many are ignorant or wrong-headed, but on whether their leaders are less ignorant or less wrong-headed. No doubt the Wise are few; and the leaders are few; but it hardly follows that the leaders are wise. Before we reject the publicity principle because the leaders know best, we

must have reason to believe that the leaders know better. And to find that out, we must look carefully at the variety of mechanisms by which decision-making elites are actually selected. If actual selection mechanisms choose randomly between the Many and the Wise, or affirmatively disfavor the Wise, then the foolishness of the many is irrelevant: the Few in official positions have no reason to suppose that their policy brainstorms are any less foolish" (1996, 193).

7. Fanon emphasizes how the cultural vernacular of modesty within the Muslim community initially placed the unveiled women in conflict with their fathers, who saw their daughters' bare faces as a disgrace to their patriarchal role. Reframing of the unveiling as subterfuge eventually brought their fathers to understand that by feigning the French vernacular of femininity, their daughters could perform guerrilla acts of resistance more effectively than they.

8. All page references without date in this section are to "After Ten Years."

9. In "An Answer to the Question: What Is Enlightenment?" Kant (1996/1784) had posited: "*Enlightenment is the human being's emergence from his self-incurred minority* [*Unmündigkeit*, immaturity]. *Minority* [immaturity] is inability to use one's own understanding without direction from another."

10. All page references without date in this section are to "On Violence."

Chapter 4. Parrhesia at Robben Island

1. For a discussion of the rhetorical complexities attendant on truth and reconciliation in South Africa, see Doxtader (2003, 2007, 2008) and Doxtader and Villa-Vicencio (2004).

2. The Rivonia Trial, which took place in South Africa between 1963 and 1964, takes its name from a privately owned farm in Rivonia, a suburb of Johannesburg. The farm, owned by Arthur Goldreich, had served as a hideout for ANC leaders. On July 11, 1963, as ANC leaders were meeting there to plan the next steps in their opposition to the government, South Africa's Special Forces raided their meeting and took nineteen prisoners into custody. The Rivonia Trialists refers to the ten ANC leaders placed on trial for 221 acts of sabotage intended to overthrow the apartheid government.

3. Neville Alexander (1994) introduced this characterization, which recurs repeatedly in former prisoner accounts of their experience on Robben Island on deposit at the Mayibuye Archives, located at the University of the Western Cape and at the Robben Island Museum.

4. The element of passion, central to Cicero's eloquence and to the art of rhetoric in general, is implicit in Foucault's formulation of the parrhesiastes as someone with a passion for the truth, in addition to the virtue of living in truth. Although Foucault does not develop this element in relation to rhetoric, its connection is lurking at the edges of his discussion, awaiting a more robust understanding of rhetoric than Foucault provides. See Levy (2009) for discussion of how Foucault neutralizes passion in his discussion of parrhesia as a virtue.

5. The parallel between Havel's account of what constitutes truth and Foucault's attribution of truth to the ancient parrhesiastes is remarkable. See Foucault (2001, 13–15).

6. Goffman's distinctions regarding the regimes of obedience correspond to political prisoners' accounts of their treatment. I have adopted his labels for these regimes—deference obligations, personal defacement, personal disfigurement, and mortification—as a convenient descriptive template for them (Goffman 1961, 1–125).

7. The NP had established four racial categories for the organization of South African society: White; Indian, consisting of Asians; Colored, consisting of mixed-race persons; and African, consisting of black natives belonging to one of South Africa's indigenous tribes.

8. Pierre Bourdieu (1990, 127) develops this thesis as an explanation for how a *habitus* of socially approved symbolic acts regulates social practices in ways that reflect the social and political economy of power.

9. The United Nations International Convention on the Elimination of All of Racial Discrimination does not use the term "racism," but speaks of "racial discrimination," which it defines as follows: "*the term* 'racial discrimination' *shall mean any distinction, exclusion, restriction or preference based on race, colour, and fundamental freedoms in the political, economic, social, cultural or any other field of public life*" (United Nations International Convention 1966).

10. My use of the term "chronotope" is intended in the spirit of Bakhtin's theorizing of the space and time relationship created in literature. See Bakhtin (1981, 84–258). My extension of his term is grounded, however, in the rhetorical sense of place as an inventional locus and the priority of place to space as a particularized manifestation of historicity within space.

11. Quotations from prisoner narratives are as they appear in the transcripts housed at the Mayibuye Archive. I have retained their disfluencies and have not corrected for grammar. I also have included their reports of the guards' orders when given in Afrikaans where it is important to the narrative and the gist of what is being said is evident from the context.

12. This ritual, referred to by Dlamini (1984) and Naidoo (1982), and discussed in Buntman (2004), is commonly mentioned in prisoner interviews contained in the Mayibuye Archive as among the most reviled and dehumanizing of the mortification practices at the prison.

13. I discuss this incident and Naidoo's prison memoir in greater detail in chapter 7. See also Hauser (2006).

14. Certain warders were notorious in this respect. The most mentioned of them were the Kleynhans brothers. Johnson Mlambo, sentenced in 1963 to twenty years for sabotage, received international notice for the brutality of his treatment. He offers this account of the Kleynhans brothers in action: "That's another incident where I found myself buried and covered up in earth, except for the eyes. They were doing it for fun. . . . They would actually say 'Okay, you dig here.' And people find themselves digging a trench and in, the process someone is forced into that trench and he is now completely covered up with earth, the whole body except perhaps the face and the eyes so that they must be above the soil. Then they would laugh at him and sometimes they would actually come and water on his face. That is urinate on his face. So these are the type of experiences that often occurred" (Mlambo c.2000, 15).

15. Junior Certificate was generally taken by white schoolchildren around age fifteen, and they usually did not leave school until this point. The Matriculate Certification required two more years of study and qualified the student for higher education.

16. Prisoners were classified as A, B, C, or D. Upon arrival, all political prisoners, unlike common prisoners, were classified as D. Prisoners in D class were not permitted to pursue studies, while those in other classifications could petition to enroll, and frequently achieved academic success. However, orders often came to summarily demote prisoners to D class for trivial offenses or for trumped-up offenses. Neville Alexander points out that in 1974, the prison regulations were amended to subvert the spirit of the Prison Act by making permission to study purely within the discretion of the Office of Corrections. Unless lack of education was a cause of the crime, the Office of Corrections did not have to grant permission to take a course. Prisoners also were denied books, even books that were required for courses. Tuition funds were denied prisoners, even when they came from their families, which meant they

could not enroll in the courses for which permission had been granted. There was no scientific library on Robben Island, which limited the possibilities of pursuing scientific or technical education. Any work that made mention of Marxism or was written by a black was proscribed. See Alexander (1994, 47–65).

17. The PAC deeply distrusted the ANC because of its adherence to Communism; the ANC had deep disagreement with the PAC's political goal of black rule of Africa, which it saw as substituting one form of apartheid for another. The BCM, which was mostly composed of younger men who believed Africans must first liberate themselves from a sense of racial inferiority before they could liberate their country, also found itself divided from the ANC on grounds of racial exclusiveness.

18. The formal expression of this vision is found in the Freedom Charter (Congress of the People 1955), which commits to these principles: the people govern; equal rights for all; share the wealth; equal treatment before the law; equal human rights; open doors of learning and culture; and peace and friendship.

19. The visiting area consisted of two facing arenas with wire mesh from floor to ceiling. Guards patrolled the section between them. Prisoners and visitors faced each other across the divide and had to shout to be heard above the din. The consequence was noise so loud as to make hearing what was being said impossible.

Chapter 5. Women of the Small Zone and a Rhetoric of Indirection

1. "*Kairos*" is the ancient Greek term for "the opportune moment." It refers to knowing the moment to make an appeal in order to gain maximum effect. See White (1987), Kinneavy (1986), and Poulakos (1995) for elaboration on its underlying theory and implications.

2. My discussion of indirection in this section has been influenced by the work of Maurice Natanson (1965, 1978), who points out the significance of involvement and *ethos* as among its defining features.

3. The label "Todorov problem" was coined by Nadia Kaneva in a graduate seminar paper at the University of Colorado at Boulder. My account is a brief summary of her more elaborate and convincing analysis, now in published form. See Kaneva (2007).

4. "Carriages for transportation of prisoners, introduced by Pyotr Stolypin, Russian Minister of Internal affairs, 1906–11. Each carriage is divided into nine cubic meter compartments, which were shared by an average of four prisoners in Tsarist times and twelve in Soviet times. Records exist of compartments holding twenty-nine people" (Ratushinskaya 1989, 9, n.1).

5. All page references without date are to *Grey Is the Color of Hope*.

6. Communication "on the pipe" is accomplished by placing the base of an empty mug on the pipe and listening to hear what is being said. To talk, you reverse the process by speaking into the mug.

7. Prisoners were permitted only three visitations a year, one of which was an extended visit that could last between one and three days.

8. Making legal appeals occurs at times in all cultures, but it was distinctively common for political prisoners and dissidents in Communist states of Central and Eastern Europe to write to officials and official bodies citing explicit clauses of the constitution, penal code, and laws that were being violated. The framers of Charter 77 (Library of Congress 1977) lodged their protest to the government in terms of violations of the Czech constitution and failure to comply with human rights treaties it had signed. In the USSR, Anatoli Scharansky, a defendant in

a show trial, sent a flurry of petitions and complaints to the various legal and political offices with jurisdiction over his treatment, as did his family and supporters. In Schransky's case, his supporters in the United States put the Soviet government on trial for violation of the state constitution. The three eminent jurists who heard the case found it guilty. Although such efforts invariably proved fruitless, legal appeals to the state and its predictable rejection of them played an important role in condemning the government before a national and international audience of onlookers and kept alive the prospect of international pressure on the state to protect the prisoners' rights.

Chapter 6. Passive Aggression of Bodily Sufficiency

1. I am indebted to Samuel McCormick for suggesting this term. Conversation with McCormick on his own work on passive aggression was suggestive for how to think about the Provo resistance in Maze prison, and I am pleased to acknowledge his prodding. I alone am responsible for the argument developed here.

2. The parallel between the POC's use of the body and bodily displays in demonstrations of passive resistance is evident, and suggests that this rhetorical mechanism may harbor interpretive insights when extended to passive resistance in general.

3. Quintilian offers advice on how to evoke strong emotion through bringing the scene of bodily mayhem before the judge's eyes in *Institutio Oratoria,* VI.ii, and Xenophon portrays the consequences when the ekklesia, convulsed with emotion, rendered a decision it regretted in *Hellenika,* I.7.7-35, I–II.3.10.

4. I use the term "political" to refer to the ongoing negotiation over how we shall act and interact, which is always a negotiation over the manifestations of power.

5. Serbian messianic construction of itself as a nation crucified is founded on in Serb memory of Prince Lazar, a fourteenth-century leader who was killed by the Ottoman Turks at the Battle of Kosovo in 1389. In Serb tradition, his death marks the end of Serb independence and the onset of Ottoman rule (Sells 1996, 31). During the nineteenth century, Lazar was transformed into a Christ figure. If his martyrdom symbolized the death of the Serbian nation, it could not be resurrected until his murderers were slain. On this premise hung the fate of all Muslims, who, seen as direct descendants of Ottoman Turks, were constructed as Christ slayers who must be purged from the face of the earth.

6. For a sampling of the difficulty in making sense of hunger strikes, see Annas (1982), who considers them in ethical and motivational terms; Dooley-Clarke (1981), who invokes medical ethics; O'Keefe (1984), who invokes a theological frame to consider whether they are suicide or murder; Sneed and Stonecipher (1989); Sweeney (1993), who discusses them as an Irish cult practice; and Thorpe (1994), who considers them in terms of free speech rights.

7. See issues 1 and 2 of the *Argumentation and Advocacy* (Hauser 1999c) for consideration of whether bodies can argue and the fragility/robustness of those arguments.

8. The IRA and Provisional IRA were distinct groups by the time of the Troubles. In common usage, Provisional IRA military forces and the IRA are not distinguished with respect to violence in and associated with Northern Ireland. Since IRA and Provisional IRA are not germane to this discussion, I use "Provo" and IRA interchangeably to refer to the Provisional IRA, rather than introduce a new, and possibly confusing, locution.

9. One might point to self-immolation as another, more graphic possibility. However, it is not a culturally resonant form of resistance within Irish culture, whereas the hunger strike is.

10. For a discussion of these differences in public memory, see McKeever, Joseph, and McCormack (1993) and Kovalcheck (1987).

11. The solidarity of the Armaugh women prisoners with the dirty protest at Maze, although celebrated by Republicans at one level, was a source of consternation within Republican Irish male culture, which had difficulty accepting women smearing menstrual blood along with excreta on their cell walls. See Aretxaga (1997) for a discussion of the tensions surrounding the Armaugh women's dirty protest.

12. This exchange between James Lamond, MP, and Donald Concannon, secretary of state for Northern Ireland, is illustrative of the government's defense of prisoner treatment in Maze based on the prison's palatial attributes juxtaposed to prisoner behavior to support laudatory claims about conditions in Maze.

> Mr. Lamond: Is my hon. Friend aware of the concern that has been expressed by the Northern Ireland Civil Rights Association about the conditions affecting all prisoners in this type of block? Is he satisfied that his Department could meet any criticisms that might come from an international inquiry into conditions there from such a body as, say, the Red Cross?
>
> Mr. Concannon: I am satisfied that the prison conditions provided in the H block units in the Maze are amongst the best in the United Kingdom. The units cost over 1 million each. Associated with them are recreational facilities that include a 100,000 indoor sports hall and two all-weather sports pitches. By observing the rules, through working and wearing prison clothes, prisoners can have weekly visits and can wear their own clothes, of an approved type, during recreational periods or when seeing their visitors. These are privileges which are not allowed in the rest of the United Kingdom.

The protests consist of some prisoners deliberately setting out to create bad conditions out of good conditions and then to make propaganda out of those conditions. Of the 300 prisoners who urinate, smear the walls of their cells with excreta, break up their furniture and take the springs out of their beds, 74 have been convicted of murder or attempted murder, 80 of firearms offences, and 82 of explosives offences, including 47 of causing explosions. In Hansard (1978).

13. An extensive collection of newspaper articles, editorials, pamphlets, broadsides, posters, and other materials is located at Belfast's Linen Hall Library in its Northern Ireland Political Collection. See especially the Chris Ryder collection. Back issues of the *News Letter* also are housed at Linen Hall Library.

14. The IRA prisoners maintained a military chain of command with the OC serving as their leader. The prisoners would only deal with the prison official through the OC, forcing the prison to conform to the same lines of communication with them as it would were they officially recognized as POWs

15. The prisoners of Long Kesh had developed an effective system of communication that relied on several mediums. In addition to Gaelic, they relied on written messages composed on cigarette paper and smuggled to other prisoners or the outside by enclosing them in plastic food wrap and hiding them in the orifices of the body. By scheduling at least one outside visit per day to each section of the H-Blocks, the prisoners were able to get a message out, receive a reply, and respond in the course of a single day. They also had smuggled radio receivers about the size of the barrel of a small pen into the prison. This was an additional source of public information. See Beresford (1987), Coogan (1997/1980), and O'Malley

(1990) for accounts of how the Provo prisoners smuggled information and contraband in and out of Maze prison.

16. The incredulous claims of Secretary Atkins notwithstanding, the Royal Ulster Constabulary Chief Constable Report shows there was increased violence in May 1981, when Sands died. Looked at in terms of annual violent activity reported, 1981 generally continued a downward trend since 1979 in overall terrorist violence reported. Data for these years show the following with respect to known terrorist activity.

Republican	1979	1980	1981
Murders	91	53	69
Att. Murders	204	188	461
Explosions	414	260	159
Loyalist			
Murders	16	13	12
Att. Murders	19	15	26
Explosions	8	20	3

During May 1981, however, there was an increase in terrorist activity. There were 132 incidents of terrorist explosions recorded, fully one-third of the 398 total incidents reported for that year. The report also shows that attacks on RUC personnel spiked in May, with 3,813 attacks on members while on duty (40.4 percent of annual total). These included the lowest total of physical assaults for the year on RUC personnel (11 incidents, or 2.8 percent), but 37.6 percent (2,116 incidents) of attacks with stones, 54.8 percent (1,575 incidents) of attacks with petrol bombs, 21.7 percent (46 incidents) of attacks with explosives, and 19.2 percent (66 incidents) of attacks with gunfire (Royal 1980, 65; 1981, 54–55).

17. For a discussion of the distinctions between power, strength, authority, violence, and force, see Arendt (1969).

Chapter 7. Display Rhetoric and the Fantasia of Demonstrative Displays

1. All references to *Institutio Oratoria* are provided in the text.

2. The Greeks provided foundation for this view when they characterized epideictic as a *deictic* form, or mode of proof, that is distinguishable from other modes of proof. Thus, rhetorical displays were *epideictic logoi*, demonstrations were *apodeictic logoi*, and historical indications were *endeictic logoi*. Moreover, in contrast with the Greek view, the Romans considered demonstration to be a mode of reasoning whose premises were grounded in the minds of judging audiences rather than in the nature of the subject undergoing demonstration. As Quintilian notes, speeches demonstrate through praise and blame the "nature of the object with which they [that is, the audience members] are concerned" (III.iv.14). The idea that standards for judgment of whatever is "demonstrated" are located within the audience rather than in some extrinsic metaphysical or epistemological foundation has as its corollary the need to discover resources for "proving" through rhetorical invention. An important example of this innovation is found in Cicero's consideration of *loci* as an extension of Aristotle's metaphysically grounded topical theory.

3. In *Topica* II.6, Cicero pays homage to Aristotle in a way that situates his work as an extension of Aristotle's theory. He argued, contrary to the Stoics (and Aristotle's *Topica*, which he ostensibly was appropriating), that a method for inventing claims to be tested was required

prior to testing their truth. His upbraiding of the Stoics for neglecting the other half of Aristotle's system, coupled with his assertion that Aristotle founded the subject and that he regards his work as following Aristotle's, suggests Cicero thought he was advancing Aristotle's system. However, his specific complaint, that the Stoics' almost exclusive focus on judgment paid insufficient attention to invention, ignores Aristotle's fixing the ends of dialectic as criticism and belief (albeit provisionally so), and that the emphasis of Aristotle's *Topica* is on testing the opponent's argument, or judgment. See Cicero (1968).

4. See McKeon (1966, 365–73), for a discussion of this shift as illustrated by the four stasis questions. McKeon argues that the stases, which are central to Roman rhetorical theory, are permutations of Aristotle's metaphysically based questions that guide scientific inquiry.

5. Newton encouraged the moral philosophers of the Enlightenment to use the observational method for investigating the workings of the mind, which he explicitly recommended to them at the close of his *Optics*. See Newton (1803/1729, 1931/1730). The British empiricists' observation-based speculations on the workings of the mind, in turn, influenced the rhetorical and aesthetic theorists of the Scottish Enlightenment's psychological school. Speculative treatises by Archibald Allison, James Beattie, Hugh Blair, George Campbell, Alexander Gerard, Joseph Priestly, and Adam Smith, to mention the more noteworthy, maintained that qualities of vivid display rendered rhetorical and aesthetic creations mimetic of nature. I have discussed this relationship with regard to the centrality of visualization in Hauser (1972). For a provocative extension of this visual line of thought, see McDaniel (2000).

6. Discourse is "dialogized" when the privileged positions of prevailing power structures and ideologies are challenged, making us aware of competing positions and interpretations. These radiant engagements instigate a dialogue among the respective cultural languages "that mutually and ideologically interanimate each other," giving new possibilities for understanding and expressing reality. As such, Bakhtin holds, all discourse is heteroglossic. Its situatedness provides an unrepeatable set of conditions that make its meanings to particular listeners at a particular time unlike any before or since. See Bakhtin (1981, 47, 284–85, and editor's glossary 426–27).

7. *Island in Chains* was published in 1982 by Penguin Books in Britain, and Random House in the United States and Canada. Its publication by commercial presses suggests that its contents were not dictated by the ANC, as might be alleged were it to have appeared from a press under its influence or control.

8. The reader will recognize the account to follow as waterboarding, a hotly debated form of treatment used by the CIA during the Bush administration to gain information from detainees suspected of being members of the Taliban or al-Qaeda. The debated issue was whether waterboarding was torture. I will leave the reader to draw his or her own conclusions from Naidoo's account. See chapter 8 for a more detailed discussion of the treatment of U.S. military detainees during the Iraq War and the memoranda authorizing these "enhanced" interrogation techniques.

9. Naidoo reports that efforts to complain to external authorities were rebuked as trivial, seldom transmitted, never responded to as serious, frequently dismissed with fabricated notations that the prisoner chose to drop the complaint, and carried consequences for being lodged. When outside observers came to monitor the prisoners' treatment, the authorities carefully orchestrated where the visitors went and whom they interviewed to craft a perception of humane conditions. It was not until the airing of *90 Days* on BBC in 1966 and subsequent

public concern expressed by Helen Sussman in the South African parliament that national and world attention to Afrikaner treatment of political prisoners became a topic of public concern (Naidoo 1982, 162–63). Barbara Harlow (1996) also notes the visit of a Red Cross official who counteracted misleading government statements by filing a report highly critical of conditions in the prison.

10. Political prisoners commonly circumvent restrictions on communication by smuggling messages hidden in the body's orifices. Guards attempt to prevent this by subjecting prisoners to body searches. Prisoners regard this practice, even when performed without explicitly demeaning rituals such as the "*tausa!,*" as a humiliating invasion of their bodies.

11. Naidoo's ignorance of Afrikaans may have been a ruse, since he recounts in Afrikaans what the guard was saying and uses Afrikaans throughout the book.

12. Neville Alexander (1994, 15–27) discusses the political inflection of "*Baas.*" According to Alexander, "Just as a nonpolitical prisoner's life would be worth nothing if he did not do this [that is, call the warder '*Baas*' or a similar term of submission], so in 1962–1964 the political prisoners who refused to kow-tow in this manner courted death in the most literal sense. Many assaults were caused by refusal to say Baas. Virtually all prisoners used this searingly, readily debasing terminology until a stand was taken by certain prisoners and followed by the rest" (27).

13. Naidoo's account of this event is referred to in several of the Robben Island prisoner narratives. The prisoner most referenced, Johnson Phillip Mlambo, claims he was not the only one made victim to such treatment. See Mlambo (c. 2000, 15).

Chapter 8. Quo Vadis America

1. I am indebted to Virginia Sanprie, who collaborated with me on a project that considered the rhetorical frames of women warriors. See Hauser and Sanprie (2007)

2. "Black sites" is the term used in White House, CIA, DOJ, and congressional documents to refer to secret locations outside the United States where prisoners were taken for interrogation. Their existence and location are known to only a handful of officials.

3. Extraordinary rendition involves the secret and extrajudicial transfer of a person from one state to another. The state that takes custody of the prisoner, such as Egypt or Syria, is one known to engage in torture; hence the practice is sometimes referred to as torture by proxy. Despite Bush administration denials that it engaged in this practice, DOJ memoranda steadfastly maintained that foreign nationals held at sites outside the United States are not protected by U.S. or international law. For a more detailed discussion of this practice, see Mayer (2008, 101–38).

4. The effects of forced standing are swelling of the feet and ankles. The severity depends on length of time. Within twenty-four hours they will swell to twice their normal size, blisters form, fainting often occurs, and there may be kidney failure (Rejali 2004).

5. Two administration memos, written by Assistant Attorney General Bybee (2002) and Special Counsel to the President Yoo (2002), addressed the ways harsh treatment could avoid being labeled torture prior to Beaver's October opinion. However, memos concerning the use of torture specifically crafted to authorize harsh treatment without acknowledging it as torture and to provide legal cover for those who used these interrogation techniques were written up to the last days of the Bush administration. See also Working Group Report (2003) and Bradbury (2005, 2009).

6. All references to Gallup polling data are from the Gallup website (http://www.gallup .com/home.aspx). See "Overwhelming Support for War Continues," November 29, 2001 (http://www.gallup.com/poll/5083/overwhelming-support-war-continues.aspx); and "American Opinion: Should Saddam Be Worried? January 15, 2002 (http://www.gallup.com/poll/5176/American-Opinion-Should-Saddam-Worried.aspx).

7. Other polls showed even stronger numbers, with the CBS News poll reporting 69 percent in favor and 26 percent opposed to removing Hussein, and the Fox poll reporting 71 percent in favor and 24 percent opposed. These polling differences may have been the result of wording, with Gallup's use of "ground troops" and "invade" in its question causing some respondents to pause. Respondents also became more circumspect in their support for invading Iraq when they were reminded that the U.N. was considering the matter and asked whether the United States should wait for U.N. approval or proceed regardless, with 40 percent saying only with approval and 38 percent saying proceed even without approval. The CBS poll reported similar reserve, with 38 percent thinking the United States should act fairly soon while 60 percent thought it should give the U.N. more time to complete its inspections and pass a resolution approving invasion. See Newport (2003).

8. On May 1, 2003, Bush landed on the *USS Abraham Lincoln* in a Lockheed S-3 Viking. He became the first sitting president to make an arrested landing in a fixed-wing aircraft on an aircraft carrier. Later, he delivered a speech on the flight deck announcing the end of major combat in Iraq, with the warship's banner proclaiming "Mission Accomplished" prominent in the background.

9. These were posted at AntiWar.com (http://www.antiwar.com/news/?articleid=2444) and thememoryhole.org (http://www.thememoryhole.org/war/iraqis_tortured/index.htm).

10. The Taguba Report makes much of the stress under which the guards operated as an explanation for their behavior while placing blame squarely on the guards.

11. Posted on May 12, 2004 (http://hypertext.rmit.edu.au/~om_blog/archives/000190.html).

Bibliography

abcnews. 2006. "Seven in 10 Oppose Holding Detainees Indefinitely without Charges." June 25. http://abcnews.go.com/images/Politics/1015a2Gitmo.pdf.

Actis, Manú, Cristina Aldini, Liliana Gardella, Miriam Lewin, and Elisa Tokar. 2006. *That Inferno: Conversations with Five Women Survivors of an Argentine Torture Camp.* Translated by Gretta Siebentritt. Nashville, Tenn.: Vanderbilt University Press.

Agamben, Giorgio. 1998. *Homo Sacer.* Translated by Daniel Heller-Roazen. Palo Alto, Calif.: Stanford University Press.

———. 2005. *State of Exception.* Translated by Kevin Attell. Chicago: University of Chicago Press.

Alexander, Neville. 1994. *Robben Island Prison Dossier: 1964–1974.* Cape Town: University of Cape Town.

Alford, William P. 1992. "Making a Goddess of Democracy from Loose Sand: Thoughts on Human Rights in the People's Republic Of China." In An-Na`im 1992a, 65–80.

Amnesty International. 2007. "12 Years under House Arrest–Amnesty Demands Release of Daw Aung San Suu Kyi and All Other Prisoners of Conscience." October 24. http://www.amnesty.nl/voor_de_pers_artikel/24689.

Anderson, Benedict. 2006. *Imagined Communities.* Rev. ed. New York: Verso.

Anderson, Susan Heller, and David W. Dunlap. 1986. "A Jailed Russian Poet Inspires Poetic Protest." *New York Times,* May 26. http://select.nytimes.com.

An-Na`im, Abdullahi Ahmed, ed. 1992a. *Human Rights in Cross-Cultural Perspectives: A Quest for Consensus.* Philadelphia: University of Pennsylvania Press.

———. 1992b. "Toward a Cross-Cultural Approach to Defining International Standards of Human Rights: The Meaning of Cruel, Inhuman, or Degrading Treatment or Punishment." In An-Na`im 1992a, 19–43.

Annas, George J. 1982. Prison Hunger Strikes: Why the Motive Matters. *Hastings Center Report* 12 (December): 21–22.

Anonymous. 2011. "The Cry of the New Martyrs: A Continuing Vigil." *Orthodox America.* http://www.roca.org/OA/65/65d.htm.

Applebaum, Anne. 2003. *Gulag: A History.* New York: Doubleday.

Arendt, Hannah. 1958. *The Human Condition.* Chicago: University of Chicago Press.

———. 1964. *Eichmann in Jerusalem: A Report on the Banality of Evil.* New York: Viking Press.

———. 1968. *The Origins of Totalitarianism.* New York: Harcourt.

———. 1969. *On Violence.* New York: Harcourt, Brace & World.

———. 1977. *Between Past and Future.* Baltimore: Penguin Books.

Aretxaga, Begona. 1997. *Shattering Silence: Women, Nationalism, and Political Subjectivity in Northern Ireland.* Princeton, N.J.: Princeton University Press.

Aristotle. 2007. *On Rhetoric: A Theory of Civic Discourse.* 2nd ed. Edited, translated, and introduction by George A. Kennedy. New York: Oxford University Press.

———. 1941. *Nichomachean Ethics.* Translated by W. D. Ross. In *The Basic Works of Aristotle.* Edited by Richard McKeon, 935–1126. New York: Random House.

Asen, Robert, and Daniel C. Brouwer, eds. 2001. *Counterpublics and the State.* Albany, N.Y.: SUNY Press.

Ashforth, Adam. 1990. *The Politics of Official Discourse in Twentieth-Century South Africa.* Oxford: Clarendon Press.

Avalon Project at Yale Law School. 2011. "The Code of Hammurabi." Translated by L. W. King. http://www.yale.edu/lawweb/avalon/medieval/hammenu.htm.

Baker, Houston, Jr. 1995. "Critical Memory and the Black Public Sphere." In *The Black Public Sphere,* edited by The Black Public Sphere Collective, 7–37. Chicago: University of Chicago Press.

Bakhtin, M. M. 1981. *The Dialogic Imagination: Four Essays.* Edited by M. Holquist. Translated by C. Emerson and M. Holquist. Austin: University of Texas Press.

Balibar, Etienne. 2004. "Is a Philosophy of Human Civic Rights Possible? New Reflections on Equiliberty." *South Atlantic Quarterly* 103: 311–22.

Barrett, Patrick. 2004. "US TV Blackout Hits Litany of War Dead." *Guardian,* April 30. http://www.guardian.co.uk/media/2004/apr/30/Iraqandthemedia.usnews.

Bartley, William. 1962. *The Retreat to Commitment.* New York, Knopf, 1962.

Baudrillard, Jean. 2000. "Photography, Or the Writing of Light." Translated by Francois Debrix. *Ctheory.net,* April 12. http://www.ctheory.net/articles.aspx?id=126#note1.

Beaver, Diane. 2002. "Legal Brief on Proposed Counter-Resistance Strategies." Memorandum for Commander, Joint Task Force 170, 11 October. In Greenberg and Dostal 2005, 229–35.

Beer, Francis A., and Robert Hariman. 1996. "Refiguring Realism." In *Post-Realism: The Rhetorical Turn in International Relations,* edited by Francis A. Beer and Robert Hariman, 1–33. East Lansing: Michigan State University Press.

Beneson, Peter. 1961. "The Forgotten Prisoners." *Observer,* May 28. http://www.guardian.co.uk/uk/1961/may/28/fromthearchive.theguardian.

Benjamin, Walter. 1969. "Theses on the Philosophy of History." In *Illuminations,* edited by Hannah Arendt, 253–64. New York: Schoken.

Bentham, Jeremy. (1789) 1931. *The Theory of Legislation.* London: Paul, Trench, Trubner.

Beresford, David. 1987. *Ten Dead Men: The Story of the 1981 Irish Hunger Strike.* London: Grafton.

Biko, Steve. 1978. "On Death." In *I Write What I Like.* London: Bowerdean.

bin Laden, Osama. 2001. "Text of bin Laden Video Statement." *New York Times on the Web,* October 8. http://www.nytimes.com.

Bonhoeffer, Dietrich. 1967a. *Letters and Papers from Prison.* Rev. ed. Edited and translated by Eberhard Bethge. New York: Macmillan.

———. 1967b. "After Ten Years." In Bonhoeffer 1967a, 1–17.

———. 1967c. "Prayer for Fellow Prisoners: Christmas 1943." In Bonhoeffer 1967a, 139.

———. 1967d. "Report on Experiences during Alerts." In Bonhoeffer 1967a, 151–247.

———. 2001. *Discipleship* (1937). In *Dietrich Bonhoeffer Works*. Vol. 4. Edited by Geffrey B. Kelly and John D. Godsey. Translated by Barbara Green and Rienhard Krauss. Minneapolis: Fortress Press.

"Bottom of the Heap." 2008. *Economist*, June 21–27, 35.

Bourdieu, Pierre. 1990. *The Logic of Practice*. Translated by Richard Nice. Stanford, Calif.: Stanford University Press.

Bradbury, Steven G. 2005. "Withdrawal of Office of Legal Counsel CIA Interrogation Opinions." Memorandum for John A. Rizzo, April 15. www.justice.gov/olc/2009/withdrawal officelegalcounsel.pdf.

———. 2009. "Status of Certain OLC Opinions Issued in the Aftermath of the Terrorist Attacks of September 11, 2001." Memorandum for the Files, January 15. www.gwu.edu/~nsarchiv/torturingdemocracy//documents/20090115.pdf.

Brouwer, Daniel C. 1998. "The Precarious Visibility Politics of Self-Stigmatization: The Case of HIV/AIDS Tattoos." *Text and Performance Quarterly* 18: 114–16.

———. 2001. "ACT-ing UP in Congressional Hearings." In Asen and Brouwer 2001, 87–109.

———. 2004. "Corps/Corpse: The U.S. Military and Homosexuality." *Western Journal of Communication* 68: 411–30.

Bruner, Jerome. 1987. "Narrative as Life." *Social Research* 54:1–17.

———. 1991. "The Narrative Construction of Reality." *Critical Inquiry* 18: 1–21.

Buckley, Michael J. 1970. "Philosophic Method in Cicero." *Journal of the History of Philosophy* 8: 143–14.

Buckley, William F. 2004. "Finding Honor in Abu Ghraib." *National Review Online*, May 14. http://www.nationalreview.com/articles/210659/finding-honor-abu-ghraib/william-f-buckley-jr.

Buntman, Fran Lisa. 2004. *Robben Island and Prisoner Resistance to Apartheid*. Cambridge: Cambridge University Press.

Burke, Edmund. (1757) 1909. "A Philosophical Inquiry into the Origins of Our Ideas of the Sublime and Beautiful." In *The Works of Edmund Burke*. Vol. 1. London: George Bell & Sons.

Burke, Kenneth. (1931) 1953. *Counter-Statement*. 2nd ed. Los Altos, Calif.: Hermes Press.

———. (1950) 1969. *A Rhetoric of Motives*. Berkeley: University of California Press.

———. 1973. "The Rhetoric of Hitler's Battle." In *Philosophy of Literary Form*. 3rd ed., 191–220. Berkeley: University of California Press.

———. 1984a. *Permanence and Change: An Anatomy of Change*. 3rd ed. Berkeley: University of California Press.

———. 1984b. *Attitudes Toward History*. 3rd ed. Berkeley: University of California Press.

Bush, George W. 2001a. "Address to the Nation." September 11. PBS Online NewsHour. http://www.pbs.org/newshour/bb/military/terroristattack/bush_speech.html.

———. 2001b. "Proclamation 7462 of September 13, 2001: National Day of Prayer and Remembrance for the Victims of the Terrorist Attacks on September 11, 2001." September 13. *Federal Register* 66: 47945.

———. 2001c. "Remarks at the National Day of Prayer and Remembrance Service." September 14. *Weekly Compilation of Presidential Documents*, week ending Friday, September 14, 2001, 1309–10.

————. 2001d. "Presidential Documents, Proclamation 7463 of September 14, 2001." *Federal Register* 66: 48199.

————. 2001e. "Address before a Joint Session of the Congress of the United States: Response to the Terrorist Attacks of September 11." September 20. *Weekly Compilation of Presidential Documents*, week ending Friday, September 21, 2001, 1347–1351.

————. 2001f. "Military Order of November 3, 2001: Detention, Treatment, and Trial of Certain Non-Citizens in the War against Terrorism." In Greenberg and Dratel 2005, 25–28.

————. 2002. "Address to the United Nations General Assembly in New York City." September 12. *The American Presidency Project.* http://www.presidency.ucsb.edu/ws/index.php?pid=64069&st=&st1=.

————. 2003a. "Address Before a Joint Session of the Congress on the State of the Union." January 28. *The American Presidency Project.* http://www.presidency.ucsb.edu/ws/index.php?pid=29645&st=&st1=.

————. 2003b. "The President's Radio Address." February 8. *The American Presidency Project.* http://www.presidency.ucsb.edu/ws/index.php?pid=25133&st=&st1=.

————. 2003c. "Address to the Nation on Iraq." March 17. *The American Presidency Project.* http://www.presidency.ucsb.edu/ws/index.php?pid=63713&st=&st1=.

Butler, Judith. 2004. *Precarious Life: The Powers of Mourning and Violence.* London: Verso.

————. 2009. *Frames of War: When Is Life Grievable?* London: Verso.

Bybee, James, 2002a. "Application of Treaties and Laws to al Qaeda and Taliban Detainees." Memorandum for Alberto R. Gonzales, General Counsel to the President, and William J. Haynes, General Counsel to the Department of Defense, January 22. In Greenberg and Dratel 2005, 81–117.

————. 2002b. "Status of the Taliban Forces Under the Third Geneva Convention of 1949." Memo, Alberto R. Gonzales, February 7. In Greenberg and Dratel 2005, 136–43.

————. 2002c. "Standards of Conduct for Interrogation Under 18 U.S.C." Memorandum for Alberto R. Gonzales, August 1. In Greenberg and Dratel 2005, 172–217.

Caplan, Harry, trans. 1964. [Cicero], *Rhetorica ad Herennium.* Cambridge, Mass.: Harvard University Press.

Carter, Bill. 2004. "Pentagon Ban on Pictures of Dead Troops Is Broken." *New York Times,* April 23. http://www.nytimes.com/2004/04/23/national/23PHOT.html.

Cassius Dio Cocceianus. 1917. *Roman History.* Vol. 5. Translated by Earnest Cary. Cambridge, Mass.: Harvard University Press.

Certeau, Michel de, Luce Giard, and Pierre Mayol. 1998. *The Practice of Everyday Life.* Vol. 2, *Living and Cooking.* Rev. ed. Edited by Luce Giard. Translated by Timothy J. Tomasik. Minneapolis: University of Minnesota Press.

Cheney, Dick. 2002. Speech to VFW National Convention. August 26. *guardian.co.uk.*.

Cicero. 1968. *Topica.* Translated by H. M. Hubbell. Cambridge, Mass.: Harvard University Press.

Cixous, Hélène. 1976. "The Laugh of Medusa." Translated by Keith Cohen and Paula Cohen. *Signs* 1: 875–93.

Clark, Roger S. 2000. "How International Human Rights Law Affects Domestic Law." In *Human Rights: New Perspectives, New Realities,* edited by Adamantia Pollis and Peter Schwab, 185–207. London: Lynne Rienner.

Clarke, Thomas, Eamonn Ceannt, James Connolly, Sean Mac Diarmada, Thomas Mac-Donaugh, P. H. Pearse, and Joseph Plunkett. (1916) 1990. "Proclamation of the Republic, 24 April, 1916." In *Last Words: Letters and Statements of the Leaders Executed after the Rising at Easter 1916*, edited by Piaras F MacLochlainn, 1–3. Dublin: Stationary Office.

Clinton, William J. 1999. "Statement of President Clinton before United Nations General Assembly." September 21. In *International Human Rights in Context*, edited by Henry J. Steiner and Phillip Alston. 2nd ed., 661–62. New York: Oxford University Press.

CNN.COM. 2001. "President Tours New York Devastation." September 14. http://archives .cnn.com/2001/US/09/14/america.under.attack/.

Cohen, Joshua. 1997. "Procedure and Substance in Deliberative Democracy." In *Deliberative Democracy*, edited by James Bohman and William Rehg, 407–37. Cambridge, Mass.: MIT Press.

Cole, David. 2003. *Enemy Aliens: Double Standards and Constitutional Freedoms in the War on Terrorism*. New York: New Press.

Congress of the People. 1955. "Freedom Charter." June 26. http://www.anc.org.za/ancdocs/ history/charter.html.

Connolly, James. (1916) 1990. "Statement to Court Martial, 9 May 1916." In *Last Words: Letters and Statements of the Leaders Executed after the Rising at Easter 1916*, edited by Piaras F. MacLochlainn, 188–89. Dublin: Stationary Office.

Convention Against Torture and Other Cruel, Inhuman or Degrading Treatment or Punishment. 1984. *Audiovisual Library of International Law*. December 10. http://untreaty.un.org/ cod/avl/ha/catcidtp/catcidtp.html.

Coogan, Tim Pat. (1980) 1997. *On the Blanket: The Inside Story of the IRA Prisoners "Dirty" Protest*. Boulder, Colo: Roberts Rhinehart.

Cronin, Sea. 1980. *Irish Nationalism: A History of Its Roots and Ideology*. Dublin: Academy.

CyberUSSR. 2000. "Article 58, Criminal Code of the RSFSR (1934)." December 26. http:// www.cyberussr.com/rus/uk58-e.html.

D'Anjou, Leo. 1996. *Social Movements and Cultural Change: The First Abolition Campaign Revisited*. Hawthorne, N.Y.: Aldine de Gruyter.

Danner, Mark. 2009a. "US Torture: Voices from the Black Sites." *New York Review of Books*, April 9. http://www.nybooks.com/articles/archives/2009/apr/09/us-torture-voices-from -the-black-sites/.

———. 2009b. "The Red Cross Torture Report: What It Means." *New York Review of Books*, April 30. http://www.nybooks.com/articles/archives/2009/apr/30/the-red-cross-torture- report-what-it-means/.

Dershowotz, Alan. 2002. "Want to Torture? Get a Warrant." *San Francisco Chronicle*, January 22. http://www.sfgate.com/cgi-bin/article.cgi?file=/chronicle/archive/2002/01/22/ED53 29.DTL.

Dlamini, Moses. 1984. *Hell-Hole, Robben Island: Reminiscences of a Political Prisoner in South Africa*. Trenton, N.J.: Africa World Press.

Donnelly, Jack. 2003. *Universal Human Rights in Theory and Practice*. 2nd ed. Ithaca, N.Y.: Cornell University Press.

Dooley-Clarke, Dolores. 1981. "Medical Ethics and Political Protest." *Hastings Center Report* 11: 5–8.

Doxtader, Erik. 2000. "Characters in the Middle of Public Life: Consensus, Dissent, and Ethos." *Philosophy and Rhetoric* 33: 336–69.

———. 2001. "Making Rhetorical History in a Time of Transition: The Occasion, Constitution, and Representation of South African Reconciliation." *Rhetoric & Public Affairs* 4: 223–60.

———. 2003. "Reconciliation: A Rhetorical Conception." *Quarterly Journal of Speech* 89: 267–92.

———. 2007. "The Faith and Struggle of Beginning (with) Words: On the Turn between Reconciliation and Recognition." *Philosophy and Rhetoric* 40:119–146.

———. 2008. *Faith in the Works of Words: The Beginnings of Reconciliation in South Africa.* Cape Town: David Philip.

———. 2010. "The Rhetorical Question of Human Rights: A Question." *Quarterly Journal of Speech* 96: 353–79.

Doxtader, Erik, and Philippe-Joseph Salazar. 2007. *Truth and Reconciliation in South Africa: The Fundamental Documents.* Cape Town: David Philip.

Doxtader, Erik, and Charles Villa-Vicencio, eds. 2004. *To Repair the Irreparable: Reparation and Reconstruction in South Africa.* Cape Town: David Philip.

Drumgo, Fleeta. 1971. "Letter from Fleeta." In *If They Come in the Morning: Voices of Resistance*, edited by Angela Y. Davis, 115. New York: Third Press.

Duelfer, Charles. 2004. "DCI Special Advisor Report on Iraq's WMD." Central Intelligence Agency. September 23. https://www.cia.gov/library/reports/general-reports-1/iraq_wmd _2004/index.html.

Dworkin, Ronald. 2002. "The Threat to Patriotism." *New York Review of Books*, February 28, 44–49.

Ehrenreich, Barbara. 2004. "A Uterus Is No Substitute for a Conscience." *Znet*, May 24. http://www.zcommunications.org/a-uterus-is-no-substitute-for-a-conscience-by-barbara -ehrenreich.

Eisenman, Stephen F. 2007. *The Abu Ghraib Effect.* London: Reaktion Books.

Ellmann, Maud. 1993. *The Hunger Artists.* Cambridge, Mass.: Harvard University Press.

Evans, Sara M., and Harry C. Boyte. 1992. *Free Spaces: The Sources of Democratic Change in America.* Chicago: University of Chicago Press.

Falk, Richard. 1992. "Cultural Foundations for the International Protection of Human Rights." In An-Na`im 1992a, 44–64.

Fanon, Frantz. 1952. *Black Skin, White Masks.* Translated by Charles Lam Markmann. New York: Grove Press.

———. 1963. *The Wretched of the Earth.* Preface by Jean-Paul Sartre. Translated by Constance Farrington. New York: Grove Press.

———. 1965. "Algeria Unveiled." In *A Dying Colonialism.* Translated by Haakon Chevalier. New York: Grove Press.

Farrell, Thomas B. 1993. *Norms of Rhetorical Culture.* New Haven, Conn.: Yale University Press.

———. 2008. "The Weight of Rhetoric: Studies in Cultural Delirium." *Philosophy & Rhetoric* 41: 467–87.

Feldmann, Allen. 1991. *Formations of Violence: The Narrative of Body and Political Terror in Northern Ireland.* Chicago: University of Chicago Press.

Fihla, Nkosinati Benson. c. 2000. "Interview with B. Fihla." Mayibuye Archive, EPP Collection. Bellville, S.A.: University of the Western Cape.

Fisher, Ian. 2004. "The Struggle for Iraq: Iraqi Inmate Recounts Hours of Abuse by U.S. Troops." *New York Times*, May 5. http://www.nytimes.com/2004/05/05/world/the-struggle-for-iraq-inmate-iraqi- recounts-hours-of-abuse-by-us-troops.html?pagewanted=1.

Fleischer, Ari. 2002. Press Briefing. December 2. *The American Presidency Project.* http://www.presidency.ucsb.edu/ws.index.php?pid=47457

———. 2003. Press Briefing. January 9. *The American Presidency Project.* http://www.presidency.ucsb.edu/ws/index.php?pid=61619.

Foucault, Michel. 1972. *The Archeology of Knowledge.* Translated by A. M. Sheridan. New York: Pantheon Press.

———. 1973. *Madness and Civilization: A History of Insanity in the Age of Reason.* Translated by Richard Howard. New York: Vintage Press.

———. 1975. *The Birth of the Clinic: An Archeology of Medical Perception.* Translated by A. M. Sheridan Smith. New York: Vintage Press.

———. 1977. Discipline and Punish: The Birth of the Prison. Translated by Alan Sheridan. New York: Vintage Press.

———. 1980. *The History of Sexuality.* Vol. *1, An Introduction.* Translated by Robert Hurley. New York: Vintage Press.

———. 1983. "The Meaning and Evolution of the Word 'Parrhesia.'" In *Discourse and Truth: The Problematization of Parrhesia.* http://foucault.info/documents/parrhesia

———. 1988. "The Political Technology of Individuals." In *Technologies of the Self: A Seminar with Michel Foucault,* edited by Luther Martin, Huck Gutman, and Patrick H. Hutton, 145–62. Amherst: University of Massachusetts Press.

———. 1991. "Governmentality." In *The Foucault Effect: Studies in Governmentality,* edited by Graham Burchell, Colin Gordon, and Peter Miller, 87–104. Hemel Hempstead: Harvester Wheatsheaf.

———. 2001. *Fearless Speech.* Los Angeles: Semiotext(e).

———. 2008. *The Birth of Biopolitics: Lectures at the College de France, 1978–1979.* Edited by Michel Seneleart. Translated by Graham Burchell. New York: Pelgrave Macmillan.

Fredrickson, George M. 1995. *Black Liberation: A Comparative History of Black Ideologies in the United States and South Africa.* New York: Oxford University Press.

Gamson, William A., and Andre Modigliani. 1989. "Media Discourse and Public Opinion on Nuclear Power: A Constructionist Approach." *American Journal of Sociology* 95:1–37.

Gamson, William A., David Croteau, William Hoynes, and Theodore Sasson. 1992. "Media Images and the Social Construction of Reality." *Annual Review of Sociology* 18:373–93.

Gandhi, Mahatma. (1910) 1997. *Hind Swaraj and Other Writings.* Cambridge: Cambridge University Press.

Geertz, Clifford. 1987. "Deep Play: Notes on the Balinese Cockfight." In *Interpretive Social Science: A Second Look,* edited by Paul Rabinow and William M. Sullivan, 195–240. Berkeley: University of California Press. Originally published in *Daedalus* (1972), 101: 1–37.

Glendon, Mary Ann. 2001. *A World Made New: Eleanor Roosevelt and the Universal Declaration of Human Rights.* New York: Random House.

Goffman, Erving. 1959. *The Presentation of Self in Everyday Life.* Garden City, N.Y.: Doubleday.

———. 1961. *Asylum: Essays on the Social Situation of Mental Patients and Other Inmates.* Garden City, N.Y.: Anchor Books.

———. 1974. Frame Analysis: An Essay on the Organization of Experience. Cambridge, Mass.: Harvard University Press.

Goldstein, Richard. 2004. "Bitch Bites Man! Why Lynndie England Is the Public Face of Torturegate." *Village Voice,* May 4. http://www.villagevoice.com/2004-05-04/news/bitch -bites-man/1/.

Gonzalez, Alberto R. 2002. "Decision RE Application of the Geneva Convention of Prisoners of War to the Conflict with al Quaeda and the Taliban." Memorandum for the President. January 25. http://www1.umn.edu/humanrts/OathBetrayed/policies-index.html.

Gore, Al. 2004. "Remarks by Al Gore." *MoveOn PAC,* May 26. http://pol.moveon.org/gorere marks052604.html

Greenberg, Karen J. 2006. "Split Screen, The American Prospect Online." April 10. http:// prospect.org/cs/articles?article=split_screens.

Greenberg, Karen J., and Joshua L. Dratel, eds. 2005. *The Torture Papers: The Road to Abu Ghraib.* New York: Cambridge University Press.

Griffin, Leland M. 1952. "The Rhetoric of Historical Movements." *Quarterly Journal of Speech* 38: 184–88.

Gutmann, Amy. 2001. "Introduction." In Ignatieff et al., 2001, vii–xxviii.

Hall, Peter M., and John P. Hewit. 1970. "The Quasi-Theory of Communication and the Management of Dissent." *Social Problems* 18:17–27.

Hamdan v. Rumsfeld, 548 U. S. (2006).

Hansard. 1978. "Maze." May 11. http://hansard.millbanksystems.com/commons/1978/may/ 11/maze-prison.

———. 1986. "Common Sitting: Petitions." June 11. http://hansard.millbanksystems.com/ commons/1986/jul/11/irina-ratushinskaya.

Hardin, Garrett. 1968. "The Tragedy of the Commons." *Science* 162: 1243–48.

Harding, Vincent. 1981. *There Is a River: The Black Freedom Struggle in America.* New York: Harcourt.

Hariman, Robert. 1995. *Political Style.* Chicago: University of Chicago Press.

Hariman, Robert, and John Louis Loucaites. 2007. *No Caption Needed: Iconic Photographs, Public Culture, and Liberal Democracy.* Chicago: University of Chicago Press.

Harlow, Barbara. 1996. *After Lives.* London: Verso.

Harris-Lacewell, Melissa. 2004. *Barbershops, Bibles, and BET: Everyday Talk and Black Political Thought.* Princeton, N.J.: Princeton University Press.

Hasian, Marouf, Jr., and Lisa A. Flores. 2000. "Mass Mediated Representations of the Susan Smith Trial." *Howard Journal of Communication* 11: 163–78.

Hauser, Gerard A. 1972. "Empiricism, Description, and the New Rhetoric." *Philosophy and Rhetoric* 5: 24–44.

———. 1999a. "Aristotle on Epideictic: The Formation of Public Morality." *Rhetoric Society Quarterly* 29: 5–23.

———. 1999b. *Vernacular Voices: The Rhetoric of Publics and Public Opinion.* Columbia: University of South Carolina Press.

———, ed. 1999c. *Body Argument. Argumentation and Advocacy* 36: 1–100.

———. 2001. "Prisoners of Conscience and the Counterpublic Sphere of Prison Writing: The Stones That Start the Avalanche." In Asen and Brouwer 2001, 35–58.

————. 2006. "Demonstrative Displays of Dissident Rhetoric: The Case of Prisoner 885/63." In *The Rhetoric of Display*, edited by Lawrence Prelli, 229–54. Columbia: University of South Carolina Press.

Hauser, Gerard A., and Donald P. Cushman. 1973. "McKeon's Philosophy of Communication: The Architectonic and Interdisciplinary Arts." *Philosophy and Rhetoric* 6: 211–34.

Hauser, Gerard A., and Virginia Sanprie. 2007. "Women in Combat: Arguments against Military Women in Combat through Media Depictions of Jessica Lynch and Lynndie England." *Proceedings of the Sixth Conference of the International Society for the Study of Argument*, edited by Frans. H. van Eemeren and Peter Houtlosser, 583–90. Amsterdam: Sic Sat.

Havel, Vaclav. 1977. "Manifesto of Charter 77." Translated by anonymous in the *Times* of London, January 7. http://lcweb2.loc.gov/frd/cs/czechoslovakia/cs_appnd.html.

————. 1986a. "An Anatomy of Reticence." In Havel 1986b, 164–95.

————. 1986b. *Living in Truth*. Edited by Jan Vladislav. Translated by Paul Wilson. Boston: Faber and Faber.

————. 1986c. "The Power of the Powerless." In Havel 1986b, 36–122.

————. 1989. *Letters to Olga*. Translated by Paul Wilson. New York: Henry Holt.

————. 1992. "'I Take the Side of Truth:' An Interview with Antoine Spire." In *Open Letters: Selected Writings, 1965–1990*, edited and translated by Paul Wilson. New York: Vintage Press.

————. 1998a. *The Art of the Impossible: Politics as Morality in Practice*. Translated by Paul Wilson and others. New York: Fromm International.

————. 1998b. "New Year's Address to the Nation, January 1, 1990." In Havel 1998a, 3–9.

————. 2000. "Address by Vaclav Havel, President of the Czech Republic in Acceptance of an Honorary Degree from the University of Michigan." September 5. Mindfully.org. http://www.mindfully.org/Reform/Vaclav-Havel-Truth-5sep00.htm.

Haynes, William R., II. 2002. "Counter Resistance Techniques." In Greenberg and Dratel 2005, 237.

Henken, Louis. 2000. "Human Rights: Ideology and Aspiration, Reality and Prospect." In *Realizing Human Rights: Moving from Inspiration to Impact*, edited by Samantha Power and Graham Allison, 3–38. New York: St. Martin's Press.

Hersh, Seymour. 2004. "Torture at Abu Ghraib." *New Yorker,* May 10. http://www.newyorker.com/fact/content/?040510fafact.

Hoffmann, Georg. 1964. "Report on the Visit to 'Robbeneiland' (Robben Island) Prison on the 1st May, 1964, by Mr. G. Hoffmnn, Delegate General of the International Committee of the Red Cross." Institute of Commonwealth Studies, Ruth First Papers, RF 2/9/12. London: University of London.

Homer. 1990. *The Iliad*. Translated by Robert Fagles. New York: Viking Penguin.

Houreld, Katharine. 2008. "Kenyan Children Abducted, Tortured." *ABC News*, June 25. http://abcnews.go.com/International/wireStory?id=5240894.

Howard, Rhoda E. 1992. "Dignity, Community, and Human Rights." In An-Na`im 1992a, 85–102.

Hower, Edward, William Kennedy, Alison Lurie, Kenneth McClane, James McConkey, and Jon Stallworthy. 1983. "The Ratushinskaya Case." *New York Review of Books*, June 30. http://www.nybooks.com/articles/6168.

H.R. 3162. 2001. "Uniting and Strengthening America by Providing Appropriate Tools Required to Intercept and Obstruct Terrorism (USA PATRIOT ACT) Act of 2001." Library of Congress.

Hubbard, Howard. 1968. "Five Long Hot Summers and How They Grew." *Public Interest* 12:3–24.

Human Rights Watch. 2002. "U.S.: Growing Problem of Guantánamo Detainees." May 29. http://www.hrw.org/en/news/2002/05/29/us-growing-problem-guantanamo-detainees.

Hyde, Michael. 2001. The Call of Conscience: Heidegger and Levinas: Rhetoric and the Euthanasia Debate. Columbia: University of South Carolina Press.

Hylton, Wil. 2006. "The Conscience of Joe Darby." *GQ,* September.

Ignatieff, Michael. 1997. *The Warrior's Honor: Ethnic War and the Modern Conscience.* New York: Henry Holt.

———. 1999. "Human Rights: The Midlife Crisis." *New York Review of Books,* May 20, 58–62.

———. 2001a. "Dignity as Agency." In Ignatieff et al. 2001, 161–73.

———. 2001b. "Human Rights as Idolatry." In Ignatieff et al. 2001, 53–98.

———. 2002. "The Rights Stuff." *New York Review of Books,* June 13, 18.

———. 2004. *The Lesser Evil: Political Ethics in an Age of Terror.* Princeton, N.J.: Princeton University Press.

Ignatieff, Michael, K. Anthony Appiah, David A. Hollinger, Thomas Laquer, and Diane Orentlicher. 2001. *Human Rights as Politics and Idolatry.* Edited by Amy Gutmann. Princeton, N.J.: Princeton University Press.

International Committee of the Red Cross. 2004. "Report of the International Committee of the Red Cross (ICRC) on the Treatment by the Coalition Forces of the Prisoners of War and Other Protected Persons by the Geneva Conventions in Iraq During Arrest, Interrogation and Internment." May 11. http://www.indybay.org/newsitems/2004/05/11/168047 91.php

———. 2007. "ICRC Report on the Treatment of 14 'High Value Detainees' in CIA Custody." Washington, D.C.: ICRC, February 14. http://www.nybooks.com/media/doc/2010/04/22/icrc-report.pdf

International Defense and Aid Fund. 1967. "South African Prisons and the Red Cross Investigation: An Examination by International Defense and Aid fund, with Prisoners' Testimony." Mayibuye Archive, Bunting Collection, Police and Prisons file, 2.35.1.15. Bellville, S.A.: University of the Western Cape.

Iyengar, Shanto. 1991. *Is Anyone Responsible? How Television Frames Political Issues.* Chicago: University of Chicago Press.

Jacobs, Dale. 2005. "What's Hope Got to Do with It? Towards a Theory of Hope and Pedagogy." *JAC: Journal of Rhetoric, Writing, Culture, Politics* 25: 783–802.

———. 2008. "The Audacity of Hospitality." *JAC: Journal of Rhetoric, Writing, Culture, Politics* 28: 563–81.

Jingsheng, Wei. 2000. "Human Rights: Not Merely and Internal Affair." In *Realizing Human Rights: Moving from Inspiration to Impact,* edited by Samantha Power and Graham Allison, 39–47. New York: St. Martin's Press.

Johnstone, Henry, W. 1990. "Rhetoric as Wedge: A Reformulation." *Rhetoric Society Quarterly* 20: 333–38.

Jones, Anthony, and George R. Fay. 2004. "Investigation of the Abu Ghraib Detention Facility and 205th Military Intelligence Brigade." In Greenberg and Dratel 2005, 987–1131.

Kaneva, Nadia. 2007. "Remembering Communist Violence: The Bulgarian Gulag and the Conscience of the West." *Communication Inquiry* 31: 44–61.

Kant, Immanuel. (1784) 1996. "An Answer to the Question: What Is Enlightenment?" In *Practical Philosophy*, edited and translated by Mary J. Gregor, 17–22. Cambridge: Cambridge University Press.

Kawash, Samira. 1999. "Terrorists and Vampires: Fanon's Spectral Violence of Decolonization." In *Frantz Fanon: Critical Perspectives*, edited by Anthony C. Alessandrini, 235–57. London: Routledge.

Keane, John. 2000. *Vaclav Havel: A Political Tragedy in Six Acts*. New York: Basic Books.

Kempton, Kathryn. 2005. "Bridge Over Troubled Waters: Canadian Law on Aboriginal and Treaty 'Water' Rights, and the Great Lakes Annex" (2005) http://www.thewaterhole.ca/publications/Aboriginal%20water%20rights%20and%20annex%20paper%20final.pdf.

Kennedy, George, trans. 2007. *Aristotle on Rhetoric: A Theory of Civic Discourse*. 2nd ed. New York: Oxford University Press.

Kennedy, John. 1963. "Ich bin ein Berliner." June 26. In *American Rhetoric: Top 100 Speeches*, edited by Stephen Lucas and Martin Medhurst. http://www.americanrhetoric.com/speeches/jfkberliner.html.

Kinneavy, James L. 1986. "*Kairos*: A Neglected Concept in Classical Rhetoric." In *Rhetoric and Praxis: The Contribution of Classical Rhetoric to Practical Reasoning*, edited by Jean Dietz Moss, 79–105. Washington, D.C.: Catholic University of America Press.

King, Martin Luther, Jr. 1963a. "Letter from Birmingham Jail." April 16. http://www.h-net.org/~hst306/documents/letter.html.

———. 1963b. "I Have a Dream." August 28. *American Rhetoric: Top 100 Speeches*, edited by Stephen Lucas and Martin Medhurst. http://www.americanrhetoric.com/speeches/mlkihaveadream.htm.

Kitson, Ian. 1993. "Ian David Kitson Interview." Mayibuye Archives, Oral History of Exiles Project, MCA 6–297a, tape 2. Bellville, S.A.: University of the Western Cape.

Klein, Jonathan. 2010. "Photos That Changed the World." TED, April. http://www.ted.com/talks/jonathan_klein_photos_that_changed_the_world.html.

Kleinman, Arthur, and Joan Kleinman. 1997. "The Appeal of Experience; the Dismay of Images: Cultural Appropriation of Suffering in Our Times." In *Social Suffering*. Edited by Arthur Kleinman, Veena Das, and Margaret Lock, 1–23. Berkeley: University of California Press.

Kovalcheck, Kassian A. 1987. "Catholic Grievances in Northern Ireland: Appraisal and Judgment." *British Journal of Sociology* 38: 77–87.

Kull, Steven. 2004. "The Separate Realities of Bush and Kerry Supporters." Program on International Policy Attitudes, April 21. http://www.googlesyndicatedsearch.com/u/pipa?q=The+Separate+Realities+of+Bush+and+Kerry+Supporters&sa=Search.

Kundera, Milan. 1981. *The Book of Laughter and Forgetting*. Translated by M. Henry Heim. Baltimore: Penguin Books.

Kuron, Jacek, and Karol Madzelewski. (1965) 1982. *Solidarnosc: The Missing Link? The Classic Open Letter to the Party*. London: Bookmarks.

Kurtz, Howard. 2003. "Embedded Reporter's Role in Army Unit's Actions Questioned by Military." *Washington Post*, June 25, C01.

Lash, Joseph P. 1972. *Eleanor: The Years Alone*. New York: Signet.

Lazzarato, Maurizio. 2002. "Foucault: Madness/Sexuality/Biopolitics." *Warwck Journal of Philosophy* 13. http://www.generation-online.org/c/fcbiopolitics.htm.

Leary, Virginia A. 1992. "Postliberal Strands in Western Human Rights Theory: Personalist-Communitarian Perspectives." In An-Na`im 1992a, 105–32.

Leff, Michael. 2003. "Rhetoric and Dialectic in Martin Luther King's 'Letter from Birmingham Jail.'" In *Proceedings of the Fifth Conference of the International Society for the Study of Argumentation.* Edited by Frans. H. van Eemeren and Peter Houtlosser, 671–77. Amsterdam: Sic Sat.

Lesage, Julia. 2009. "Sabrina Harman Speaking." *Jump Cut: A Review of Contemporary Media,* 51. http://www.ejumpcut.org/archive/jc51.2009/TortureDocumentaries/5.html.

Levi, Primo. 1959. *If This Is a Man.* Translated by Stuart Woolf. New York: Orion Press.

———. 1988. *The Drowned and the Saved.* Translated by Raymond Rosenthal. New York: Summit Books.

Lévy, Carlos. 2009. "From Politics to Philosophy and Theology: Some Remarks About Foucault's Interpretation of *Parrhesia* in Two Recently Published Seminars." *Philosophy and Rhetoric* 42:313–25.

Limbaugh, Rush. 2004. Media Matters for America. May 5. http://mediamatters.org/items/200405050003.

Linfield, Susie. 2010. *The Cruel Radiance: Photography and Political Violence.* Chicago: University of Chicago Press.

Lizhi, Feng. 2011a. "My 'Confession.'" Translated by Perry Link. *New York Review of Books,* June 23, 23–24.

———. (1989) 2011b. "The Past and the Future." Translated by Perry Link. *New York Review of Books,* June 23. http://www.nybooks.com/articles/archives/2011/jun/23/past-and-future/.

Locke, John. (1699) 1988. *Two Treatises of Government.* 2nd ed. Edited by Peter Laslett. Cambridge: Cambridge University Press.

Loraux, Nicole. 1986. *The Invention of Athens: The Funeral Oration in the Classical City.* Translated by Alan Sheridan. Cambridge, Mass.: Harvard University Press.

Los Angeles Times. 1986. "Dissident Poet Given Early Release from Soviet Prison." October 11.

Luban, David. 1996. "The Principle of Publicity." In *The Theory of Institutional Design,* edited by Robert E. Goodin, 154–98. Cambridge: Cambridge University Press.

———. 2005. "Liberalism, Torture, and the Ticking Bomb." *Virginia Law Review* 91: 1425–61.

———. 2007. "The Defense of Torture." *New York Review of Books,* March 15, 37–40.

Lyons, F. S. L. (1963) 1985. *Ireland since the Famine.* London: Fontana.

Macey, David. 2000. *Frantz Fanon: A Biography.* New York: Picador.

Magazine. 2008. "Abu Ghraib." *New Yorker,* March 24. http://www.newyorker.com/online/2008/03/24/abughraib.

Malinowski, Bronislaw. 1946. "The Problem of Meaning in Primitive Languages." In Ogden and Richards 1946, 196–236.

Mandela, Nelson. 1961. "The Struggle Is My Life." June 26. http://www.un.org/en/events/mandeladay/struggle.shtml.

———. 1994. *Long Walk to Freedom.* New York: Little, Brown.

Mascirotte, Gloria-Jean. 2004. "Bitches' Brew: The Emasculation of Iraqi Prisoners Shows How Far American Women Still Have to Go." *Providence Phoenix,* June 4–10. http://www.providencephoenix.com/features/other_stories/documents/03892683. Asp.

Mati, Joseph. 2000. "Prisoner 398/64: Joseph Faniso Mati." In *Plain Tales from Robben Island*, edited by Jan K Coetzee, 14–33. Pretoria: Van Schaik.

Mayer, Jane. 2008. *The Dark Side: The Inside Story of How the War on Terror Turned into a War on American Ideals.* New York: Doubleday.

McAdam, Doug. 2000. "Movement Strategy and Dramaturgic Framing in Democratic States: The Case of the American Civil Rights Movement." In *Deliberation, Democracy, and the Media*, edited by Simone Chambers and Anne Costain, 117–33. New York: Rowman & Littlefield.

McAdam, Doug, John D. McCarthy, and Mayer N. Zald, eds. 1996. *Comparative Perspectives on Social Movements: Political Opportunity, Mobilizing Structures and Cultural Framings.* New York: Cambridge University Press.

McCann, Jim. 2009. "What Really Happened at Long Kesh." April 7. Ceartais. http://ceartais.blogspot.com/.

McDaniel, James P. 2000. "Fantasm: The Triumph of Form (An Essay on the Democratic Sublime)." *Quarterly Journal of Speech* 86: 48–66.

McDonnell, Patrick J. 2004. "Abuse Inquiry Focuses on New Head of Iraq Jails." *Los Angeles Times*, May 19. http://articles.latimes.com/2004/may/19/world/fg-miller19.

McKeever, C. F., S. Joseph, and J. McCormack. 1993. "Memory of Northern Irish Catholics and Protestants for Violent Incidents and Their Explanations of the 1981 Hunger Strike." *Psychological Reports* 73: 463–66.

McKeon, Richard. 1954. "Dialectic, Political Thought and Action." *Ethics* 65: 1–33.

———. 1960. "The Ethics of International Influence." *Ethics* 70: 187–203.

———. 1966. "The Methods of Rhetoric and Philosophy: Invention and Judgment." In *The Classical Tradition: Literary and Historical Studies in Honor of Harry Caplan*, ed. Luitpold Wallach, 365–73. Ithaca, N.Y.: Cornell University Press.

———. 1968. "Discourse, Demonstration, Verification, and Justification, and Proceedings." *Logique et Analyse* 11: 37–92.

Mgabela, Johnson. 2000. "Prisoner 353/64: Johnson Malcomess Mgabela." In *Plain Tales from Robben Island*, edited by Jan K. Coetzee, 34–52. Pretoria: Van Schaik.

Mhabala, Raymond. 2002. "Political Imprisonment: Lessons in African Leadership." Ideal Pictures. Cape Town: Robben Island Museum.

Michnik, Adam. 1981. "What We Want to Do and What We Can Do." *Telos* 47: 66–77.

———. 1985a. *Letters from Prison and Other Essays.* Translated by Maya Latynski. Berkeley: University of California Press.

———. 1985b. "Why You Are Not Signing." In Michnik 1985a, 3–15.

Milam, Michael C. 2004. "Torture and the American Character." *Humanist*, July–August. http://findarticles.com/p/articles/mi_m1374/is_4_64/ai_n6170956/?tag=content;col1.

Milbank, Dana. 2003. "Curtains Ordered for Media Coverage of Returning Coffins." *Washington Post*, October 21. http://www.washingtonpost.com/ac2/wp-dyn/A55816-2003Oct20.

Miller, Greg. 2002. "Many Held at Guantanamo Not Likely Terrorists." *Los Angeles Times*, December 22. http://articles.latimes.com/2002/dec/22/nation/na-gitmo22.

"Minutes." 1971. June 19. Mayibuye Archive, Brian Bunting Collection, MCH 64–17. Bellville, S.A.: University of the Western Cape.

Mlambo, Johnson. c.2000. "Interview with Mr. Johnson Phillip Mlambo." Mayibuye Archive, EPP Collection. Bellville, S.A.: University of the Western Cape.

Morrison, Craig, and Martin Bright. 2005. "Secret Gas Was Issued for IRA Prison Riots." *Observer*, January 23. guardian.co.uk home. http://www.guardian.co.uk/politics/2005/jan/23/uk.past.

Naidoo, Indres. 1968. "Letter to Officer Commanding." February 19. Mayibuye Archive, Oral History of Exiles Project, MCH 64–17. Bellville, S.A.: University of the Western Cape.

———. 1982. *Island in Chains: Ten Years on Robben Island.* As told to Albie Sachs. London: Penguin Books.

Nair, Billy. 1995. "Billy Nair Interview." Mayibuye Archive, Oral History of Exiles Project, MCA 6–337e. Bellville, S.A.: University of the Western Cape.

Nash, Graham. 1970. "Chicago."

Natanson, Maurice. 1965. "Rhetorical and Philosophical Argumentation." In *Philosophy, Rhetoric, and Argumentation*, edited by Maurice Natanson and Henry W. Johnstone Jr., 149–56. University Park: Pennsylvania State University Press.

———. 1978. "The Arts of Indirection." In *Rhetoric, Philosophy, and Literature*, edited by Don M. Burks, 35–48. West Lafayette, Ind.: Purdue University Press.

National Commission on Terrorist Attacks on the United States. 2004. The 9/11 Commission Report. http://govinfo.library.unt.edu/911/report/index.htm.

National Security Archive. 2005. "Return of the Fallen." April 28. http://www.gwu.edu/~nsarchiv/NSAEBB/NSAEBB152/index.htm.

NCBuy. 2004. "Everybody's Doing the 'Lynndie.'" September 2. http://www.ncbuy.com/news/2004-09-02/1010479.html.

Nelson, Thomas, and Donald R. Kinder. 1996. "Issue Frames and Group-Centrism in American Public Opinion." *Journal of Politics* 58: 1055–78.

Nelson, Thomas E., Zoe Oxley, and Rosalee A. Clawson. 1997. "Toward a Psychology of Framing Effects." *Political Behavior* 19: 221–46.

Newman, Robert P. 1995. *Truman and the Hiroshima Cult.* East Lansing: Michigan State University Press.

Newport, Frank. 2003. "Public Opinion on Iraq, Unemployment, Investor Optimism, Death Penalty, Abortion, Energy Prices." *Gallup*, March 11. http://www.gallup.com/poll/7978/Public-Opinion-Iraq-Unemployment-Investor- Optimism-Death-Penalty.aspx.

Newton, Isaac. (1729) 1803. *The Mathematical Principles of Natural Philosophy.* Translated by Andrew Motte. London: H. D. Symonds.

———. (1730) 1931. *Optiks.* 4th ed. corrected. London: G. Bell & Sons.

Ngxiki, Canzibe Rosebury. 2000. "Prisoner 212/64: Caibe Rorsebury (RB) Ngxiki." In *Plain Tales from Robben Island, edited by Jan K.* Coetzee, 90–104. Pretoria: Van Schaik.

Nussbaum, Martha. 1986. *The Fragility of Goodness: Luck and Ethics in Greek Tragedy and Philosophy.* New York: Cambridge University Press.

nytonline. 2004. "The Shame of Abu Ghraib: Voices of Revulsion." May 4. http://www.nytimes.com/2004/05/04/opinion/l-the-shame-of-abu-ghraib-voices-of-revulsion-466417.html.

Oberschall, Anthony. 1996. "Opportunity and Framing in the Eastern European Revolts of 1989." In McAdam, McCarthy, and Zald 1996, 93–121.

Ogden, C. K., and I. A. Richards. 1946. Th*e Meaning of Meaning*. 8th ed. New York: Harcourt, Brace & World.

O'Keefe, Terrence M. 1984. "Suicide and Self-Starvation." *Philosophy* 59: 349–63.

Okrent, Daniel. 2005. "No Picture Tells the Truth: The Best Do Better Than That." *NY Times online*, January 9. http://www.nytimes.com/2005/01/09/weekinreview/09bott .html.

Oliver, Kelly. 2004. "Witnessing and Testimony." *Parallax* 10: 79–88.

O'Mally, Padraig. 1990. *Biting at the Grave: The Irish Hunger Strike and the Politics of Despair.* Boston: Beacon.

Ono, Kent A., and John M. Sloop. 1995. "The Critique of Vernacular Discourse." *Communication Monographs* 62: 19–46.

O'Sullivan, Niamh. 2007. *Every Dark Hour: A History of Kilmainham Jail.* Dublin: Liberties Press.

"Our Women Must Be Protected." 2008. *Economist*, April 26–May 2, 64–65.

Outram, Dorinda. 1989. *The Body and the French Revolution: Sex, Class and Political Culture.* New Haven, Conn.: Yale University Press.

Peters, John Durham. 2005. *Courting the Abyss: Free Speech and the Liberal Tradition.* Chicago: University of Chicago Press.

Philbin, Patrick F., and John Yoo. 2001. "Possible Habeas Jurisdiction over Aliens Held in Guantánamo Bay, Cuba." Memorandum for William J. Haynes II, General Counsel, Department of Defense, December 28. In Greenberg and Dratel 2005, 29–37.

Plato. 1986. *The Republic*. Translated by Benjamin Jowett. Buffalo, N.Y.: Prometheus Books.

Pollis, Adamantia. 2000. "A New Universalism." In *Human Rights: New Perspectives, New Realities*, edited by Adamantia Pollis and Peter Schwab, 9–30. London: Lynne Rienner.

Poulakos, John. 1995. *Sophistical Rhetoric in Classical Greece.* Columbia: University of South Carolina Press.

Powell, Colin. 2003a. "Address by Secretary of State Colin Powell to the United Nations Security Council." February 5. *The American Presidency Project.* http://www.presidency.ucsb.edu/ ws/index.php?pid=84876&st=Colin+Powe\l&st1=United+Nations.

———. 2003b. "Powell Discusses Iraq with Radio France International." February 28. United States Diplomatic Mission to Italy. http://www.usembassy.it/file2003_02/alia/a3022 808.htm.

———. 2003c. Comments at UN Security Council Meeting, S/PV.4714. March 7, 2003. UN Security Council. http://www.un.org/Depts/dhl/resguide/scact2003.htm.

Power, Samantha. 2002. *"A Problem from Hell" America and the Age of Genocide.* New York: Basic Books.

Price, Robert M. 1991. *The Apartheid State in Crisis: Political Transformation in South Africa, 1975–1990.* Oxford: Oxford University Press.

Public Law 107–40 115 Stat. 224. 2001. "To Authorize the Use of United States Armed Forces against Those Responsible for the Recent Attacks Launched against the United States." September 18. U.S. Government Printing Office. http://www.gpo.gov/fdsys/search/ searchresults.action;jsessionid=489990543e75816d11414d176b14a3ea3fb0c52ecbd22376 b9a17f73efb9f9a6.e38Kb3eQa30Nb40PchqRahuTaNj0?st=Pub.L.+107–40%2C +115+Stat.+224.

Pulvers, Roger. 2006. "Has America's Conscience Fallen Victim to 9/11?" *Japan Times Online*, February 26. http://search.japantimes.co.jp/cgi-bin/fl20060226rp.html.

Quintilian. 1958. *Institutio Oratoria*. Translated by H. E. Butler. Cambridge, Mass.: Harvard University Press.

Ranciere, Jacques. 2004. "Who Is the Subject of the Rights of Man." *South Atlantic Quarterly* 103:298–309.

Ratushinskaya, Irina. 1989. *Grey Is the Color of Hope*. Translated by Aloyna Kopjevnikov. New York: Random House.

Referees Union. 1971. June 8. Mayibuye Archive, Brian Bunting Collection, MCH 64- 17. Bellville, S.A.: University of the Western Cape.

Reid, Tim. 2010. "George W. Bush 'Knew Guantánamo Prisoners were Innocent.'" *Sunday Times*, April 9.

Rejali, Darius. 2004. "Of Human Bondage." *Salon.com*, June 18. http://dir.salon.com/opinion/feature/2004/06/18/torture_methods.

Rejali, Darius, and Paul Gronke. 2009. "U.S. Public Opinion on Torture, 2001–2009." May 2. cforjustice.org/wp-content/uploads/2010/01/TortureWhitePaperV2.pdf.

Richards, I. A. (1936) 1965. *The Philosophy of Rhetoric*. New York: Oxford University Press.

Ricoeur, Paul. 1990. *Time and Narrative*. 3 vols. (1984–88). Translated by Kathleen Blamey and David Pellauer. Chicago: University of Chicago Press.

Romanov, Leonid. 2000. "Opening Totalitarian Societies to the Outside World: A View from Russia." In *Realizing Human Rights: Moving from Inspiration to Impact*, edited by Samantha Power and Graham Allison, 63–73. New York: St. Martin's Press.

Roosevelt, Eleanor. (1961) 1992. *The Autobiography of Eleanor Roosevelt*. New York: Da Capo Press.

Roth, Kenneth. 2002. "Letter to President Bush." December 26. Human Rights Watch Website. http://www.hrw.org/en/news/2002/12/26/united-states-reports-torture-al-qaeda-suspects-0.

Rousseau, Jean-Jacques. (1762) 1997. *On the Social Contract and Other Political Writings*. Edited and translated by Victor Gourevitch. Cambridge: Cambridge University Press.

Royal Ulster Constabulary Chief Constable. 1980–81. Royal Ulster Constabulary Chief Constable's Report. Fiche 2787. Northern Ireland Political Collection. Belfast: Linen Hall Library.

Ryder Collection. N.d. Northern Ireland Political Collection. Belfast: Linen Hall Library.

Sands, Bobby. 1983. *Writings from Prison*. Boulder, Colo: Roberts Rinehart.

Sands, Philippe. 2008. *Torture Team: Rumsfeld's Memo and the Betrayal of American Values*. New York: Pelgrave Macmillan.

Scarry, Elaine. 1985. *The Body in Pain: The Making and Unmaking of the World*. New York: Oxford University Press.

Schell, Jonathan. 1985. Introduction to Michnik 1985, xviii–xlii.

Scherer, Michale, and Mark Benjamin. 2006. "The Abu Ghraib Files: Other Government Agencies." *Salon*, March 14. http://911research.wtc7.net/cache/post911/attacks/salon_otheragencies.html.

Schlesinger, James. 2004. "Final Report of Independent Panel to Review DoD Detention Operations." In Greenberg and Dratel 2005, 908–75.

Schulweis, Harold M. 2008. *Conscience: The Duty to Obey and the Duty to Disobey*. Woodstock, Vt.: Jewish Lights.

Schulz, William F. 2003. *Tainted Legacy: 9/11 and the Ruin of Human Rights*. New York: Thunder's Mouth Press/Nation Books.

Scott, James C. 1990. *Domination and the Arts of Resistance: Hidden Transcripts*. New Haven, Conn.: Yale University Press.

Sells, Michael A. 1996. *The Bridge Betrayed: Religion and Genocide in Bosnia*. Berkeley: University of California Press.

Sennett, Richard. 1979. *The Fall of Public Man*. New York: Vintage Press.

———. 1994. *Flesh and Stone: The Body and City in Western Civilization*. New York: Norton.

Sentilles, Sarah. 2008. "He Looked Like Jesus Christ: Crucifixion, Torture, and the Limits of Empathy as a Response to the Photographs from Abu Ghraib." *Harvard Divinity Bulletin* 36, April 24.

Sheldrake, Philip. 2001. *Spaces for the Sacred: Place, Memory and Identity*. Baltimore: Johns Hopkins University Press.

Shklar, Judith N. 1984. *Ordinary Vices*. Cambridge, Mass.: Belknap Press.

Sidlayiya, Chris. c.1994. "Interview w/ Rachidi Molapo about His Arrest and Imprisonment on R.I." Mayibuye Archives, Oral History of Exiles Project, MCA 1–1056a. Bellville, S.A. University of the Western Cape.

Silwane, Philip Fumanekile. 2000. "Robben Island Interview." Mayibuye Archive, EPP Collection. Bellville, S.A.: University of the Western Cape.

Smith, W. Thomas, Jr. 2004. "No Excuses." *National Review Online*. http://www.national review.com/articles/210653/no-excuses/w-thomas-smith-jr.

Sneed, D., and H. Stonecipher. 1989. "Prisoner Fasting as a Symbolic Act: The Ultimate Speech-Action Test." *Howard Law Journal* 32: 549–62.

Snow, David A., and Robert D. Benford. 1988. "Ideology, Frame Resonance, and Participant Mobilization." *International Social Movement Research* 1:197–217.

Solzhenitsyn, Aleksandr I. 1974–76. *The Gulag Archipelago, 1918–1956: An Experiment in Literary Investigation*. Translated by Thomas P. Whitney. New York: Harper & Row.

Sontag, Susan. 1973. "Photography." *New York Review of Books online*, October 18. http://www.nybooks.com/articles/archives/1973/oct/18/photography/.

———. 1990. *On Photography*. New York: Anchor/Doubleday.

———. 2003. *Regarding the Pain of Others*. New York: Farrar, Straus and Giroux.

Sophocles. 1973. *Antigone*. Translated by Richard Emil Braun. London: Oxford University Press.

South African History Online. N.d. "Apartheid Legislation 1850s-1990s." http://www.sa history.org.za/pages/chronology/chronology.htm.

Soyinka, Wole. 1972. *The Man Died*. New York: Farrar, Straus, and Giroux.

State of Northern Ireland. 1972. *Report of the Commission to Consider Legal Procedures to Deal with Terrorist Activities in Northern Ireland*. CAIN Web Service. http://cain.ulst.ac.uk/hmso/diplock.htm.

Stern, Fritz. 1987. "National Socialism as Temptation." In *Dreams and Delusions*, 147-91. New York: Knopf.

Stevenson, Jonathan. 1996. *"We Wrecked the Place:" Contemplating an End to the Northern Irish Troubles*. New York: Free Press.

Stolberg, Sheryl Gay. 2004. "Senate Backs Ban on Photos of G.I. Coffins." *New York Times*, June 22. http://query.nytimes.com/gst/fullpage.html?res=990DE2DB1339F931A15755 C0A9629C8–63.

Stump, Eleanore. 1978. *Boethius's de Topicus Differentius.* Ithaca, N.Y.: Cornell University Press.

"Sudanese President Is Charged with Genocide." 2008. *MSNBC,* July 14. http://www.msnbc.msn.com/id/25671505/.

Sweeney, George. 1993. "Irish Hunger Strikes and the Cult of Self-Sacrifice." *Journal of Contemporary History* 28: 421–37.

Taguba, Antonio. 2004. "Articles 15–6 Investigation of the 800th Military Police Brigade." In Greenberg and Dratel 2005, 405–556.

Tanzer, Joshua. 2008. "Sub-Standard." May 18. http://www.offoffoff.com/film/2008/standard_operating_procedure.php

Taylor, Charles. 1999. "Conditions of an Unforced Consensus on Human Rights." In *The East Asian Challenge for Human Rights,* edited by Joanne R. Bauer and Daniel A. Bell. Cambridge: Cambridge University Press.

Taylor, Peter. 1997. *Behind the Mask: The IRA and Sein Fein.* New York: TV Books.

Tejirian, Ed. 2005. "Abu Ghraib: Psychological and Cross-Cultural Issues in Sexuality, Individual Conscience, and Torture." Paper presented at the American Psychological Association. http://www.maletomalefeeling.com/abughraib.html.

Terry, James P. 2004. "Rethinking Humanitarian Intervention after Kosovo: Legal Reality and Political Pragmatism." *BNET business network,* August. http://findarticles.com/p/articles/mi_m6052/is_2004_August/ai_n6253912/pg_1.

Thompson, Leonard. 1996. *A History of South Africa. 3rd ed.* New Haven, Conn.: Yale University Press.

Thorpe, J. 1994. "Prisoner—Hunger Strike—Right to Self Determination." *New Law Journal Reports,* December 9, 1695–96.

Timerman, Jacobo. 1981. *Prisoner without a Name, Cell without a Number.* Translated by Toby Talbot. New York: Knopf.

Toderov, Tzvetan. 1996. *Facing the Extreme: Moral Life in the Concentration Camps.* Translated by Arthur Denner and Abigail Pollak. New York: Metropolitan Books.

———. 1999. *Voices from the Gulag: Life and Death in Communist Bulgaria.* Translated by Robert Zaretsky. University Park: Penn State University Press.

Touraine, Alain. 1997. *What Is Democracy?* Translated by David Macey. Boulder, Colo.: Westview Press.

United Nations Convention against Torture and Other Cruel, Inhuman or Degrading Treatment or Punishment. 1985. http://www.hrweb.org/legal/cat.html.

United Nations International Convention on the Elimination of All Racial Discrimination. 1966. March 7. http://www.hri.org/docs/ICERD66.html.

United States Department of Justice. 1986. Final Report of the Attorney General's Commission on Pornography. Washington, D. C.

United States Department of State. 1999. "Introduction." 1999 Country Report on Human Rights Practices. http://www.state.gov/www/global/human_rights/1999_hrp_report/99hrp_toc.htm_1.

Urquhart, Brian. 2001. "Mrs. Roosevelt's Revolution." *New York Review of Books,* April 26, 32–34.

von Klemperer, Klemens. 1992. "'What Is the Law That Lies Behind These Words?' Antigone's Question and the German Resistance against Hitler." *Journal of Modern History,* Supplement: Resistance against the Third Reich 64:S102–11.

War Crimes Act. 1996. United States Code: Title 18, Part 1, Chapter 113C, Sections 2340, 2340A, and 2340B. http://www.law.cornell.edu/uscode/18/usc_sup_01_18_10_I_20 _113C.html.

Weimer, Walter B. 1977. "Science as Rhetorical Transaction: Toward a Nonjustificational Conception of Rhetoric." *Philosophy and Rhetoric* 10: 1–29.

Wheeler, James Scott. 1999. *Cromwell in Ireland.* New York: St. Martin's Press.

White, Eric C. 1987. *Kaironomia: On the Will to Invent.* Ithaca, N.Y.: Cornell University Press.

Wilmore, Gayraud S. 1972. *Black Religion and Black Radicalism.* Garden City, N.Y.: Doubleday.

Woodruff, Paul. 2001. *Reverence: Renewing a Forgotten Virtue.* Oxford: Oxford University Press.

Working Group Report. 2003. "Detainee Interrogations in the Global War on Terror." In Greenberg and Dratel 2005, 286–359.

Xenophon. 1989. *Hellenika* I–II. Edited and translated by Peter Krentz. Warminster, U.K.: Aris & Phillips.

Xianliang, Zhang. 1995. *Grass Soup.* Translated by Martha Avery. Boston: David R. Godine.

Yeats, W. B. 1904. *The King's Threshold.* In *The King's Threshold: And on Baile's Strand: Being Volume Three of Plays for an Irish Theatre.* London: A. H. Bullen.

Yoo, John. 2001. Memorandum Opinion for the Deputy Counsel to the President. In Greenberg and Dratel 2005, 3–24.

———. 2002. "Letter Regarding the Views of Our Office Concerning Legality, Under International Law, of Interrogation Methods to Be Used on Captured al Qaeda Operatives." Memorandum to the Honorable Alberto Gonzales, August 1. In Greenberg and Dratel 2005, 218–22.

———. 2006. *War by Other Means: An Insider's Account of the War on Terror.* New York: Atlantic Monthly Press.

Yoo, John, and Robert J. Delahunty. 2002. "Application of Treaties and Laws to al Qaeda and Taliban Detainees." Memorandum for William J. Haynes II, General Counsel, Department of Defense, January 9. In Greenberg and Dratel 2005, 38–79.

Zimbardo, P. G. 1975. "On Transforming Experimental Research into Advocacy for Social Change." In *Applying Social Psychology: Implications for Research, Practice, and Training,* edited by Morton Deutsch and H. Hornstein, 33–66. Hillsdale, N.J.: Erlbaum.

Žižek, Slavoj. 2005. "Against Human Rights." *New Left Review* 34: 115–31.

Index

CPSIA information can be obtained at www.ICGtesting.com
Printed in the USA
LVOW13s1617050114

368124LV00003B/4/P

9 781611 174380